Ayu Watanabe

L♥DK

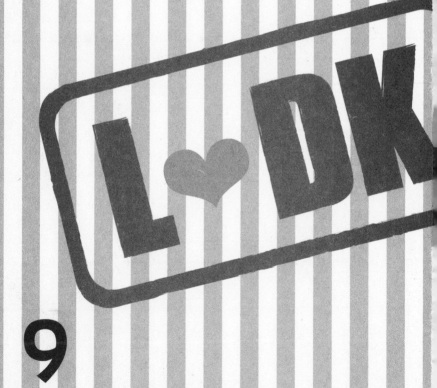

9

L♥DK
Ayu Watanabe
9

contents

#33 Naked Couple

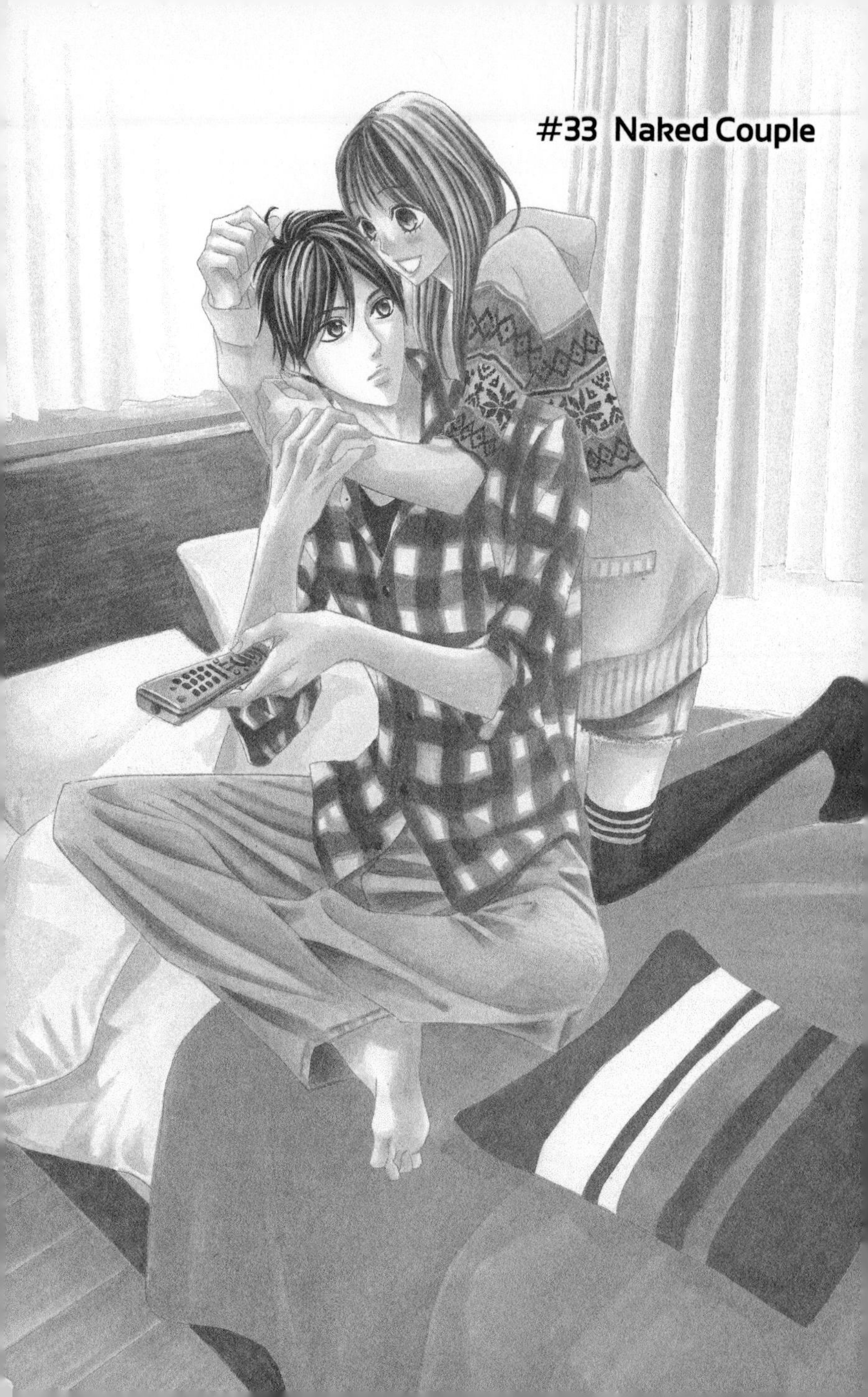

L♥DK

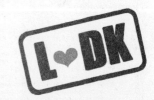

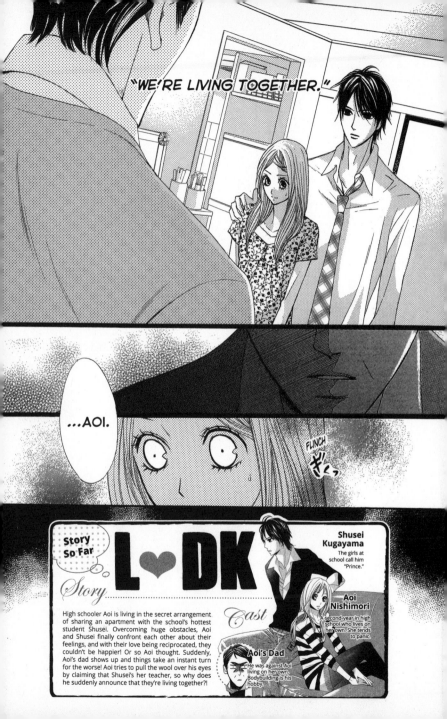

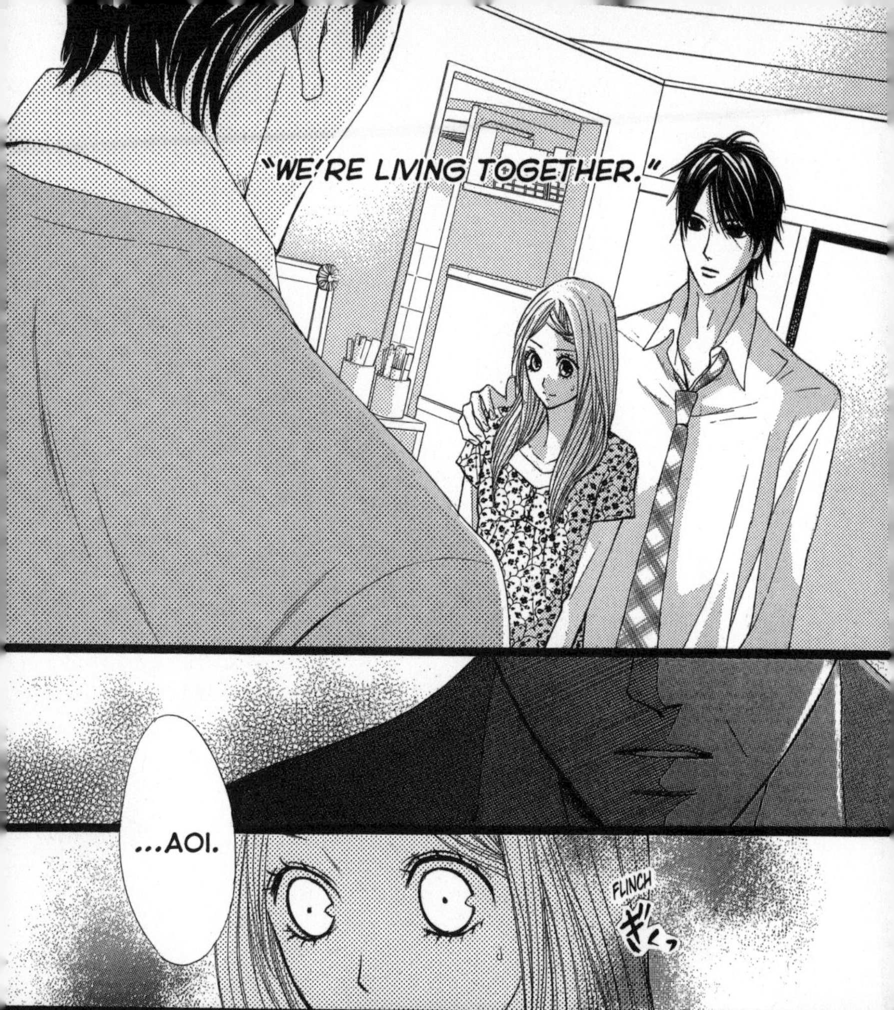
"WE'RE LIVING TOGETHER."
...AOI.
FLINCH
ぎくっ

Story So Far

L♥DK

Story

High schooler Aoi is living in the secret arrangement of sharing an apartment with the school's hottest student Shusei. Overcoming huge obstacles, Aoi and Shusei finally confront each other about their feelings, and with their love being reciprocated, they couldn't be happier! Or so Aoi thought. Suddenly, Aoi's dad shows up and things take an instant turn for the worse! Aoi tries to pull the wool over his eyes by claiming that Shusei's her teacher, so why does he suddenly announce that they're living together?!

Cast

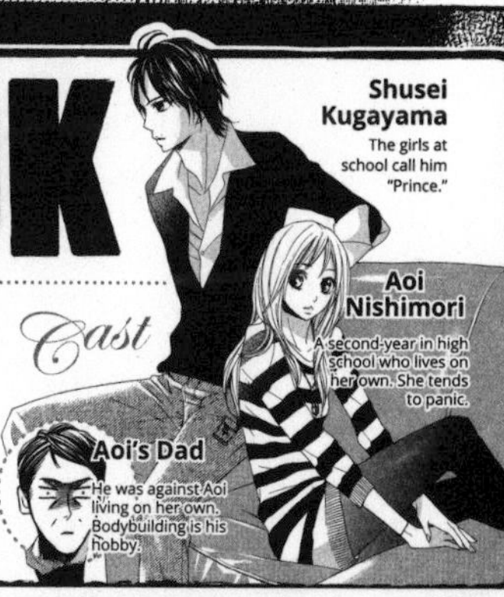

Shusei Kugayama
The girls at school call him "Prince."

Aoi Nishimori
A second-year in high school who lives on her own. She tends to panic.

Aoi's Dad
He was against Aoi living on her own. Bodybuilding is his hobby.

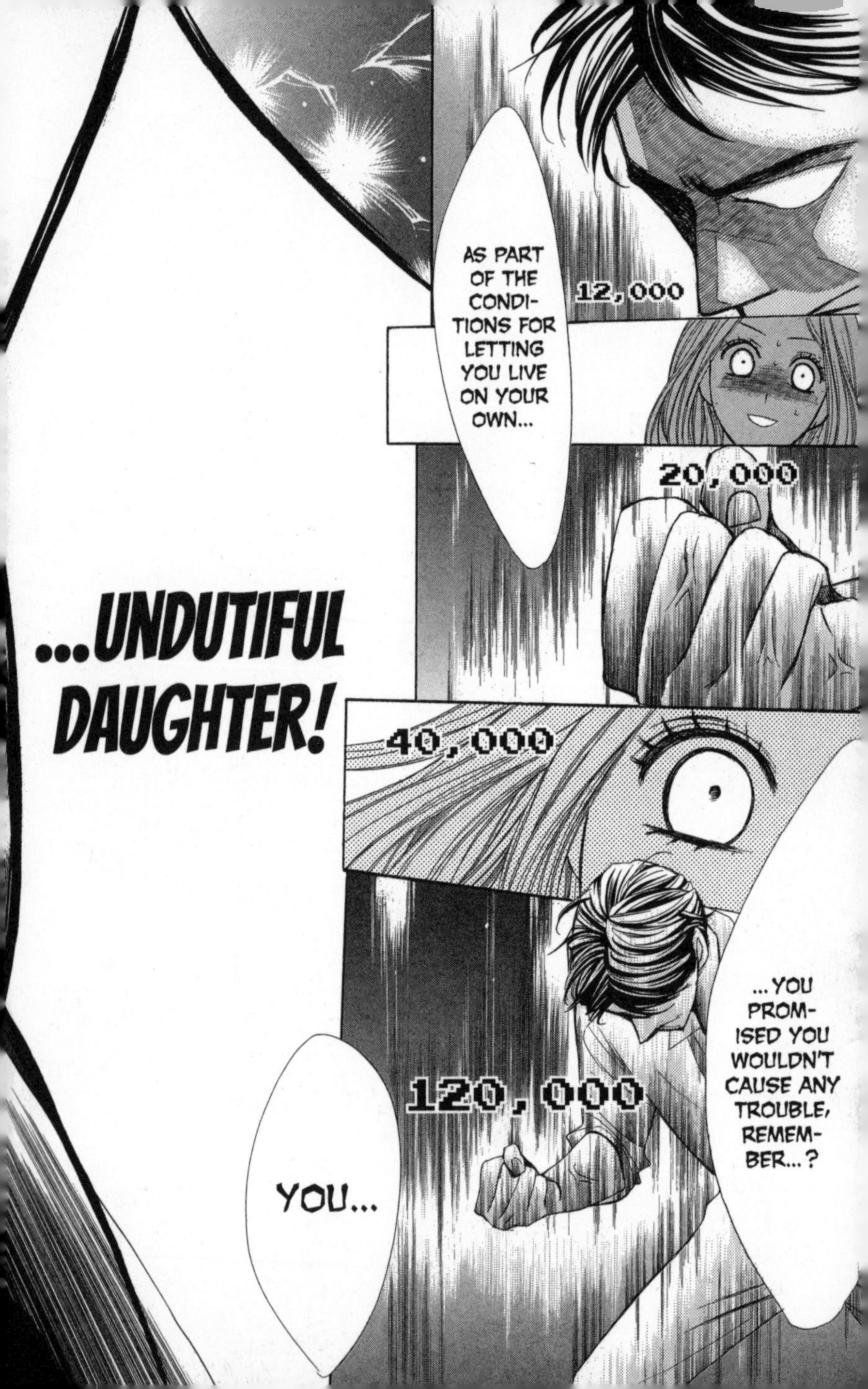
AS PART OF THE CONDITIONS FOR LETTING YOU LIVE ON YOUR OWN...
12,000
20,000
40,000
...YOU PROMISED YOU WOULDN'T CAUSE ANY TROUBLE, REMEMBER...?
120,000
YOU...
...UNDUTIFUL DAUGHTER!

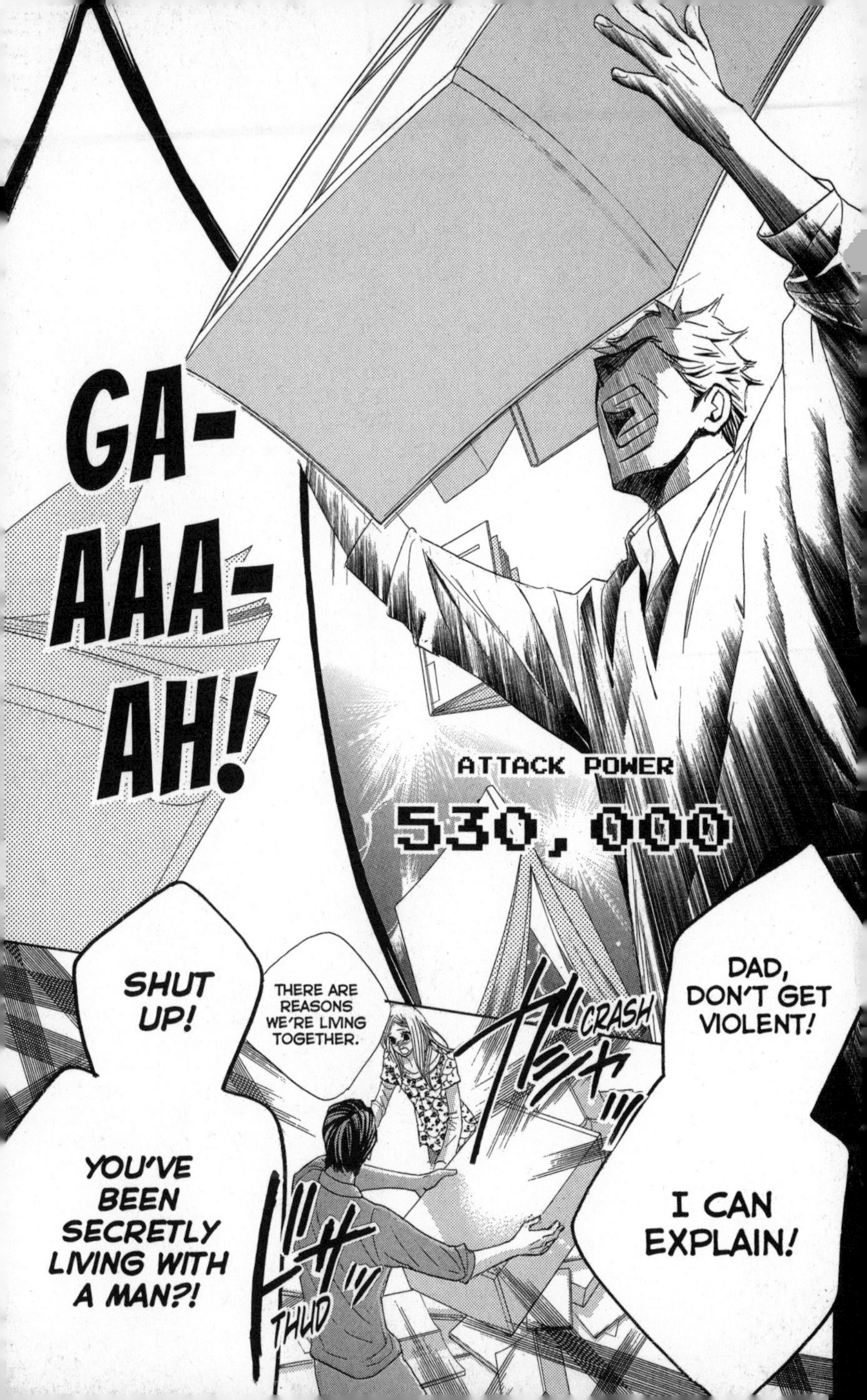
GA-AAA-AH!
ATTACK POWER
530,000
DAD, DON'T GET VIOLENT!
CRASH
THERE ARE REASONS WE'RE LIVING TOGETHER.
SHUT UP!
I CAN EXPLAIN!
THUD
YOU'VE BEEN SECRETLY LIVING WITH A MAN?!

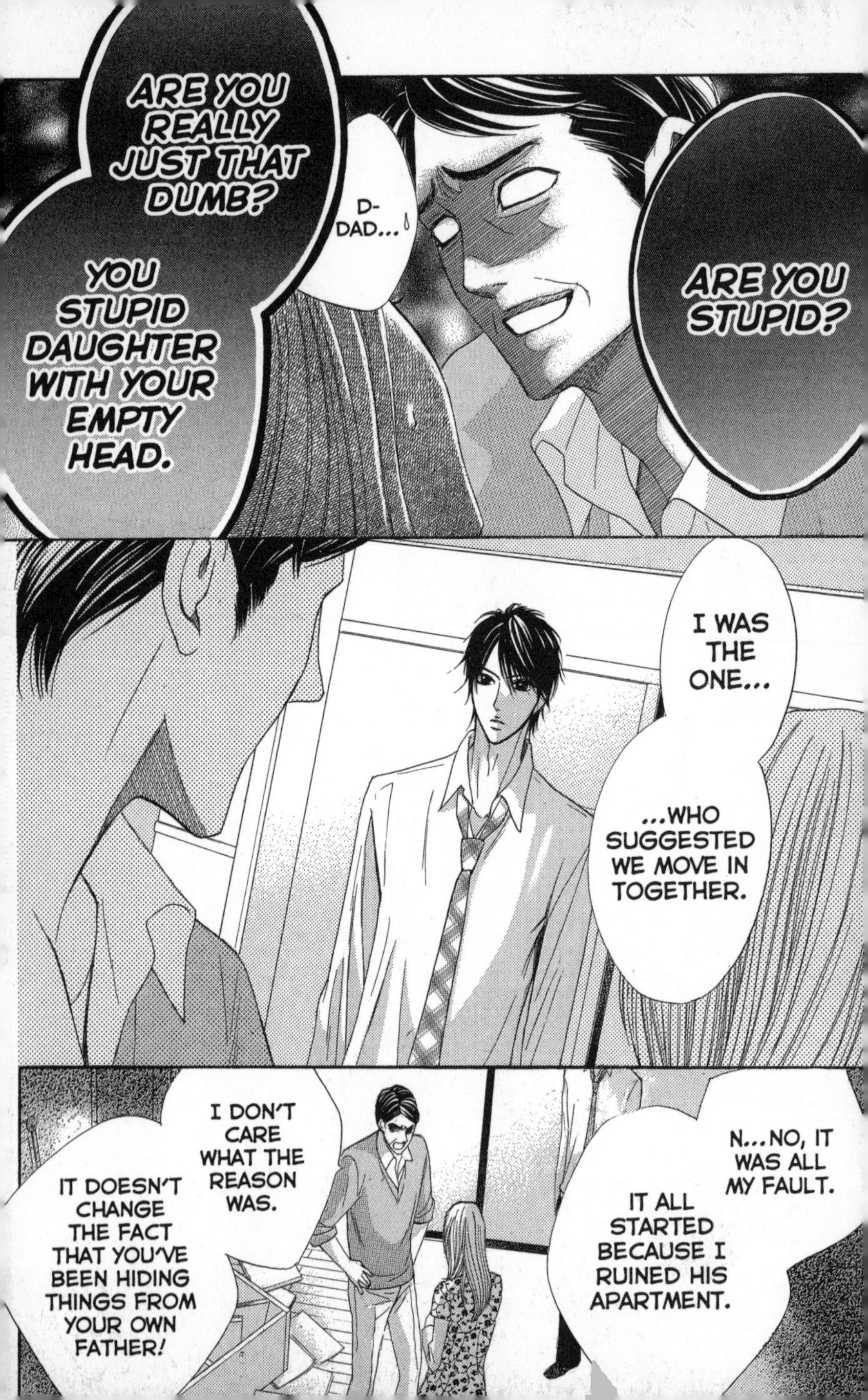
ARE YOU STUPID?
ARE YOU REALLY JUST THAT DUMB?
D-DAD...
YOU STUPID DAUGHTER WITH YOUR EMPTY HEAD.
I WAS THE ONE...
...WHO SUGGESTED WE MOVE IN TOGETHER.
N...NO, IT WAS ALL MY FAULT.
IT ALL STARTED BECAUSE I RUINED HIS APARTMENT.
I DON'T CARE WHAT THE REASON WAS.
IT DOESN'T CHANGE THE FACT THAT YOU'VE BEEN HIDING THINGS FROM YOUR OWN FATHER!

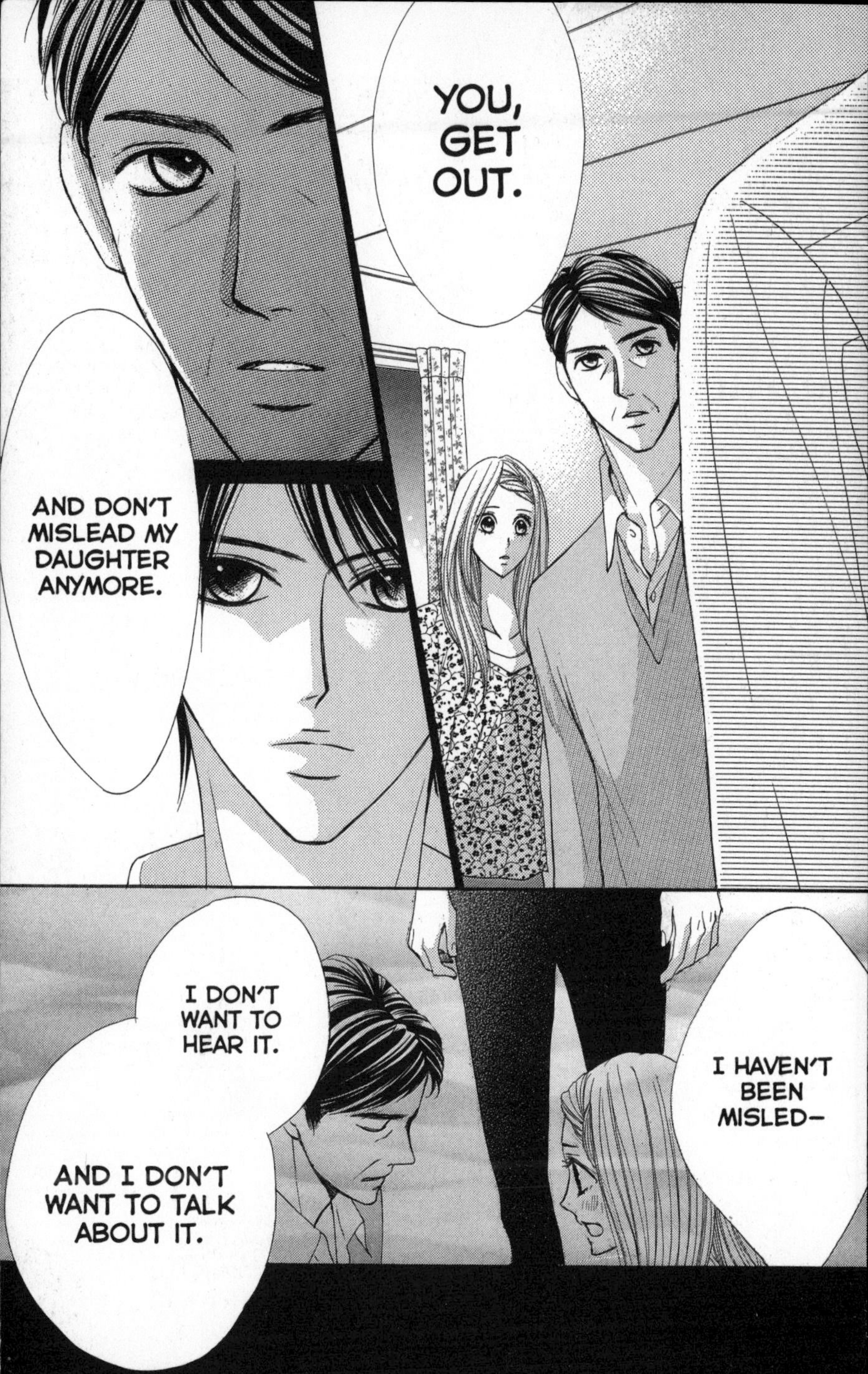
YOU, GET OUT.
AND DON'T MISLEAD MY DAUGHTER ANYMORE.
I HAVEN'T BEEN MISLED—
I DON'T WANT TO HEAR IT.
AND I DON'T WANT TO TALK ABOUT IT.

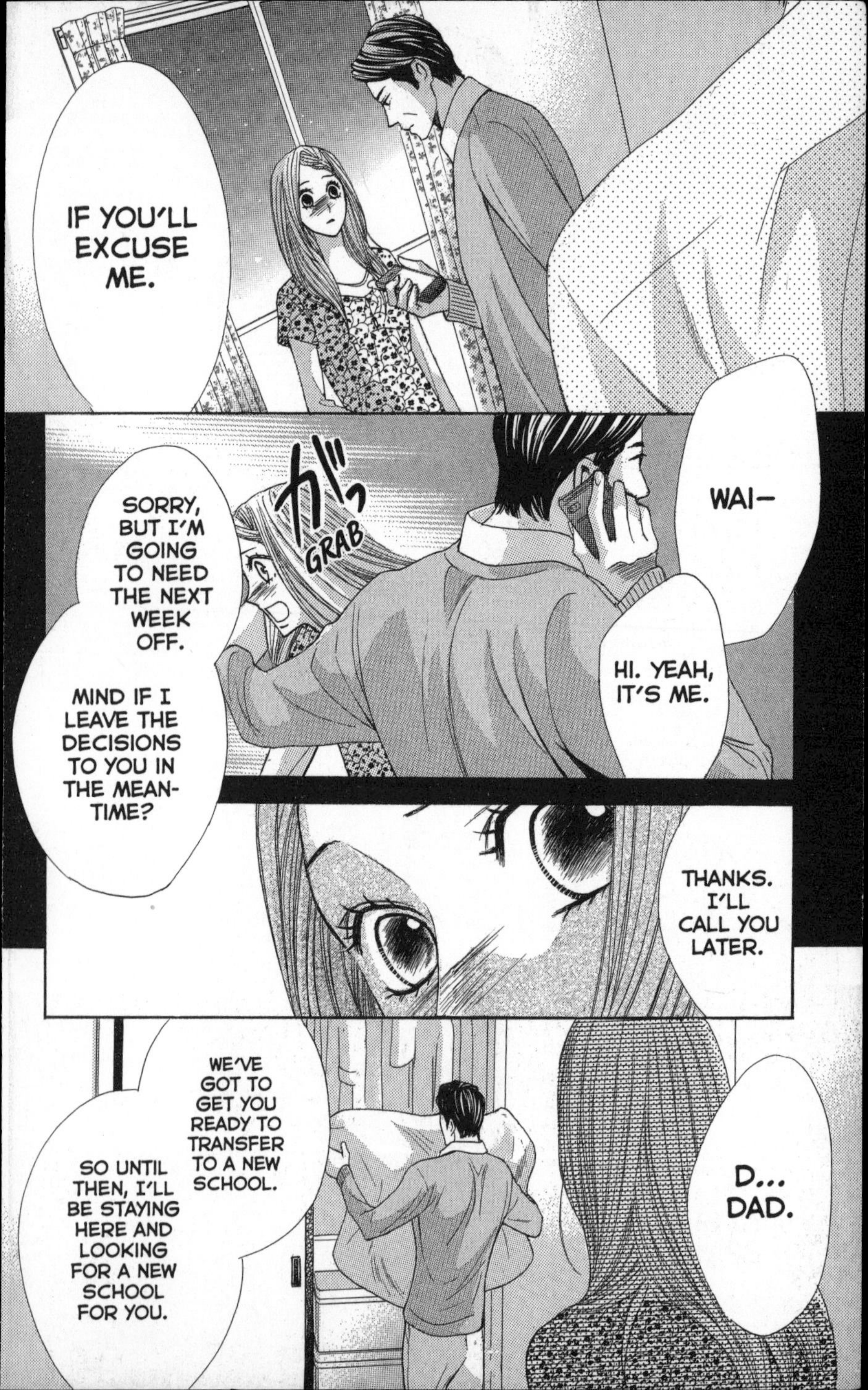
IF YOU'LL EXCUSE ME.
WAI-
ガッ
GRAB
HI. YEAH, IT'S ME.
SORRY, BUT I'M GOING TO NEED THE NEXT WEEK OFF.
MIND IF I LEAVE THE DECISIONS TO YOU IN THE MEAN-TIME?
THANKS. I'LL CALL YOU LATER.
D... DAD.
WE'VE GOT TO GET YOU READY TO TRANSFER TO A NEW SCHOOL.
SO UNTIL THEN, I'LL BE STAYING HERE AND LOOKING FOR A NEW SCHOOL FOR YOU.

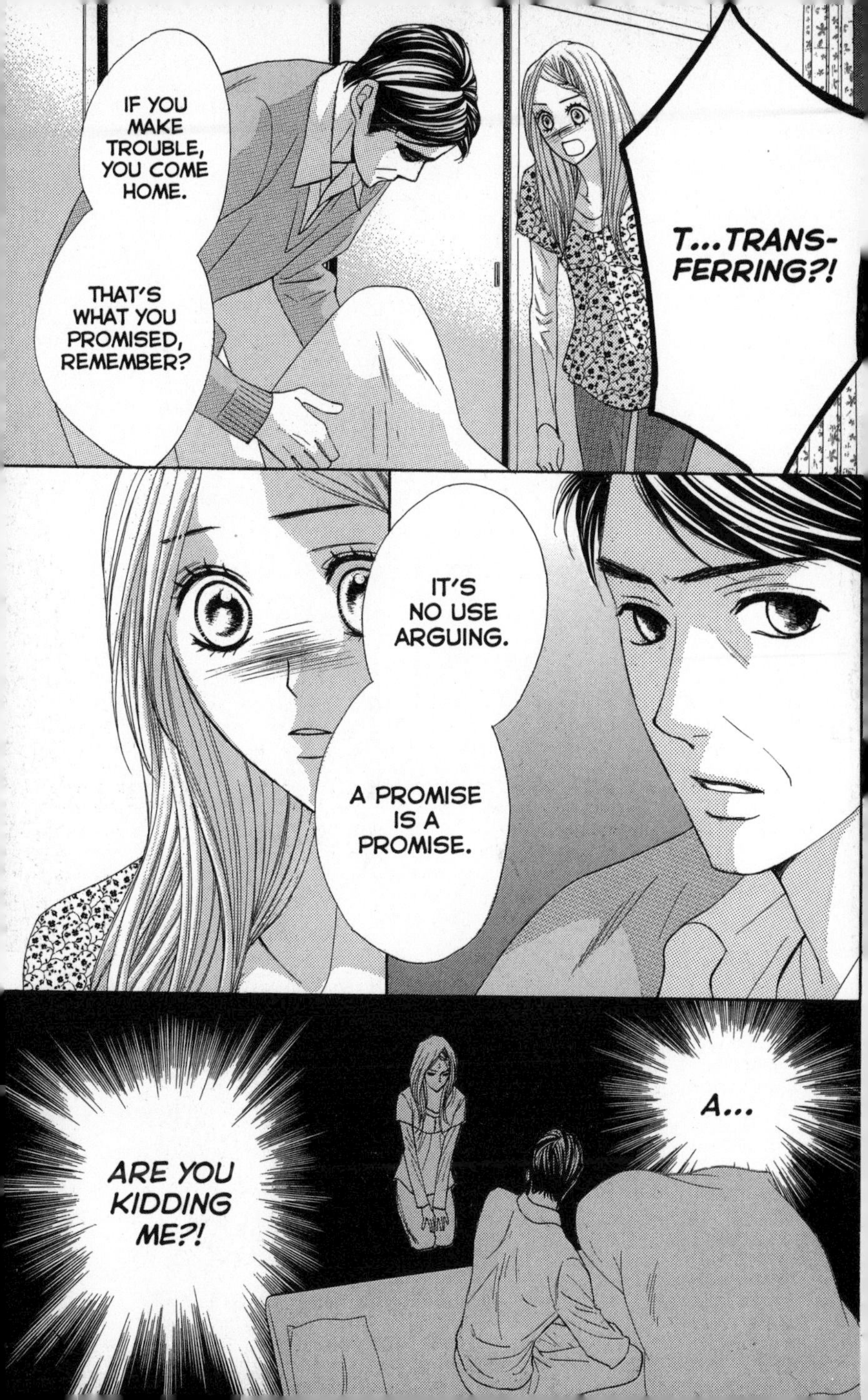
T...TRANS-FERRING?!
IF YOU MAKE TROUBLE, YOU COME HOME.
THAT'S WHAT YOU PROMISED, REMEMBER?
IT'S NO USE ARGUING.
A PROMISE IS A PROMISE.
A...
ARE YOU KIDDING ME?!

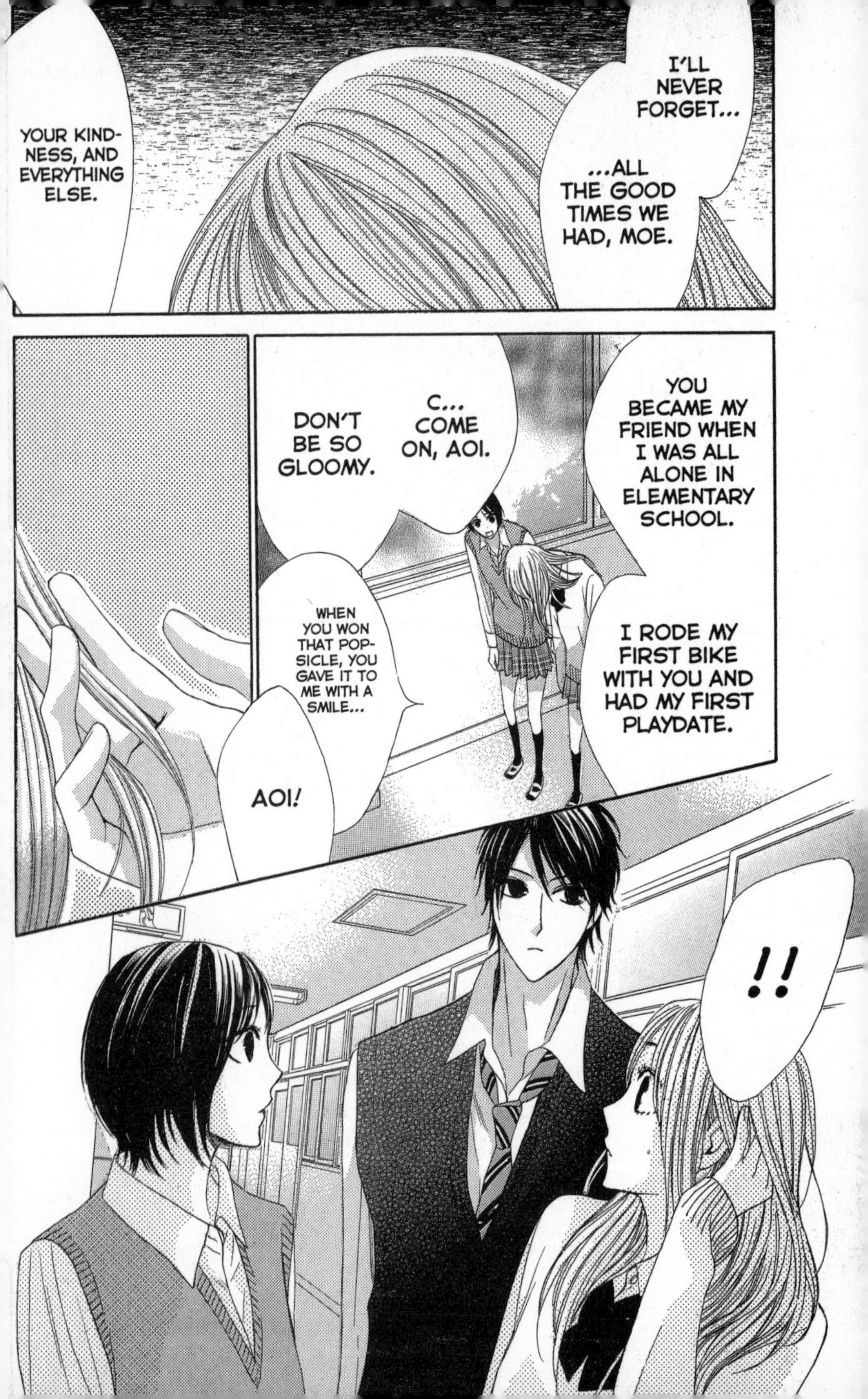
I'LL NEVER FORGET...
...ALL THE GOOD TIMES WE HAD, MOE.
YOUR KINDNESS, AND EVERYTHING ELSE.
YOU BECAME MY FRIEND WHEN I WAS ALL ALONE IN ELEMENTARY SCHOOL.
I RODE MY FIRST BIKE WITH YOU AND HAD MY FIRST PLAYDATE.
C... COME ON, AOI.
DON'T BE SO GLOOMY.
WHEN YOU WON THAT POPSICLE, YOU GAVE IT TO ME WITH A SMILE...
AOI!
!!

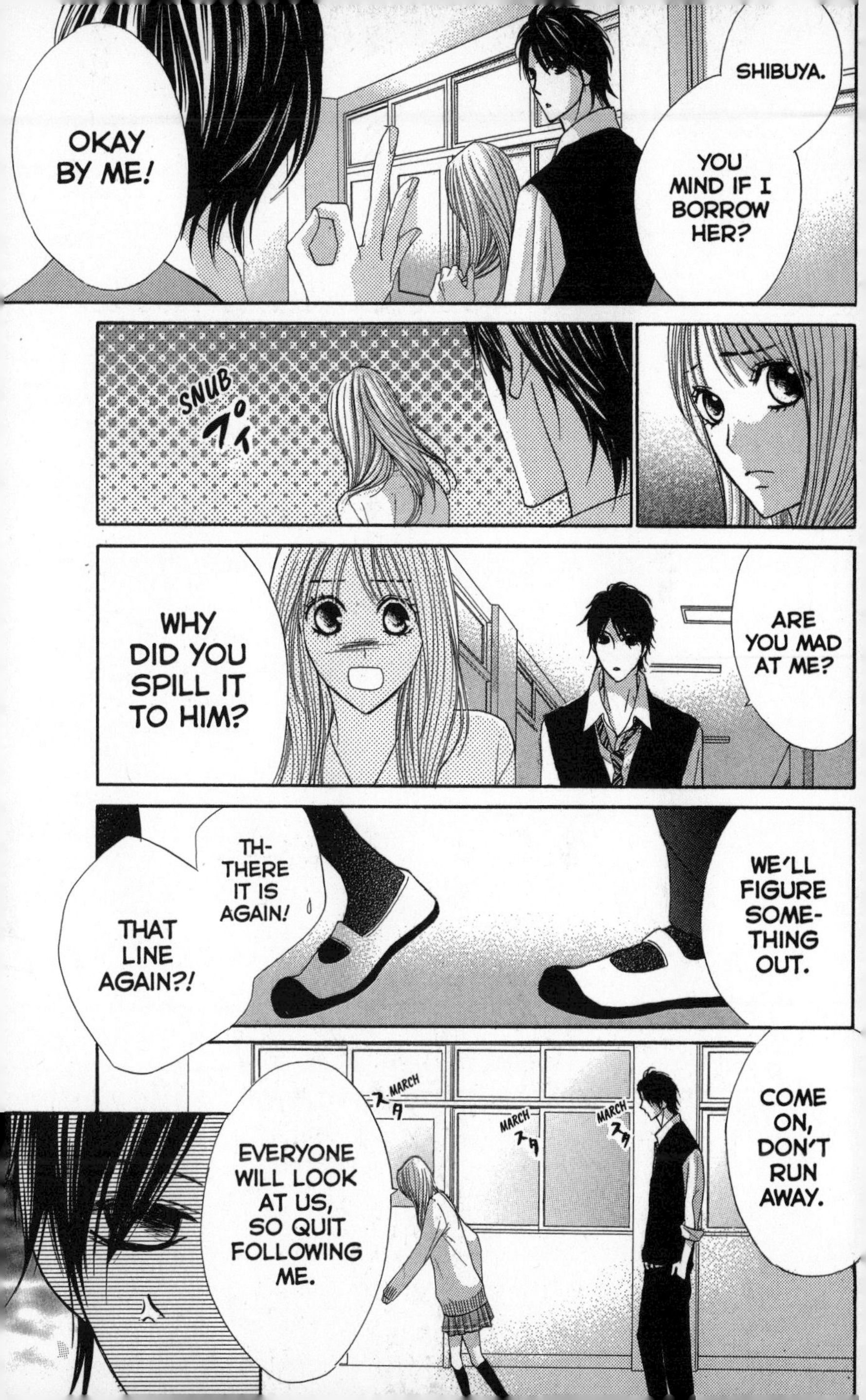
SHIBUYA.
YOU MIND IF I BORROW HER?
OKAY BY ME!
SNUB
プイ
ARE YOU MAD AT ME?
WHY DID YOU SPILL IT TO HIM?
WE'LL FIGURE SOMETHING OUT.
TH-THERE IT IS AGAIN!
THAT LINE AGAIN?!
COME ON, DON'T RUN AWAY.
MARCH
スタ
MARCH
スタ
MARCH
スタ
EVERYONE WILL LOOK AT US, SO QUIT FOLLOWING ME.

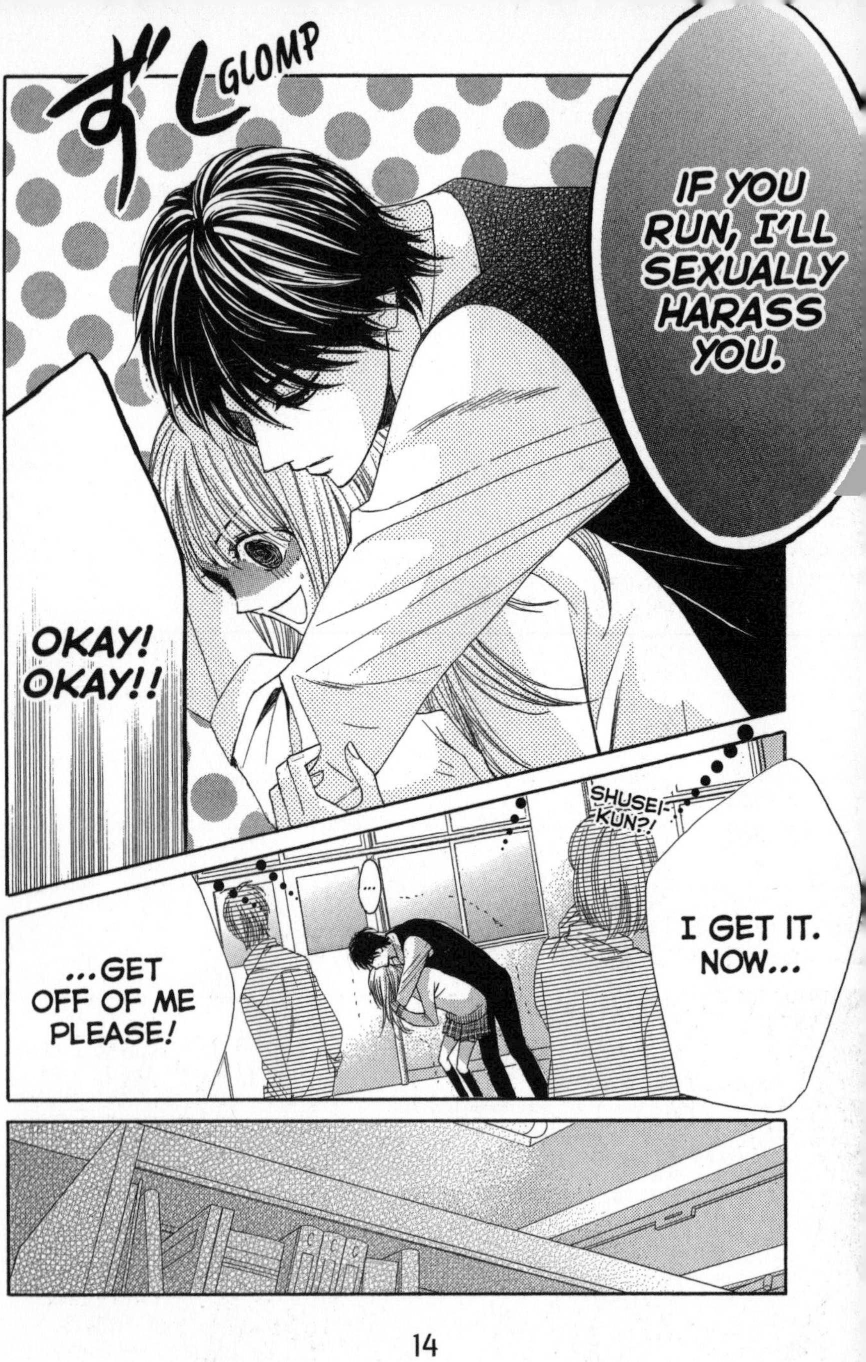
IF YOU RUN, I'LL SEXUALLY HARASS YOU.
ずし GLOMP
OKAY! OKAY!!
SHUSEI-KUN?!
I GET IT. NOW...
...
...GET OFF OF ME PLEASE!

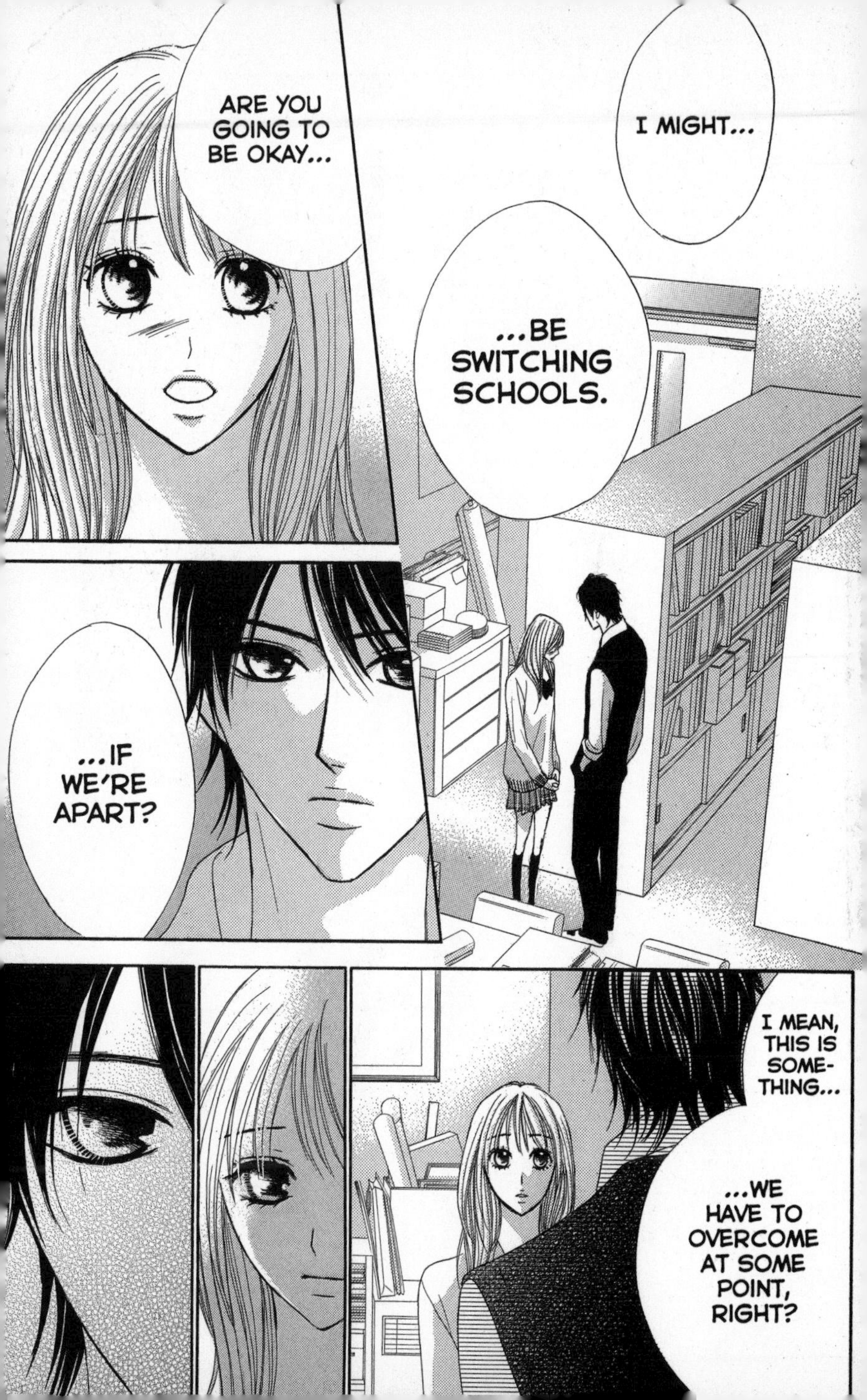
I MIGHT...
...BE SWITCHING SCHOOLS.
ARE YOU GOING TO BE OKAY...
...IF WE'RE APART?
I MEAN, THIS IS SOME-THING...
...WE HAVE TO OVERCOME AT SOME POINT, RIGHT?

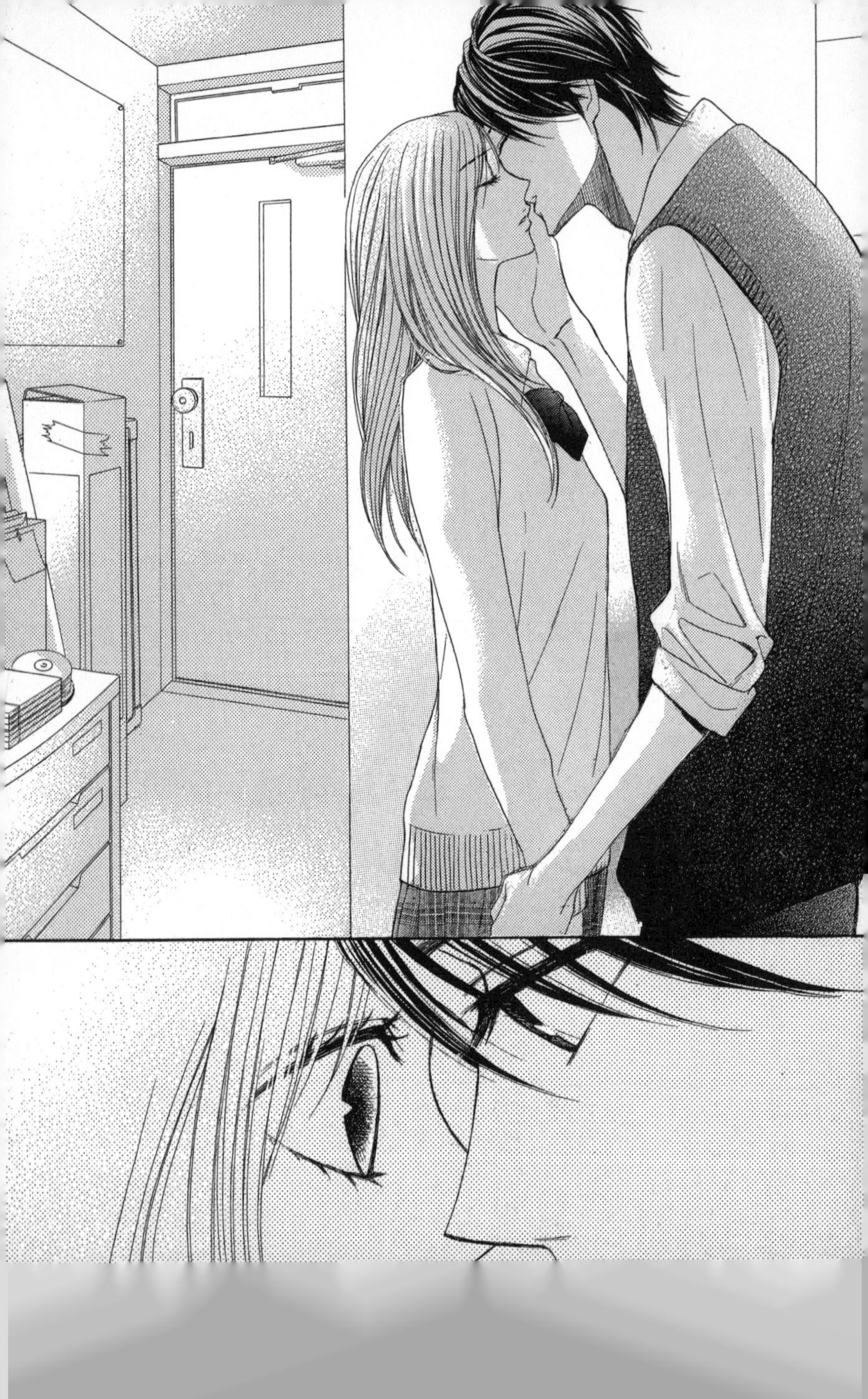

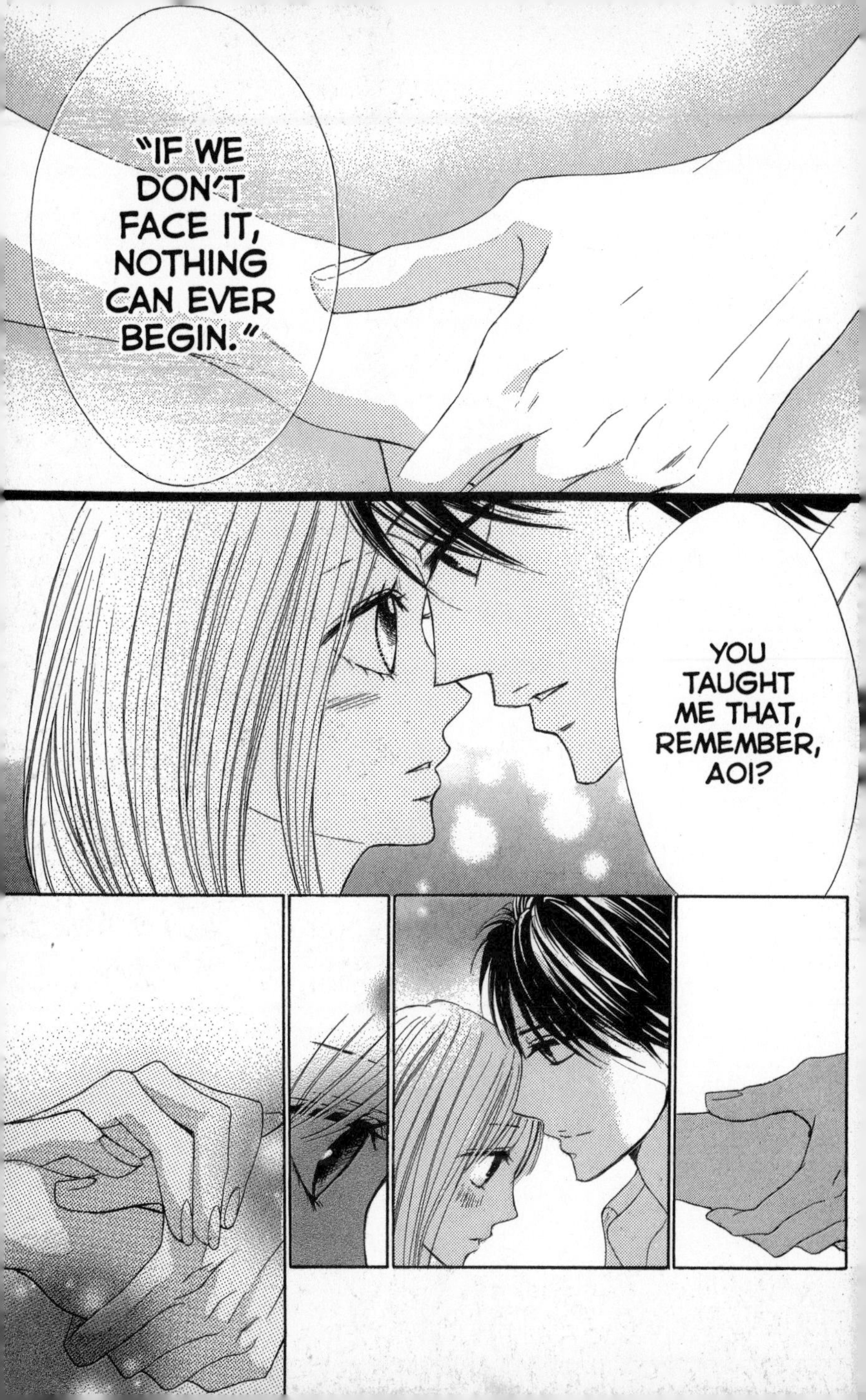
"IF WE DON'T FACE IT, NOTHING CAN EVER BEGIN."
YOU TAUGHT ME THAT, REMEMBER, AOI?

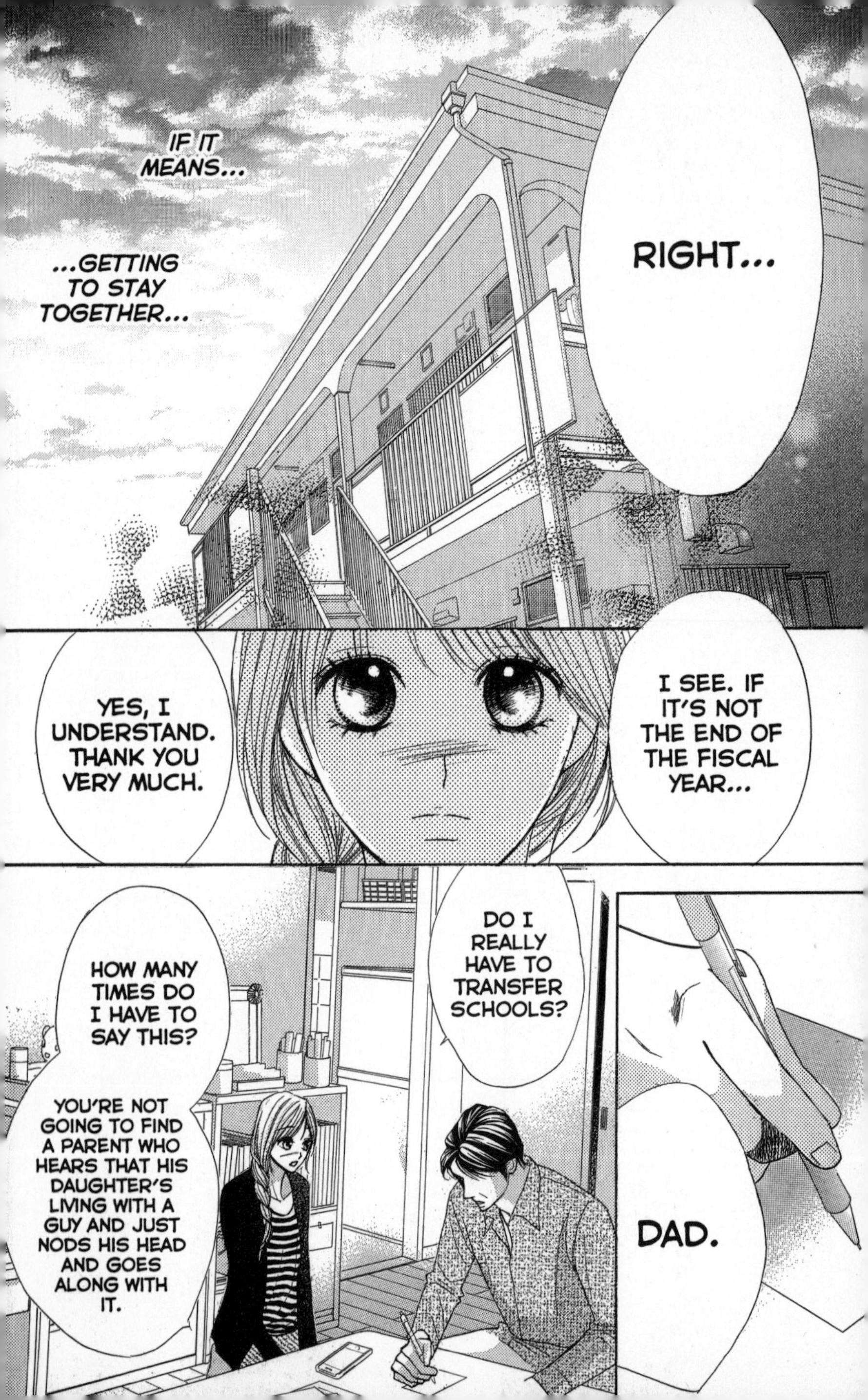
RIGHT...
IF IT MEANS...
...GETTING TO STAY TOGETHER...
I SEE. IF IT'S NOT THE END OF THE FISCAL YEAR...
YES, I UNDERSTAND. THANK YOU VERY MUCH.
DAD.
DO I REALLY HAVE TO TRANSFER SCHOOLS?
HOW MANY TIMES DO I HAVE TO SAY THIS?
YOU'RE NOT GOING TO FIND A PARENT WHO HEARS THAT HIS DAUGHTER'S LIVING WITH A GUY AND JUST NODS HIS HEAD AND GOES ALONG WITH IT.

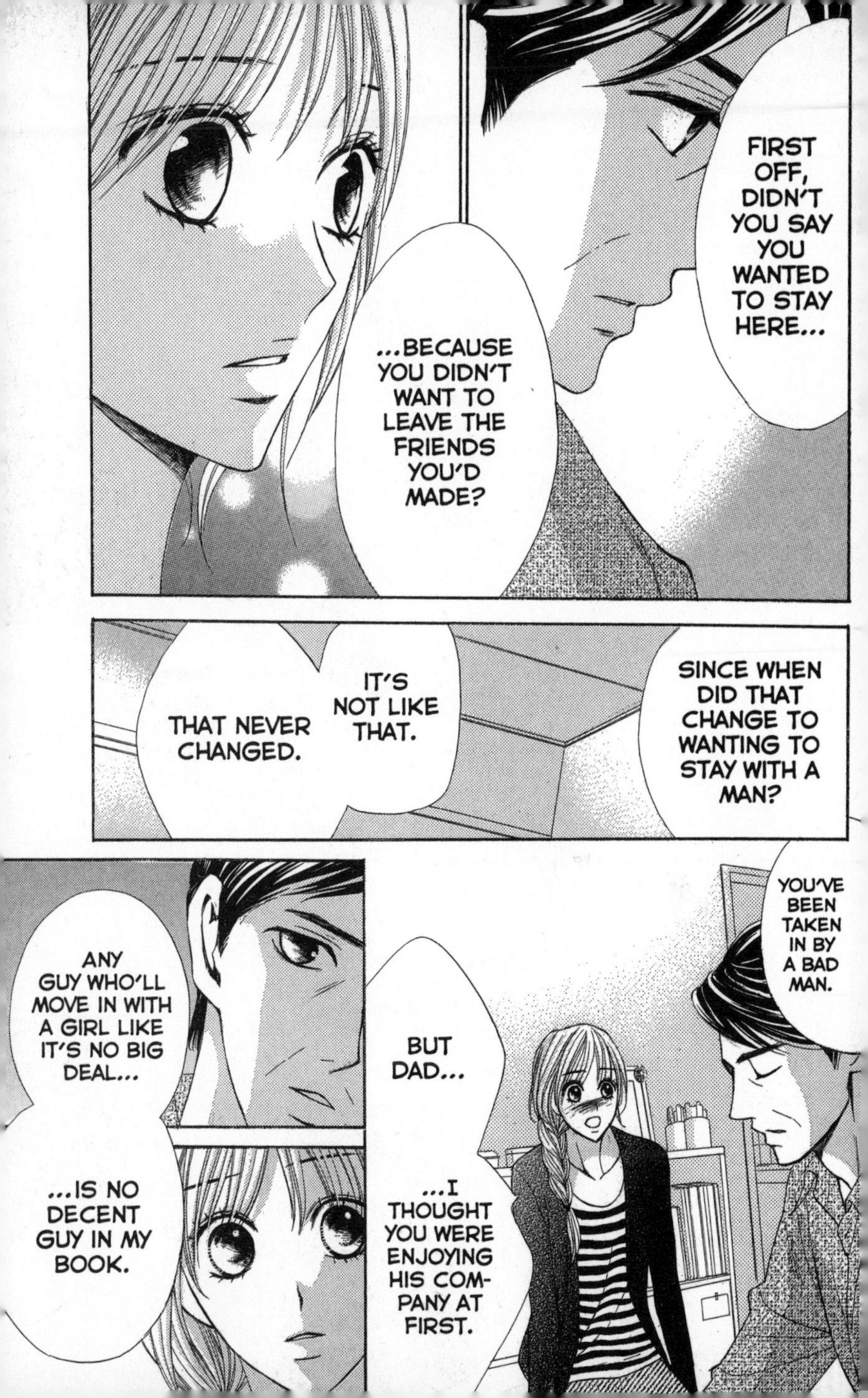
FIRST OFF, DIDN'T YOU SAY YOU WANTED TO STAY HERE...
...BECAUSE YOU DIDN'T WANT TO LEAVE THE FRIENDS YOU'D MADE?
SINCE WHEN DID THAT CHANGE TO WANTING TO STAY WITH A MAN?
IT'S NOT LIKE THAT.
THAT NEVER CHANGED.
YOU'VE BEEN TAKEN IN BY A BAD MAN.
BUT DAD...
...I THOUGHT YOU WERE ENJOYING HIS COMPANY AT FIRST.
ANY GUY WHO'LL MOVE IN WITH A GIRL LIKE IT'S NO BIG DEAL...
...IS NO DECENT GUY IN MY BOOK.

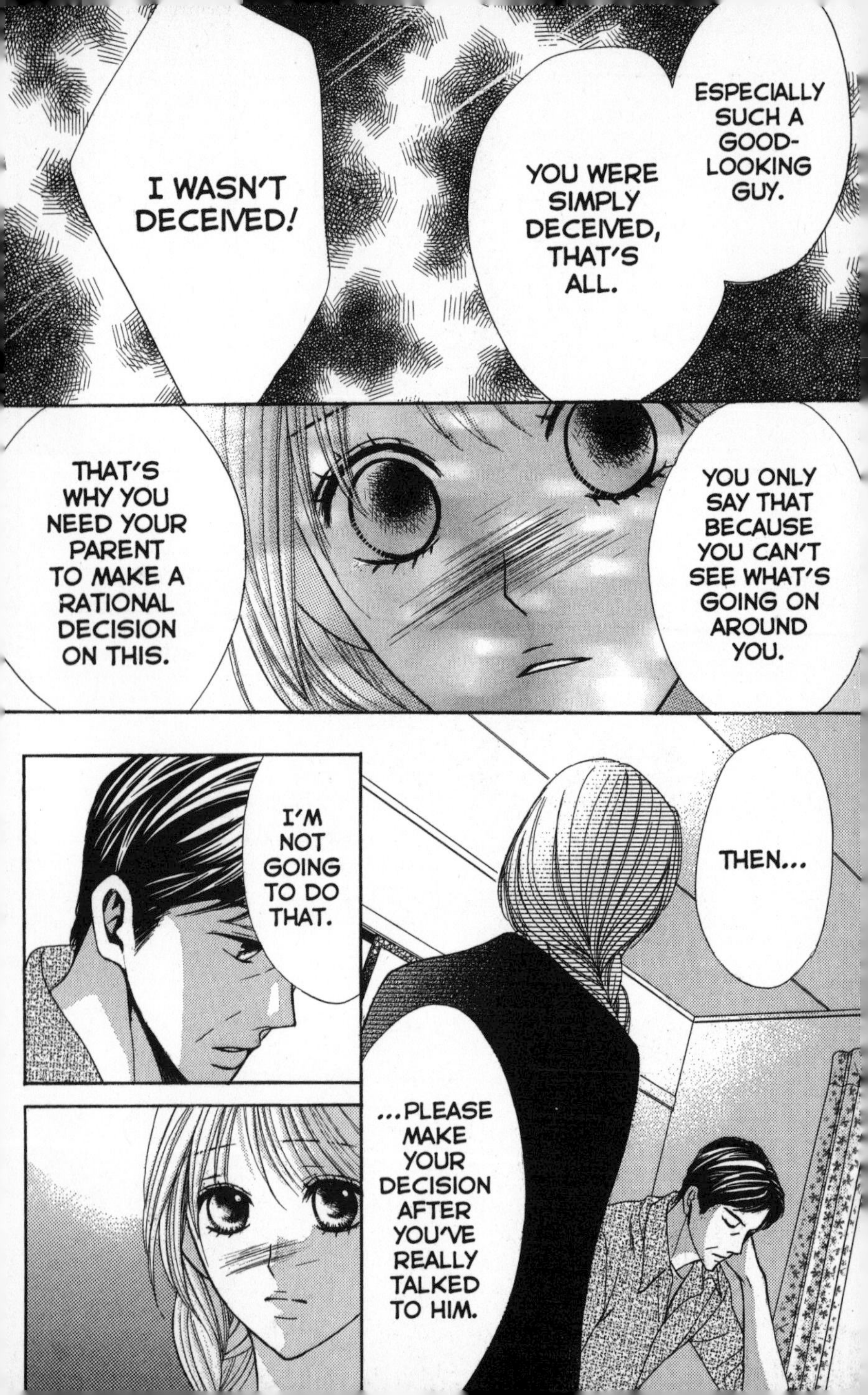

ESPECIALLY SUCH A GOOD-LOOKING GUY.
YOU WERE SIMPLY DECEIVED, THAT'S ALL.
I WASN'T DECEIVED!
YOU ONLY SAY THAT BECAUSE YOU CAN'T SEE WHAT'S GOING ON AROUND YOU.
THAT'S WHY YOU NEED YOUR PARENT TO MAKE A RATIONAL DECISION ON THIS.
I'M NOT GOING TO DO THAT.
THEN...
...PLEASE MAKE YOUR DECISION AFTER YOU'VE REALLY TALKED TO HIM.

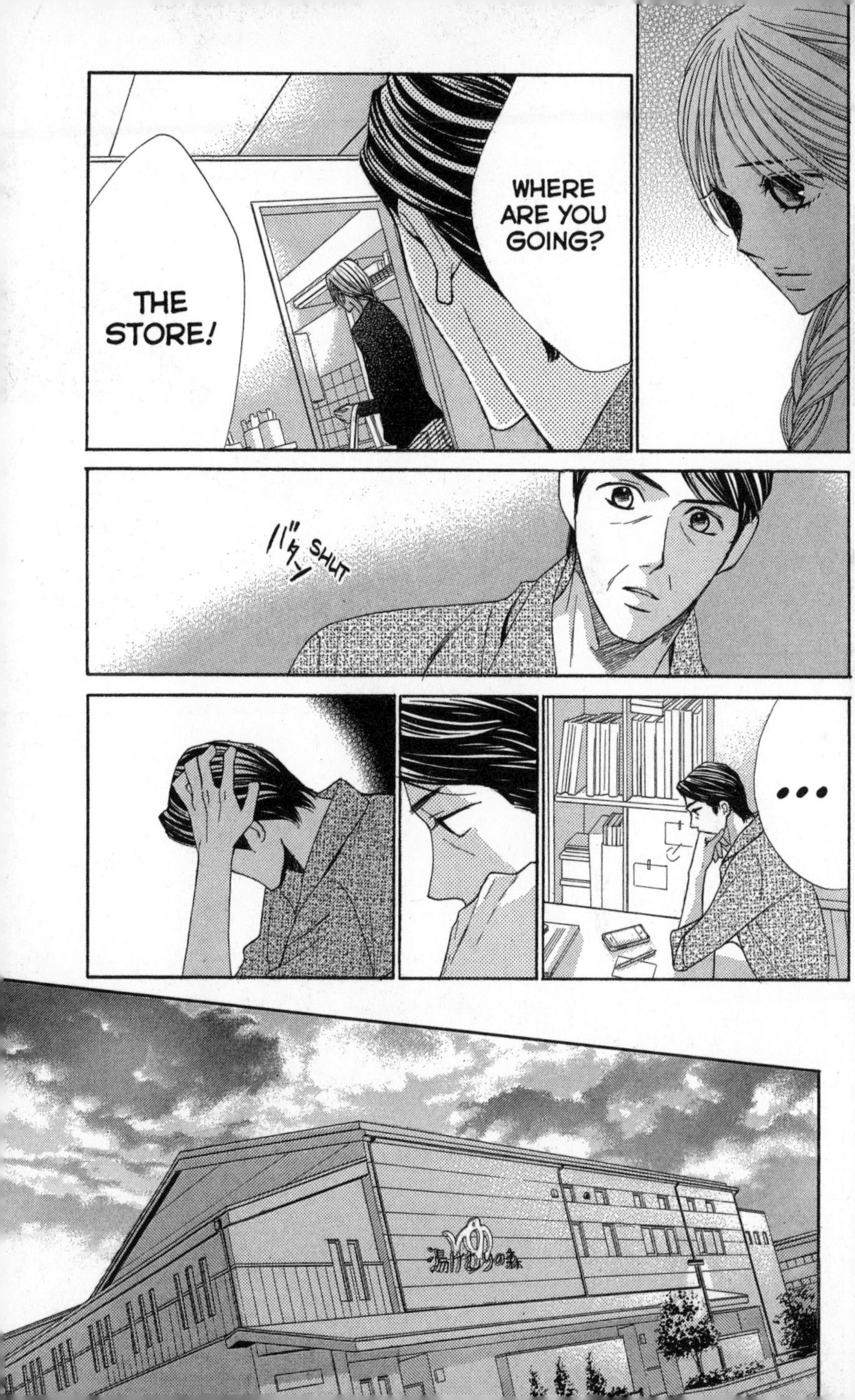
WHERE ARE YOU GOING?
THE STORE!
バタン SHUT
...
湯けむりの森

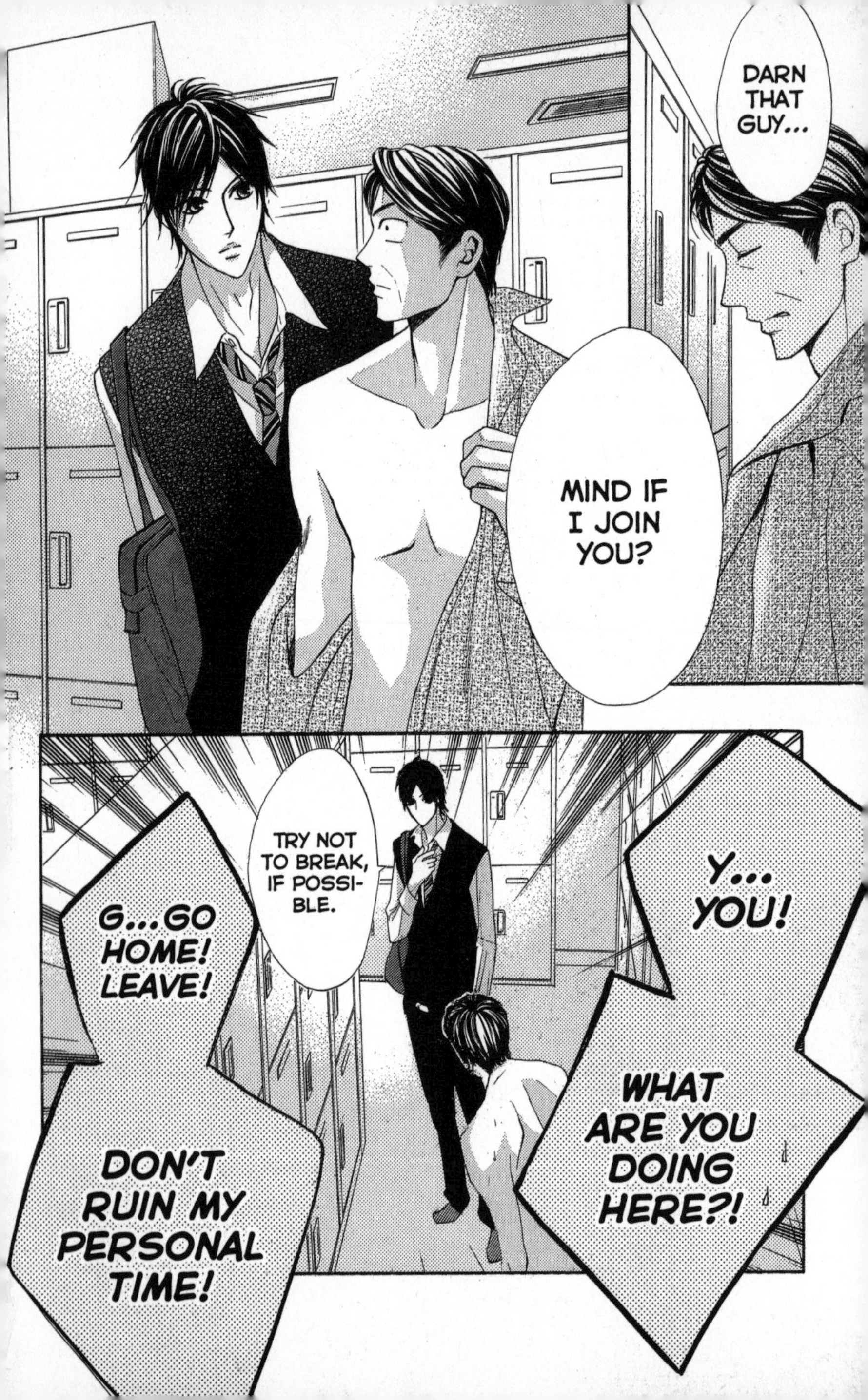
DARN THAT GUY...
MIND IF I JOIN YOU?
Y... YOU!
WHAT ARE YOU DOING HERE?!
TRY NOT TO BREAK, IF POSSI-BLE.
G...GO HOME! LEAVE!
DON'T RUIN MY PERSONAL TIME!

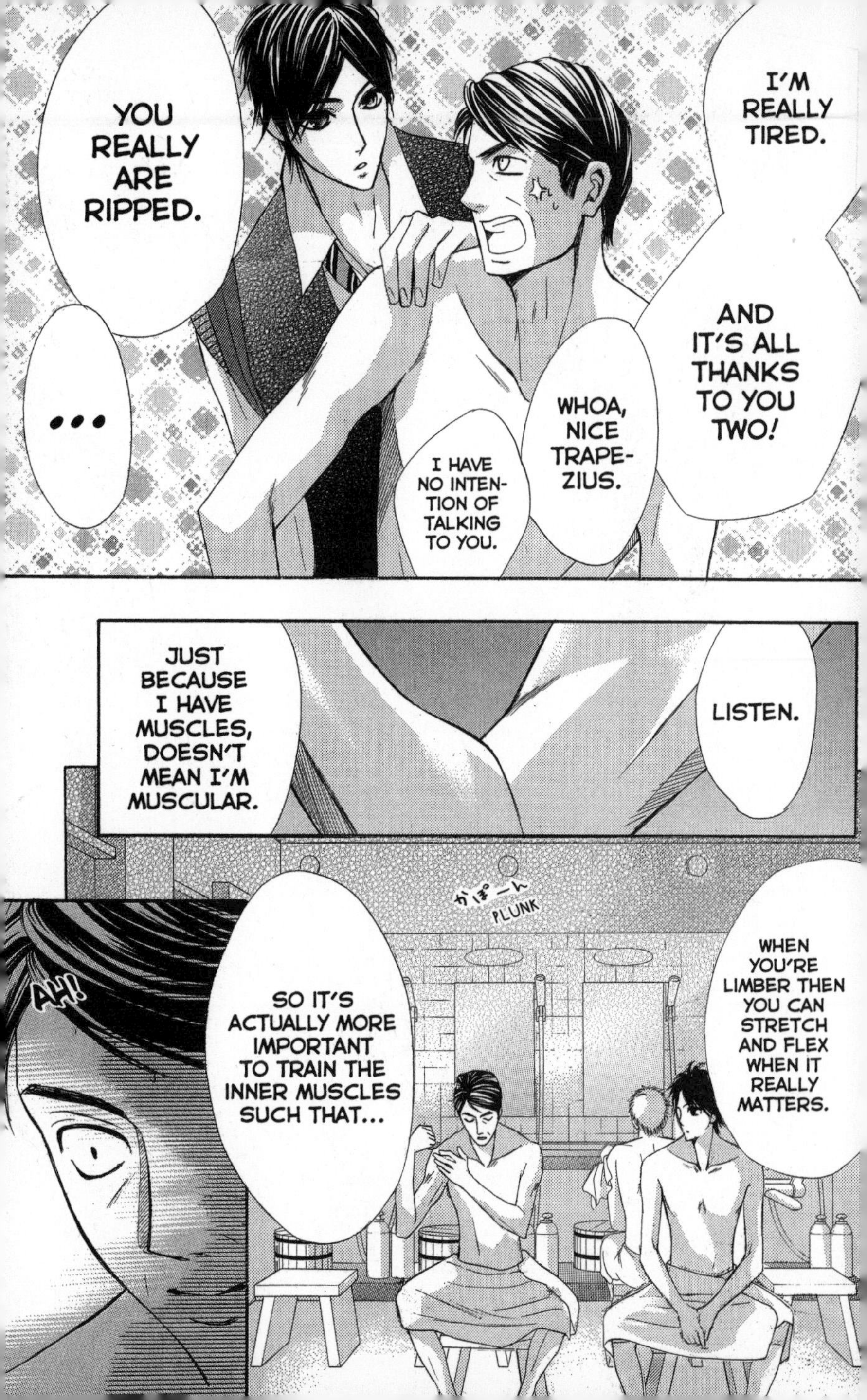

I'M REALLY TIRED.
AND IT'S ALL THANKS TO YOU TWO!
YOU REALLY ARE RIPPED.
WHOA, NICE TRAPE-ZIUS.
I HAVE NO INTEN-TION OF TALKING TO YOU.
...
LISTEN.
JUST BECAUSE I HAVE MUSCLES, DOESN'T MEAN I'M MUSCULAR.
WHEN YOU'RE LIMBER THEN YOU CAN STRETCH AND FLEX WHEN IT REALLY MATTERS.
かぽーん
PLUNK
SO IT'S ACTUALLY MORE IMPORTANT TO TRAIN THE INNER MUSCLES SUCH THAT...
AH!

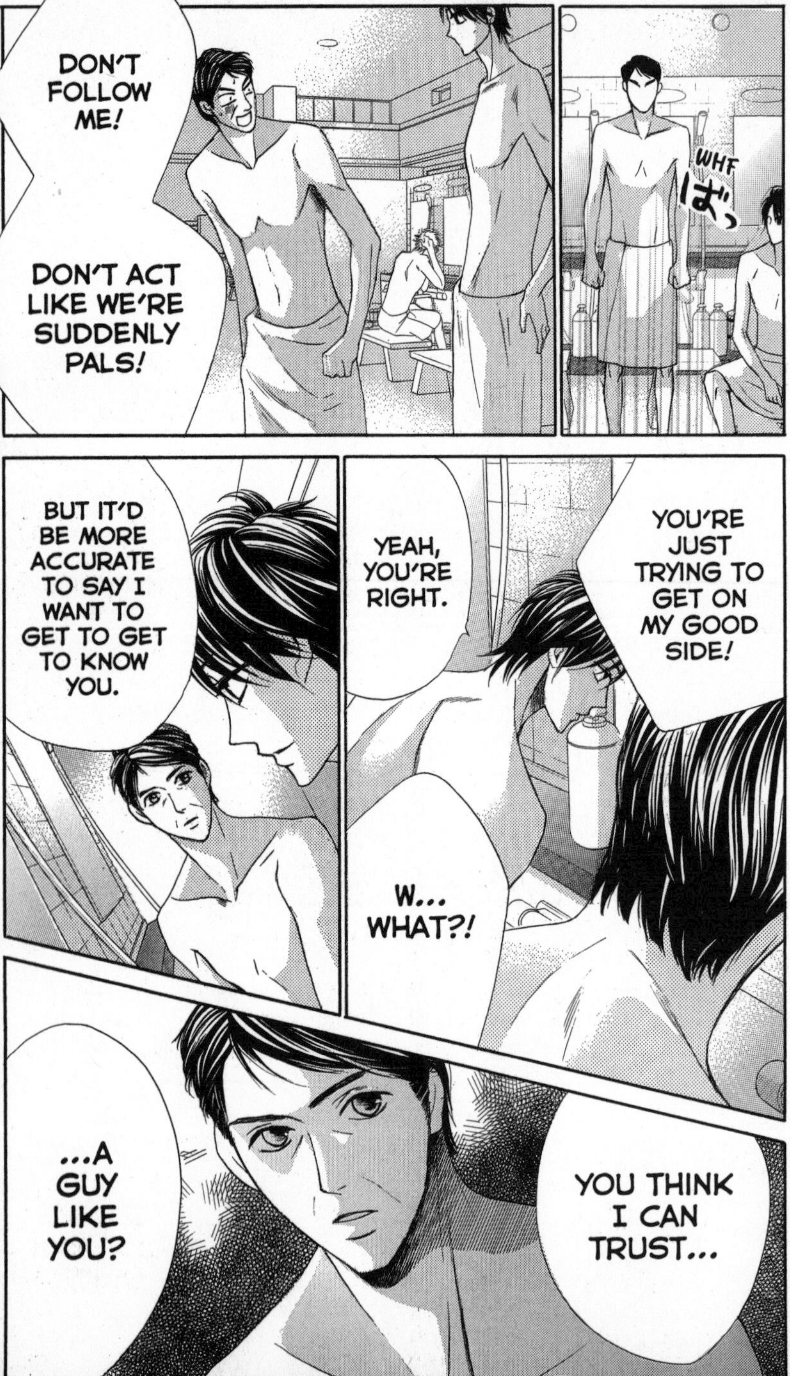
WHF
ばっ
DON'T FOLLOW ME!
DON'T ACT LIKE WE'RE SUDDENLY PALS!
YOU'RE JUST TRYING TO GET ON MY GOOD SIDE!
YEAH, YOU'RE RIGHT.
W... WHAT?!
BUT IT'D BE MORE ACCURATE TO SAY I WANT TO GET TO GET TO KNOW YOU.
YOU THINK I CAN TRUST...
...A GUY LIKE YOU?

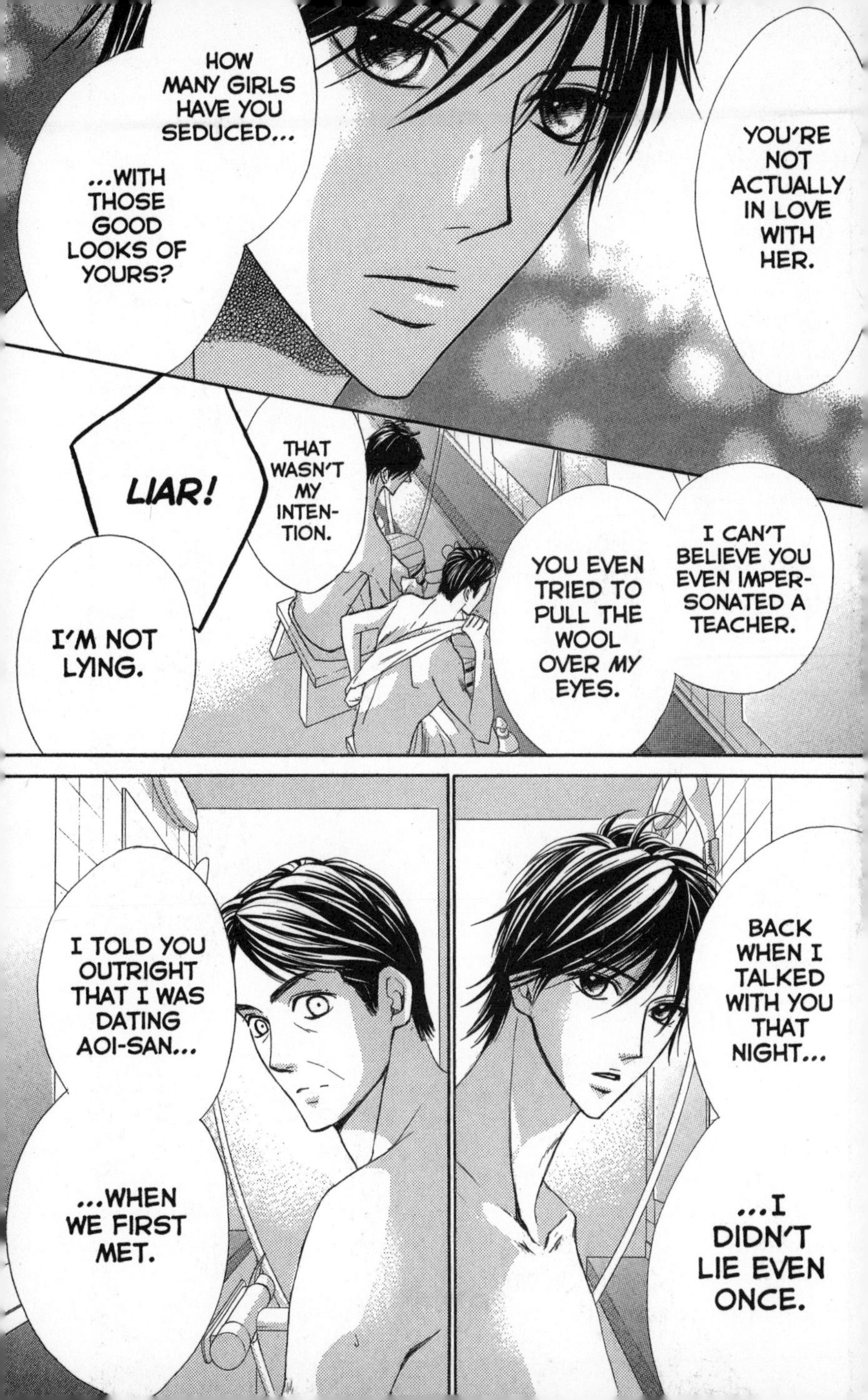
YOU'RE NOT ACTUALLY IN LOVE WITH HER.
HOW MANY GIRLS HAVE YOU SEDUCED...
...WITH THOSE GOOD LOOKS OF YOURS?
I CAN'T BELIEVE YOU EVEN IMPER-SONATED A TEACHER.
YOU EVEN TRIED TO PULL THE WOOL OVER MY EYES.
THAT WASN'T MY INTEN-TION.
LIAR!
I'M NOT LYING.
BACK WHEN I TALKED WITH YOU THAT NIGHT...
...I DIDN'T LIE EVEN ONCE.
I TOLD YOU OUTRIGHT THAT I WAS DATING AOI-SAN...
...WHEN WE FIRST MET.

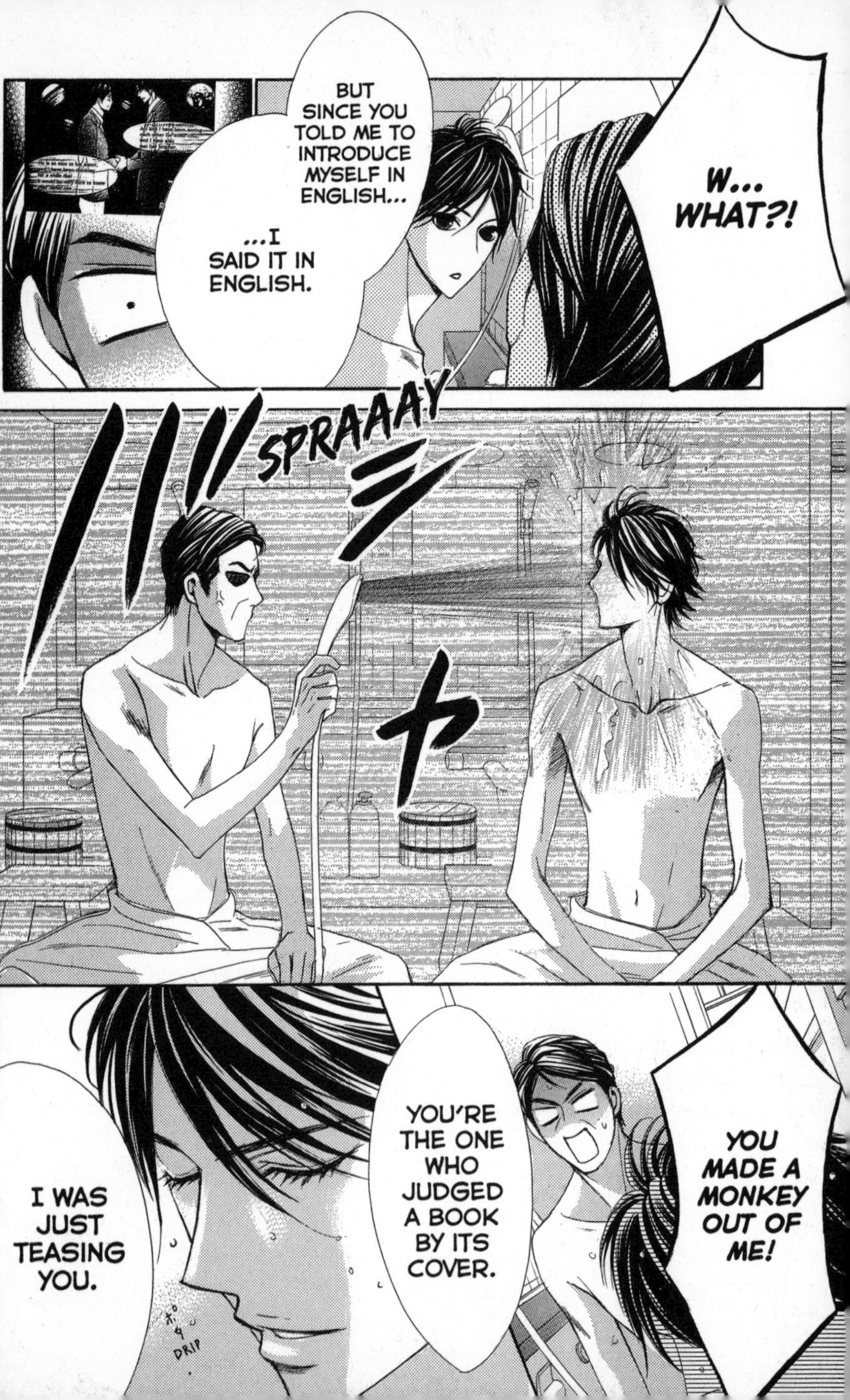
W... WHAT?!
BUT SINCE YOU TOLD ME TO INTRODUCE MYSELF IN ENGLISH...
...I SAID IT IN ENGLISH.
SPRAAAY
YOU MADE A MONKEY OUT OF ME!
YOU'RE THE ONE WHO JUDGED A BOOK BY ITS COVER.
I WAS JUST TEASING YOU.
DRIP

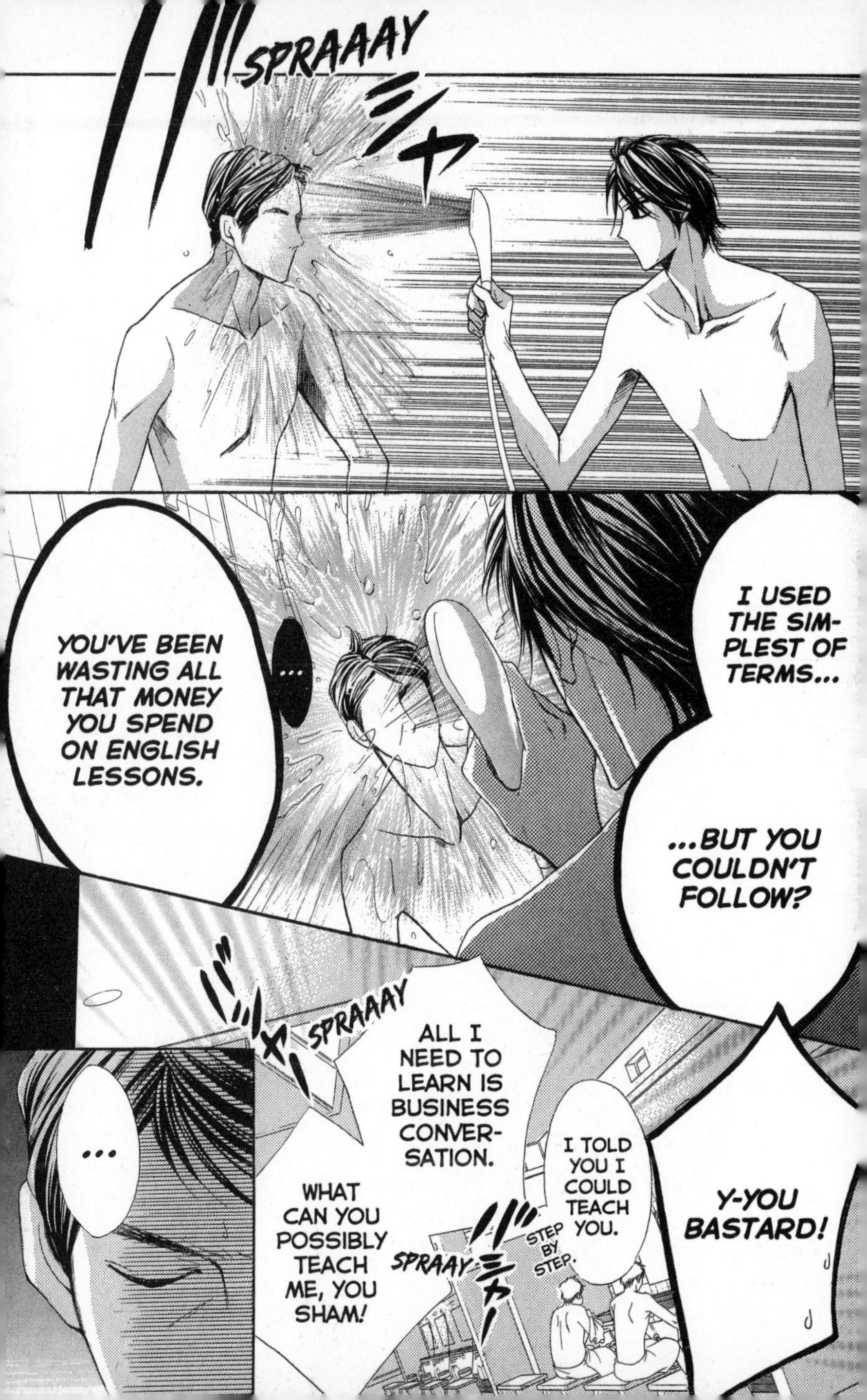
SPRAAAY
I USED THE SIM-PLEST OF TERMS...
...BUT YOU COULDN'T FOLLOW?
...
YOU'VE BEEN WASTING ALL THAT MONEY YOU SPEND ON ENGLISH LESSONS.
SPRAAAY
Y-YOU BASTARD!
I TOLD YOU I COULD TEACH YOU.
STEP BY STEP.
SPRAAY
ALL I NEED TO LEARN IS BUSINESS CONVER-SATION.
WHAT CAN YOU POSSIBLY TEACH ME, YOU SHAM!
...

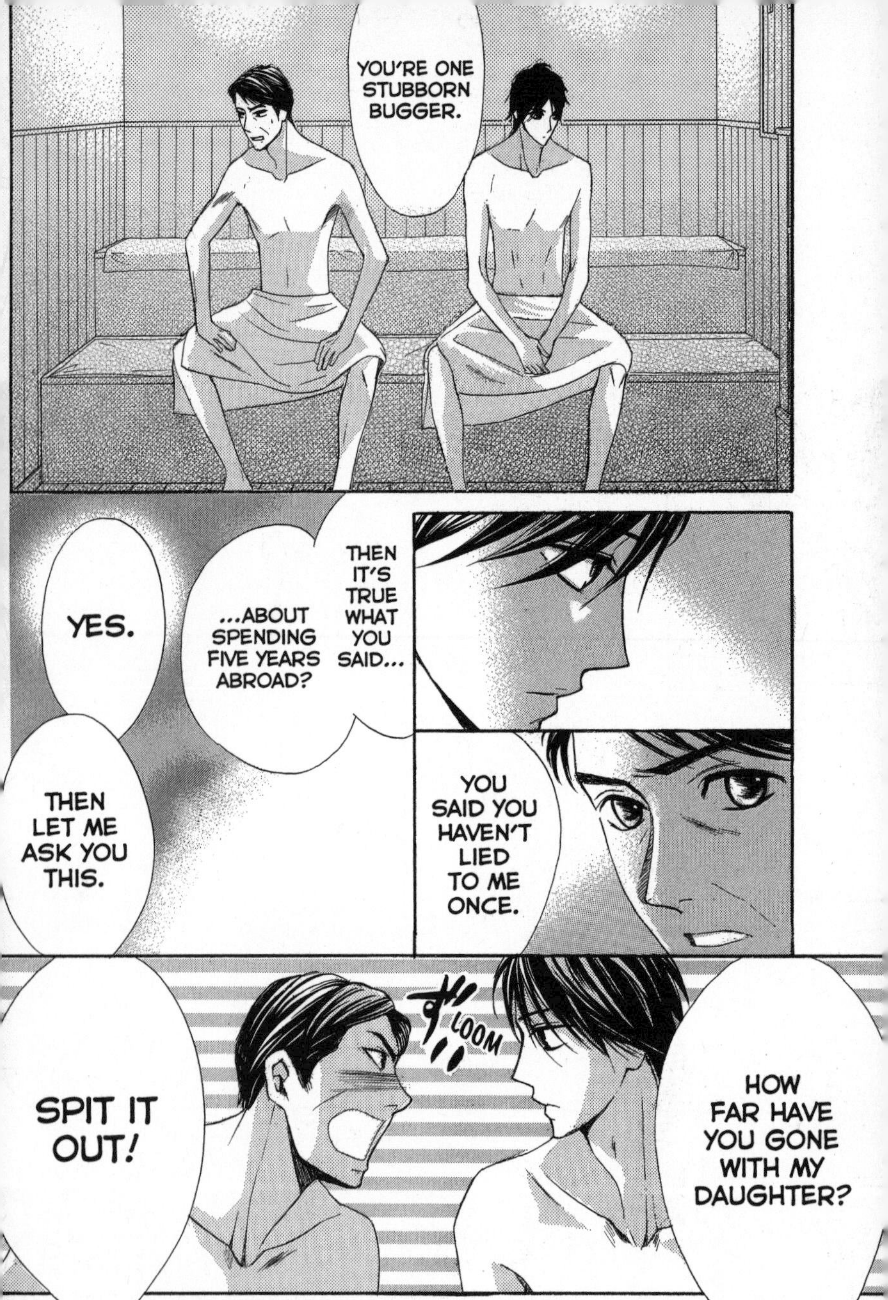
YOU'RE ONE STUBBORN BUGGER.
YOU SAID YOU HAVEN'T LIED TO ME ONCE.
THEN IT'S TRUE WHAT YOU SAID...
...ABOUT SPENDING FIVE YEARS ABROAD?
YES.
THEN LET ME ASK YOU THIS.
HOW FAR HAVE YOU GONE WITH MY DAUGHTER?
LOOM
SPIT IT OUT!

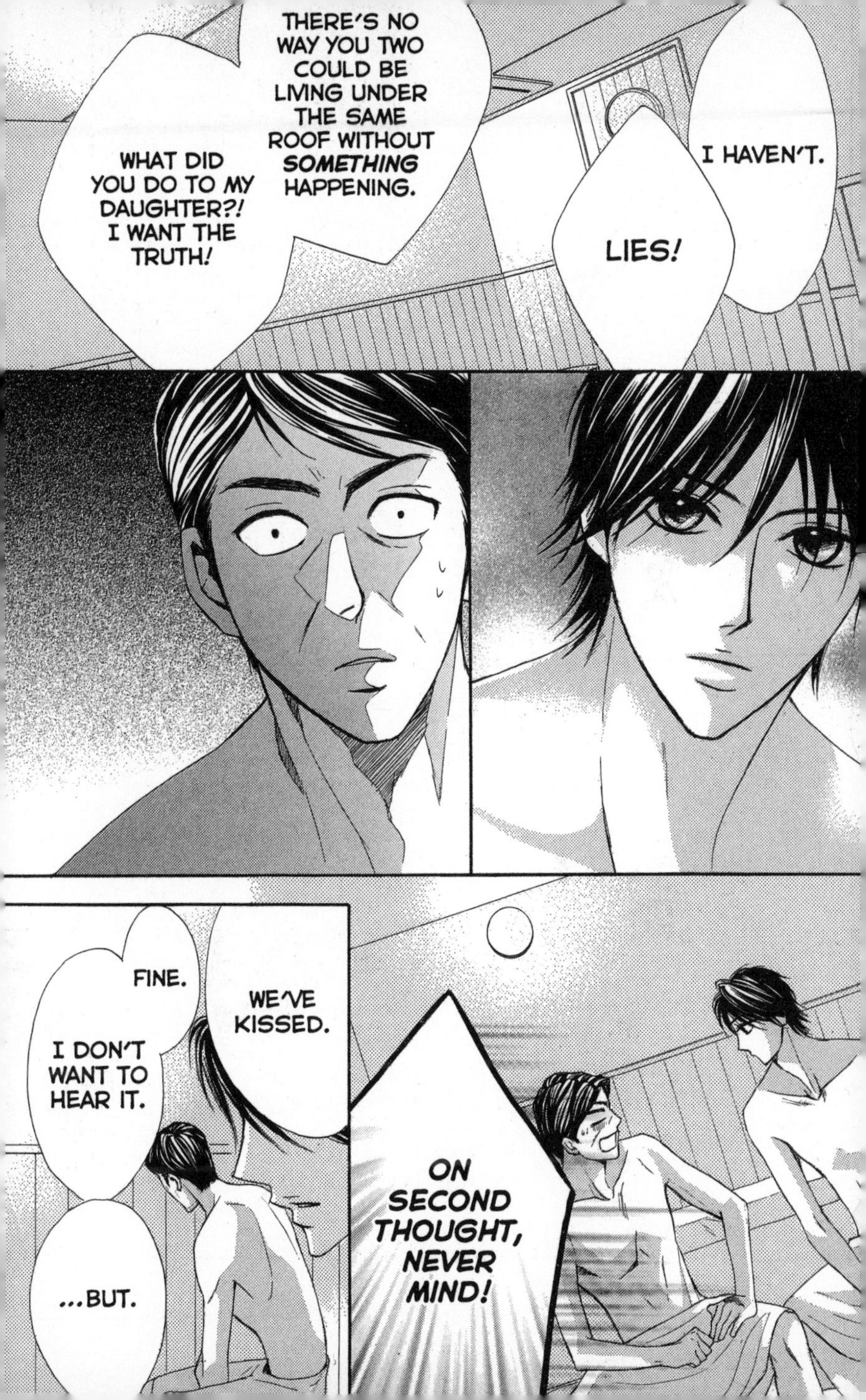
WHAT DID YOU DO TO MY DAUGHTER?! I WANT THE TRUTH!
I HAVEN'T.
LIES!
THERE'S NO WAY YOU TWO COULD BE LIVING UNDER THE SAME ROOF WITHOUT *SOMETHING* HAPPENING.
FINE.
I DON'T WANT TO HEAR IT.
...BUT.
WE'VE KISSED.
ON SECOND THOUGHT, NEVER MIND!

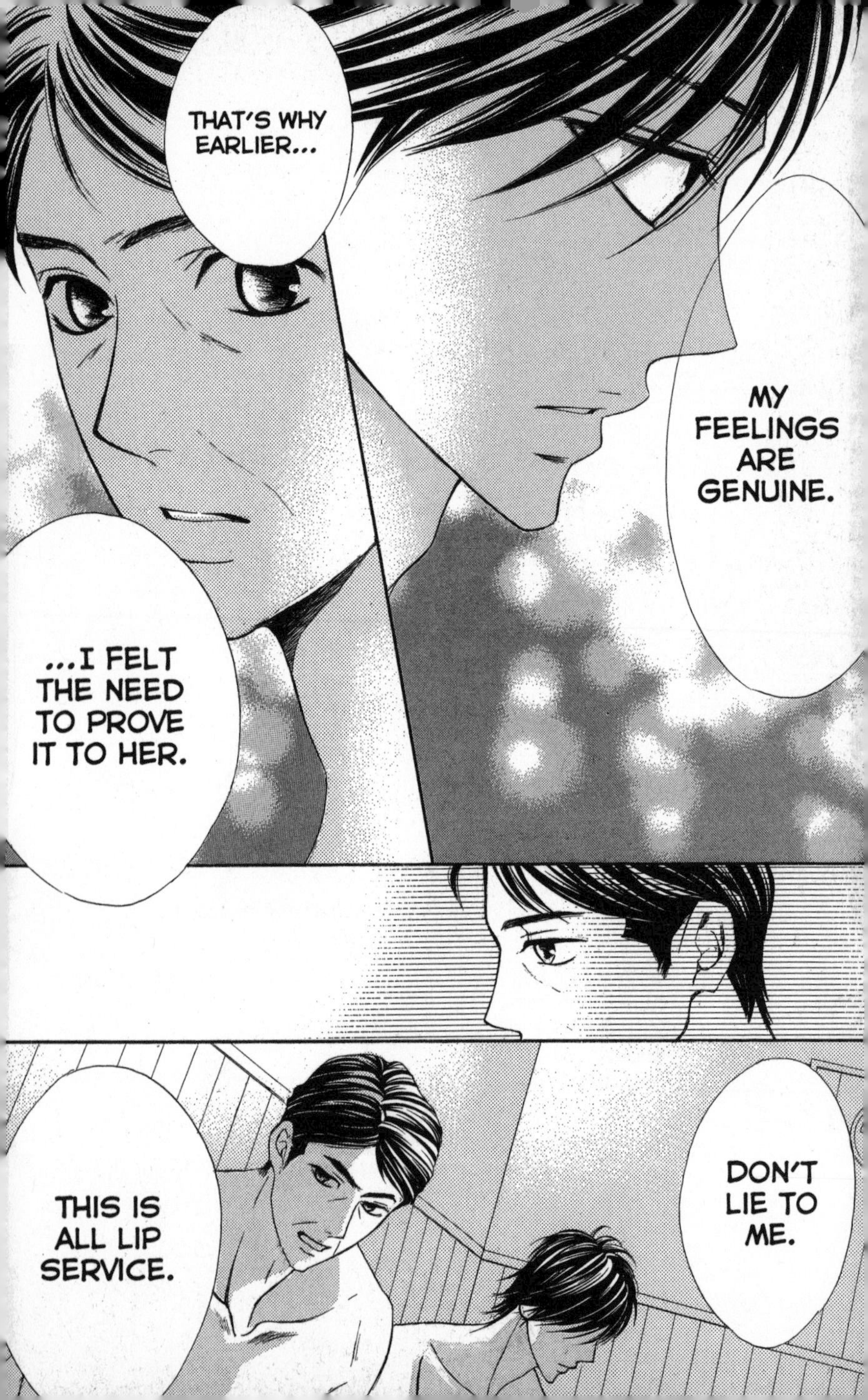
MY FEELINGS ARE GENUINE.
THAT'S WHY EARLIER...
...I FELT THE NEED TO PROVE IT TO HER.
DON'T LIE TO ME.
THIS IS ALL LIP SERVICE.

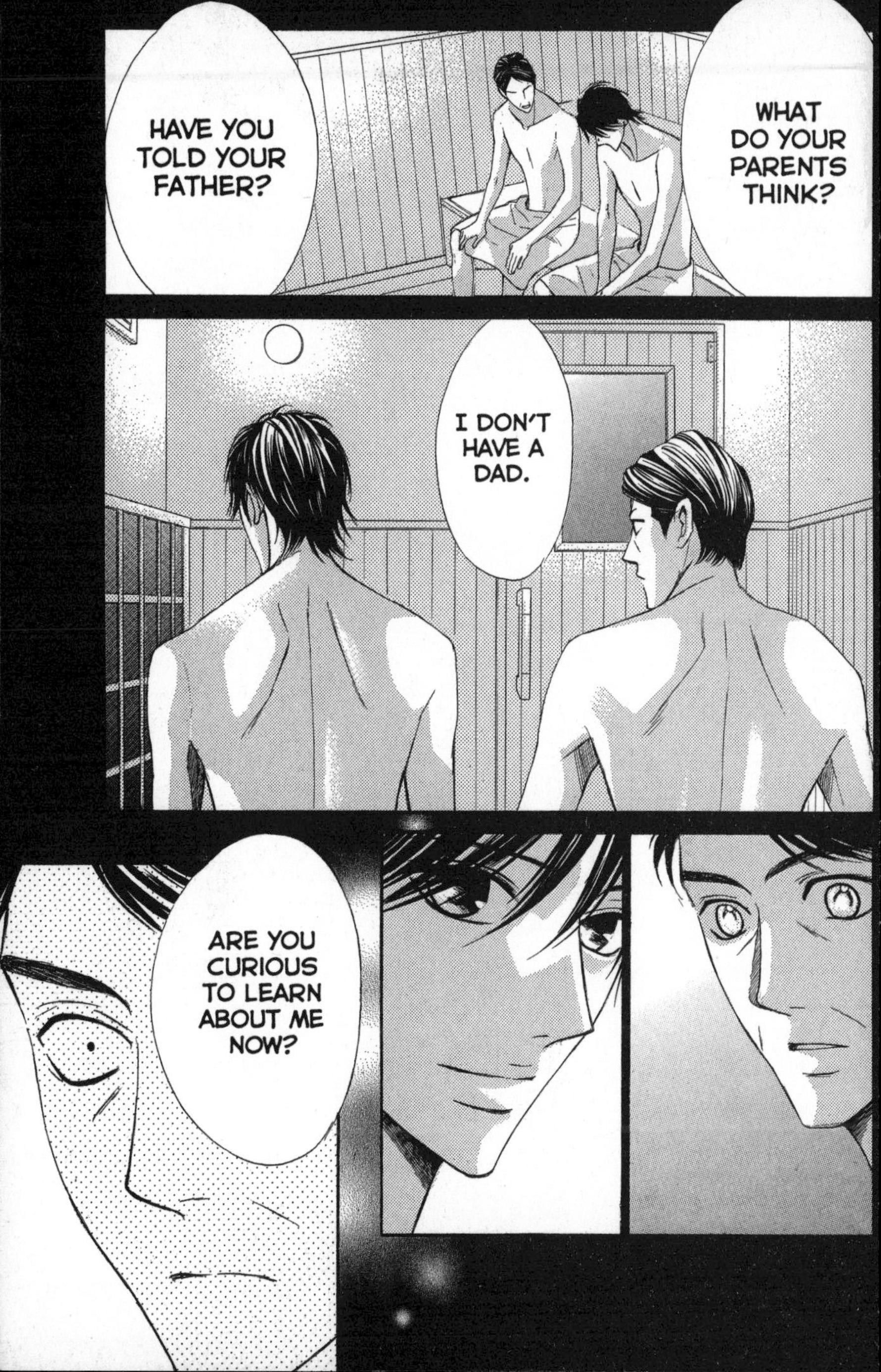
WHAT DO YOUR PARENTS THINK?
HAVE YOU TOLD YOUR FATHER?
I DON'T HAVE A DAD.
ARE YOU CURIOUS TO LEARN ABOUT ME NOW?

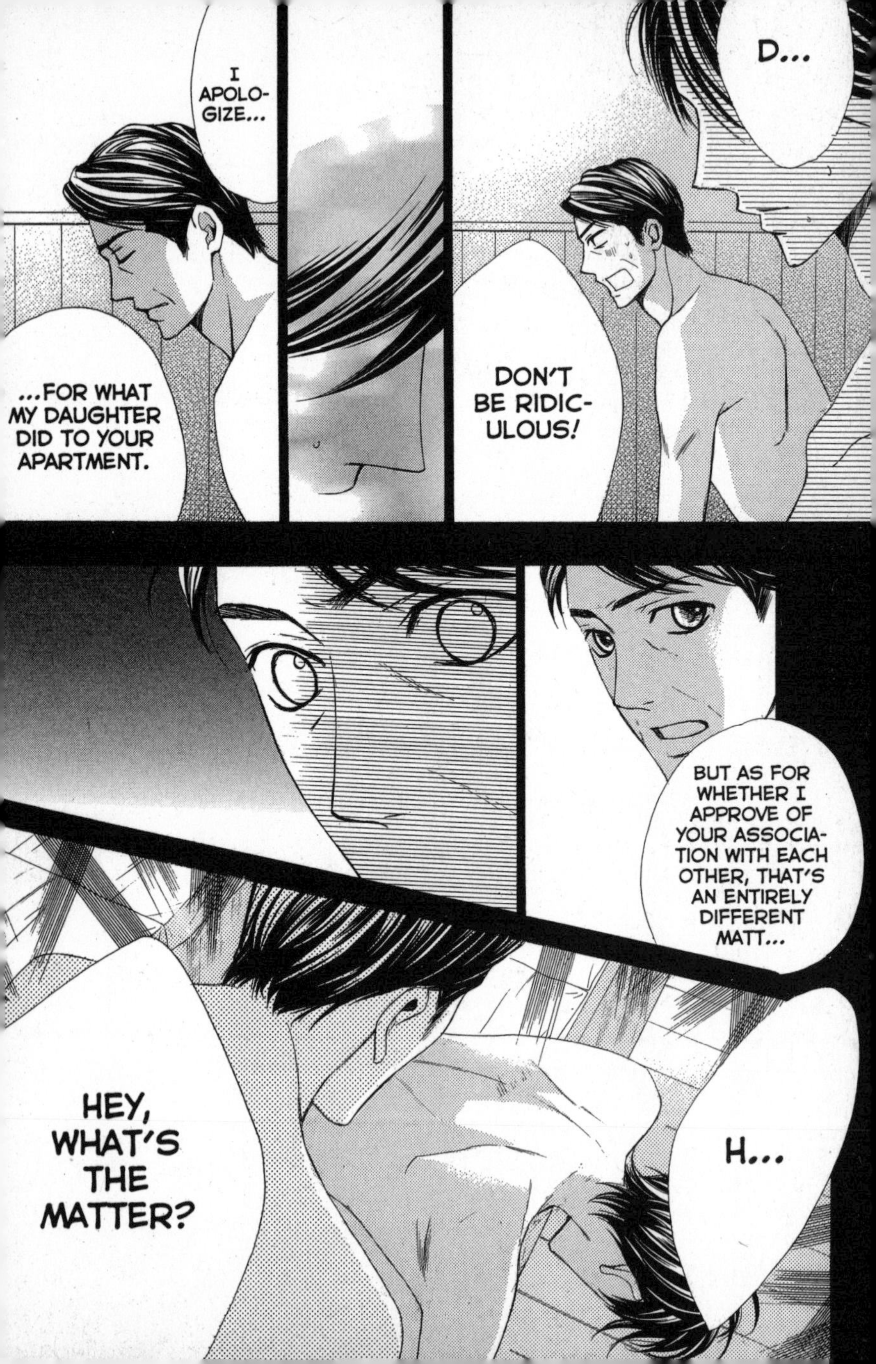
D...
DON'T BE RIDICULOUS!
I APOLOGIZE...
...FOR WHAT MY DAUGHTER DID TO YOUR APARTMENT.
BUT AS FOR WHETHER I APPROVE OF YOUR ASSOCIATION WITH EACH OTHER, THAT'S AN ENTIRELY DIFFERENT MATT...
H...
HEY, WHAT'S THE MATTER?

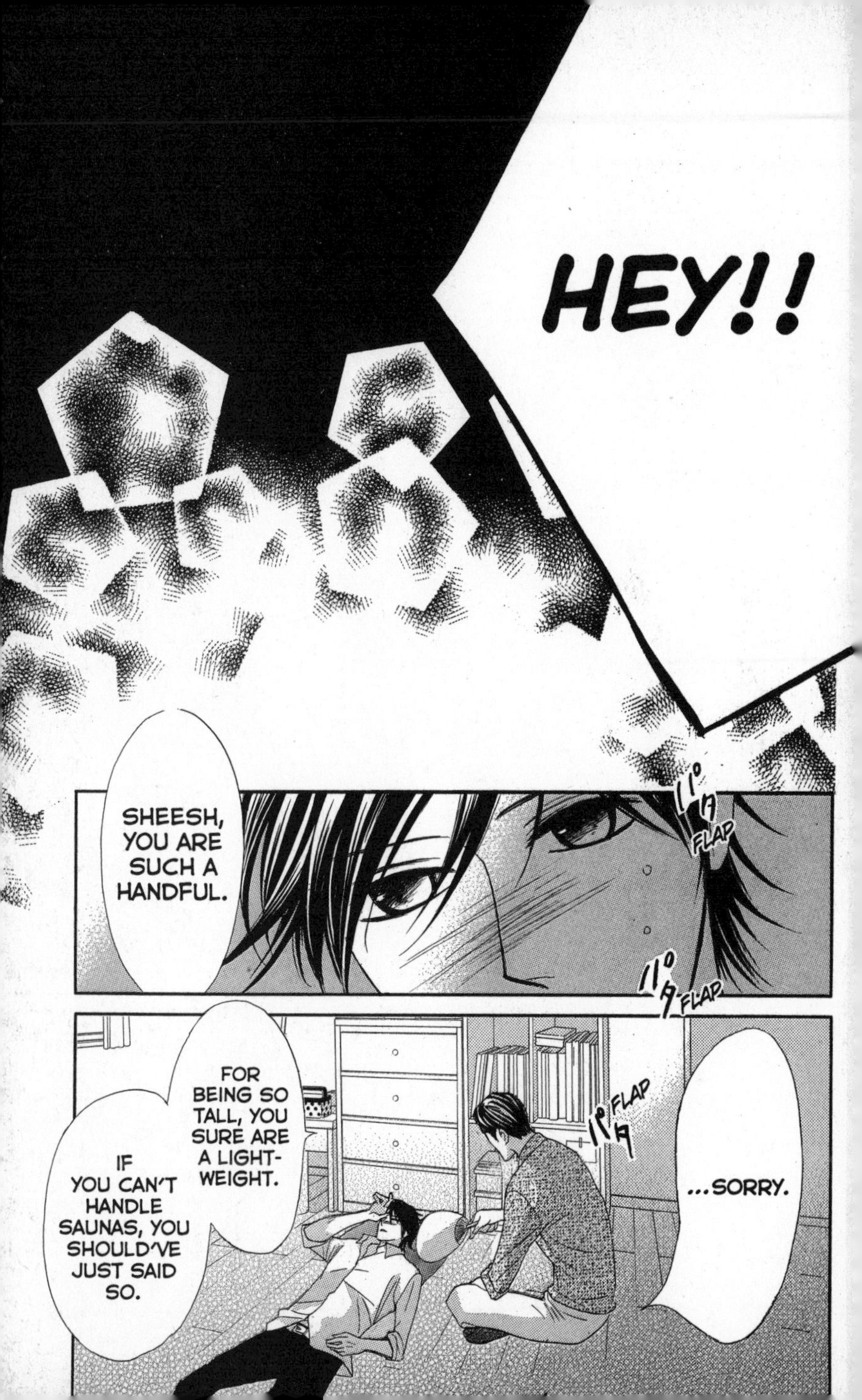
HEY!!
パタ FLAP
SHEESH, YOU ARE SUCH A HANDFUL.
パタ FLAP
...SORRY.
パタ FLAP
FOR BEING SO TALL, YOU SURE ARE A LIGHT-WEIGHT.
IF YOU CAN'T HANDLE SAUNAS, YOU SHOULD'VE JUST SAID SO.

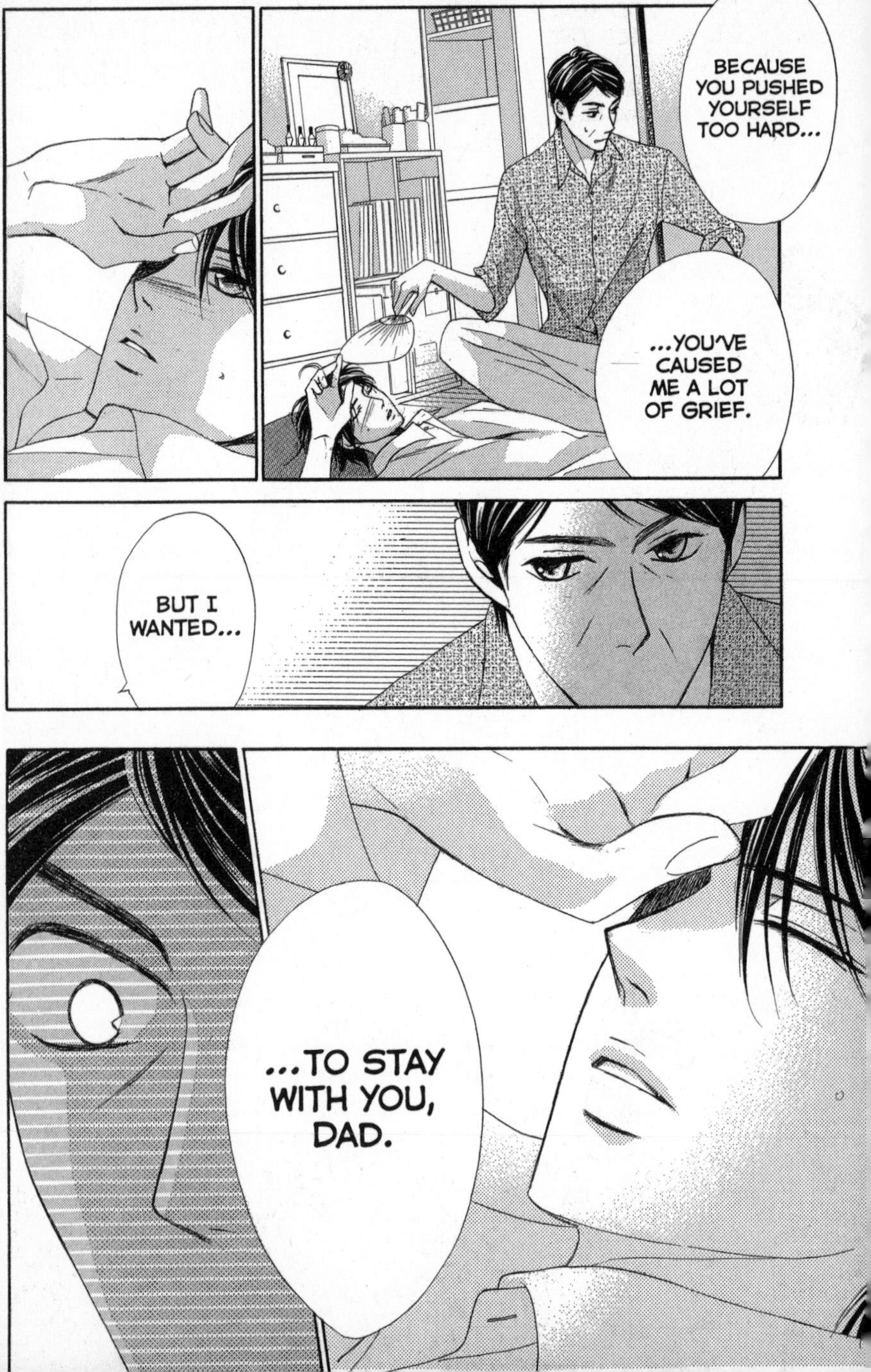
BECAUSE YOU PUSHED YOURSELF TOO HARD...
...YOU'VE CAUSED ME A LOT OF GRIEF.
BUT I WANTED...
...TO STAY WITH YOU, DAD.

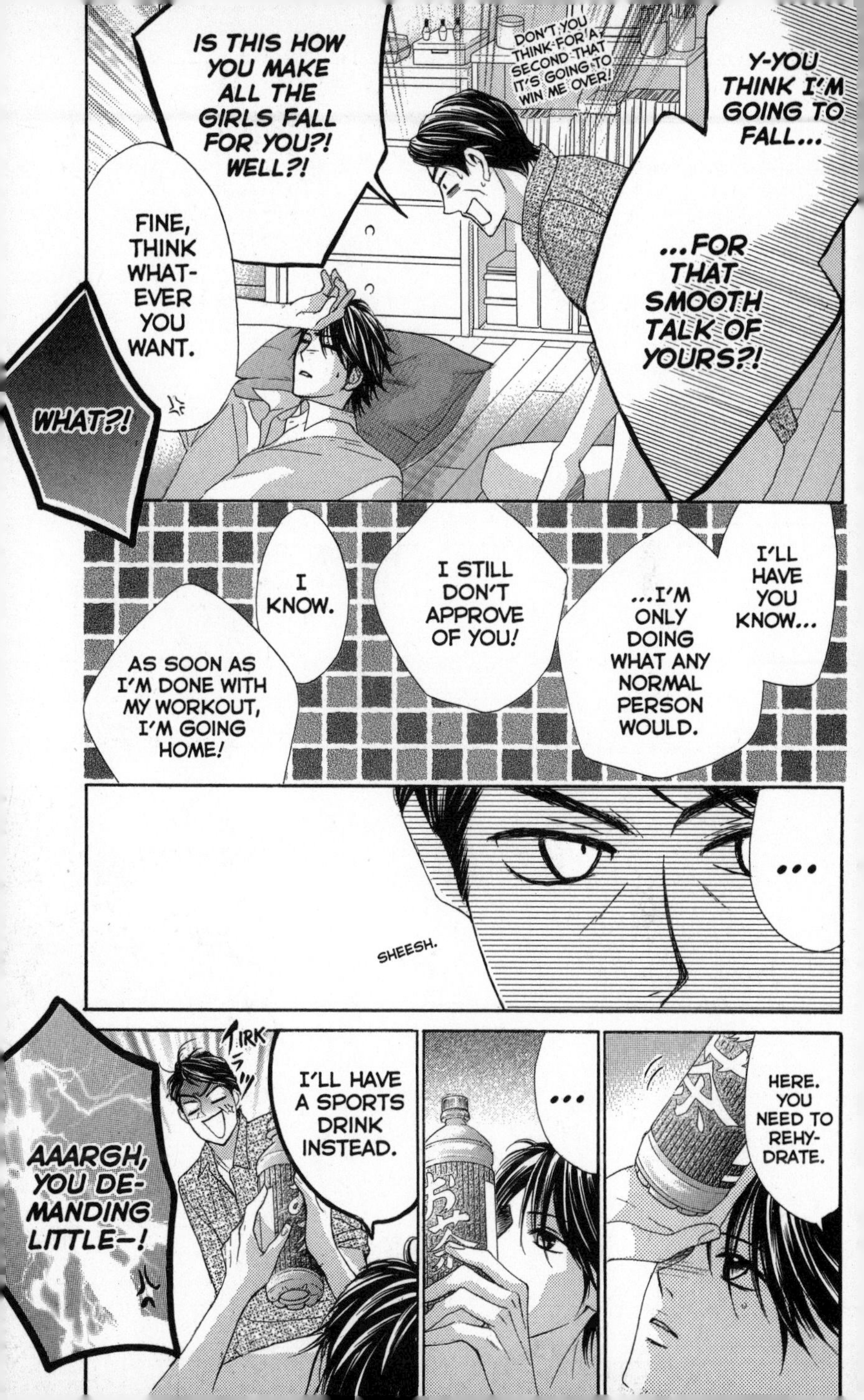

Y-YOU THINK I'M GOING TO FALL...
...FOR THAT SMOOTH TALK OF YOURS?!
DON'T YOU THINK FOR A SECOND THAT IT'S GOING TO WIN ME OVER!
IS THIS HOW YOU MAKE ALL THE GIRLS FALL FOR YOU?! WELL?!
FINE, THINK WHAT-EVER YOU WANT.
WHAT?!
I'LL HAVE YOU KNOW...
...I'M ONLY DOING WHAT ANY NORMAL PERSON WOULD.
I STILL DON'T APPROVE OF YOU!
I KNOW.
AS SOON AS I'M DONE WITH MY WORKOUT, I'M GOING HOME!
...
SHEESH.
HERE. YOU NEED TO REHY-DRATE.
...
I'LL HAVE A SPORTS DRINK INSTEAD.
IRK
AAARGH, YOU DE-MANDING LITTLE—!

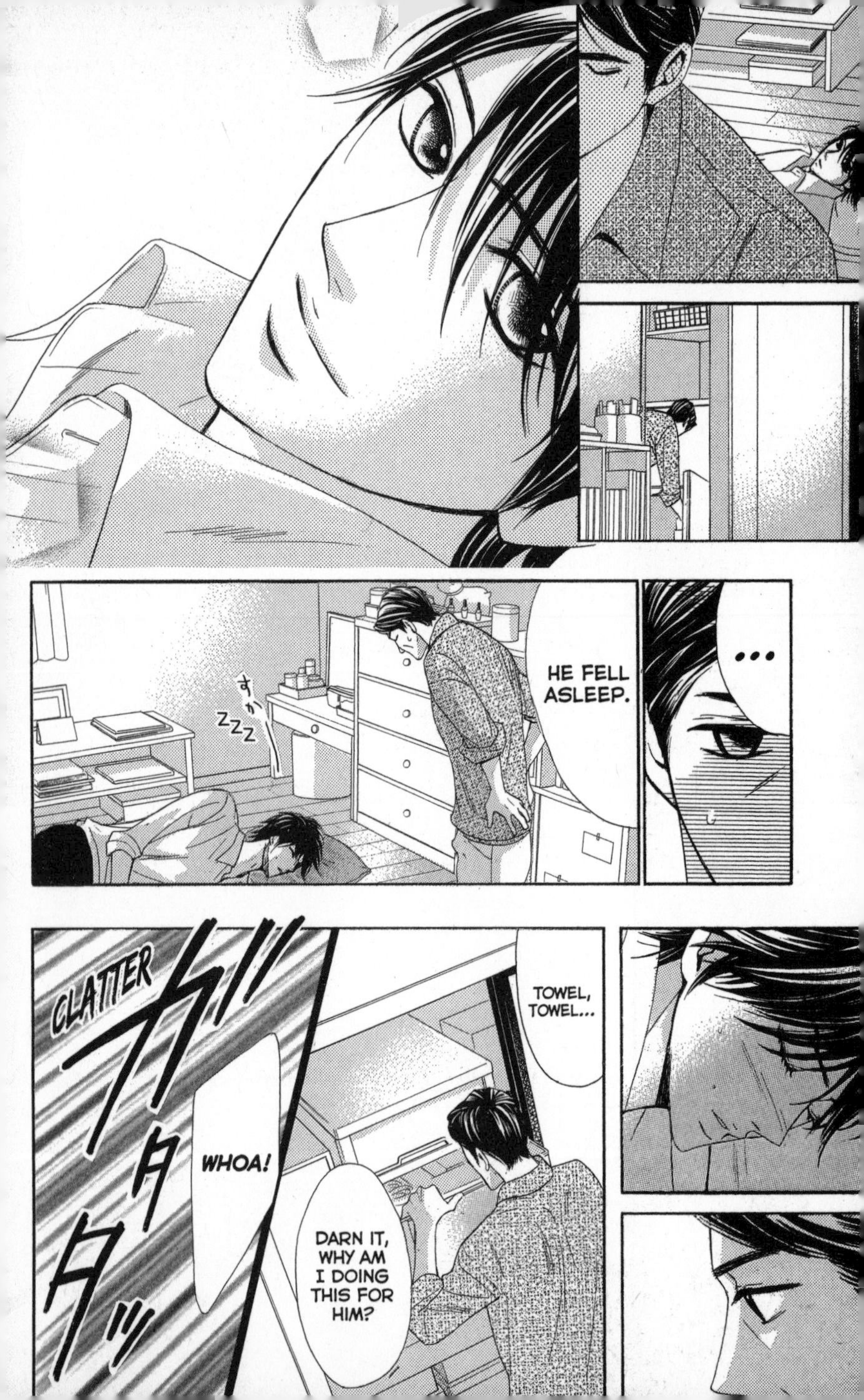

...
HE FELL ASLEEP.
すか
ZZZ
TOWEL, TOWEL...
DARN IT, WHY AM I DOING THIS FOR HIM?
WHOA!
CLATTER

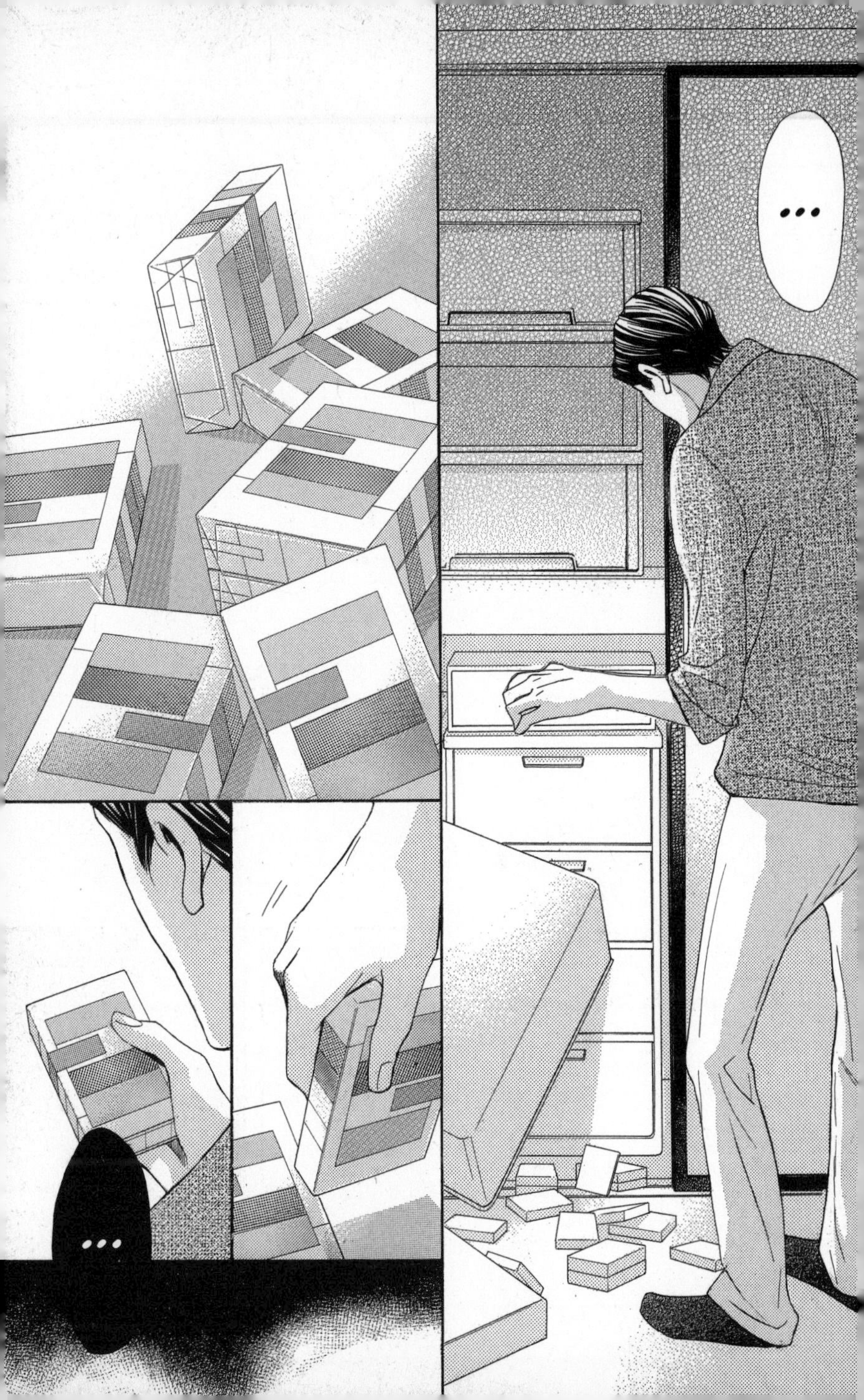
...
...

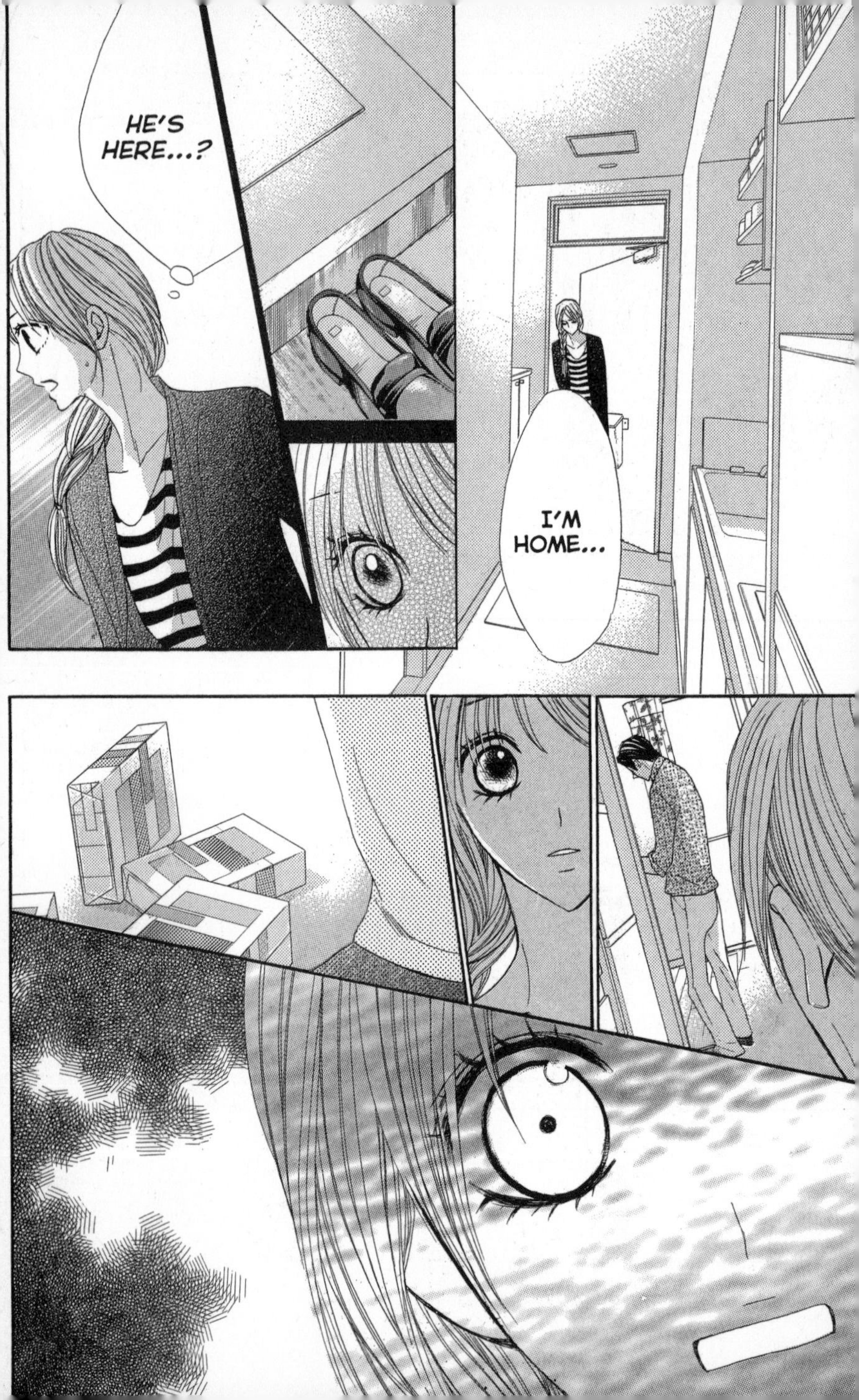
I'M HOME...
HE'S HERE...?

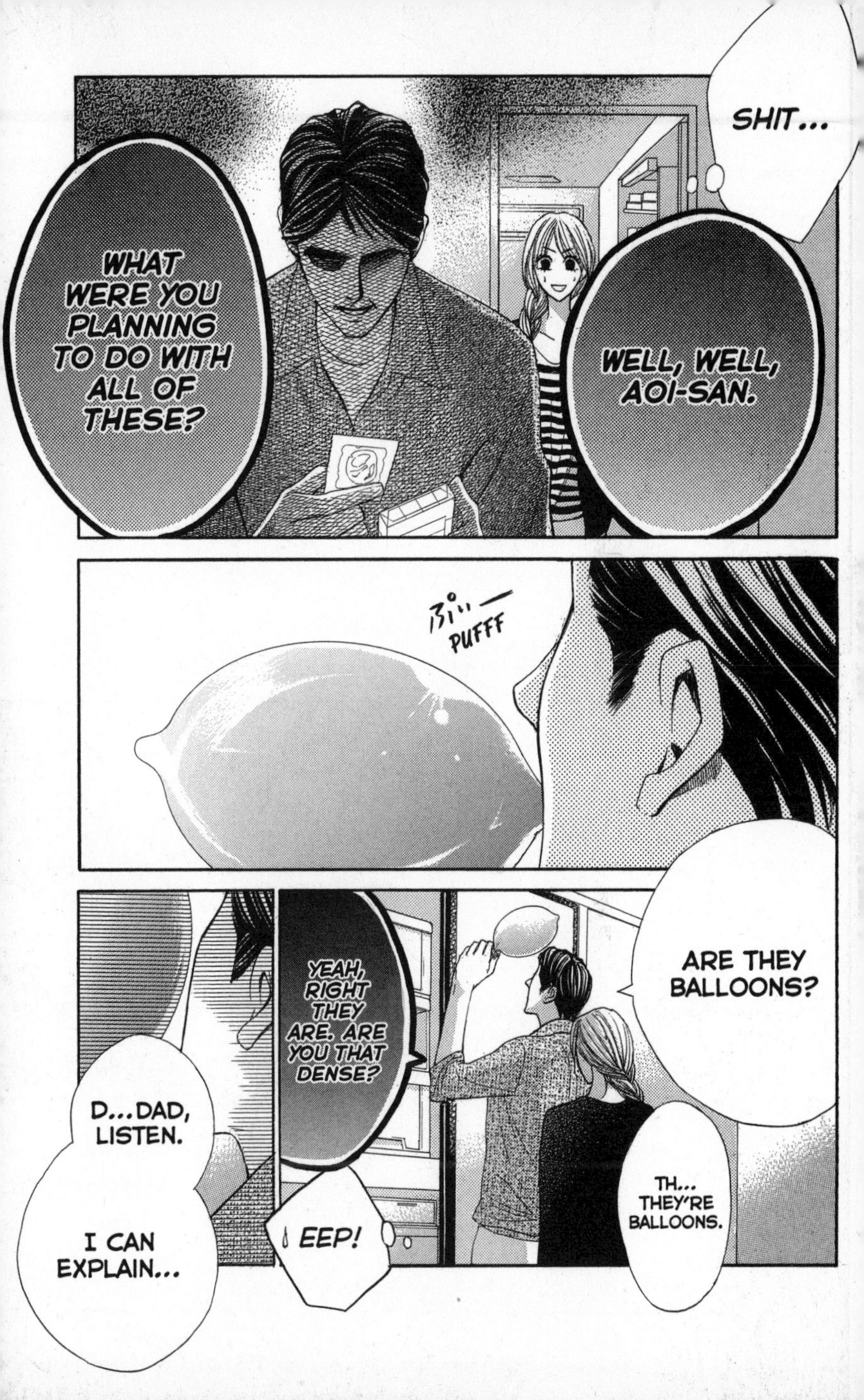
SHIT...
WELL, WELL, AOI-SAN.
WHAT WERE YOU PLANNING TO DO WITH ALL OF THESE?
ぷぃー
PUFFF
ARE THEY BALLOONS?
TH... THEY'RE BALLOONS.
YEAH, RIGHT THEY ARE. ARE YOU THAT DENSE?
EEP!
D...DAD, LISTEN.
I CAN EXPLAIN...

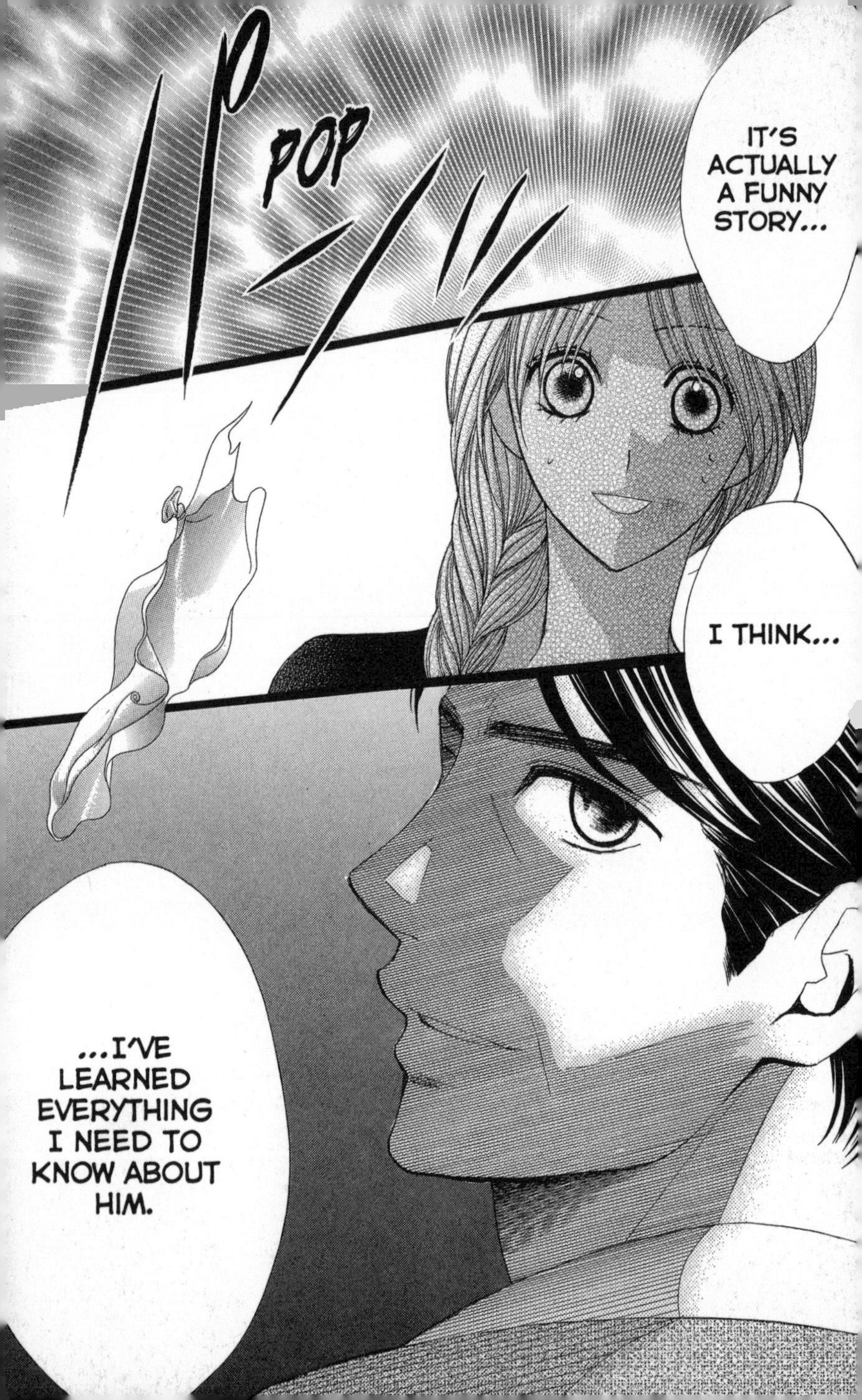
POP
IT'S ACTUALLY A FUNNY STORY...
I THINK...
...I'VE LEARNED EVERYTHING I NEED TO KNOW ABOUT HIM.

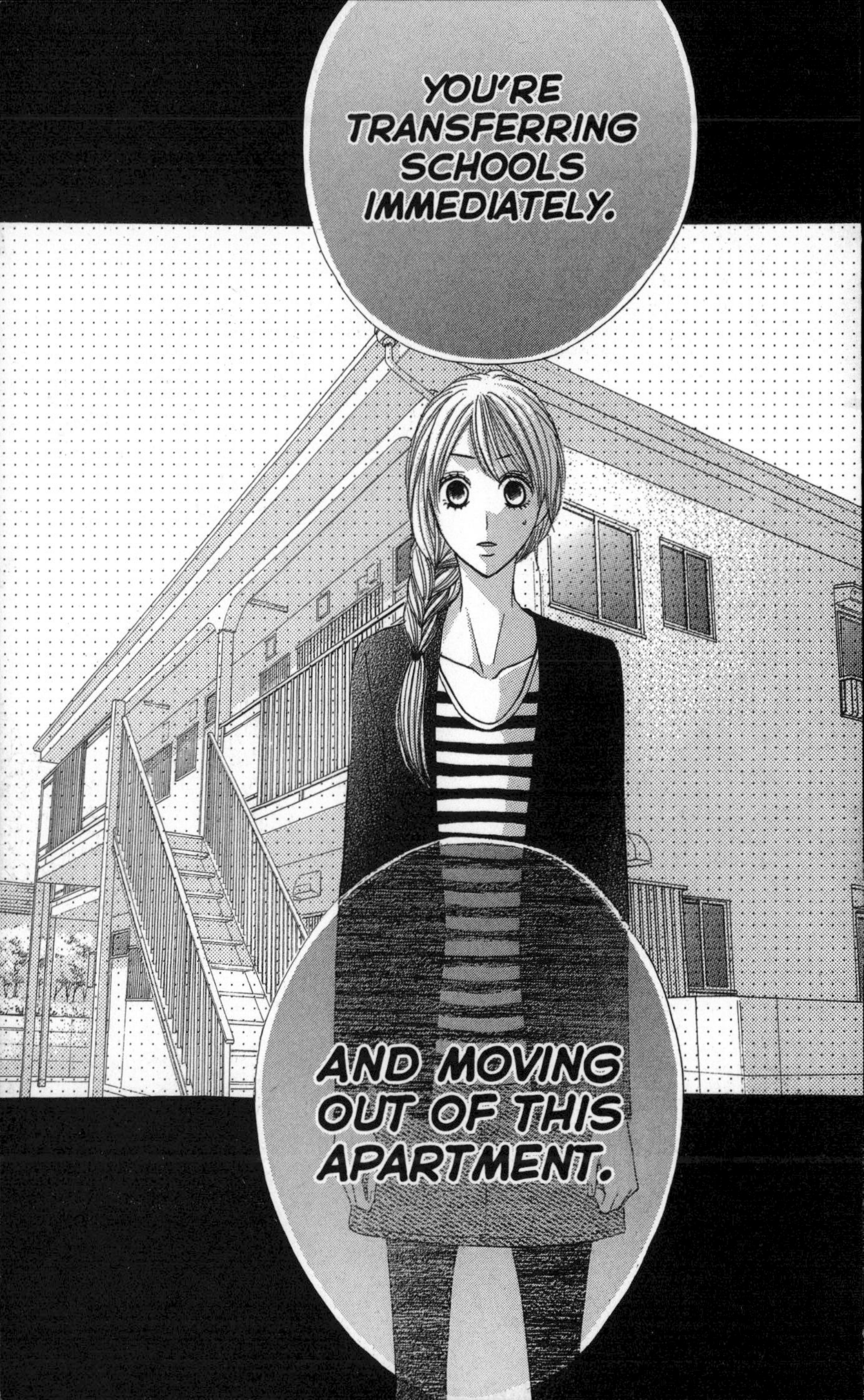
YOU'RE TRANSFERRING SCHOOLS IMMEDIATELY.
AND MOVING OUT OF THIS APARTMENT.

L♥DK

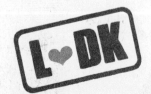

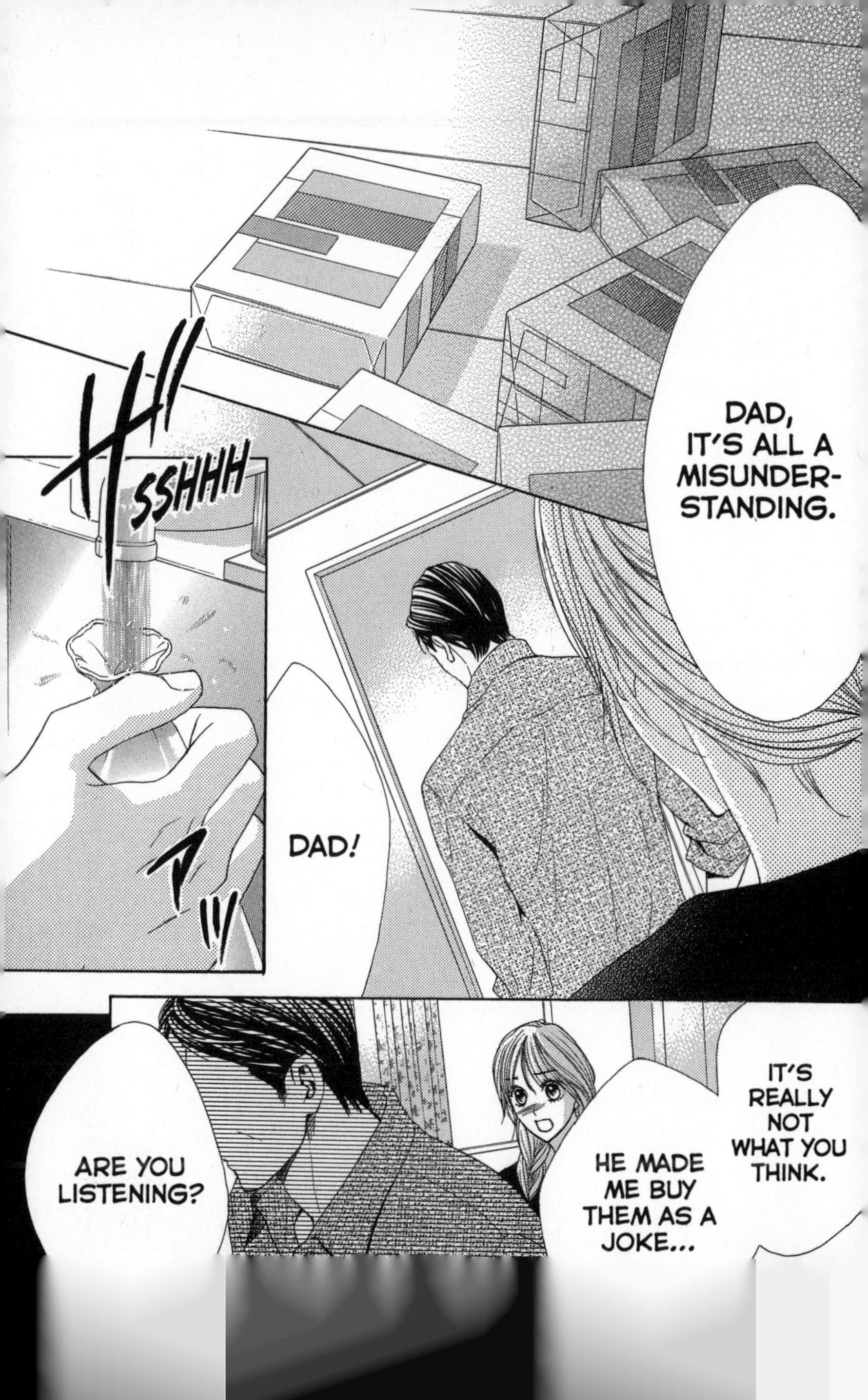
DAD, IT'S ALL A MISUNDERSTANDING.
DAD!
HSSHHH
IT'S REALLY NOT WHAT YOU THINK.
HE MADE ME BUY THEM AS A JOKE...
ARE YOU LISTENING?

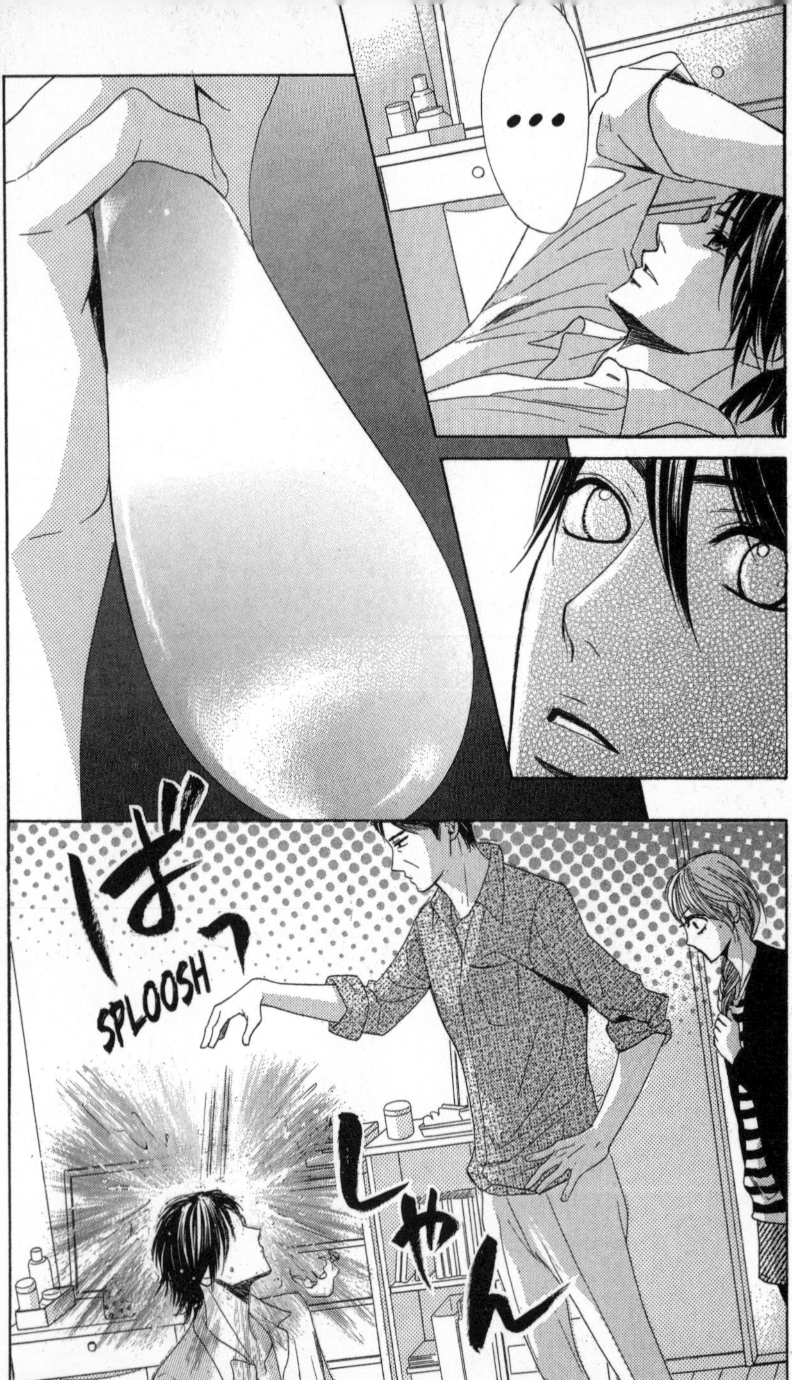
...
ばっ
SPLOOSH
しゃん

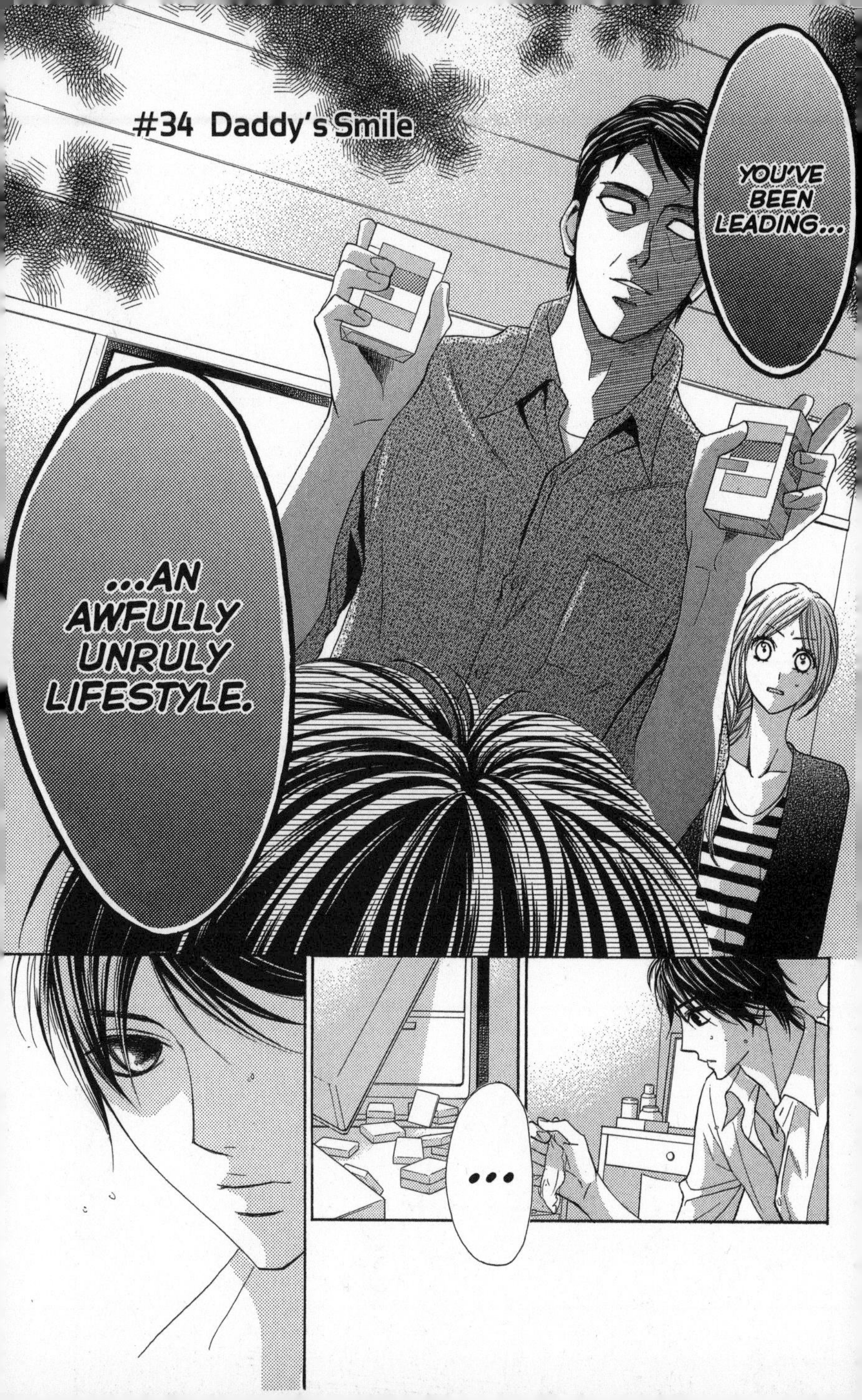
#34 Daddy's Smile
YOU'VE BEEN LEADING...
...AN AWFULLY UNRULY LIFESTYLE.
...

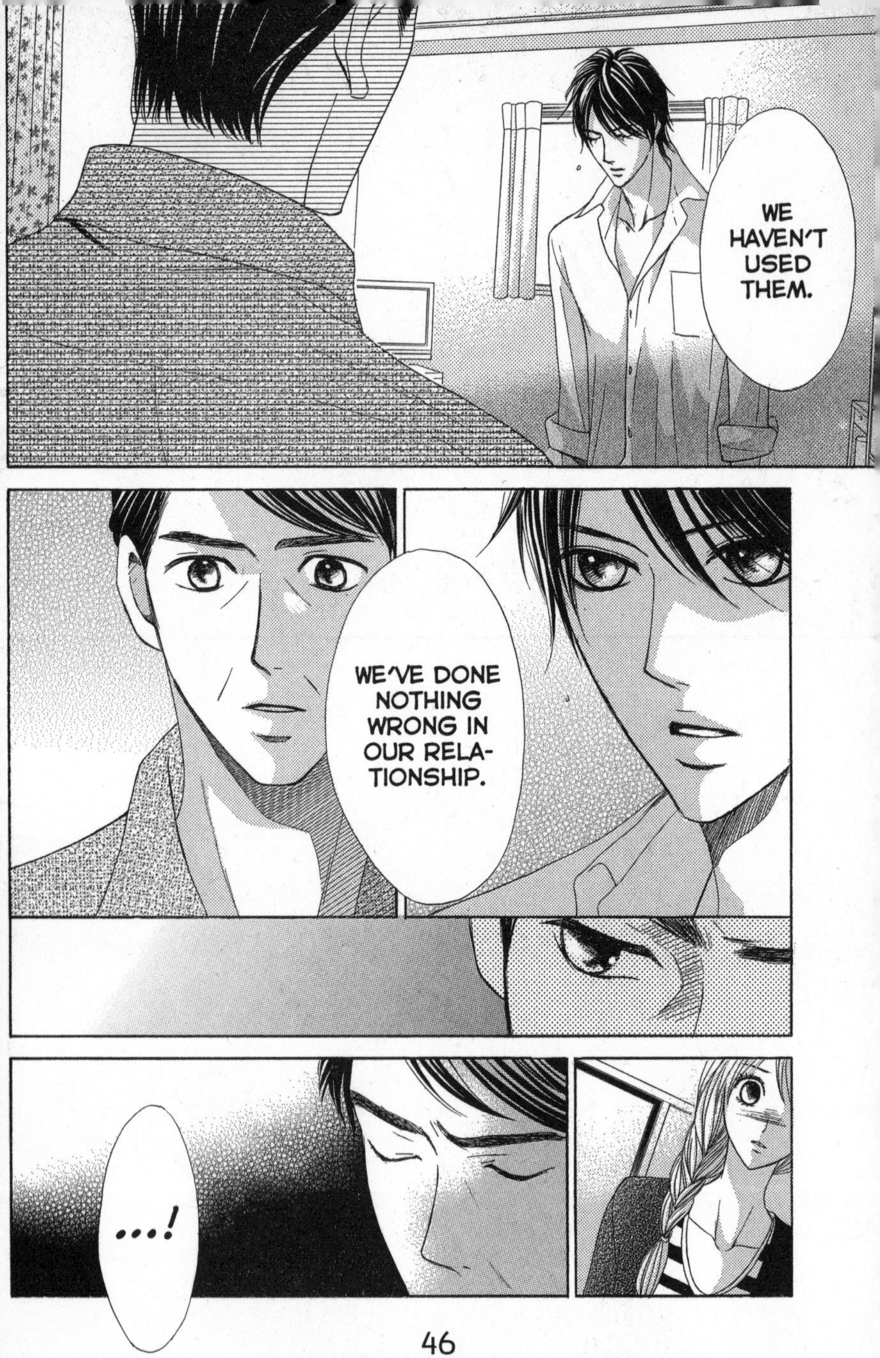
WE HAVEN'T USED THEM.
WE'VE DONE NOTHING WRONG IN OUR RELA-TIONSHIP.
...!

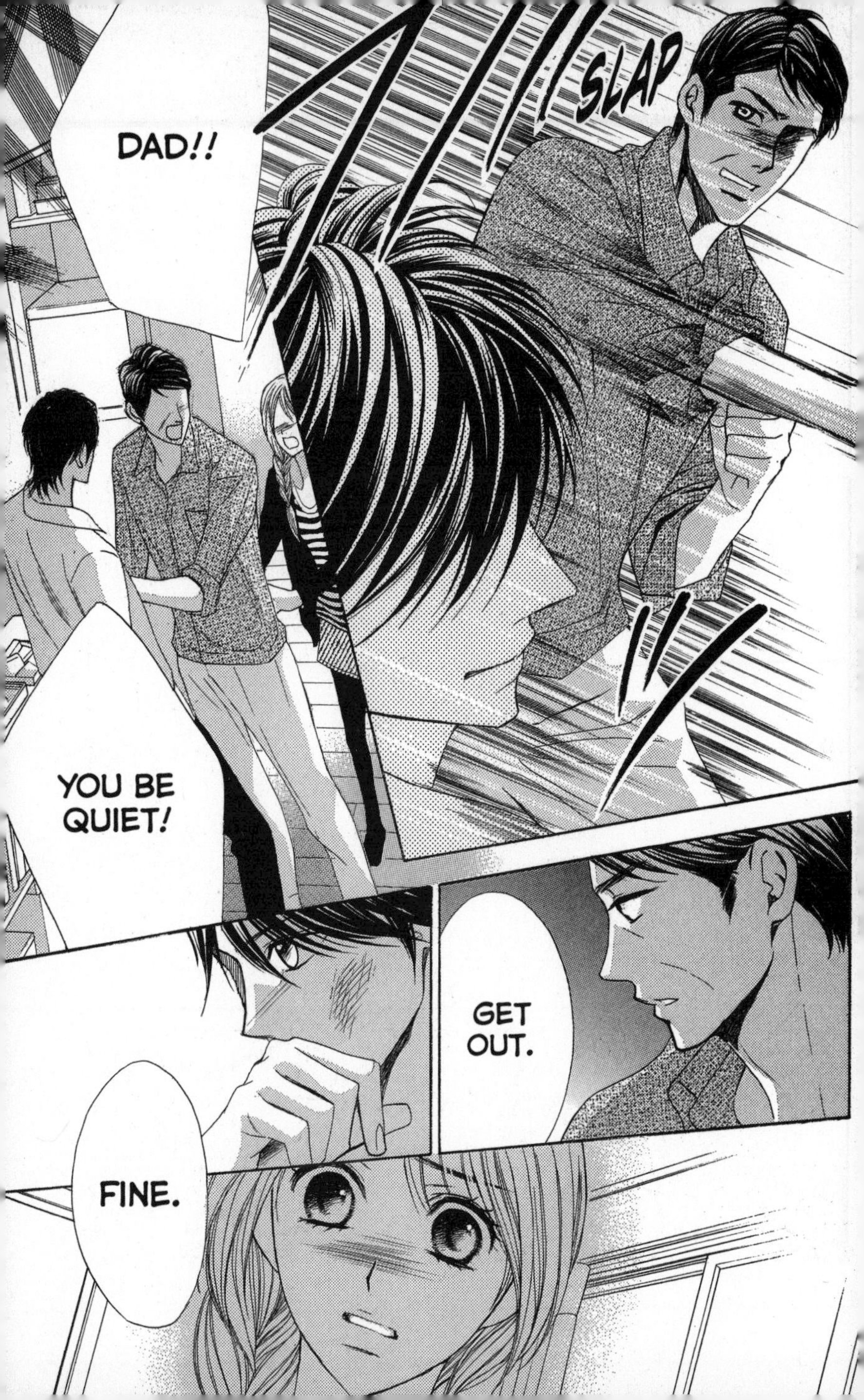
SLAP
DAD!!
YOU BE QUIET!
GET OUT.
FINE.

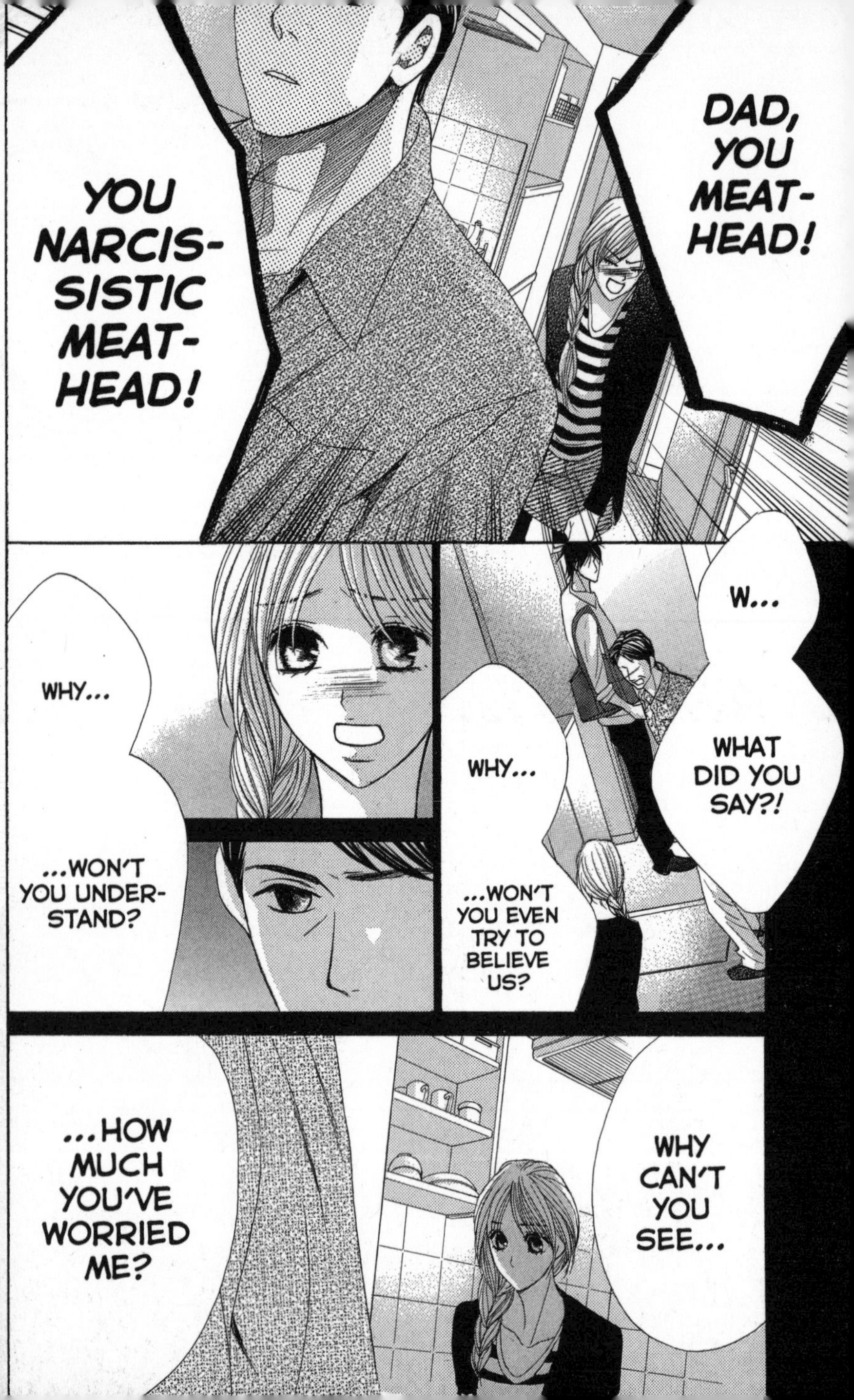
DAD, YOU MEAT-HEAD!
YOU NARCIS-SISTIC MEAT-HEAD!
W...
WHAT DID YOU SAY?!
WHY...
...WON'T YOU EVEN TRY TO BELIEVE US?
WHY...
...WON'T YOU UNDER-STAND?
WHY CAN'T YOU SEE...
...HOW MUCH YOU'VE WORRIED ME?

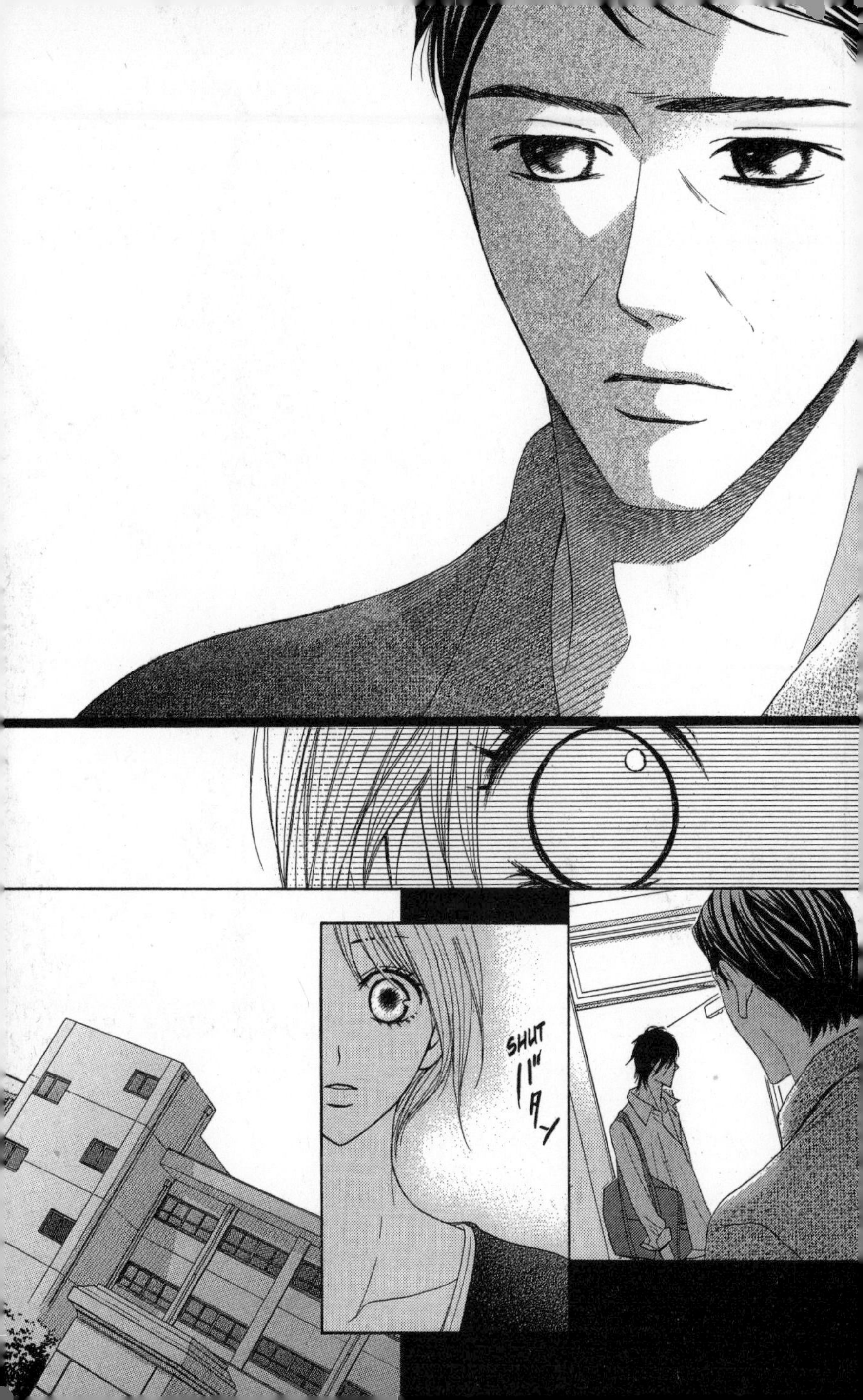
SHUT
バタン

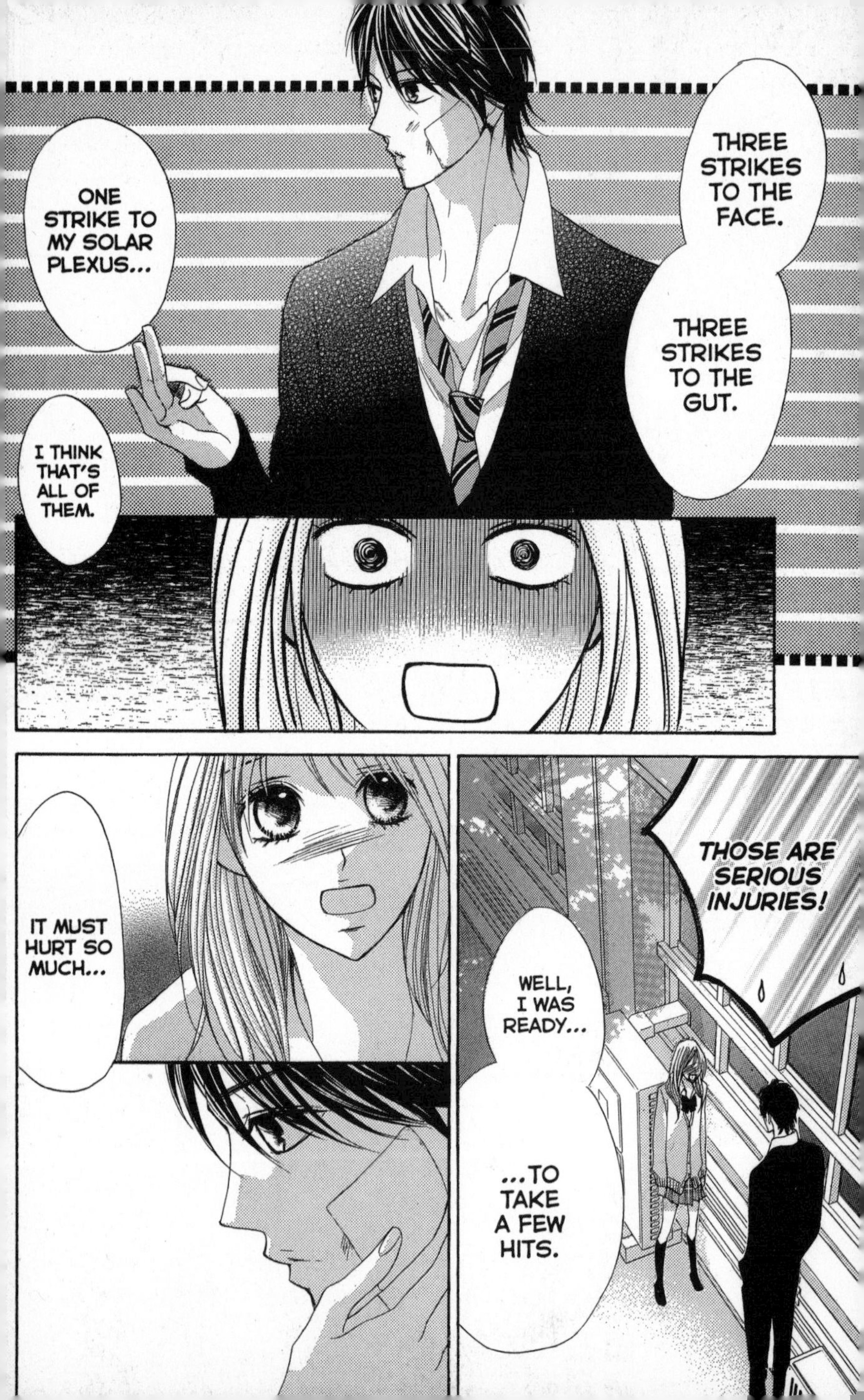
THREE STRIKES TO THE FACE.
THREE STRIKES TO THE GUT.
ONE STRIKE TO MY SOLAR PLEXUS...
I THINK THAT'S ALL OF THEM.
THOSE ARE SERIOUS INJURIES!
WELL, I WAS READY...
...TO TAKE A FEW HITS.
IT MUST HURT SO MUCH...

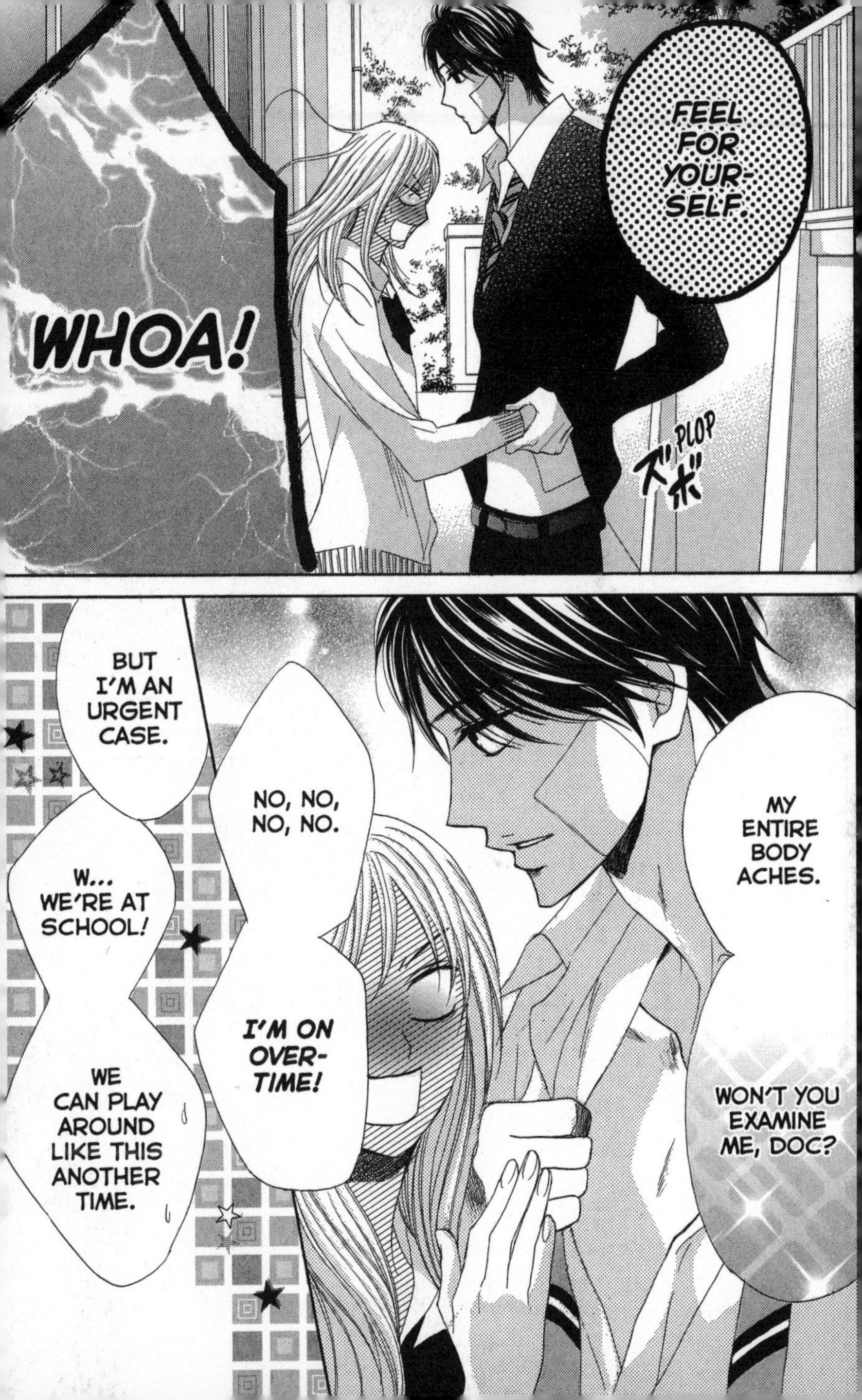
FEEL FOR YOUR-SELF.
WHOA!
PLOP
ズボ
MY ENTIRE BODY ACHES.
WON'T YOU EXAMINE ME, DOC?
NO, NO, NO, NO.
I'M ON OVER-TIME!
BUT I'M AN URGENT CASE.
W... WE'RE AT SCHOOL!
WE CAN PLAY AROUND LIKE THIS ANOTHER TIME.

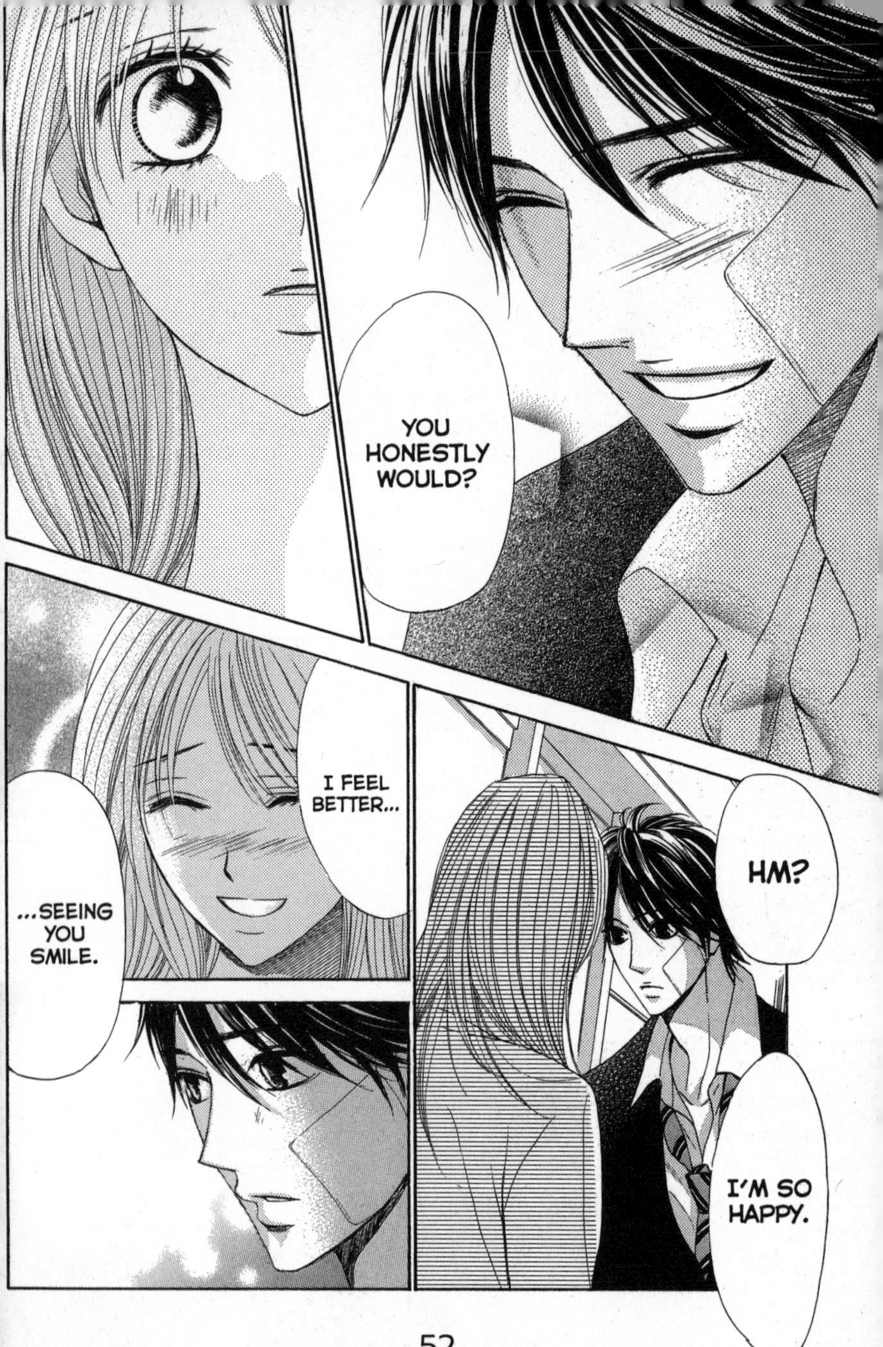
YOU HONESTLY WOULD?
HM?
I'M SO HAPPY.
I FEEL BETTER...
...SEEING YOU SMILE.

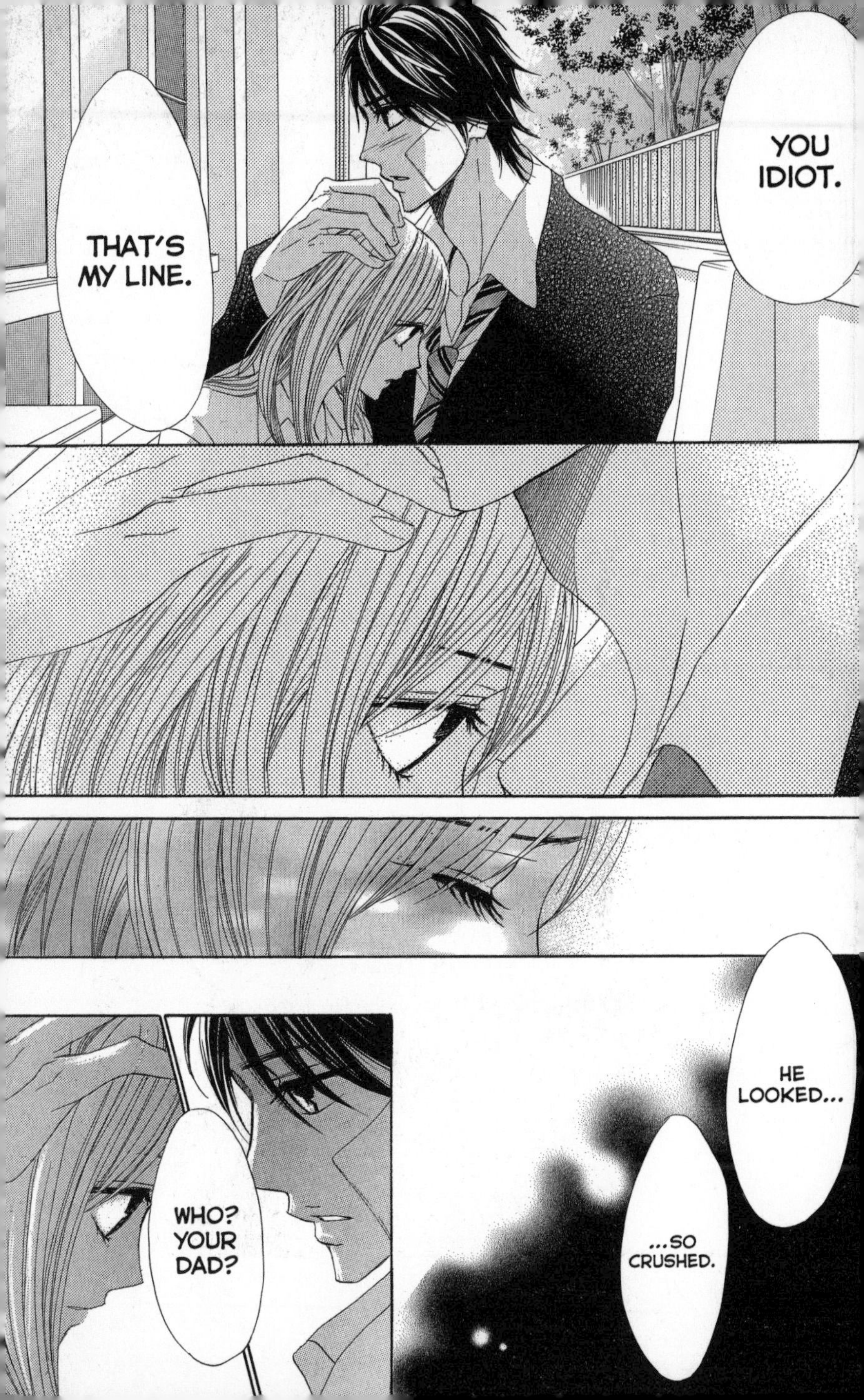
YOU IDIOT.
THAT'S MY LINE.
HE LOOKED...
...SO CRUSHED.
WHO? YOUR DAD?

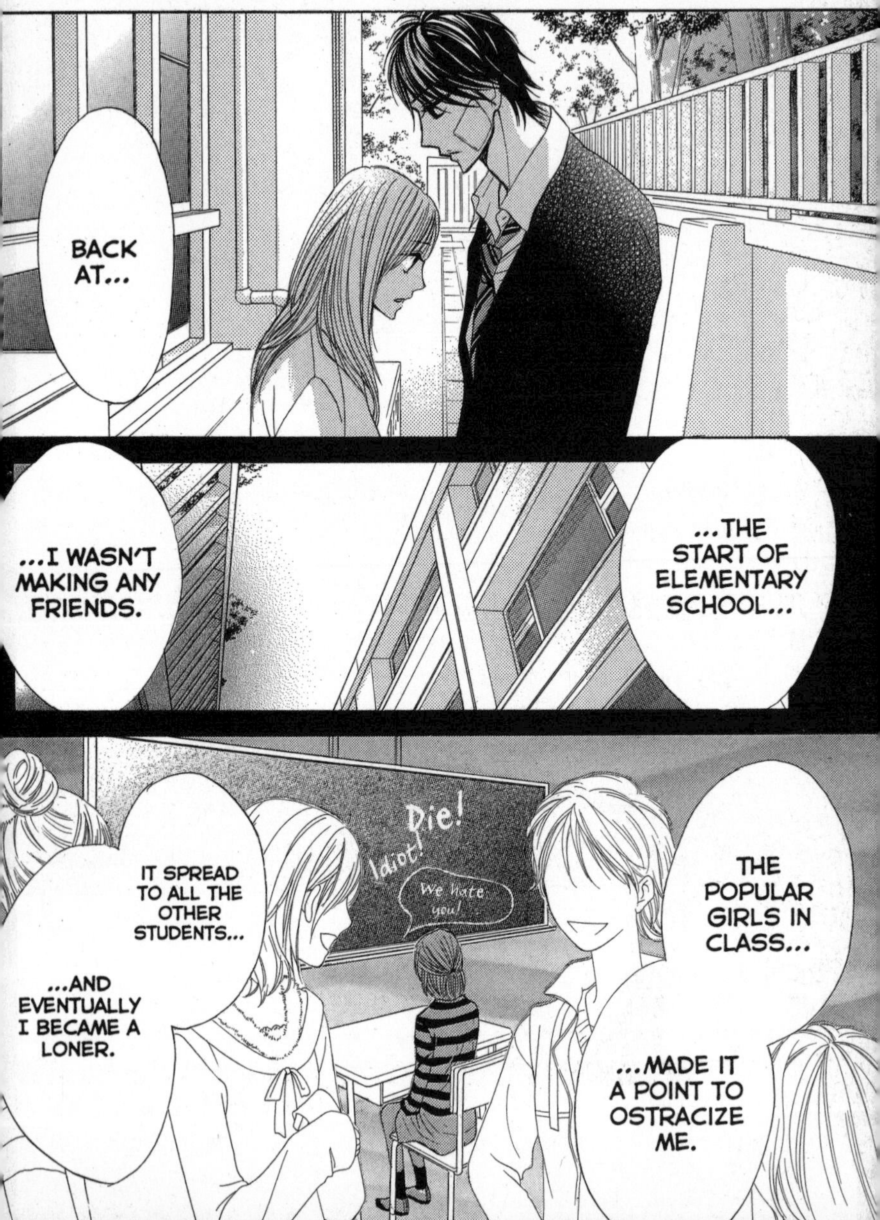
BACK AT...
...THE START OF ELEMENTARY SCHOOL...
...I WASN'T MAKING ANY FRIENDS.
THE POPULAR GIRLS IN CLASS...
...MADE IT A POINT TO OSTRACIZE ME.
Die!
Idiot!
We hate you!
IT SPREAD TO ALL THE OTHER STUDENTS...
...AND EVENTUALLY I BECAME A LONER.

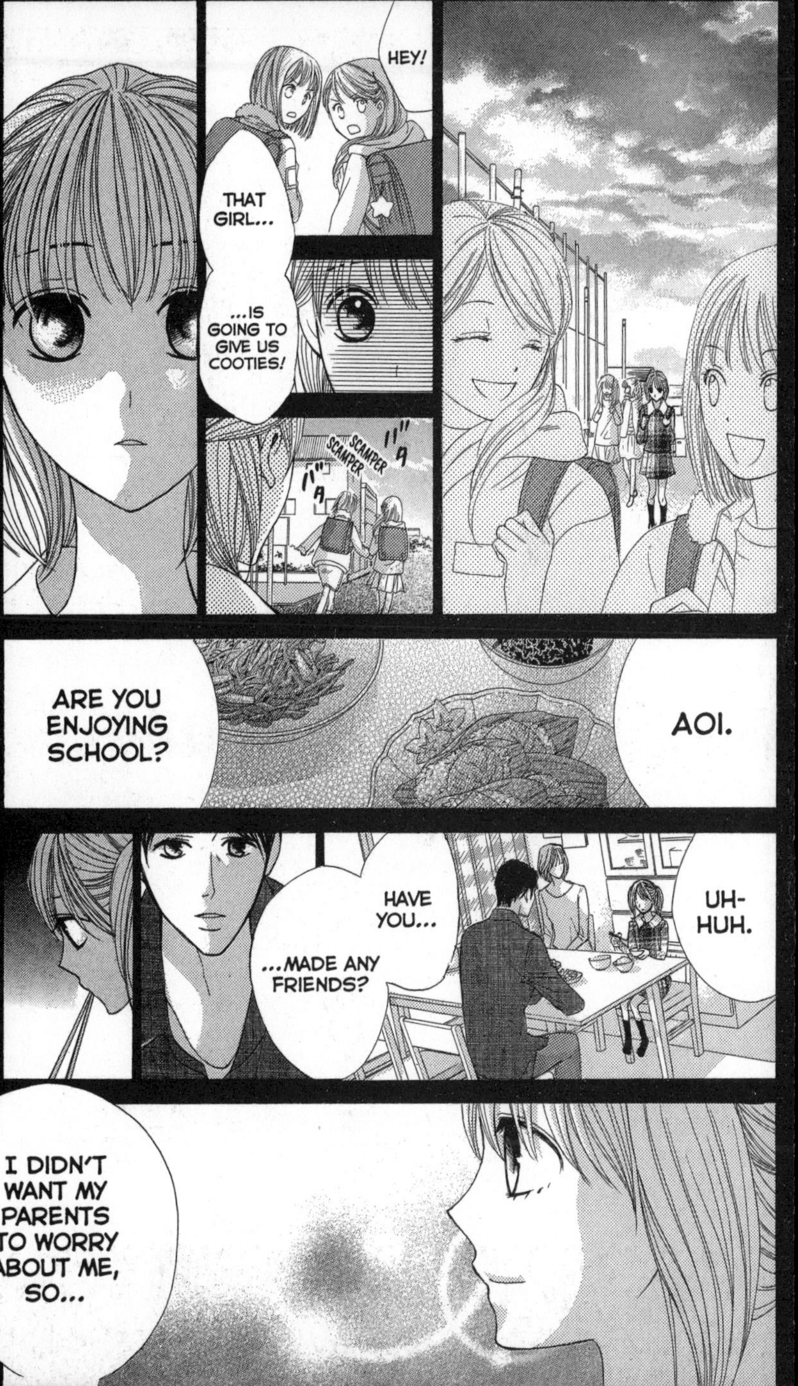
HEY!
THAT GIRL...
...IS GOING TO GIVE US COOTIES!
SCAMPER SCAMPER
AOI.
ARE YOU ENJOYING SCHOOL?
UH-HUH.
HAVE YOU...
...MADE ANY FRIENDS?
I DIDN'T WANT MY PARENTS TO WORRY ABOUT ME, SO...

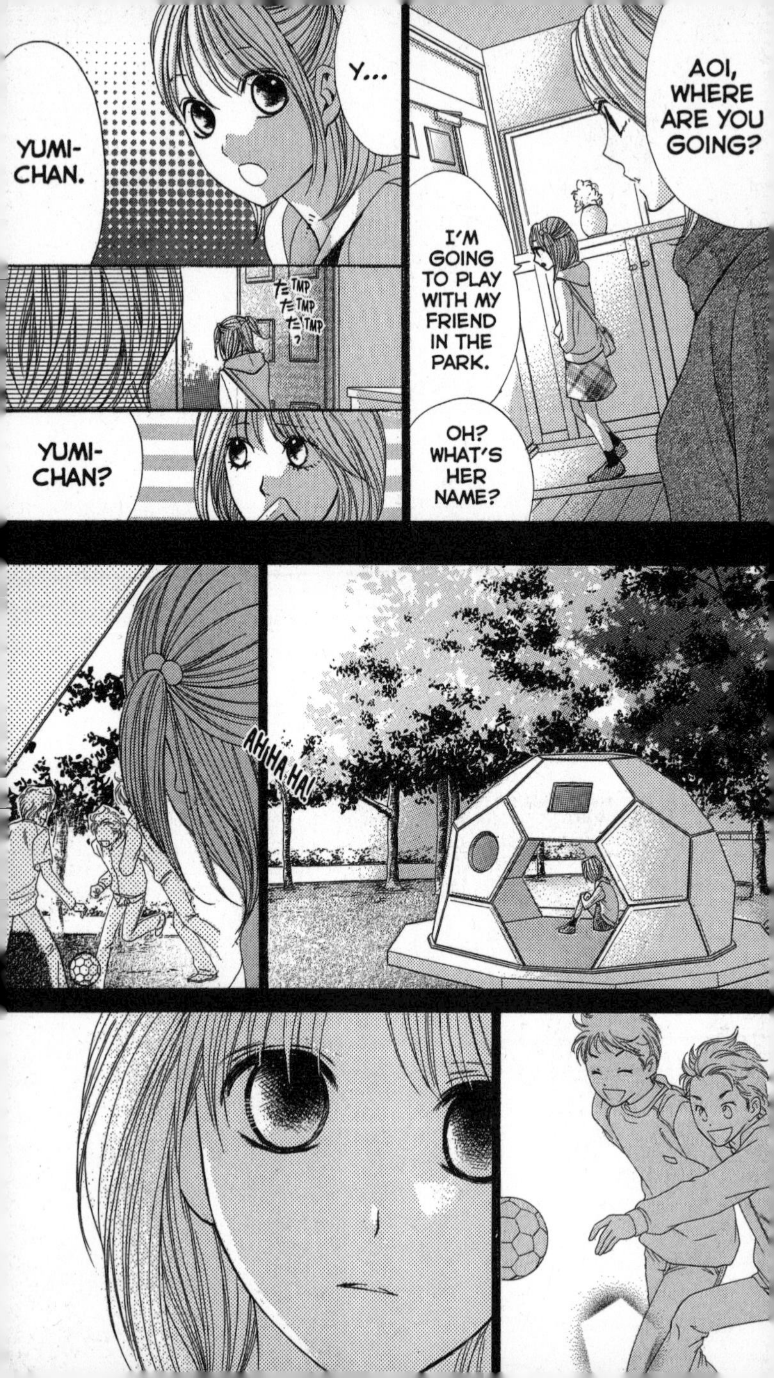
AOI, WHERE ARE YOU GOING?
I'M GOING TO PLAY WITH MY FRIEND IN THE PARK.
OH? WHAT'S HER NAME?
Y...
YUMI-CHAN.
た TMP た TMP た TMP
YUMI-CHAN?
AH HA HA!

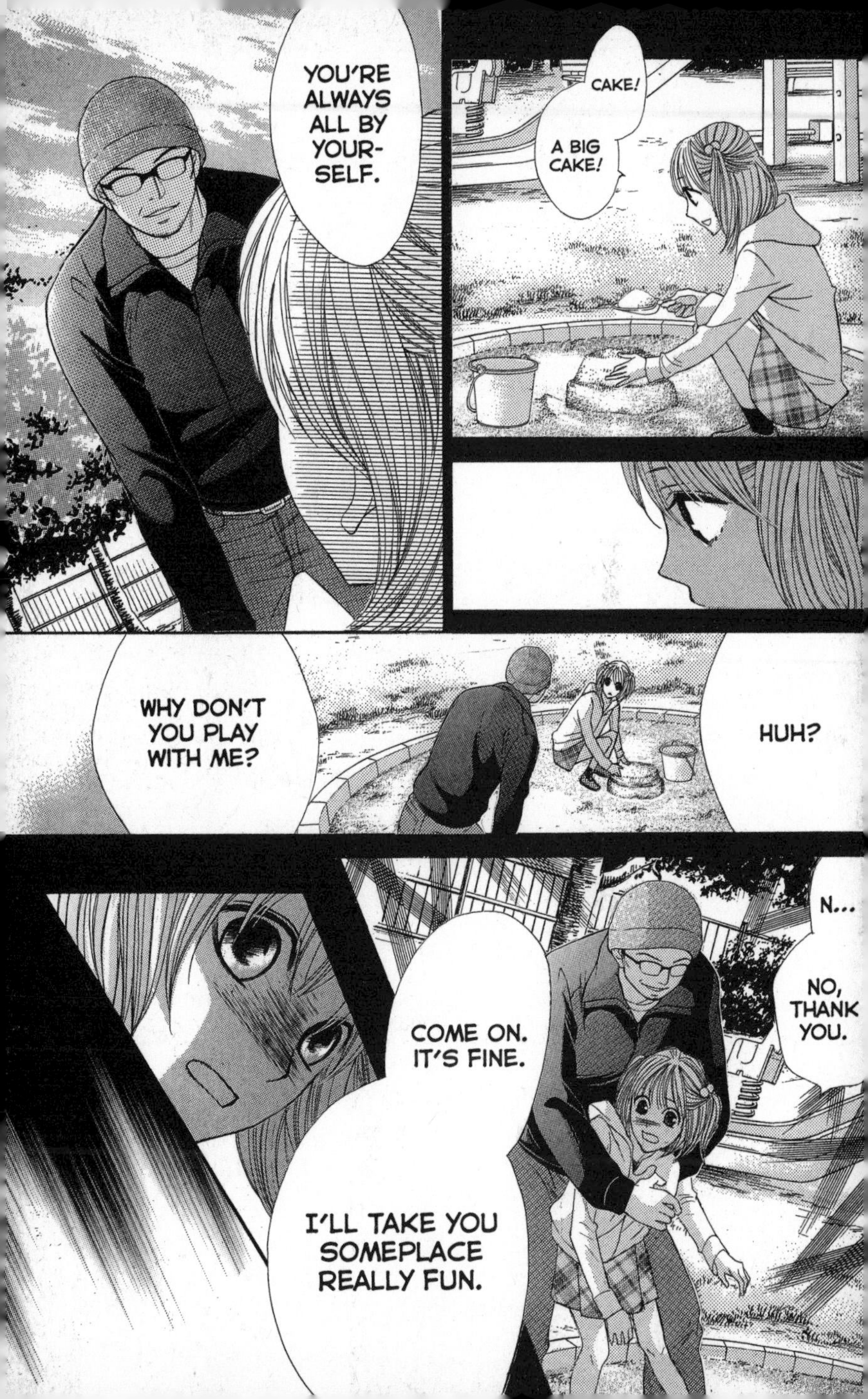
CAKE!
A BIG CAKE!
YOU'RE ALWAYS ALL BY YOUR-SELF.
HUH?
WHY DON'T YOU PLAY WITH ME?
N...
NO, THANK YOU.
COME ON. IT'S FINE.
I'LL TAKE YOU SOMEPLACE REALLY FUN.

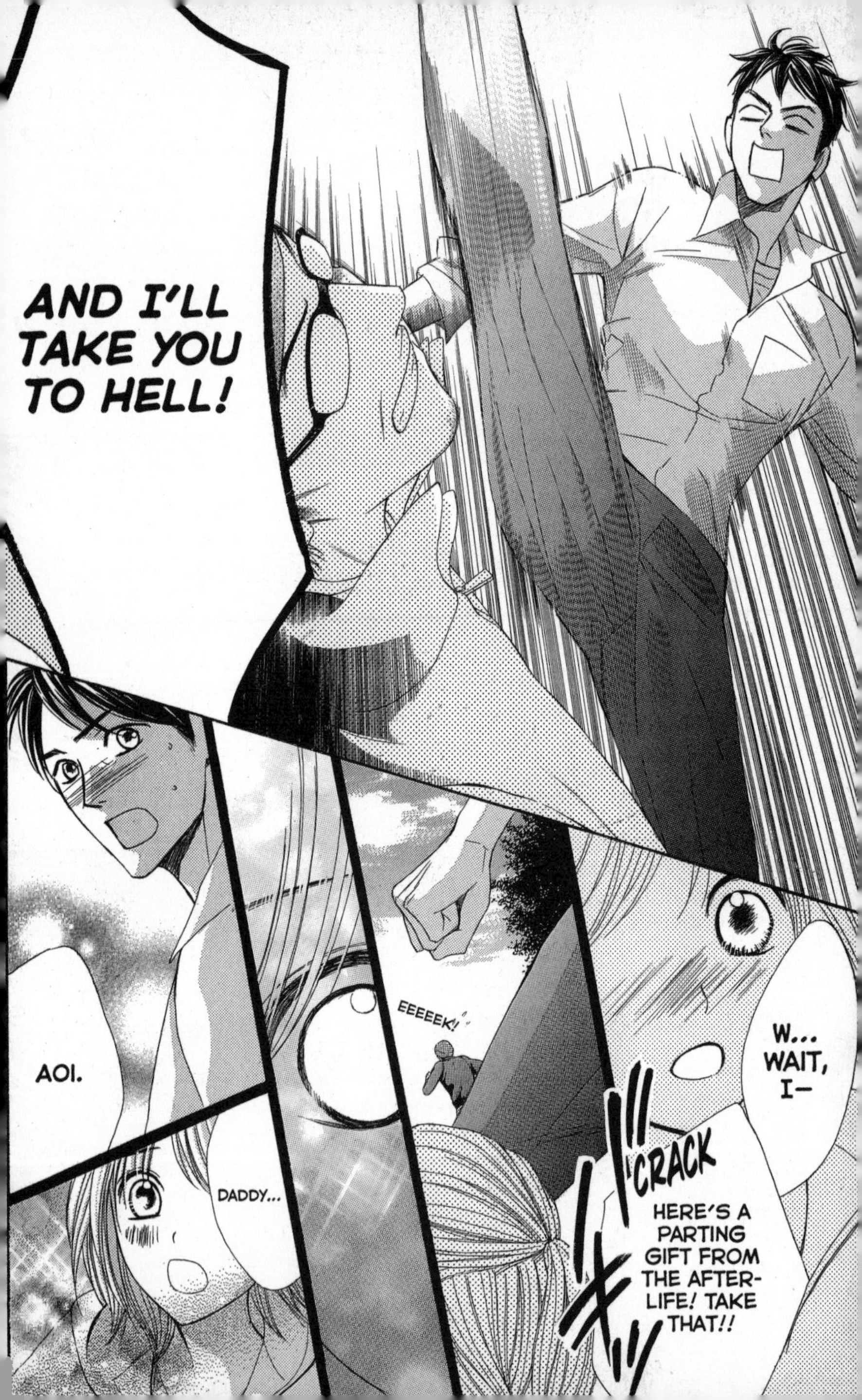
AND I'LL TAKE YOU TO HELL!
W... WAIT, I—
CRACK
HERE'S A PARTING GIFT FROM THE AFTER-LIFE! TAKE THAT!!
EEEEEK!
AOI.
DADDY...

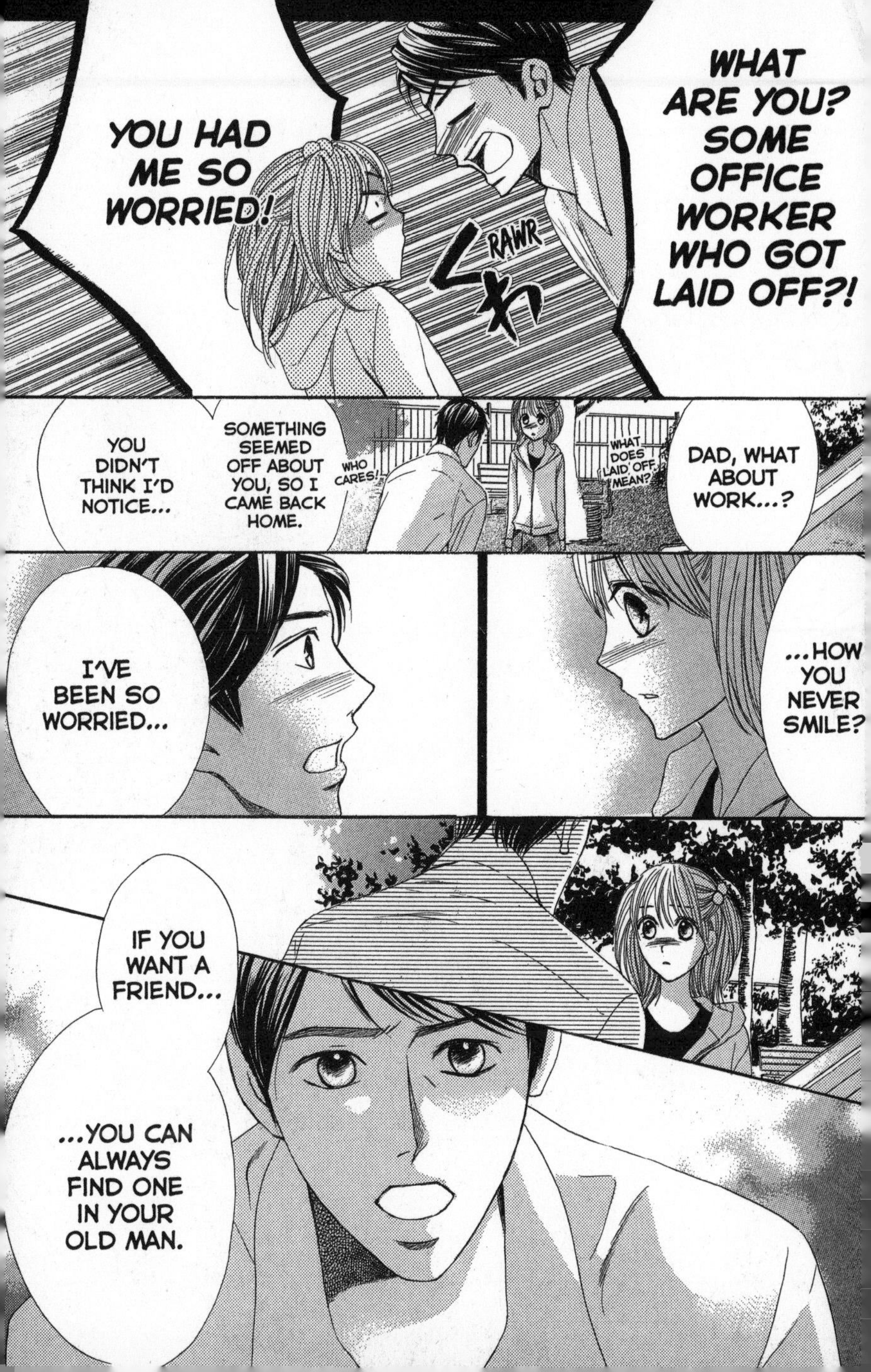

WHAT ARE YOU? SOME OFFICE WORKER WHO GOT LAID OFF?!
RAWR
YOU HAD ME SO WORRIED!
DAD, WHAT ABOUT WORK...?
WHAT DOES LAID OFF MEAN?
WHO CARES!
SOMETHING SEEMED OFF ABOUT YOU, SO I CAME BACK HOME.
YOU DIDN'T THINK I'D NOTICE...
...HOW YOU NEVER SMILE?
I'VE BEEN SO WORRIED...
IF YOU WANT A FRIEND...
...YOU CAN ALWAYS FIND ONE IN YOUR OLD MAN.

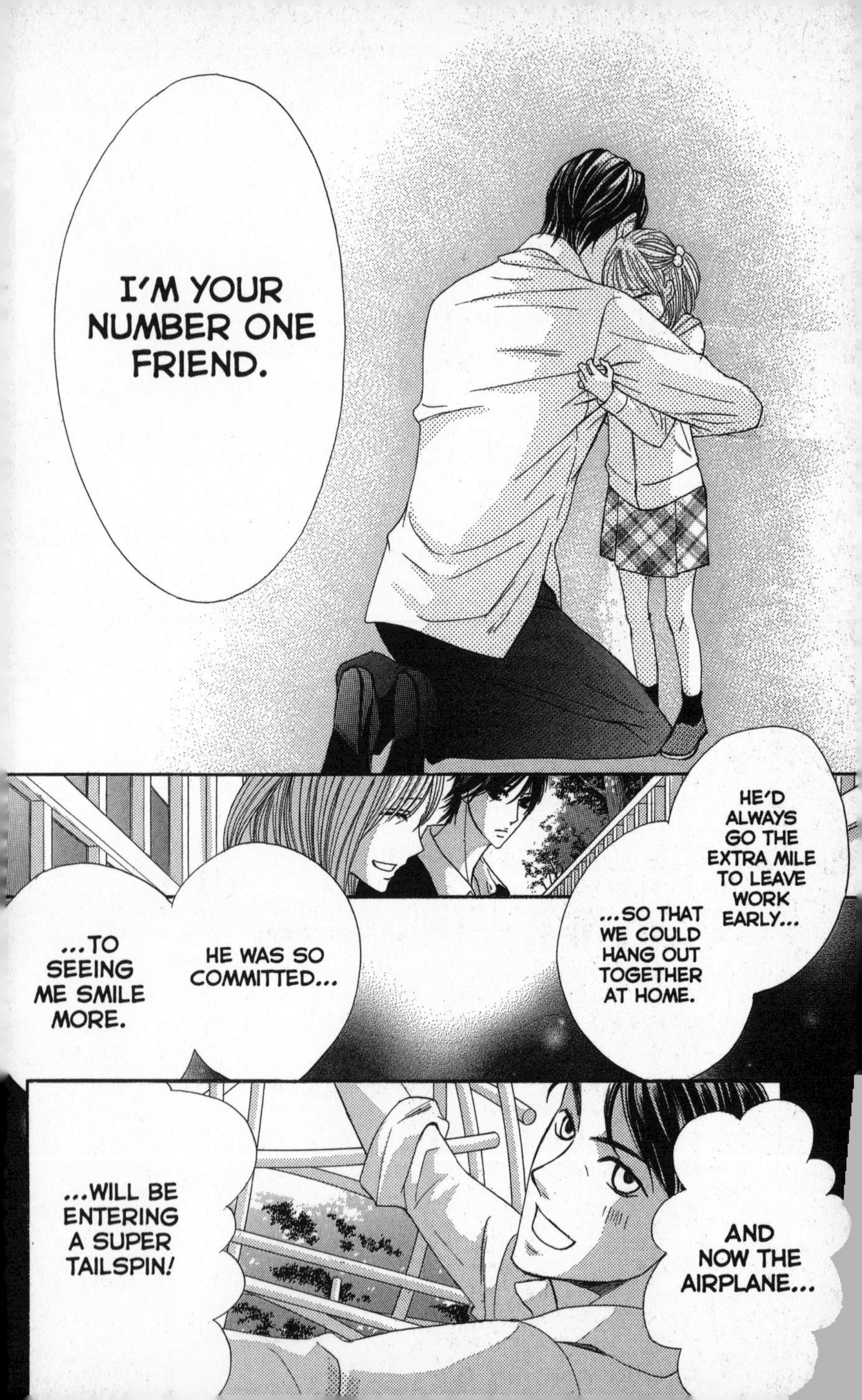
I'M YOUR NUMBER ONE FRIEND.
HE'D ALWAYS GO THE EXTRA MILE TO LEAVE WORK EARLY...
...SO THAT WE COULD HANG OUT TOGETHER AT HOME.
HE WAS SO COMMITTED...
...TO SEEING ME SMILE MORE.
AND NOW THE AIRPLANE...
...WILL BE ENTERING A SUPER TAILSPIN!

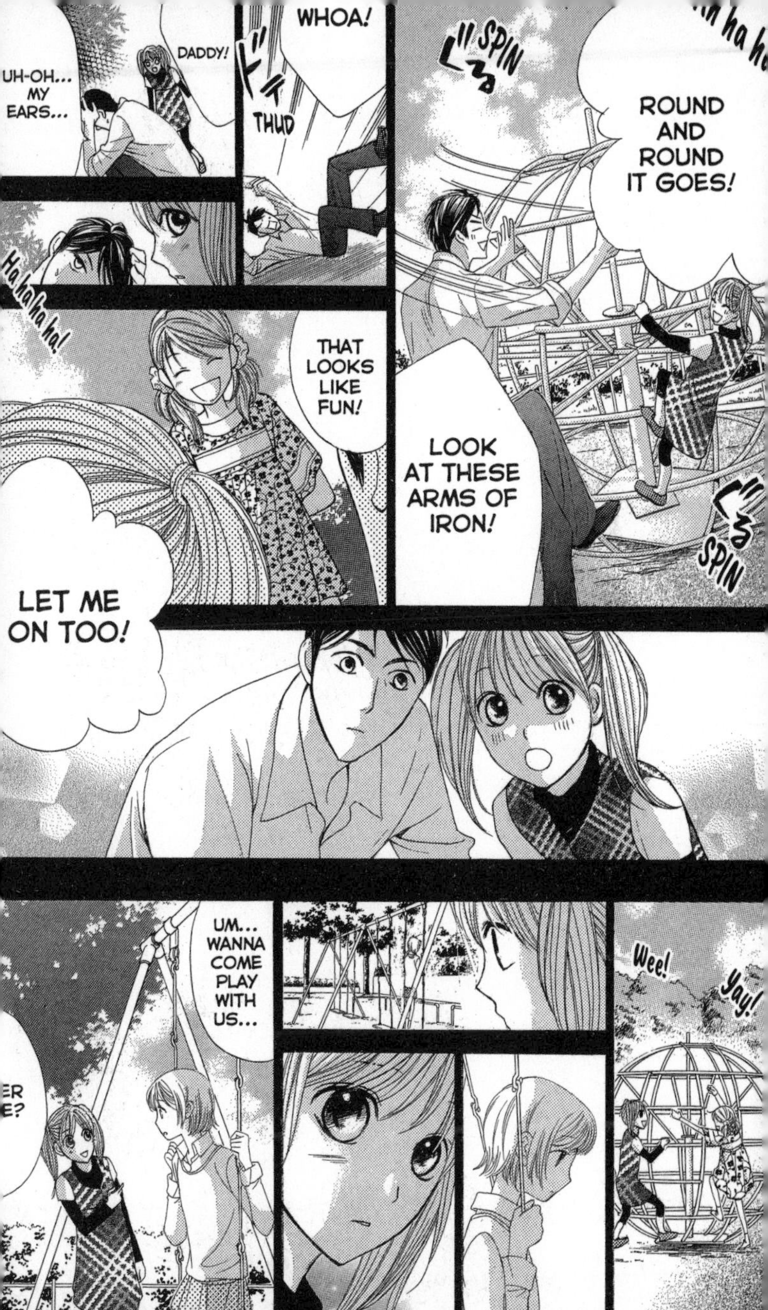
ha ha
SPIN
ROUND AND ROUND IT GOES!
LOOK AT THESE ARMS OF IRON!
SPIN
WHOA!
THUD
DADDY!
UH-OH... MY EARS...
Ha haha ha!
THAT LOOKS LIKE FUN!
LET ME ON TOO!
Wee!
Yay!
UM... WANNA COME PLAY WITH US...

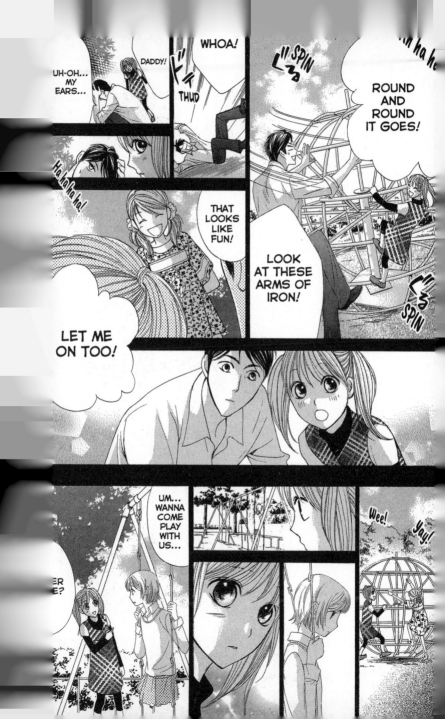

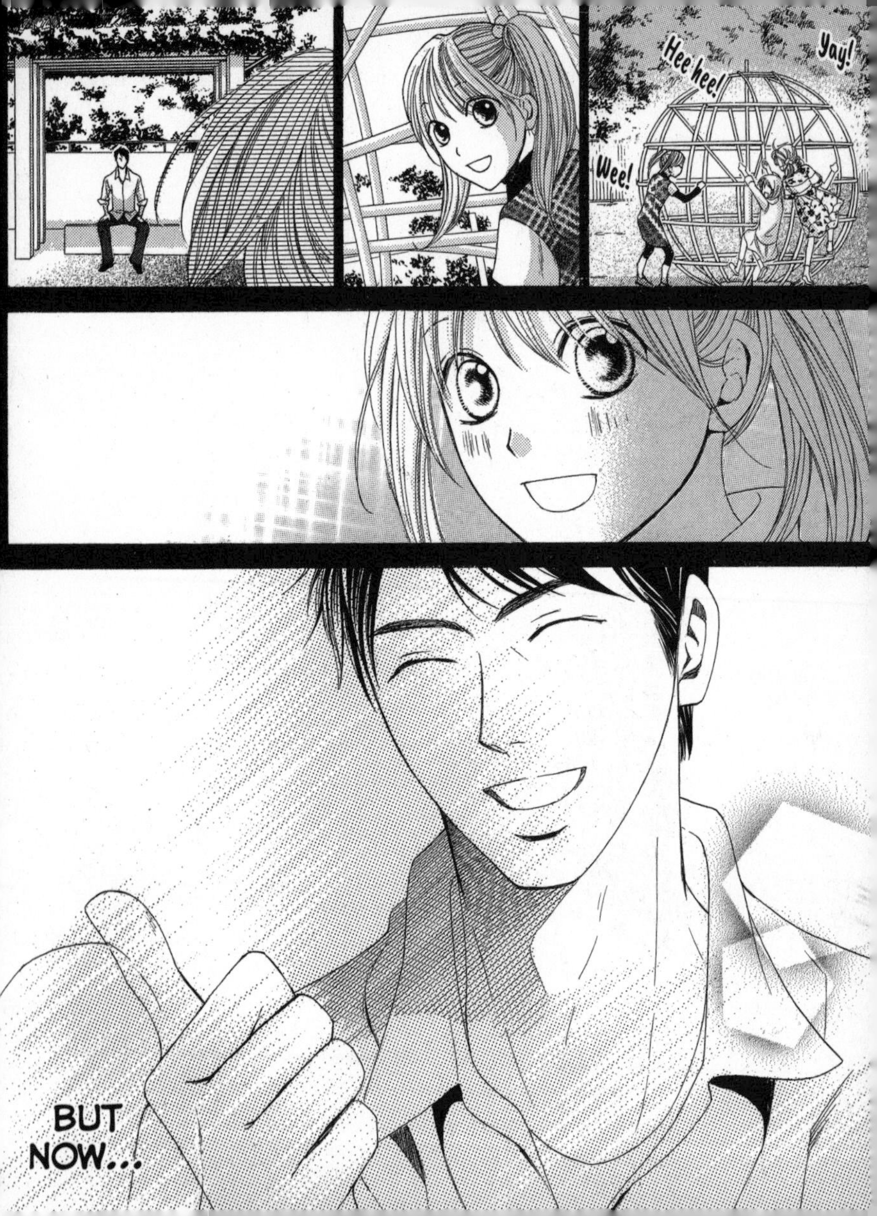
Yay!
Hee hee!
Wee!
BUT NOW...

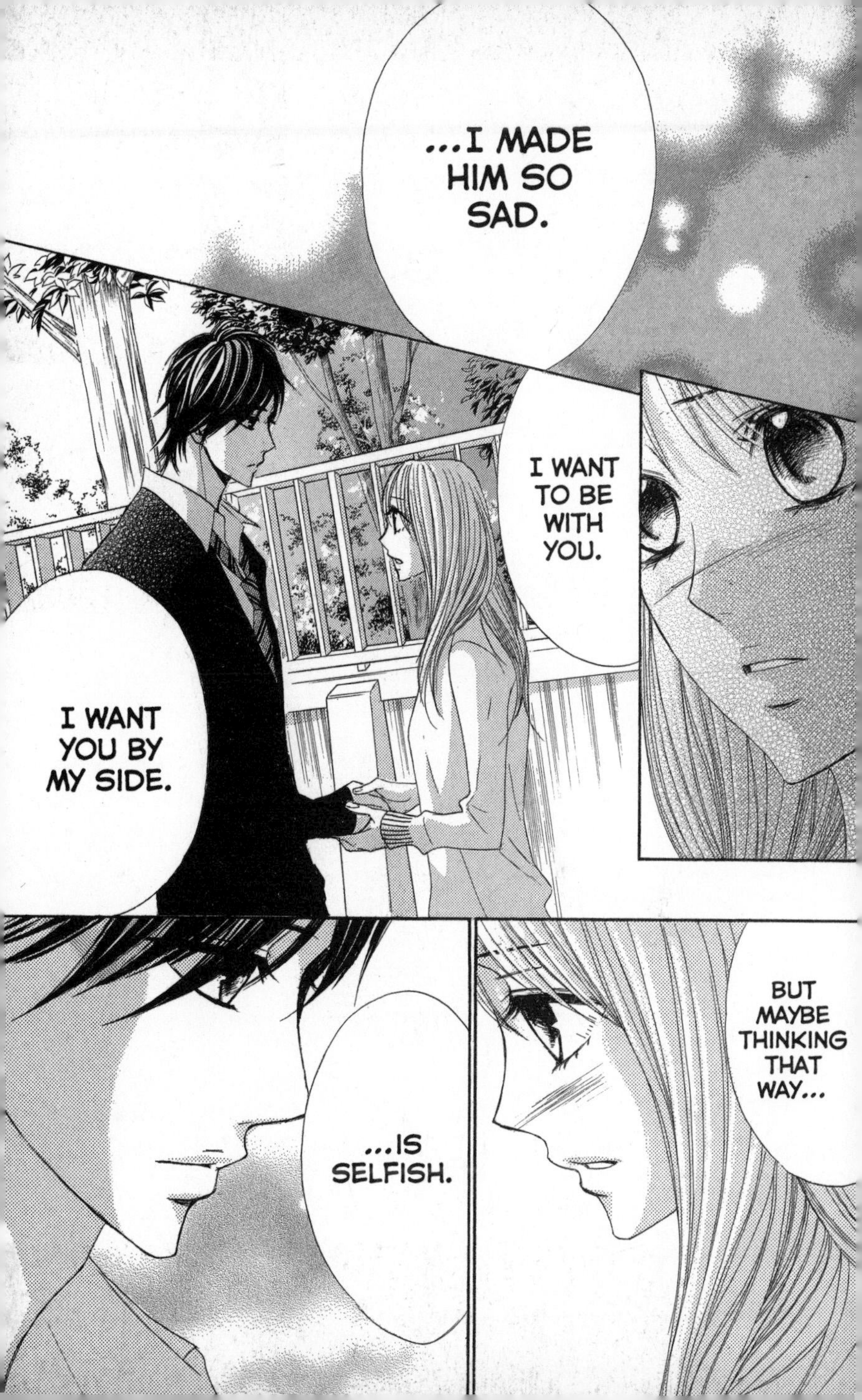
...I MADE HIM SO SAD.
I WANT TO BE WITH YOU.
I WANT YOU BY MY SIDE.
BUT MAYBE THINKING THAT WAY...
...IS SELFISH.

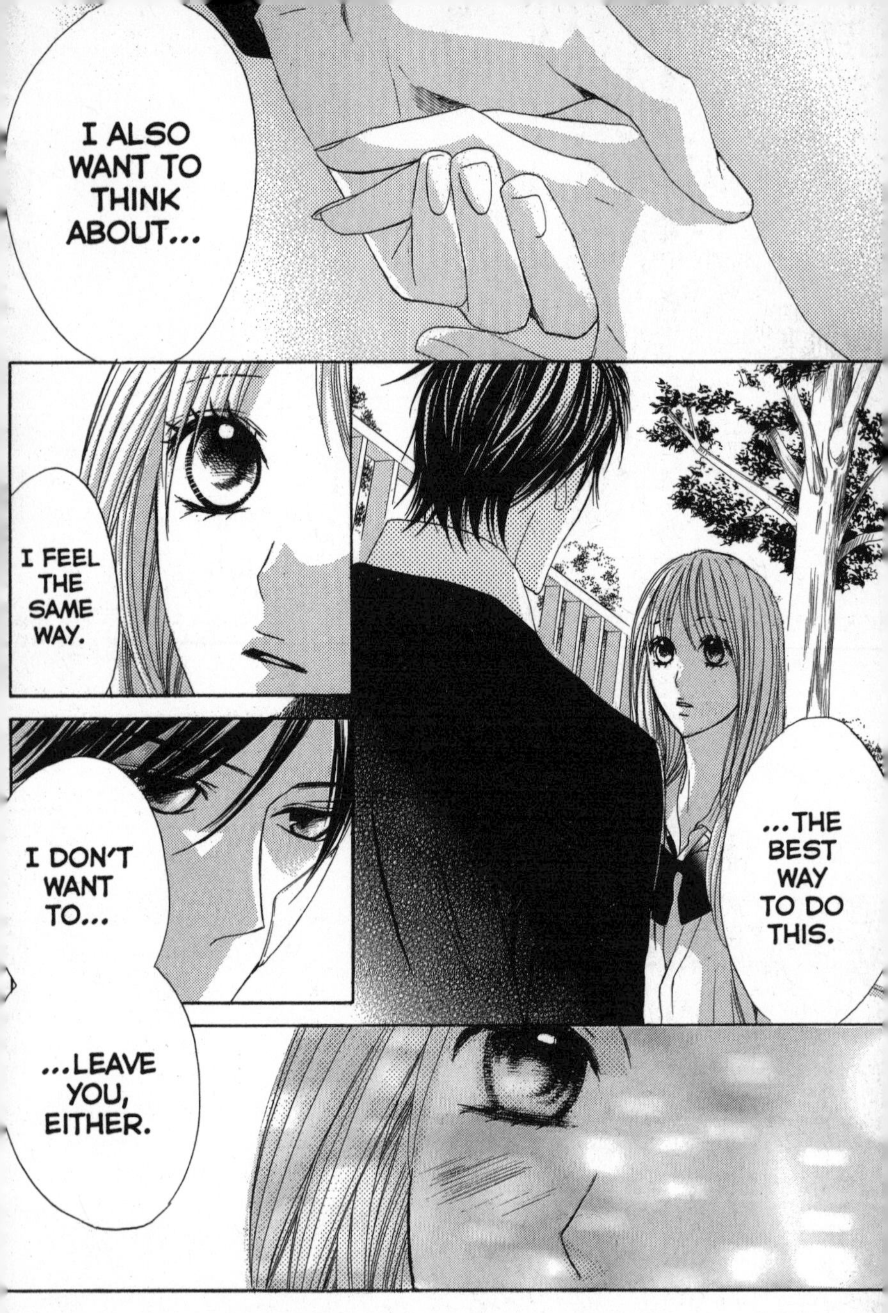
I ALSO WANT TO THINK ABOUT...
...THE BEST WAY TO DO THIS.
I FEEL THE SAME WAY.
I DON'T WANT TO...
...LEAVE YOU, EITHER.

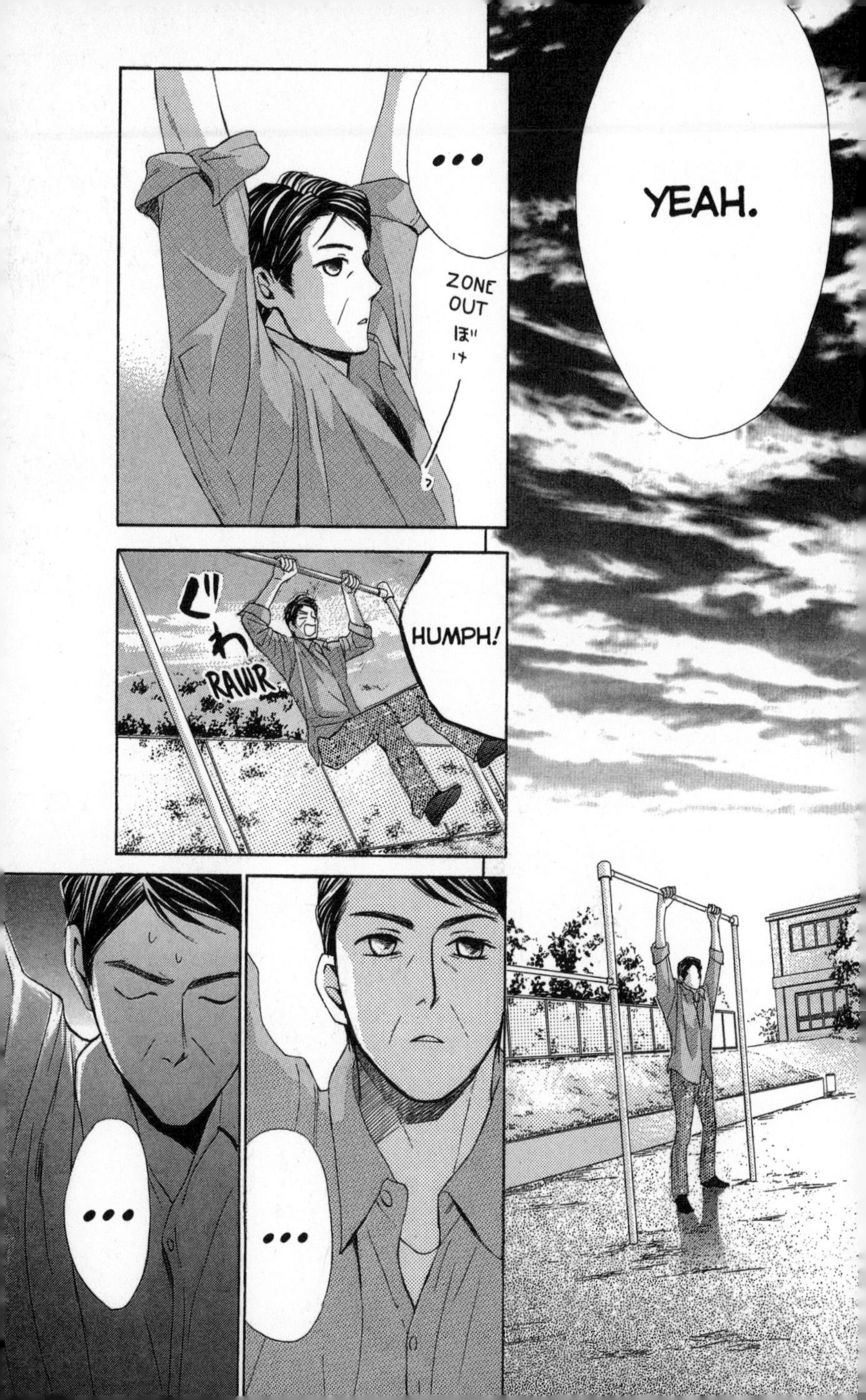
YEAH.
...
ZONE OUT
ぼけ
HUMPH!
ぐわ
RAWR
...
...

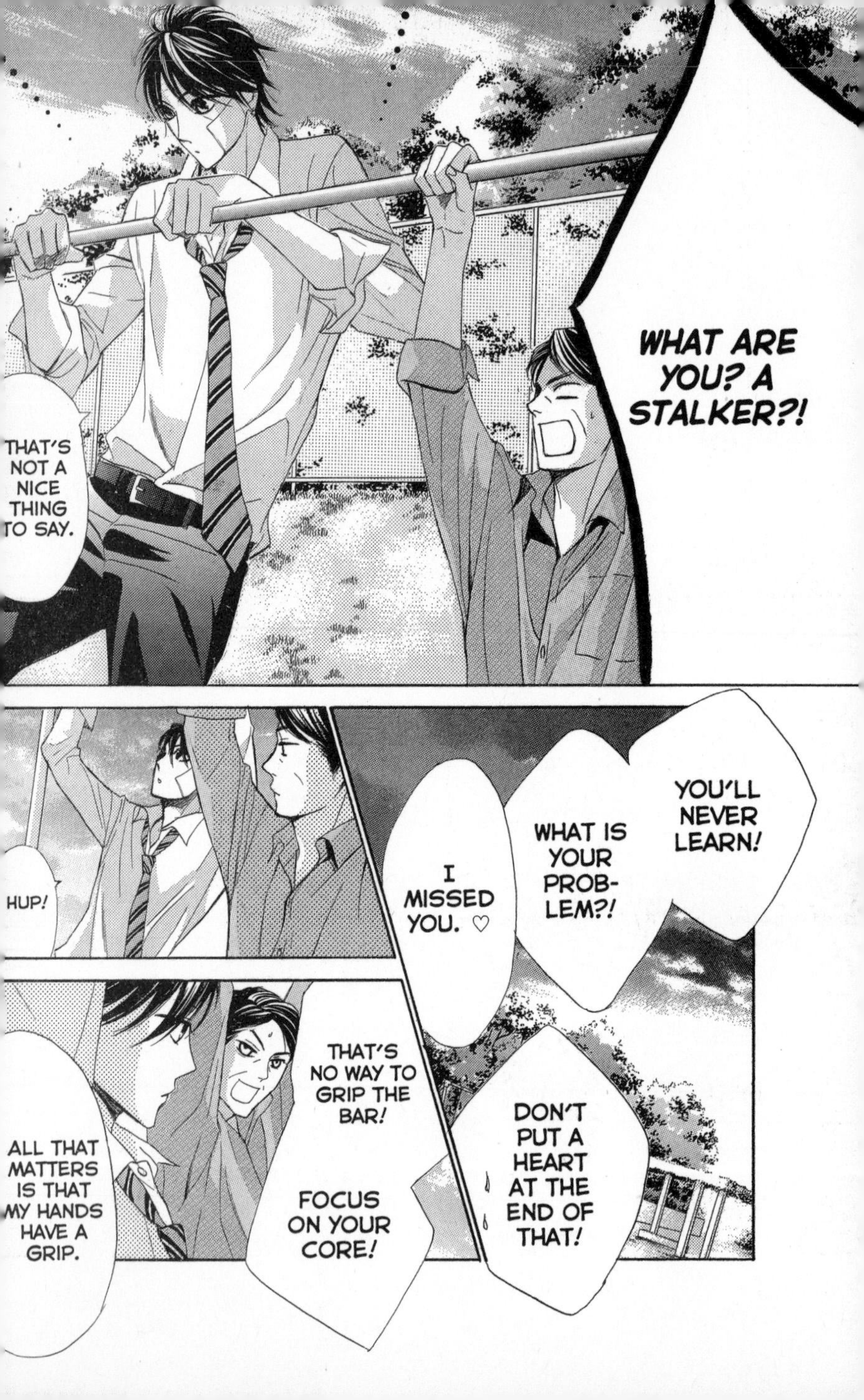
WHAT ARE YOU? A STALKER?!
THAT'S NOT A NICE THING TO SAY.
YOU'LL NEVER LEARN!
WHAT IS YOUR PROBLEM?!
I MISSED YOU. ♡
DON'T PUT A HEART AT THE END OF THAT!
HUP!
THAT'S NO WAY TO GRIP THE BAR!
FOCUS ON YOUR CORE!
ALL THAT MATTERS IS THAT MY HANDS HAVE A GRIP.

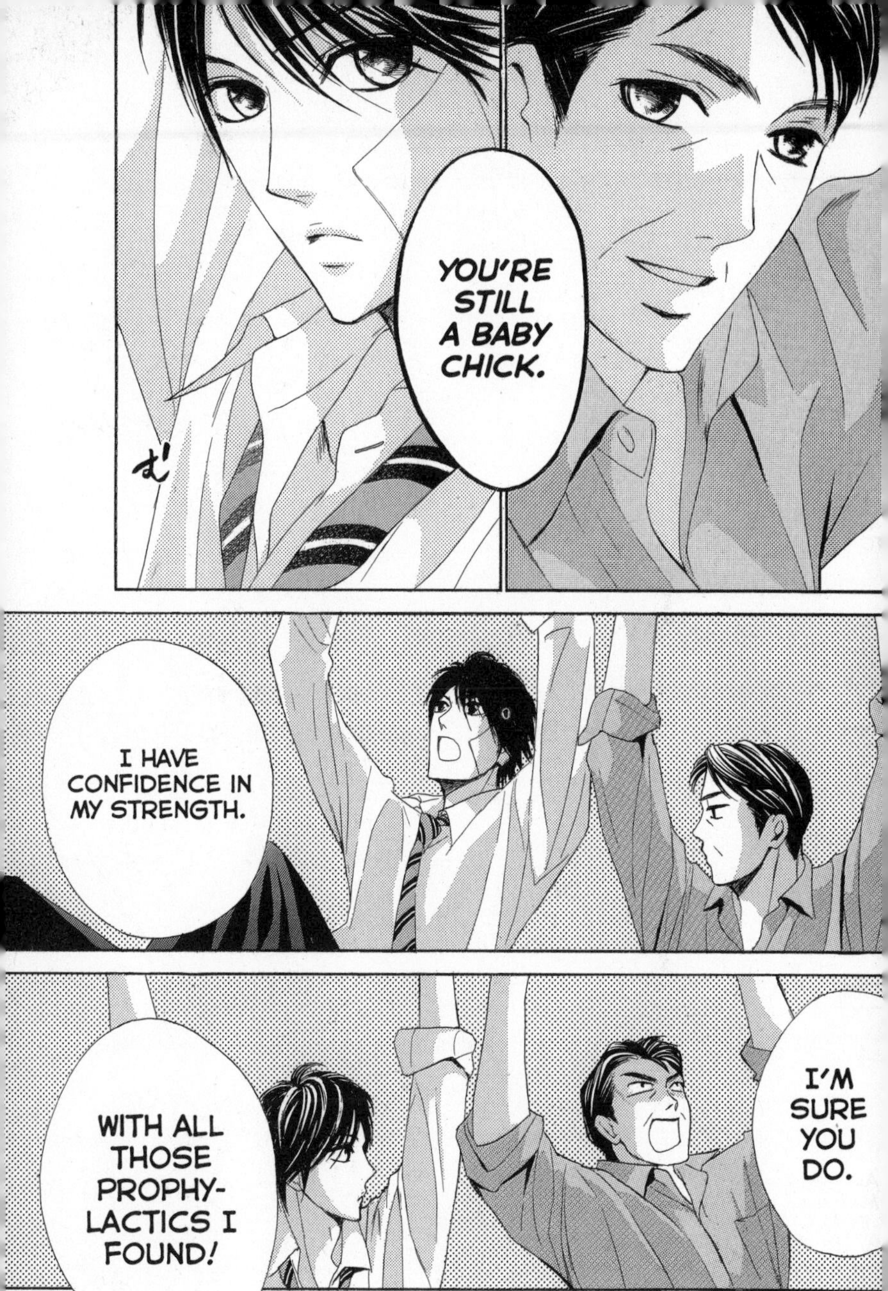
YOU'RE STILL A BABY CHICK.
む
I HAVE CONFIDENCE IN MY STRENGTH.
I'M SURE YOU DO.
WITH ALL THOSE PROPHY-LACTICS I FOUND!

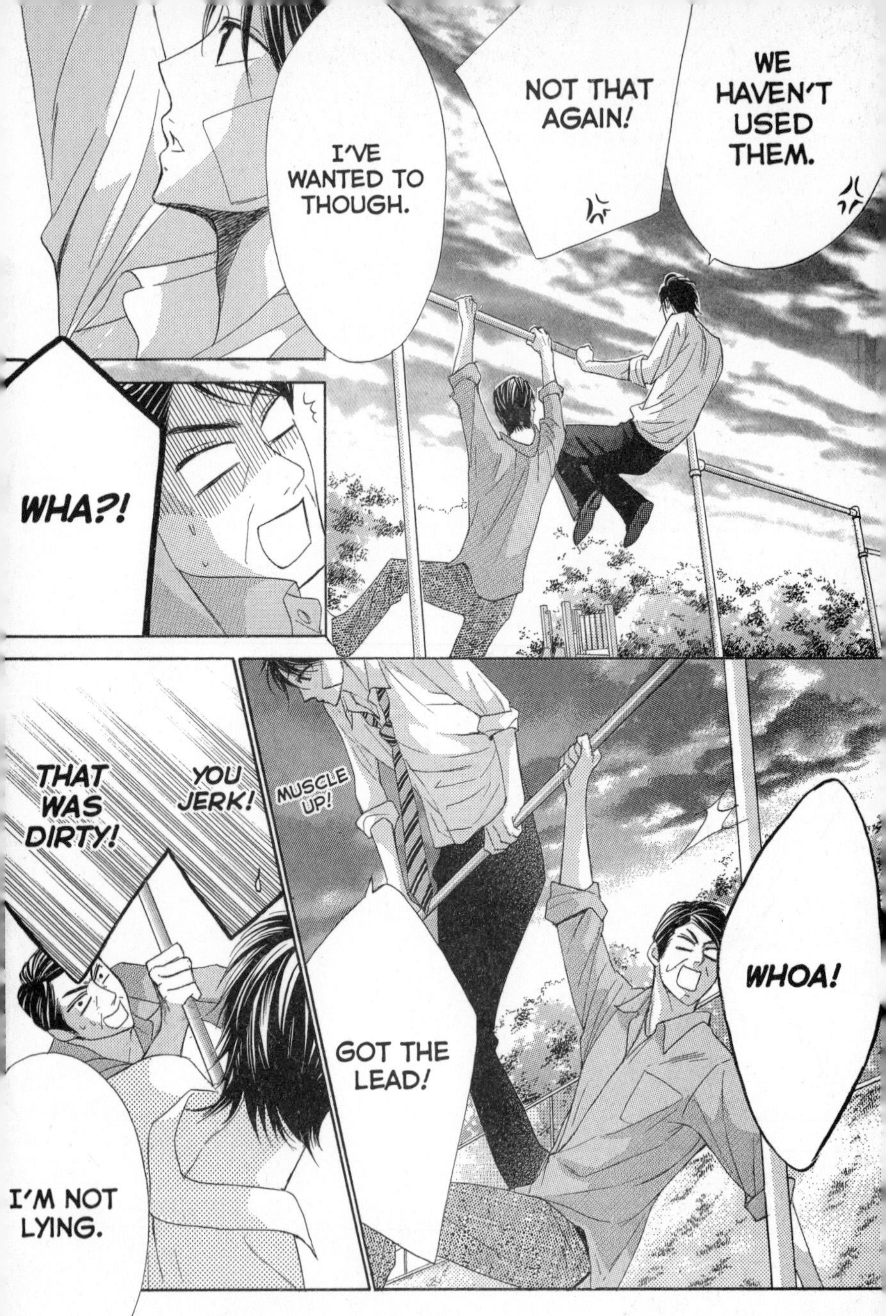
WE HAVEN'T USED THEM.
NOT THAT AGAIN!
I'VE WANTED TO THOUGH.
WHA?!
WHOA!
GOT THE LEAD!
MUSCLE UP!
YOU JERK!
THAT WAS DIRTY!
I'M NOT LYING.

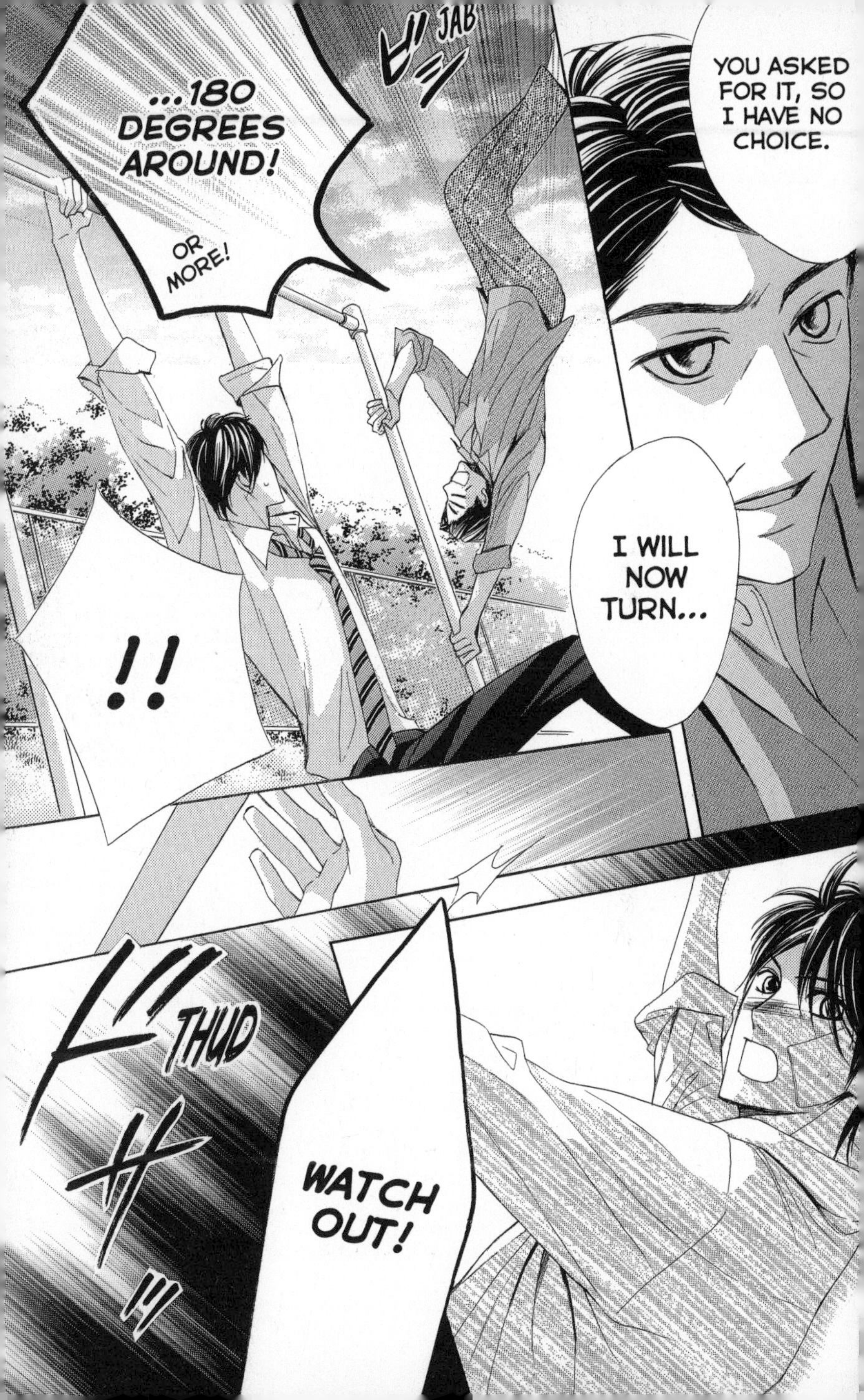
YOU ASKED FOR IT, SO I HAVE NO CHOICE.
I WILL NOW TURN...
JAB
...180 DEGREES AROUND!
OR MORE!
!!
WATCH OUT!
THUD

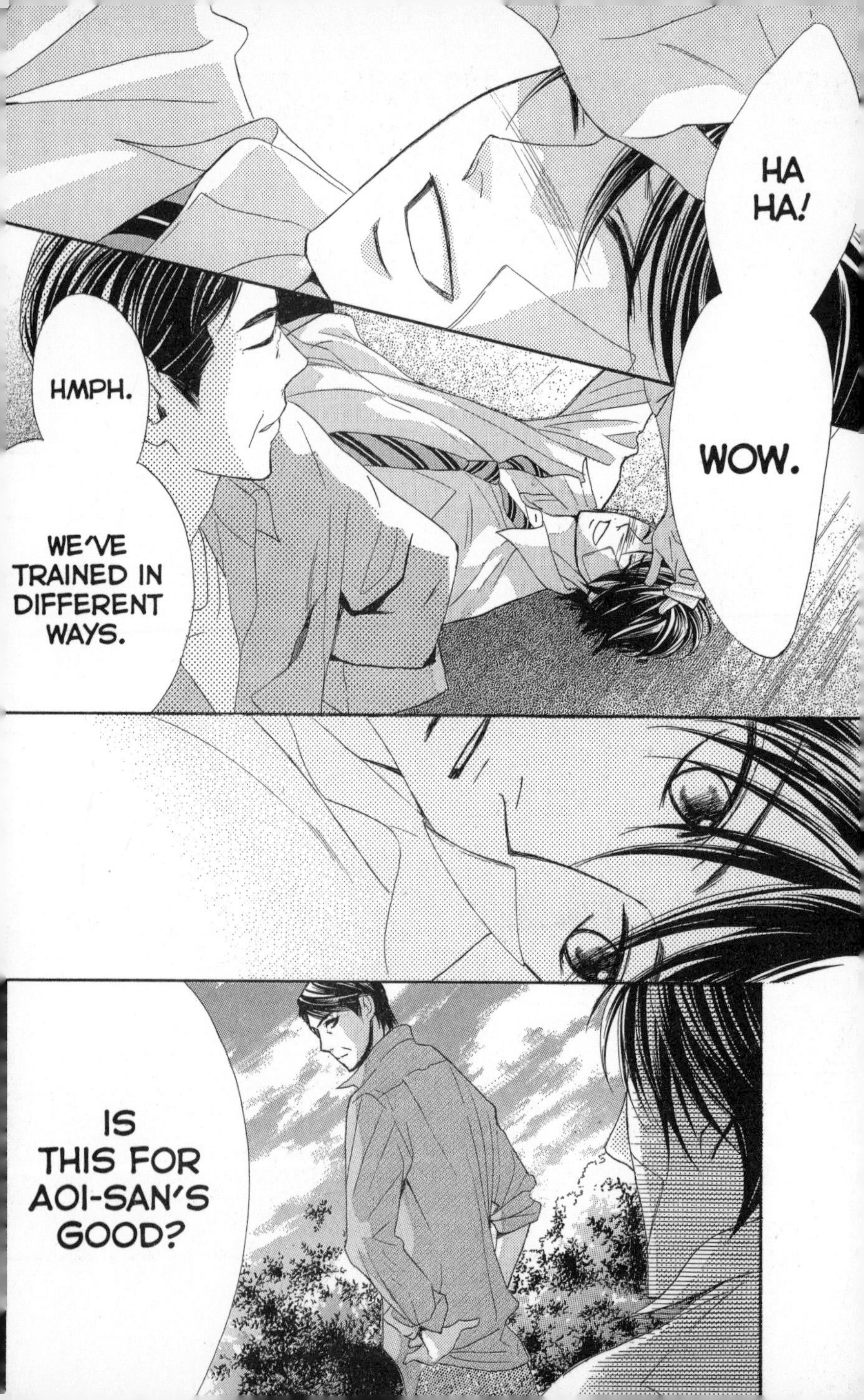
HA HA!
WOW.
HMPH.
WE'VE TRAINED IN DIFFERENT WAYS.
IS THIS FOR AOI-SAN'S GOOD?

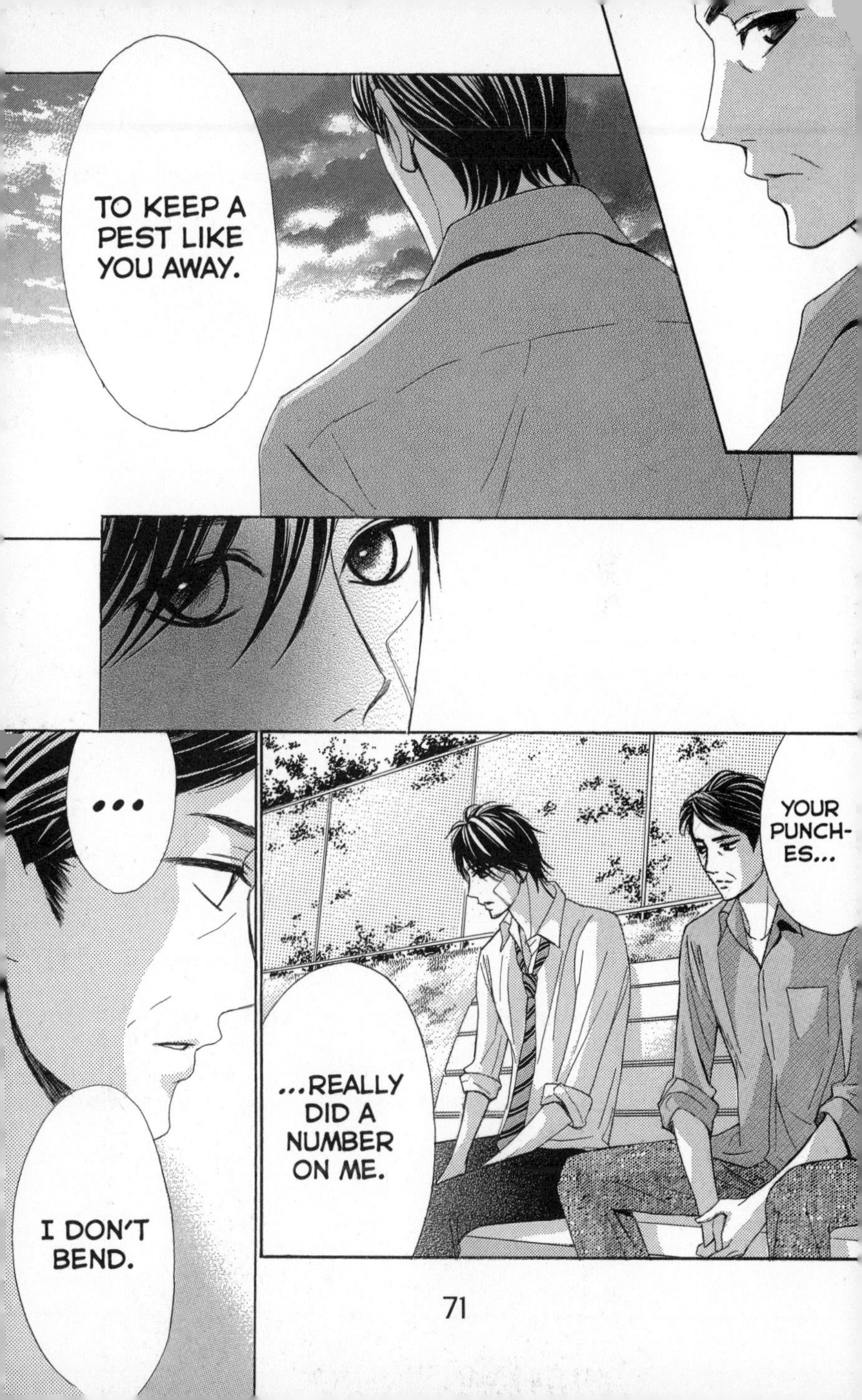
TO KEEP A PEST LIKE YOU AWAY.
YOUR PUNCH-ES...
...REALLY DID A NUMBER ON ME.
...
I DON'T BEND.

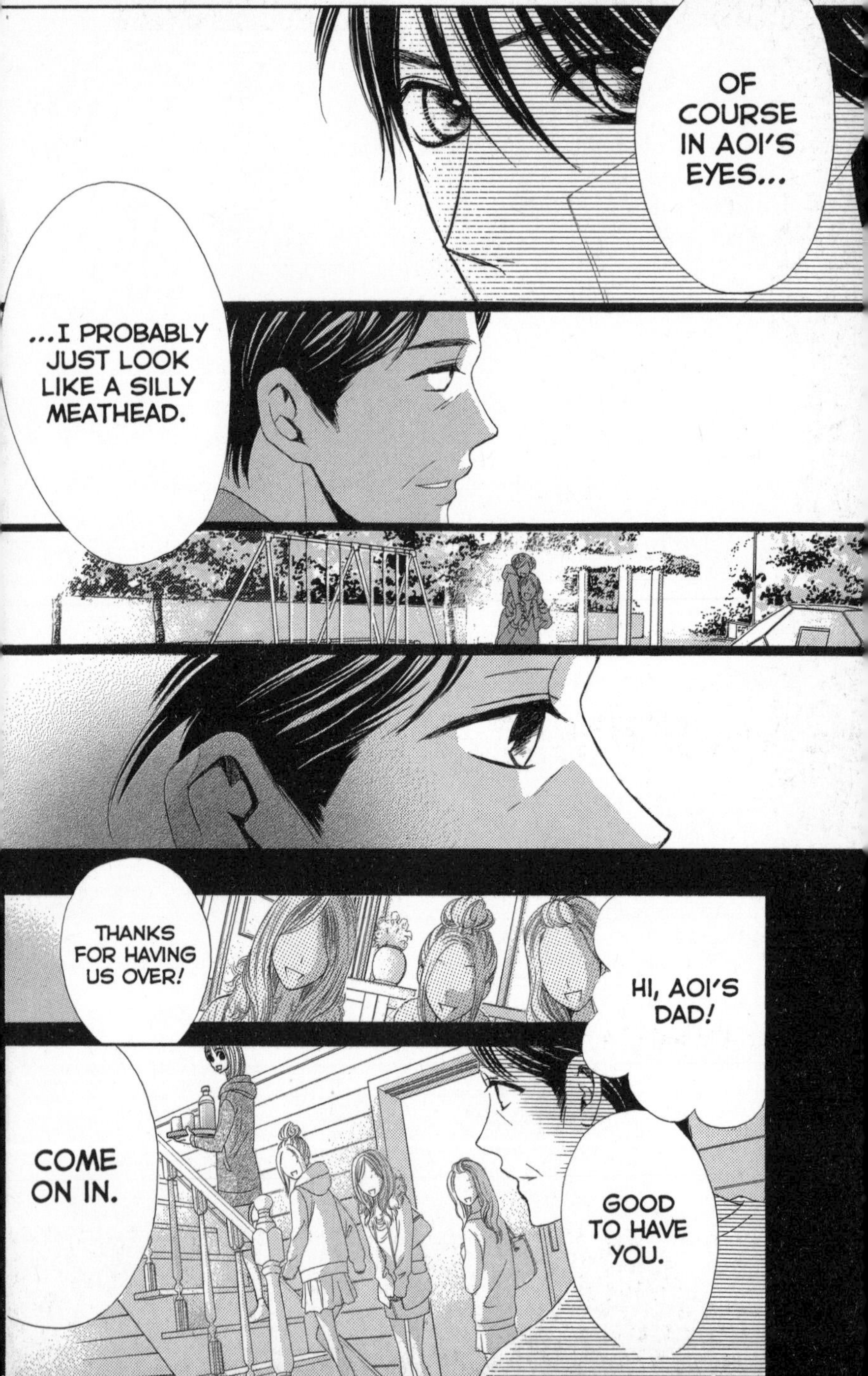
OF COURSE IN AOI'S EYES...
...I PROBABLY JUST LOOK LIKE A SILLY MEATHEAD.
HI, AOI'S DAD!
THANKS FOR HAVING US OVER!
GOOD TO HAVE YOU.
COME ON IN.

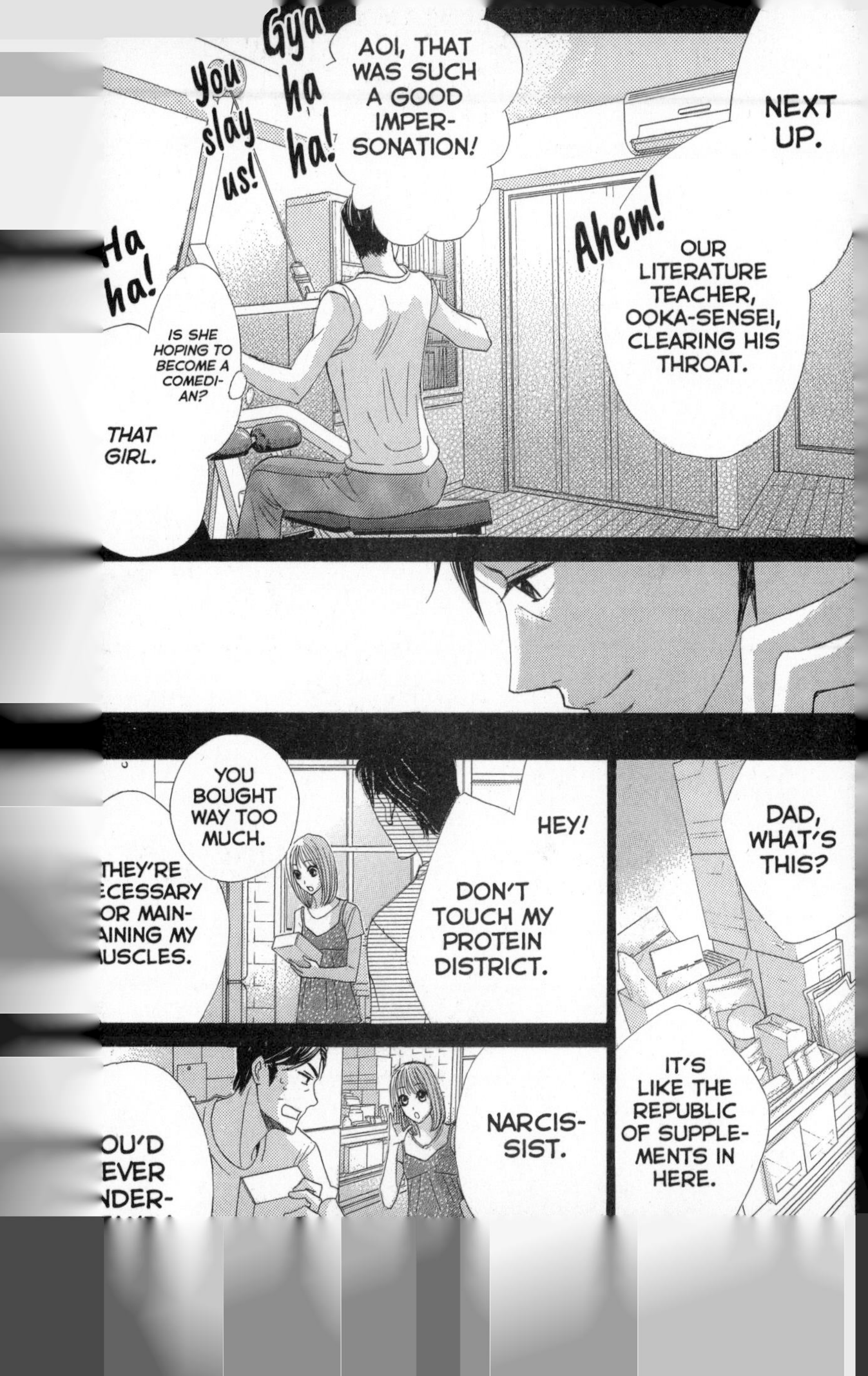
NEXT UP.
Ahem!
OUR LITERATURE TEACHER, OOKA-SENSEI, CLEARING HIS THROAT.
AOI, THAT WAS SUCH A GOOD IMPERSONATION!
Gya ha ha!
You slay us!
Ha ha!
IS SHE HOPING TO BECOME A COMEDIAN?
THAT GIRL.
DAD, WHAT'S THIS?
IT'S LIKE THE REPUBLIC OF SUPPLEMENTS IN HERE.
HEY!
DON'T TOUCH MY PROTEIN DISTRICT.
YOU BOUGHT WAY TOO MUCH.
THEY'RE ECESSARY OR MAIN- AINING MY USCLES.
NARCIS-SIST.
OU'D EVER NDER-

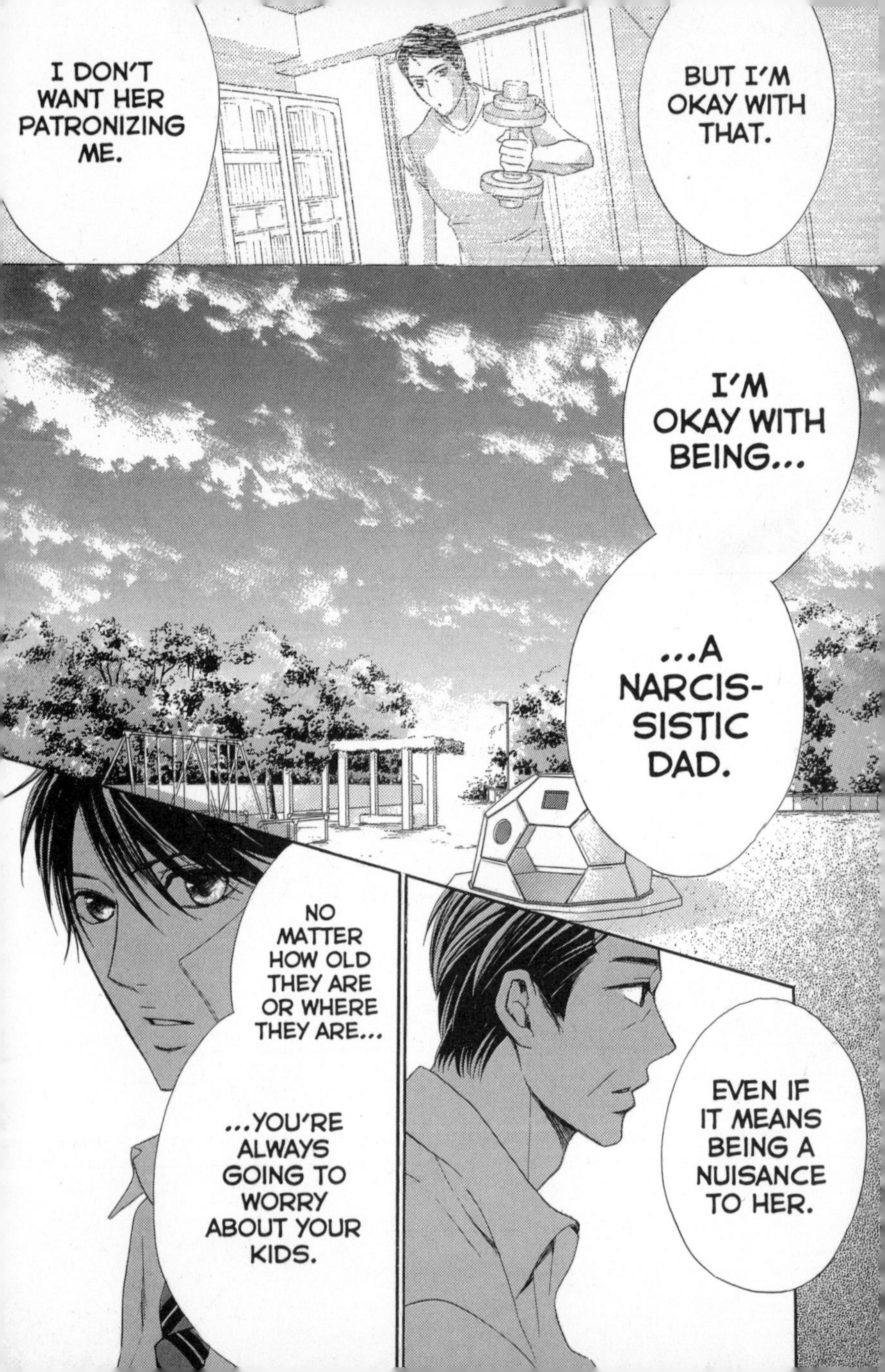
BUT I'M OKAY WITH THAT.
I DON'T WANT HER PATRONIZING ME.
I'M OKAY WITH BEING...
...A NARCIS-SISTIC DAD.
EVEN IF IT MEANS BEING A NUISANCE TO HER.
NO MATTER HOW OLD THEY ARE OR WHERE THEY ARE...
...YOU'RE ALWAYS GOING TO WORRY ABOUT YOUR KIDS.

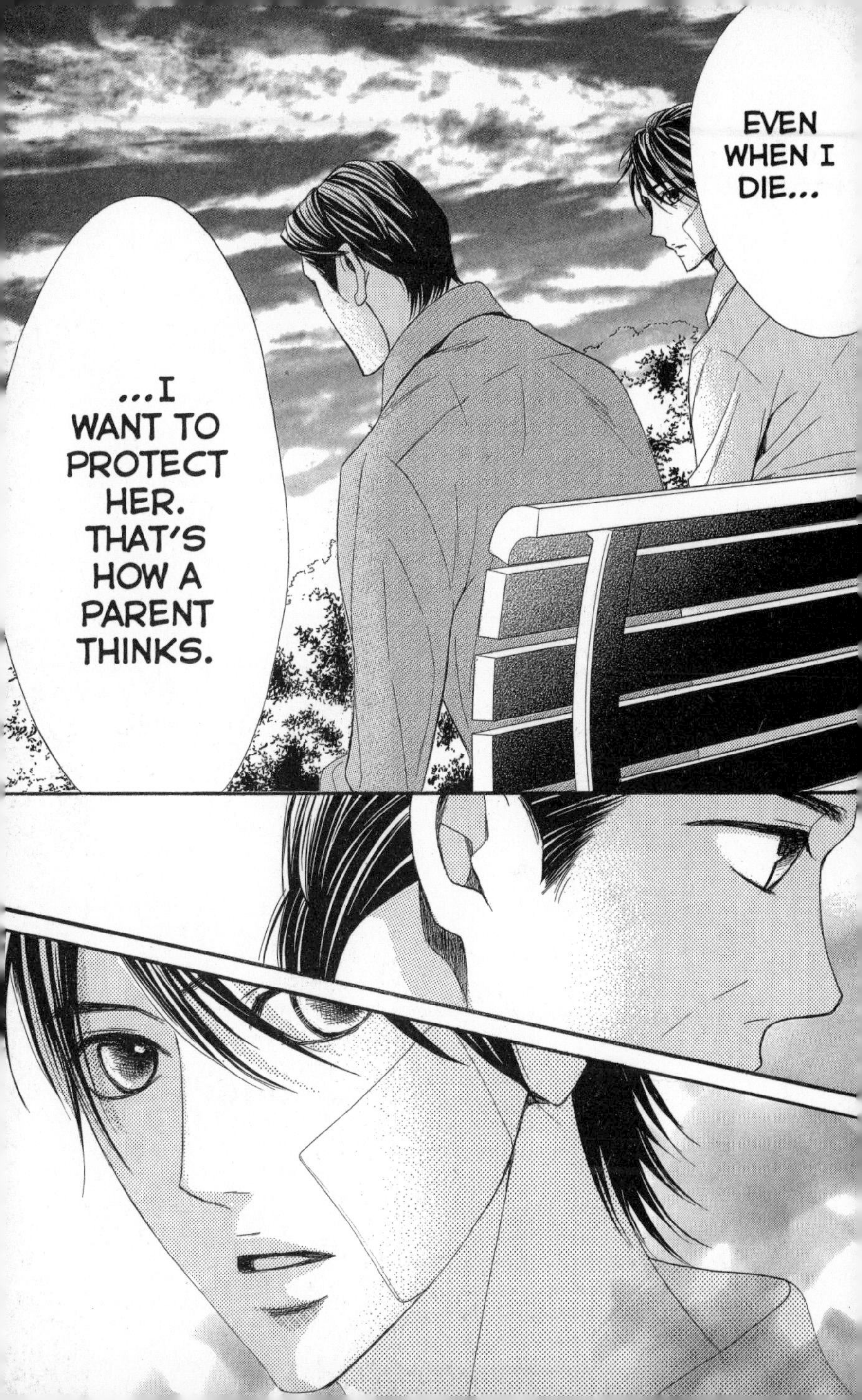
EVEN WHEN I DIE...
...I WANT TO PROTECT HER. THAT'S HOW A PARENT THINKS.

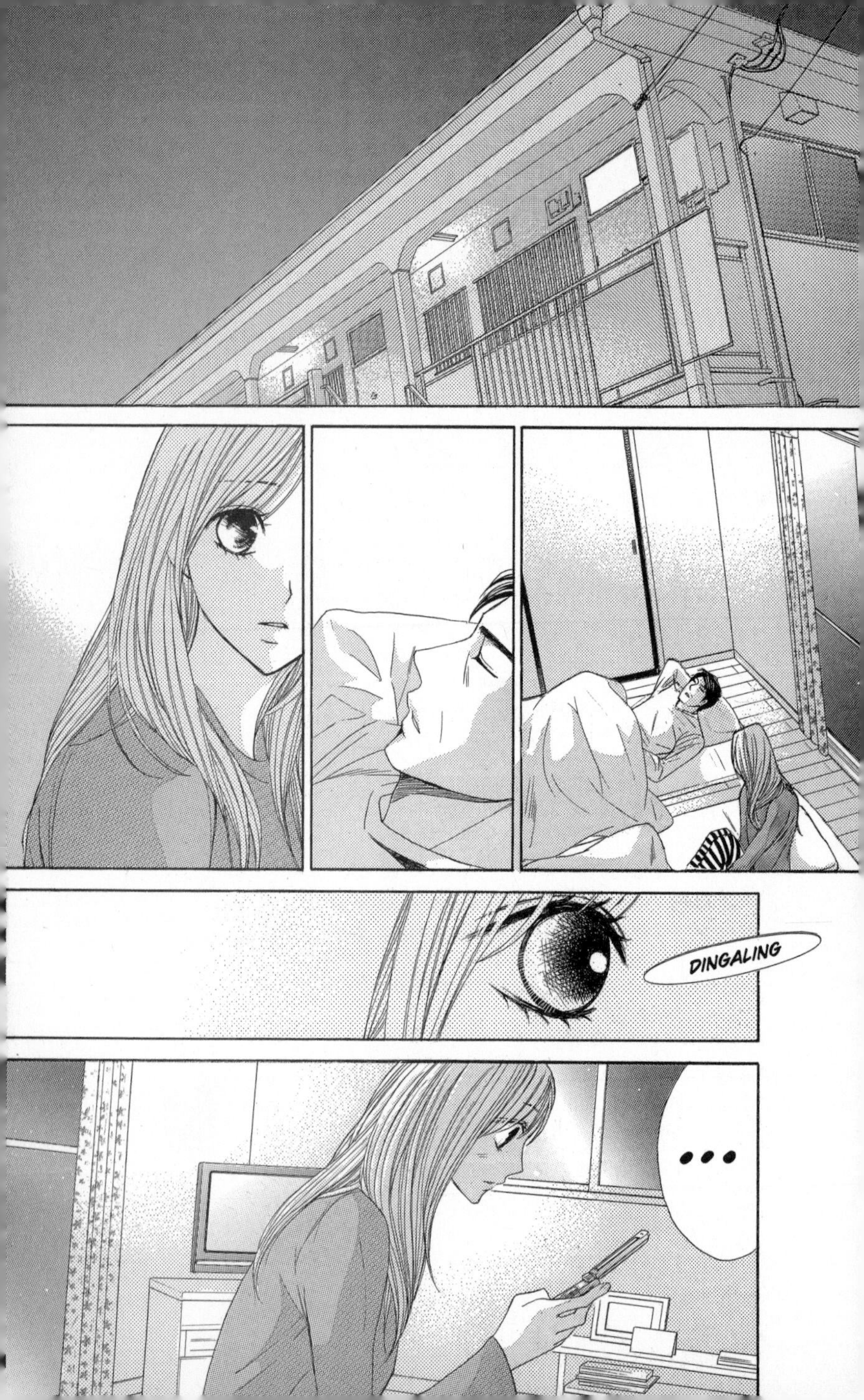
DINGALING
...

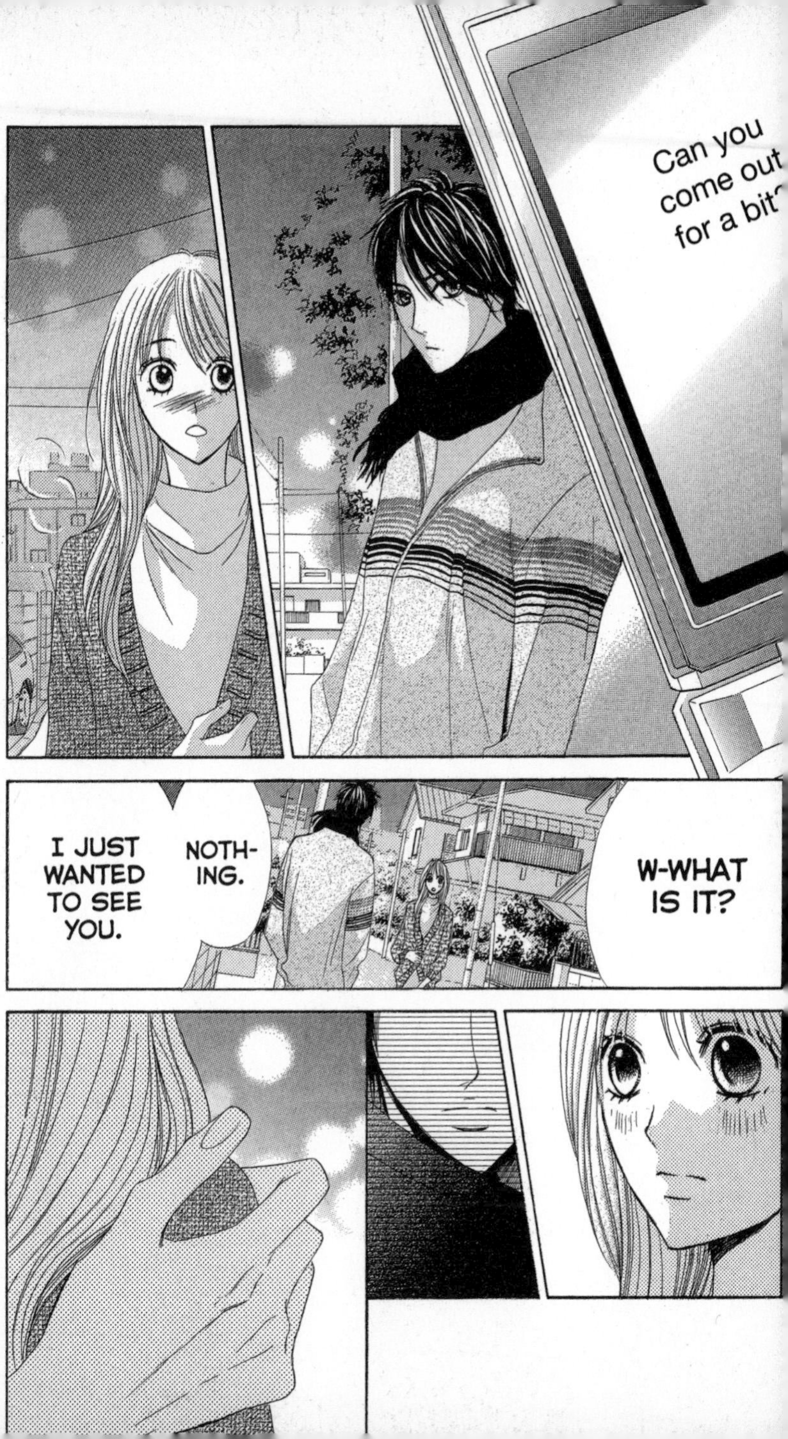
Can you come out for a bit
W-WHAT IS IT?
NOTH-ING.
I JUST WANTED TO SEE YOU.

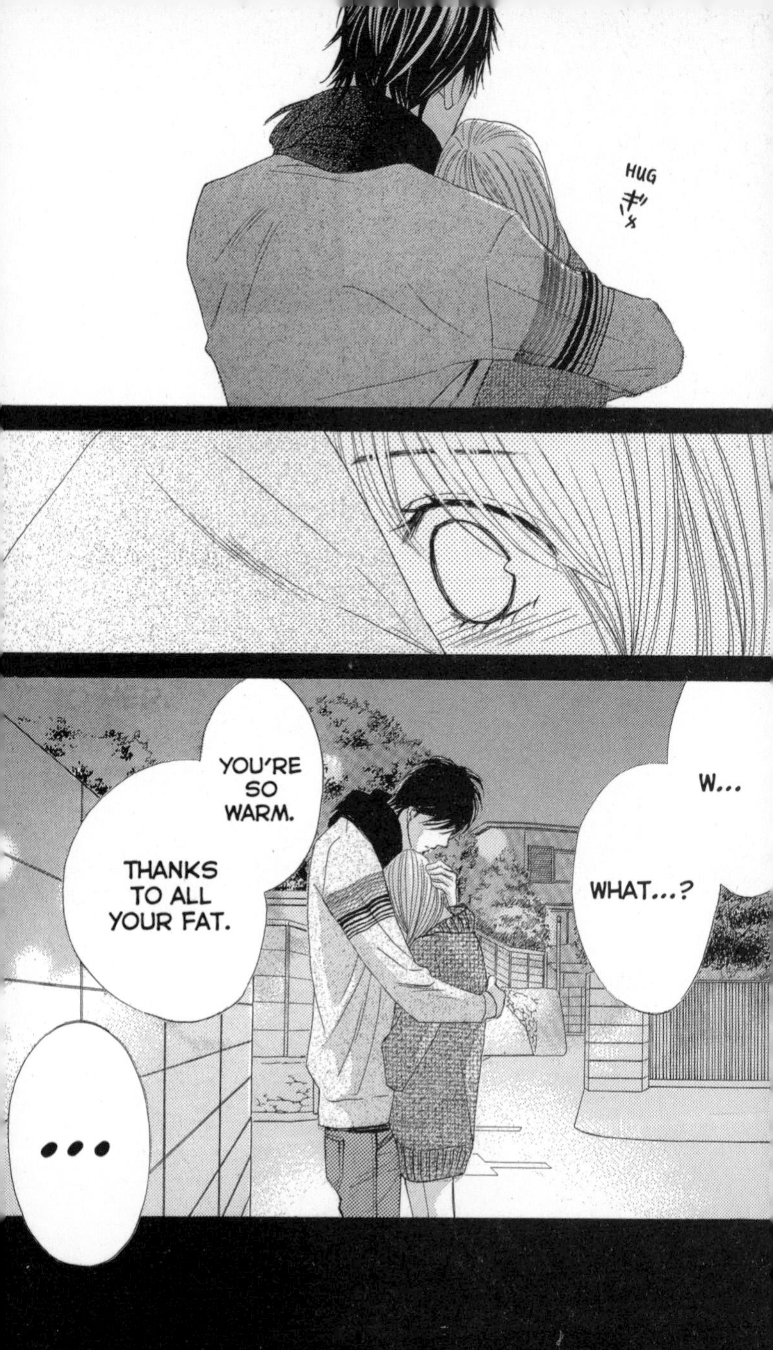
HUG
W...
WHAT...?
YOU'RE SO WARM.
THANKS TO ALL YOUR FAT.
...

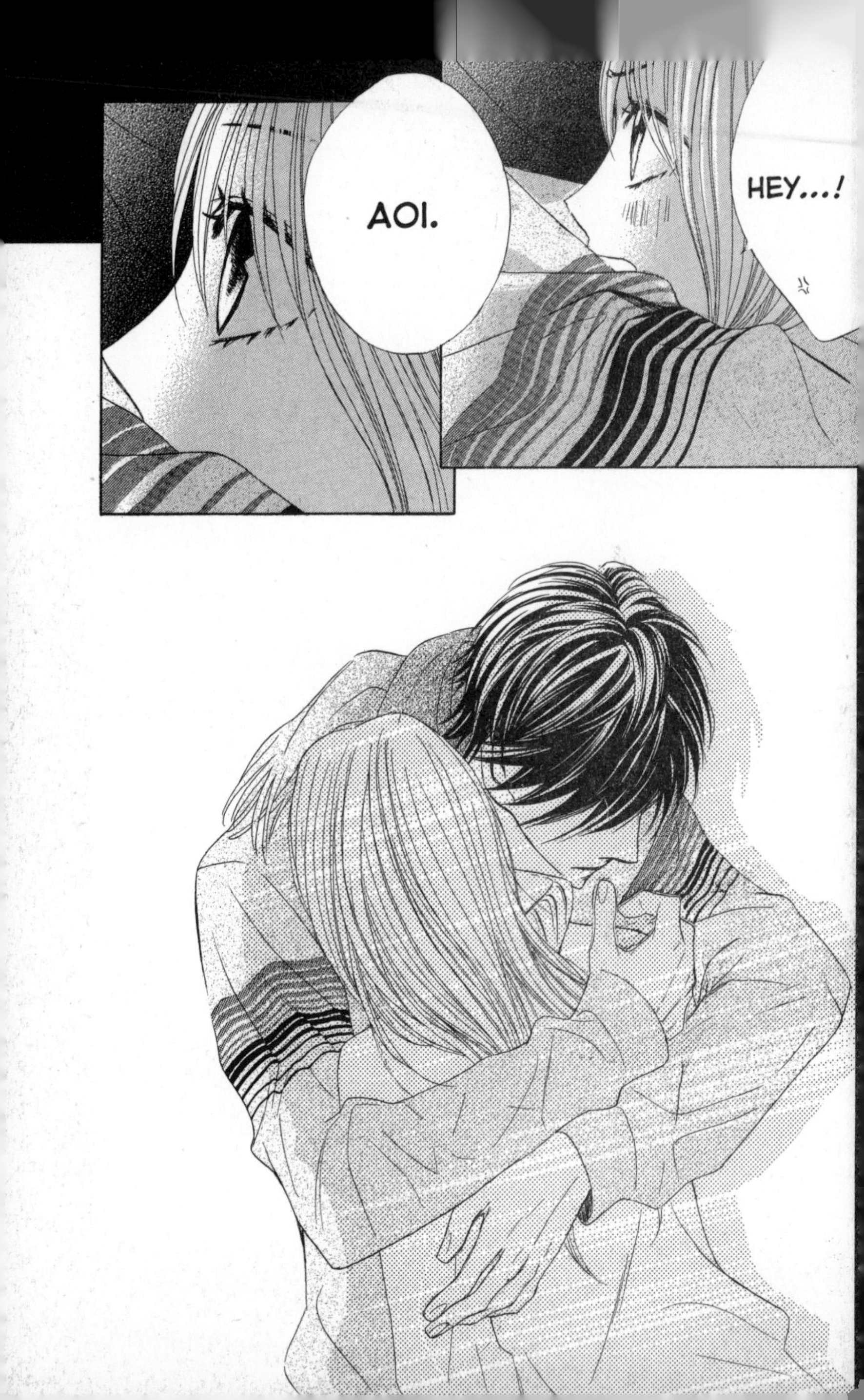
HEY...!
AOI.

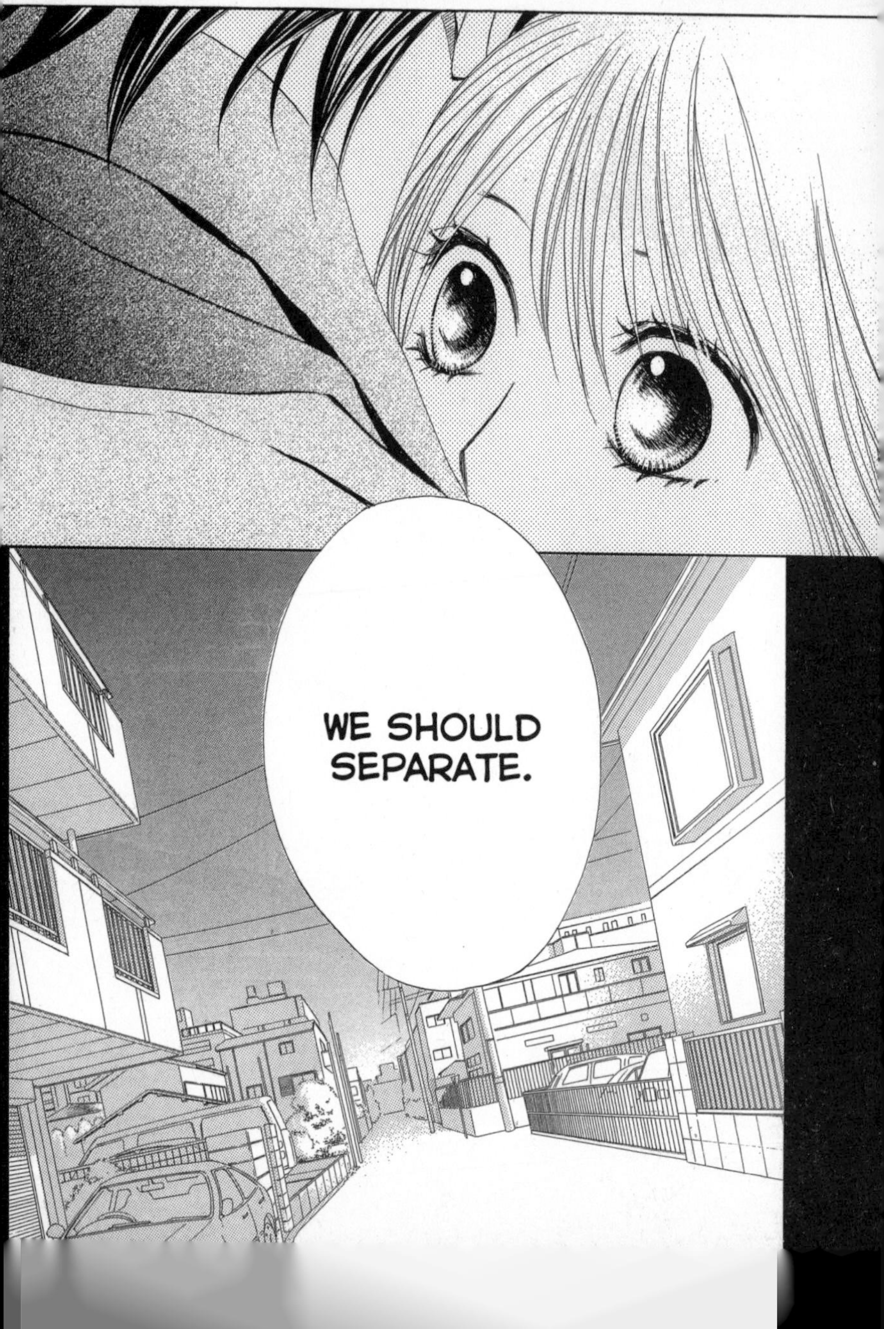
WE SHOULD SEPARATE.

L♥DK

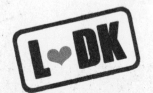

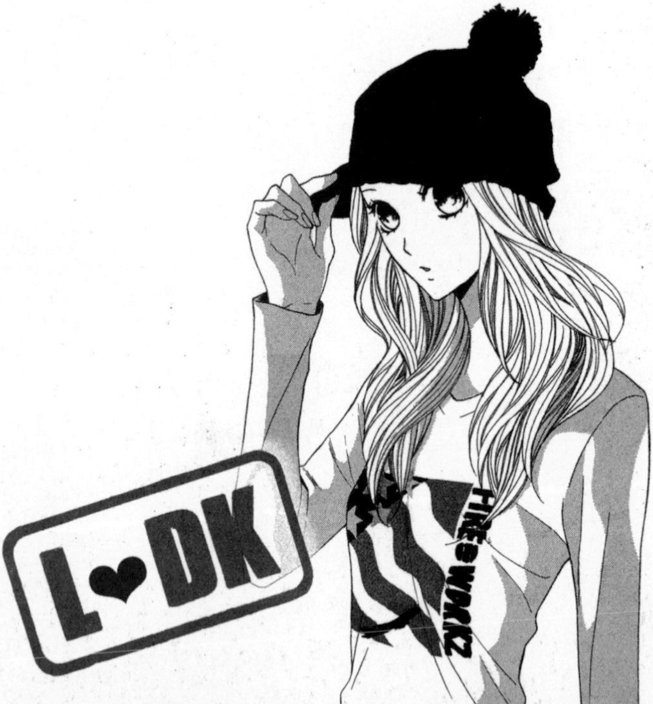
L♥DK

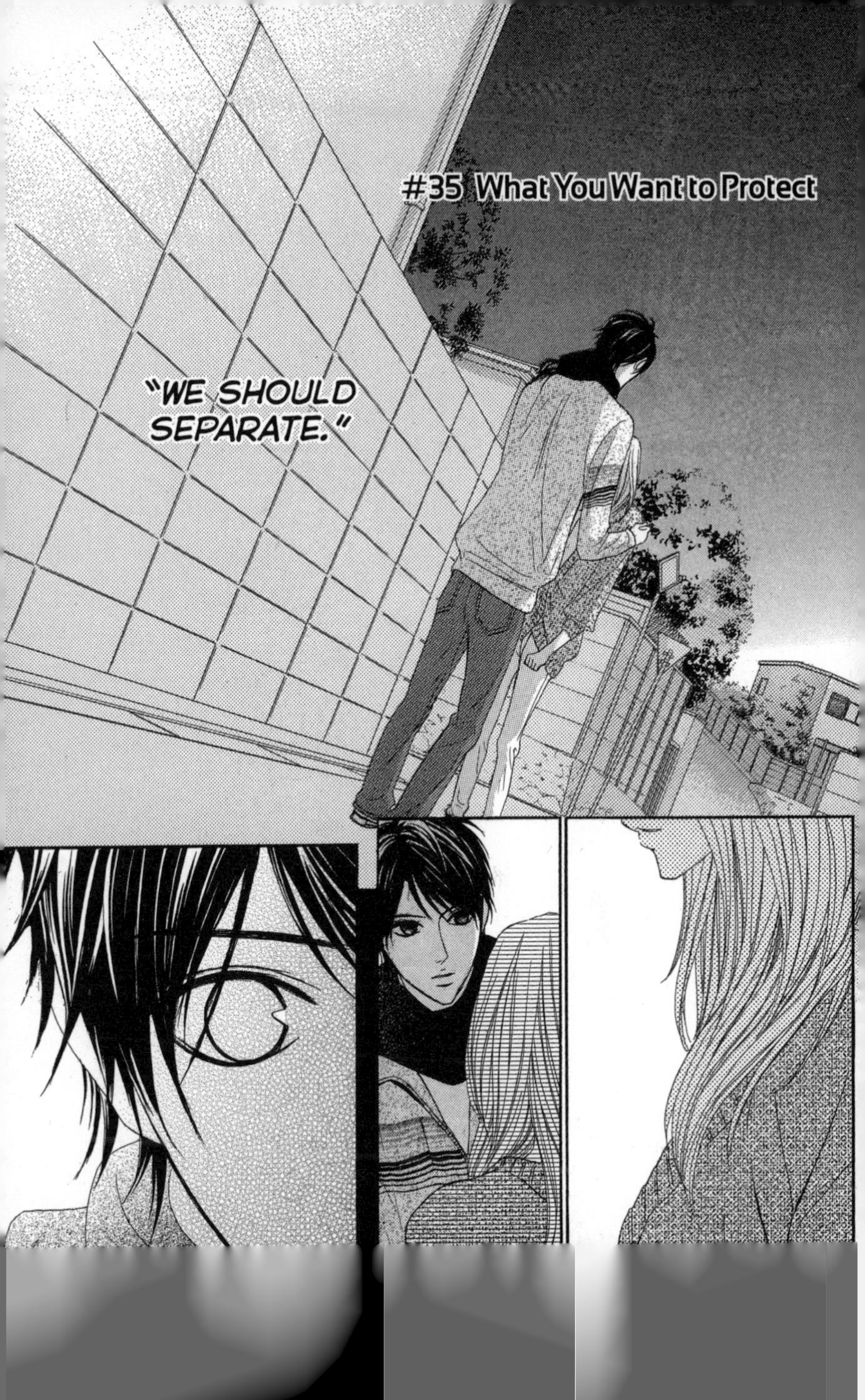
#35 What You Want to Protect
"WE SHOULD SEPARATE."

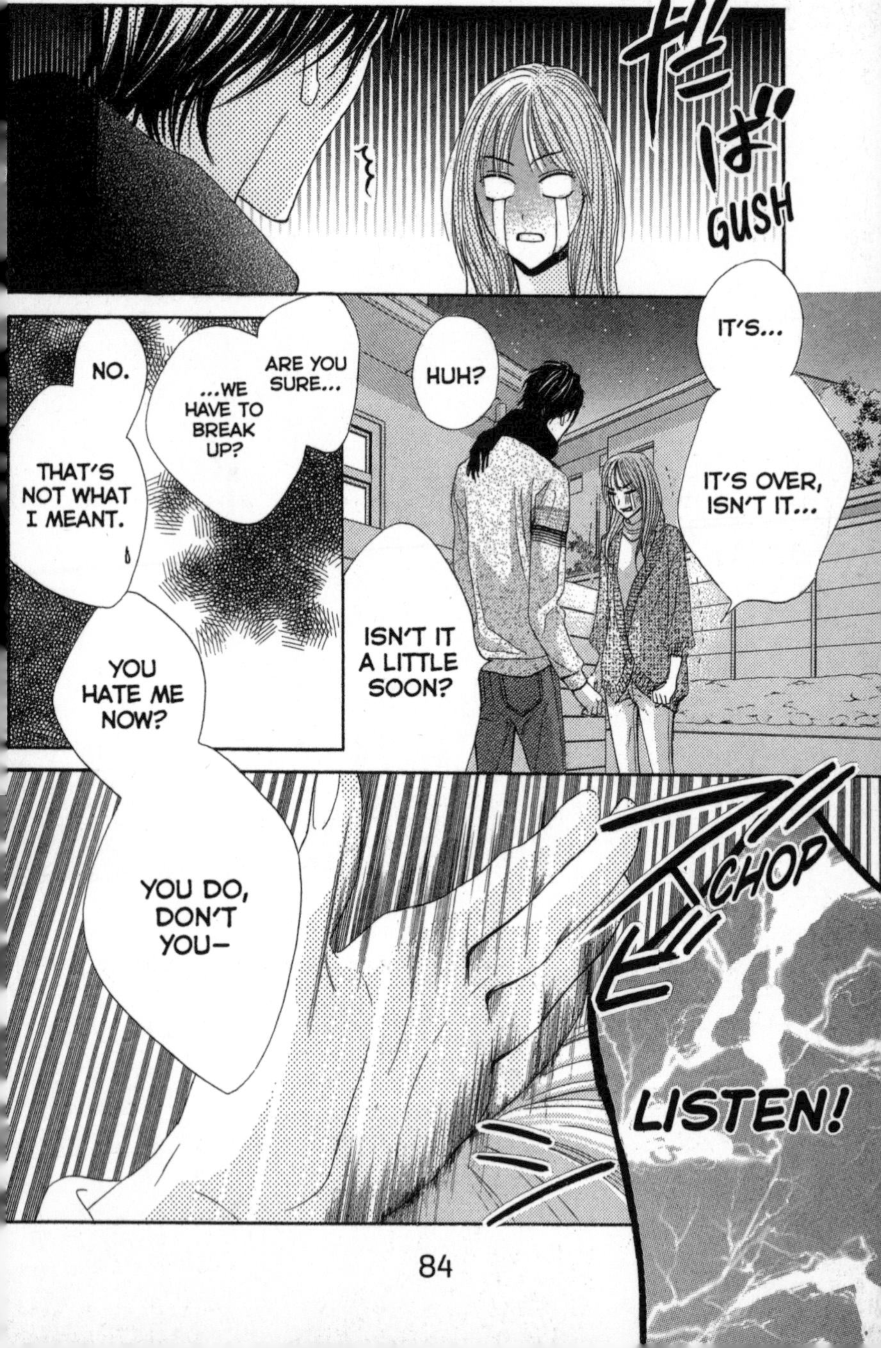
GUSH
IT'S...
IT'S OVER, ISN'T IT...
HUH?
ISN'T IT A LITTLE SOON?
ARE YOU SURE...
...WE HAVE TO BREAK UP?
NO.
THAT'S NOT WHAT I MEANT.
YOU HATE ME NOW?
YOU DO, DON'T YOU–
CHOP
LISTEN!

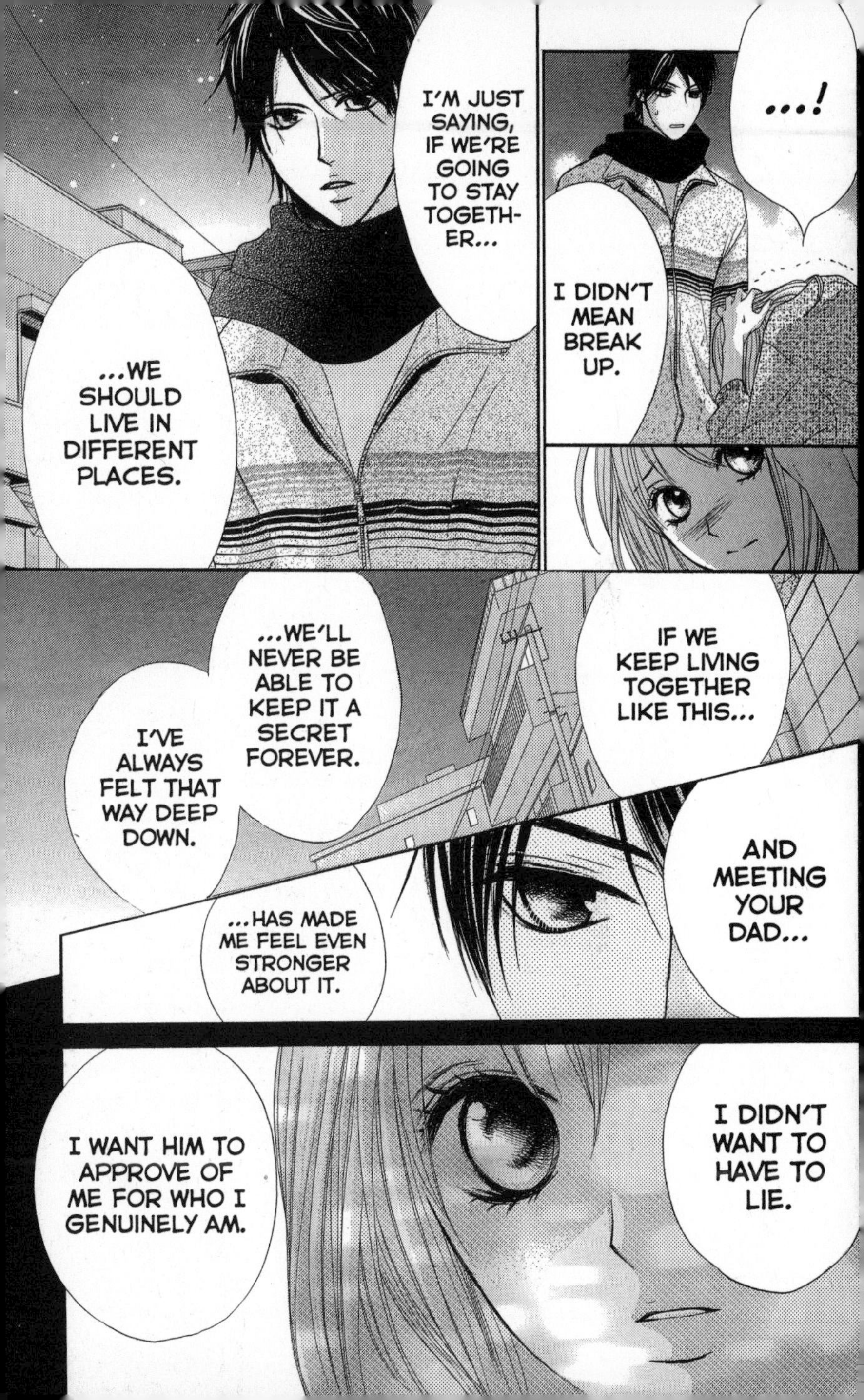
...!
I DIDN'T MEAN BREAK UP.
I'M JUST SAYING, IF WE'RE GOING TO STAY TOGETH-ER...
...WE SHOULD LIVE IN DIFFERENT PLACES.
IF WE KEEP LIVING TOGETHER LIKE THIS...
...WE'LL NEVER BE ABLE TO KEEP IT A SECRET FOREVER.
I'VE ALWAYS FELT THAT WAY DEEP DOWN.
AND MEETING YOUR DAD...
...HAS MADE ME FEEL EVEN STRONGER ABOUT IT.
I DIDN'T WANT TO HAVE TO LIE.
I WANT HIM TO APPROVE OF ME FOR WHO I GENUINELY AM.

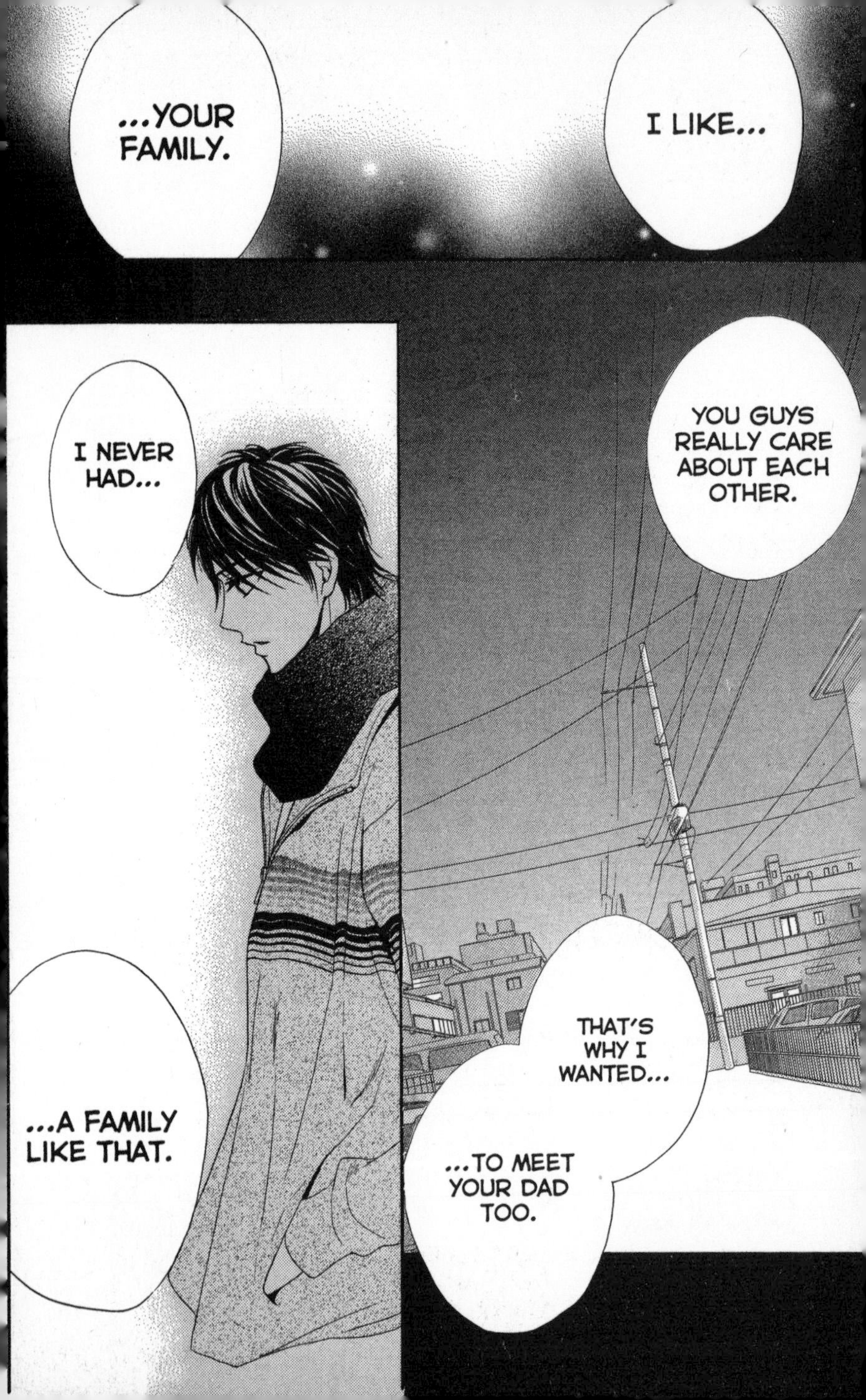
I LIKE...
...YOUR FAMILY.
YOU GUYS REALLY CARE ABOUT EACH OTHER.
THAT'S WHY I WANTED...
...TO MEET YOUR DAD TOO.
I NEVER HAD...
...A FAMILY LIKE THAT.

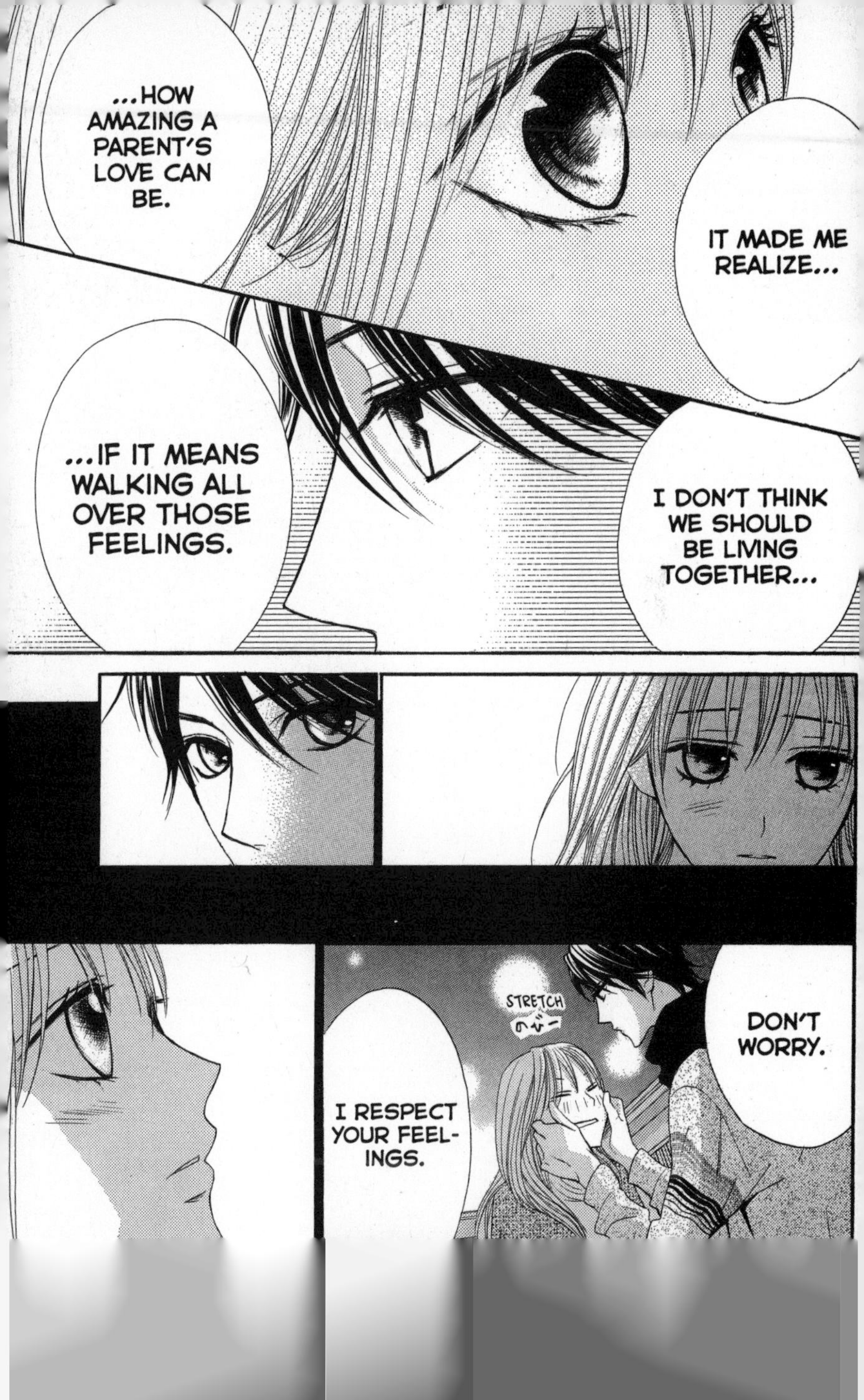
IT MADE ME REALIZE...
...HOW AMAZING A PARENT'S LOVE CAN BE.
I DON'T THINK WE SHOULD BE LIVING TOGETHER...
...IF IT MEANS WALKING ALL OVER THOSE FEELINGS.
DON'T WORRY.
STRETCH
のびー
I RESPECT YOUR FEEL-INGS.

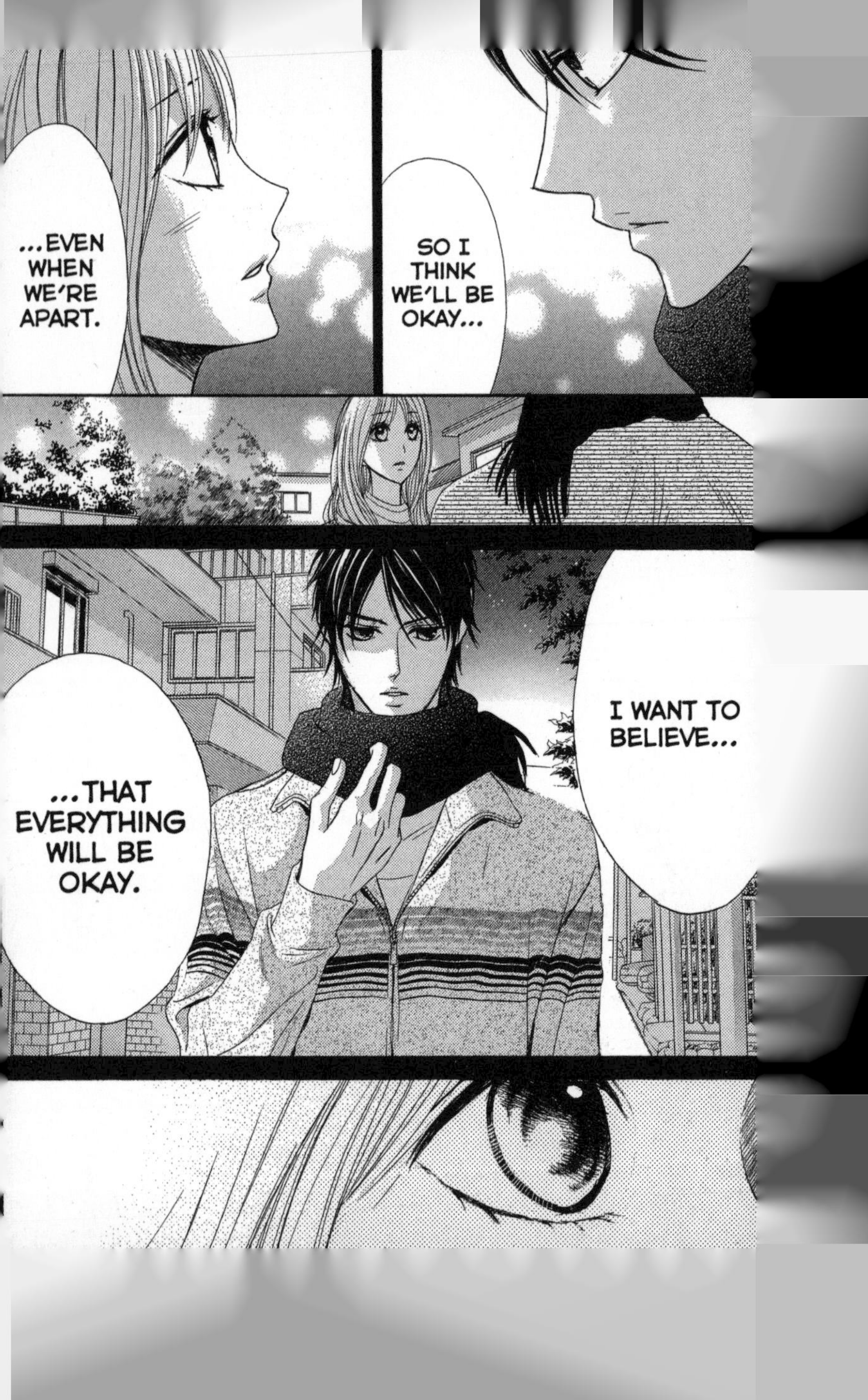
SO I THINK WE'LL BE OKAY...
...EVEN WHEN WE'RE APART.
I WANT TO BELIEVE...
...THAT EVERYTHING WILL BE OKAY.

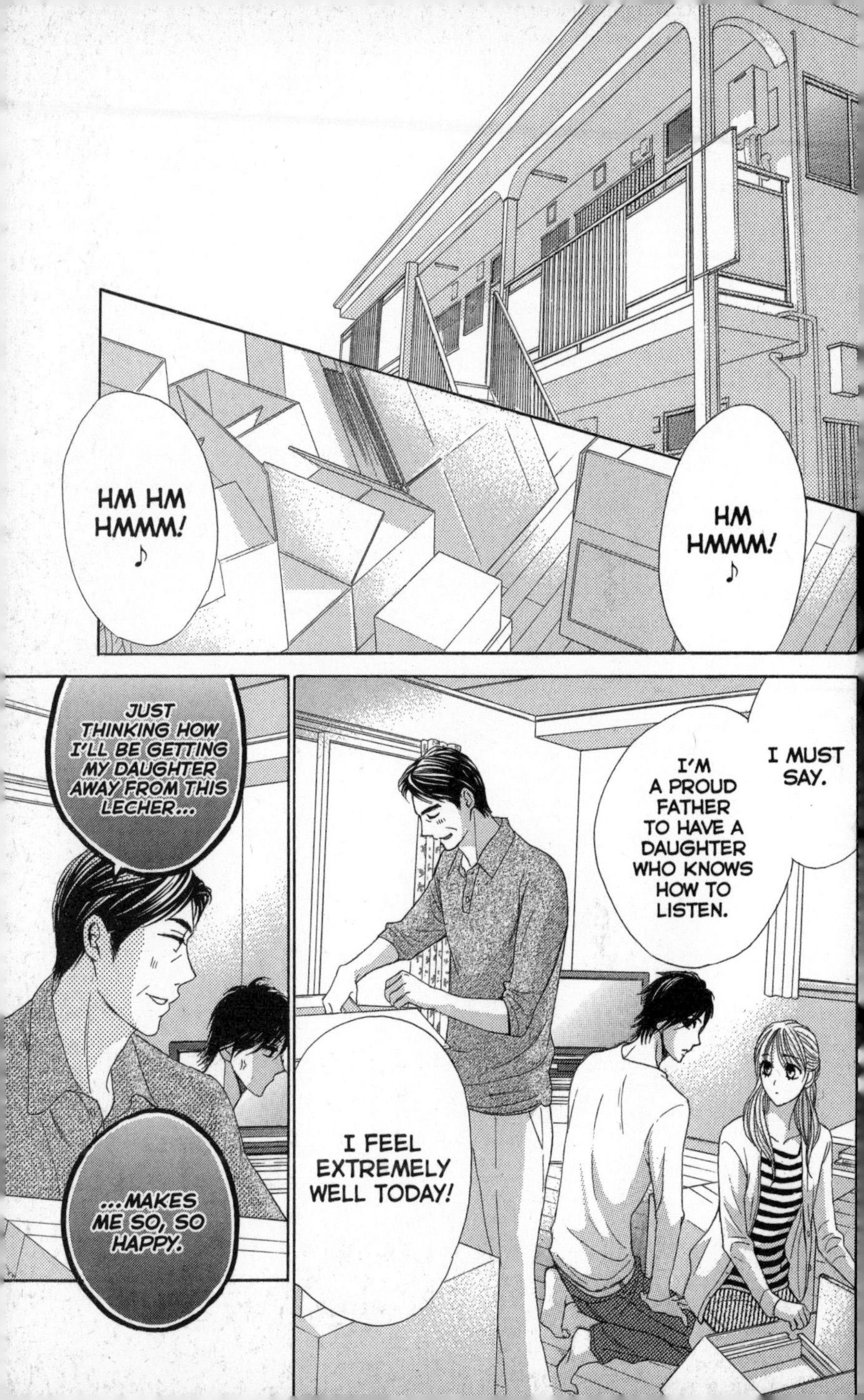
HM HMMM! ♪
HM HM HMMM! ♪
I MUST SAY.
I'M A PROUD FATHER TO HAVE A DAUGHTER WHO KNOWS HOW TO LISTEN.
I FEEL EXTREMELY WELL TODAY!
JUST THINKING HOW I'LL BE GETTING MY DAUGHTER AWAY FROM THIS LECHER...
...MAKES ME SO, SO HAPPY.

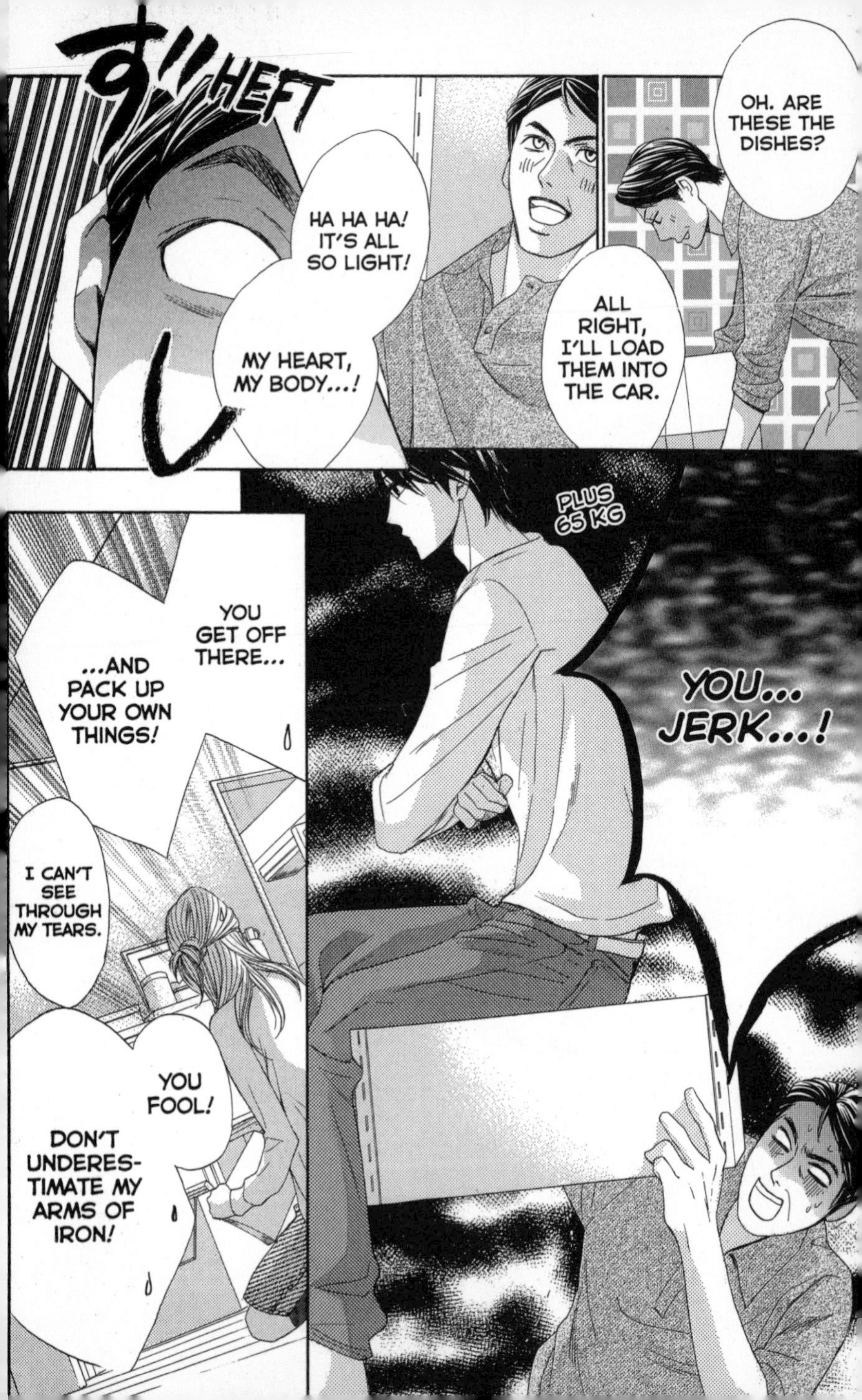
OH. ARE THESE THE DISHES?
ALL RIGHT, I'LL LOAD THEM INTO THE CAR.
HEFT
HA HA HA! IT'S ALL SO LIGHT!
MY HEART, MY BODY...!
PLUS 65 KG
YOU... JERK...!
YOU GET OFF THERE...
...AND PACK UP YOUR OWN THINGS!
I CAN'T SEE THROUGH MY TEARS.
YOU FOOL!
DON'T UNDERES-TIMATE MY ARMS OF IRON!

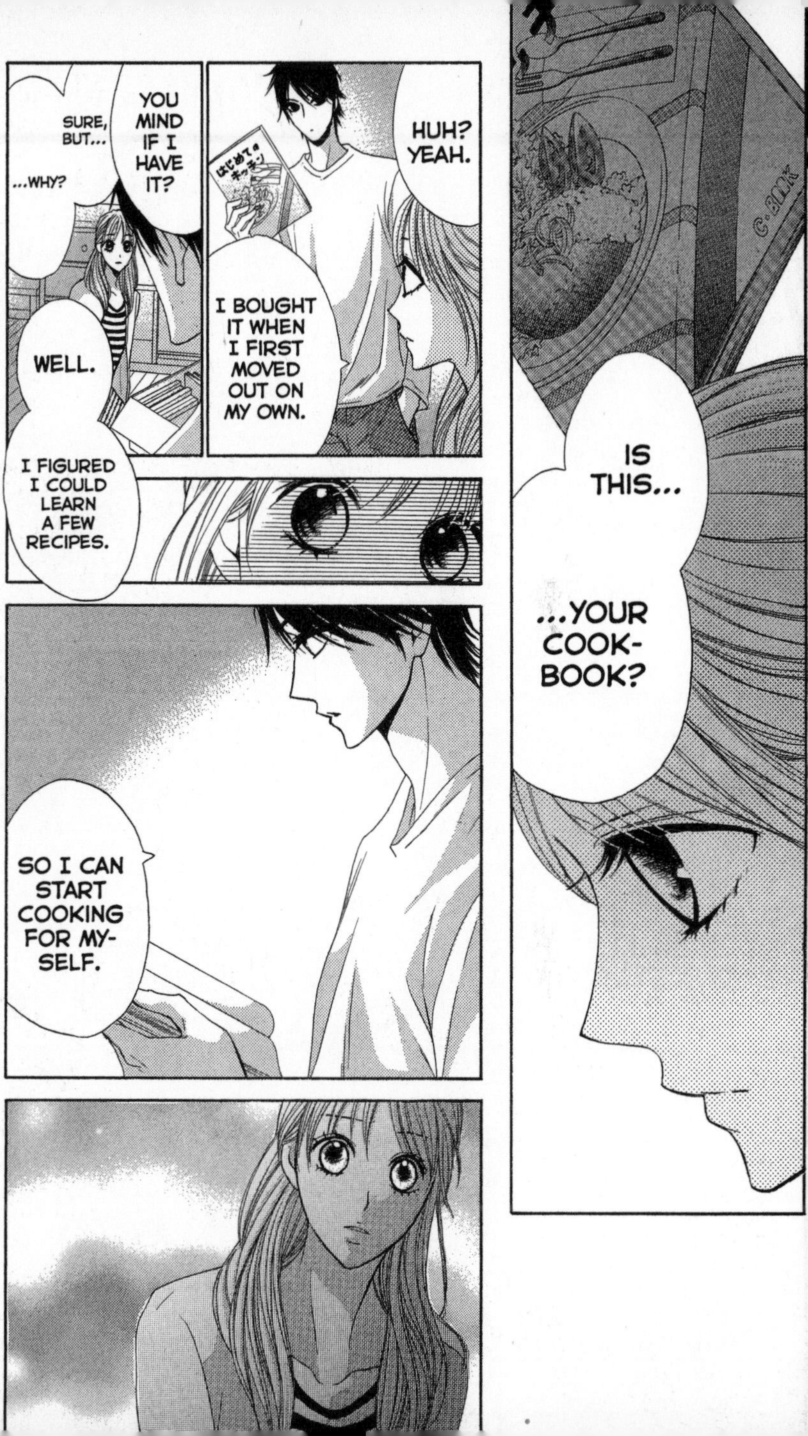
IS THIS...
...YOUR COOK-BOOK?
HUH? YEAH.
I BOUGHT IT WHEN I FIRST MOVED OUT ON MY OWN.
YOU MIND IF I HAVE IT?
SURE, BUT...
...WHY?
WELL.
I FIGURED I COULD LEARN A FEW RECIPES.
SO I CAN START COOKING FOR MY-SELF.

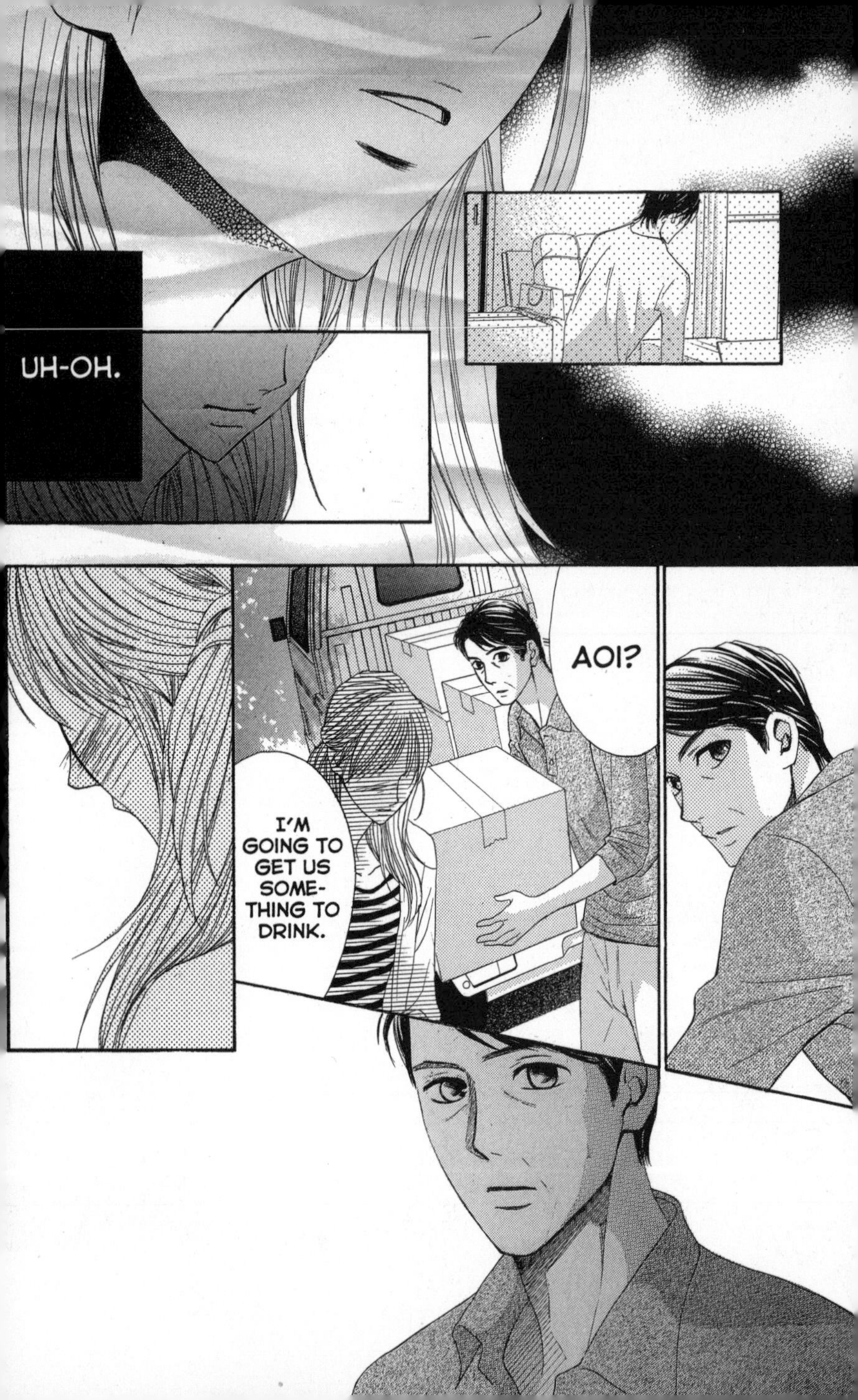
UH-OH.
AOI?
I'M GOING TO GET US SOME-THING TO DRINK.

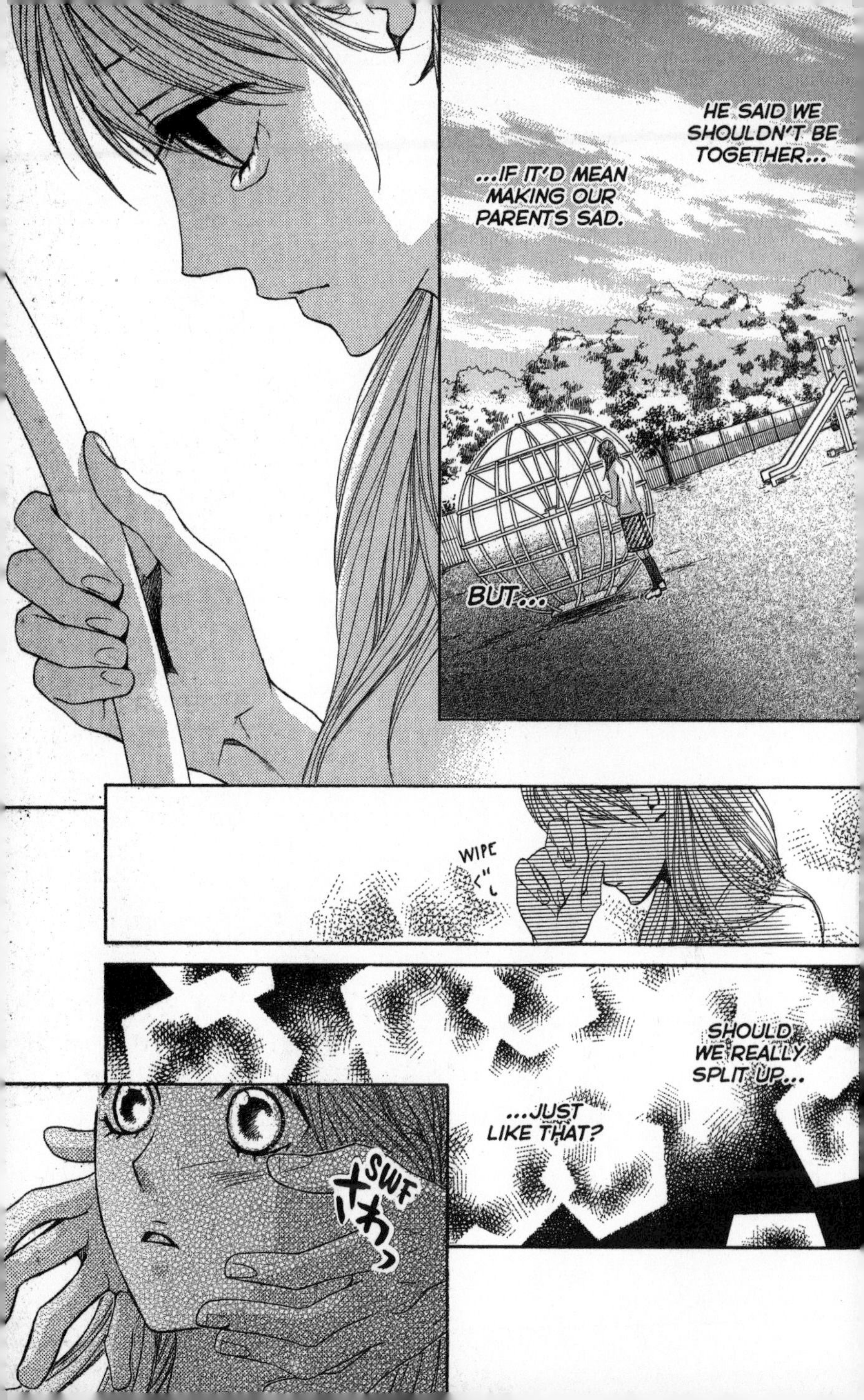
HE SAID WE SHOULDN'T BE TOGETHER...
...IF IT'D MEAN MAKING OUR PARENTS SAD.
BUT...
WIPE
SHOULD WE REALLY SPLIT UP...
...JUST LIKE THAT?
SWF
さわっ

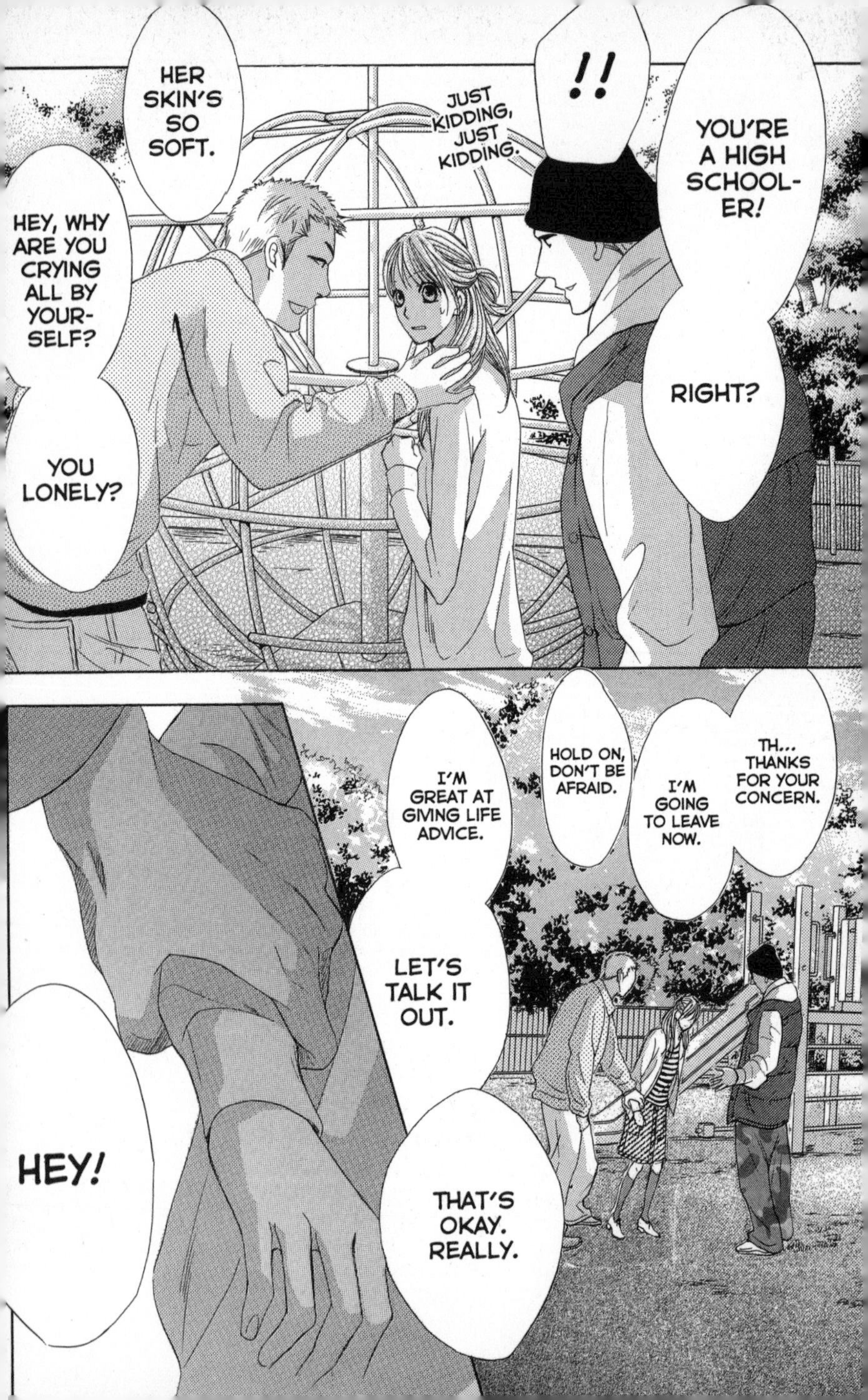
YOU'RE A HIGH SCHOOL-ER!
!!
RIGHT?
JUST KIDDING, JUST KIDDING.
HER SKIN'S SO SOFT.
HEY, WHY ARE YOU CRYING ALL BY YOUR-SELF?
YOU LONELY?
TH... THANKS FOR YOUR CONCERN.
I'M GOING TO LEAVE NOW.
HOLD ON, DON'T BE AFRAID.
I'M GREAT AT GIVING LIFE ADVICE.
LET'S TALK IT OUT.
THAT'S OKAY. REALLY.
HEY!

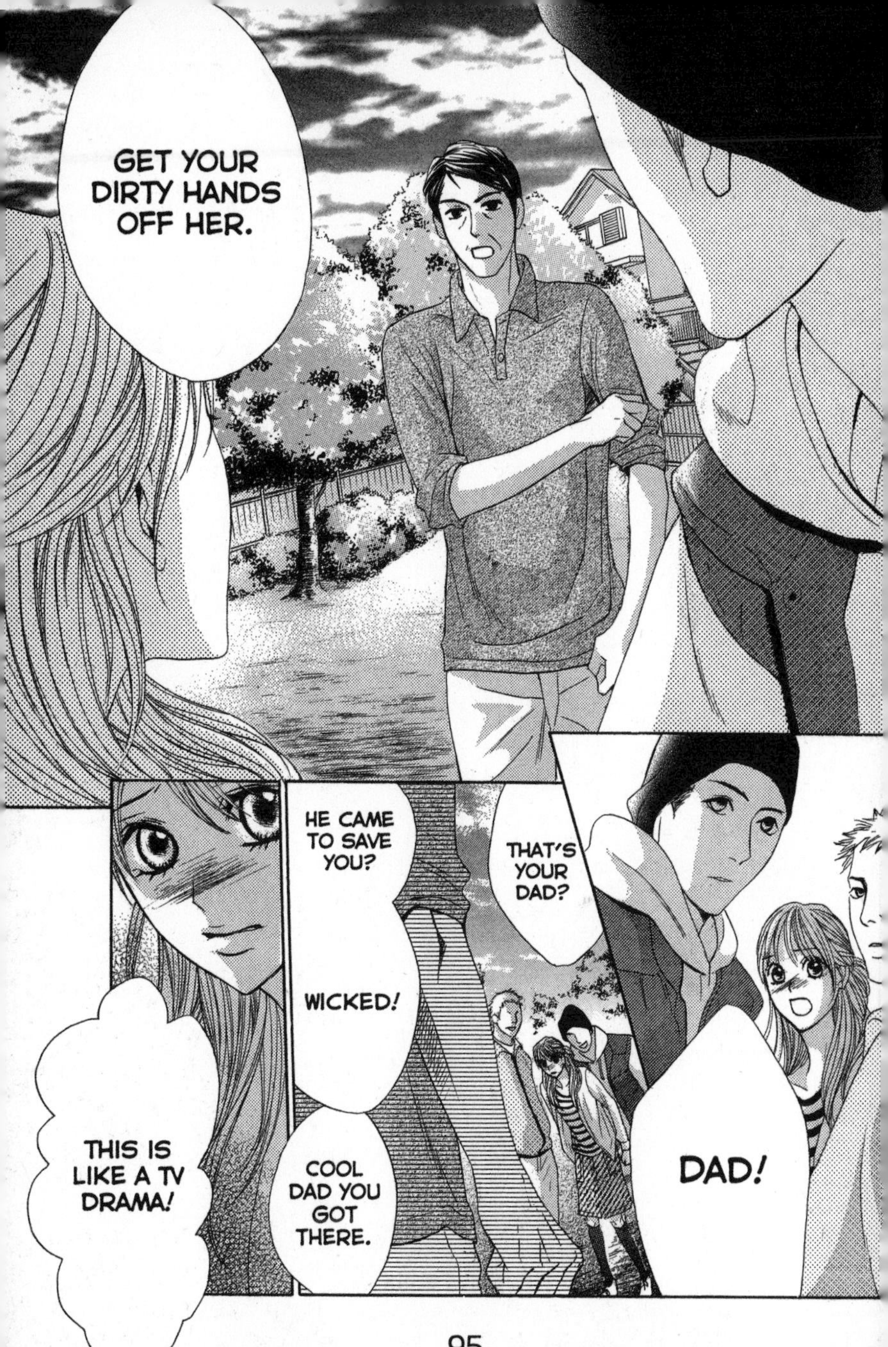
GET YOUR DIRTY HANDS OFF HER.
DAD!
THAT'S YOUR DAD?
HE CAME TO SAVE YOU?
WICKED!
COOL DAD YOU GOT THERE.
THIS IS LIKE A TV DRAMA!

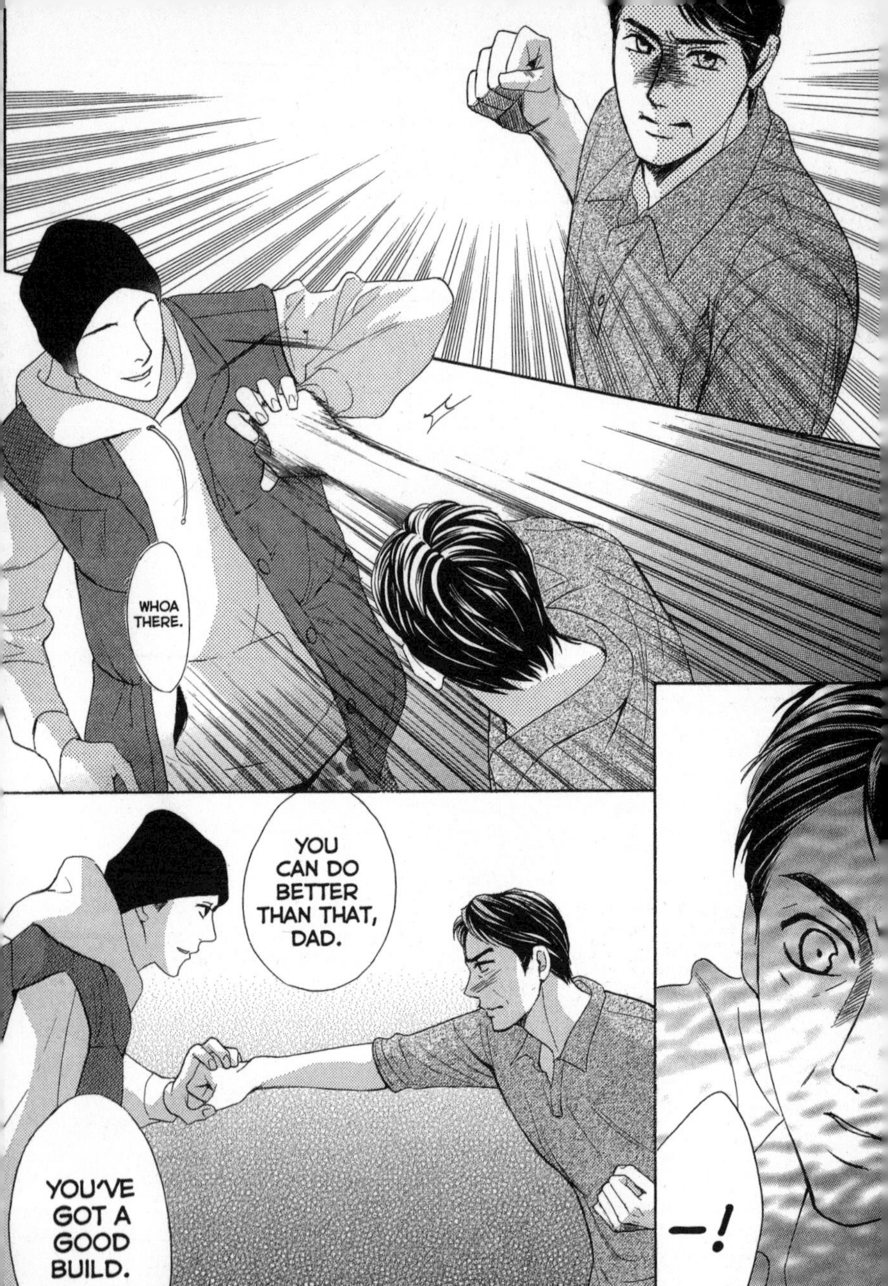
WHOA THERE.
—!
YOU CAN DO BETTER THAN THAT, DAD.
YOU'VE GOT A GOOD BUILD.

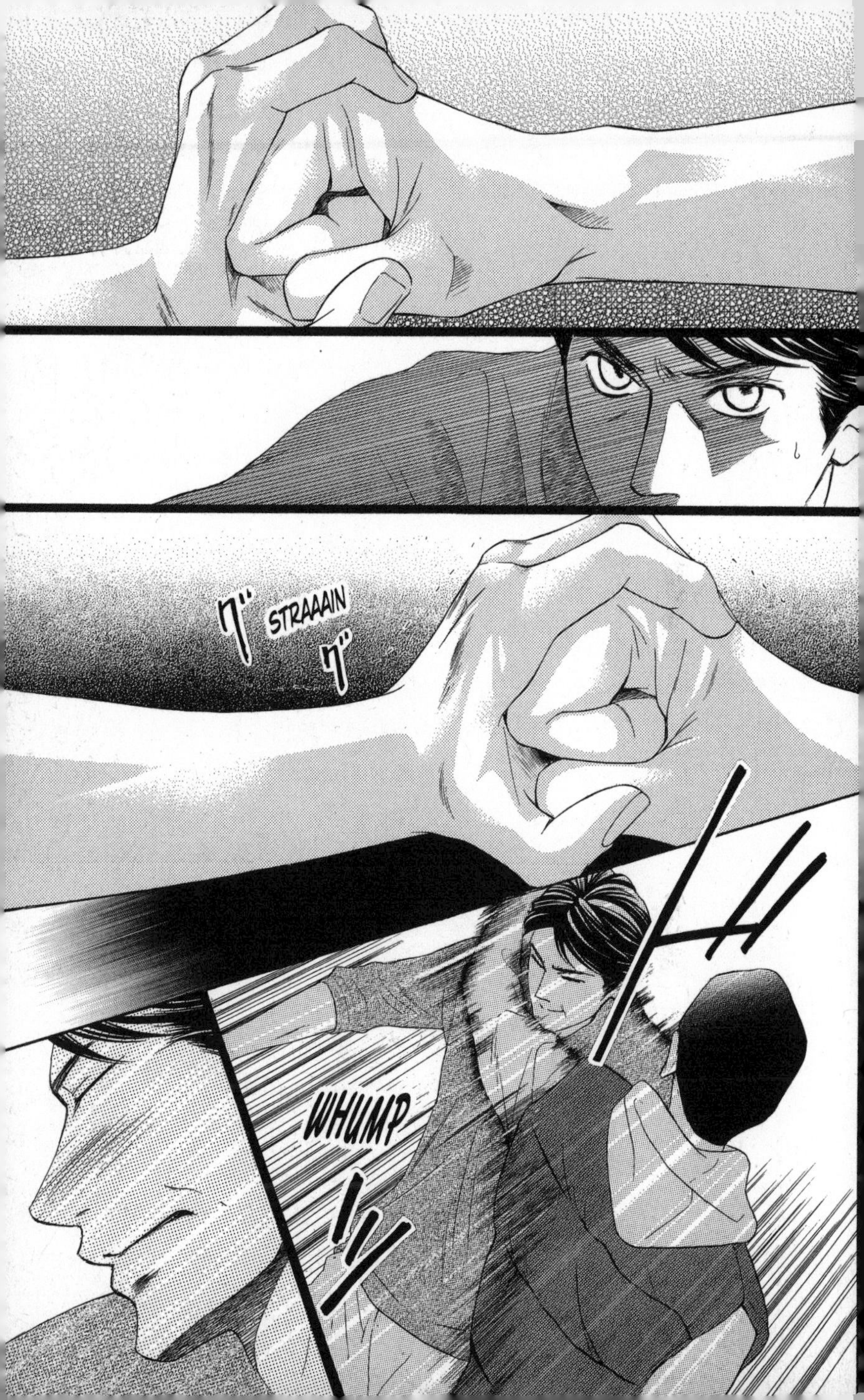
ギ STRAAAIN ギ
WHUMP

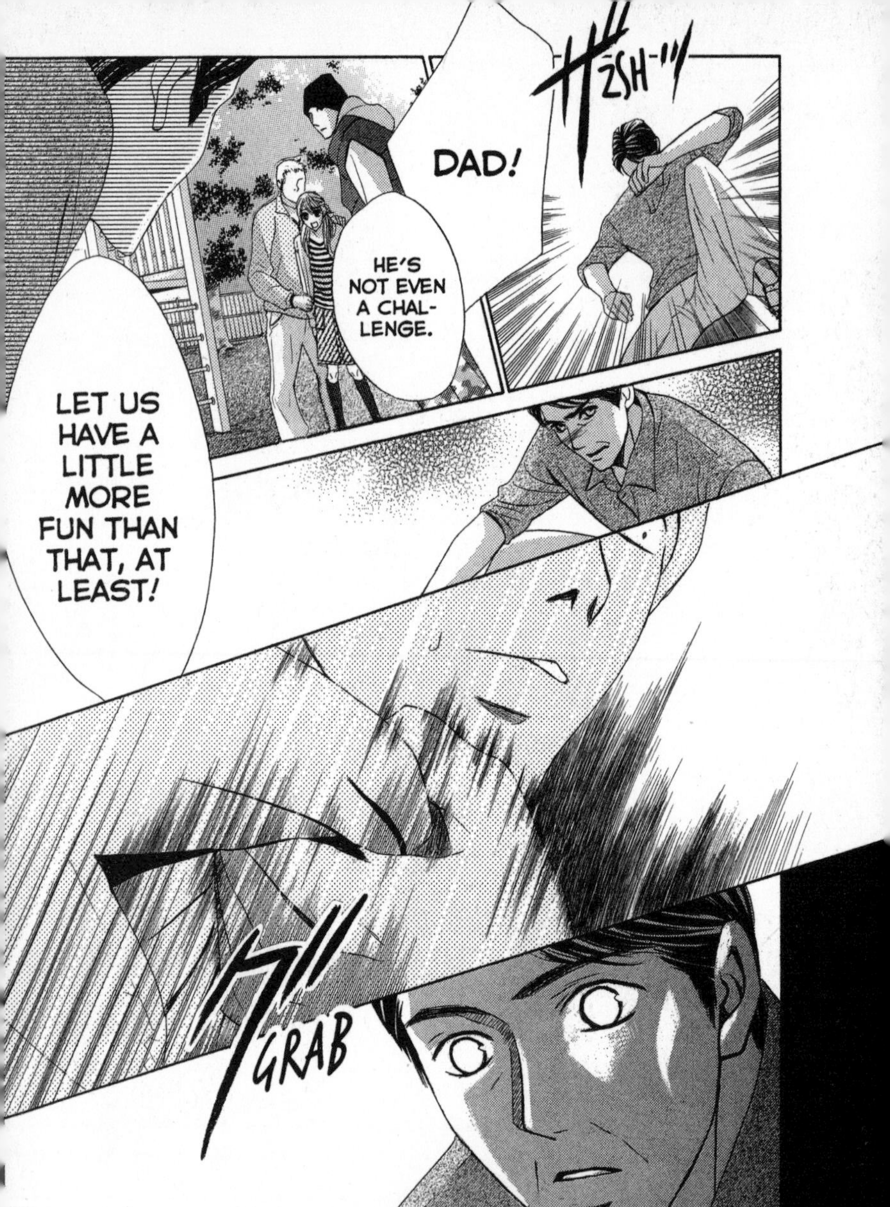
ZSH-!!
DAD!
HE'S NOT EVEN A CHAL-LENGE.
LET US HAVE A LITTLE MORE FUN THAN THAT, AT LEAST!
GRAB

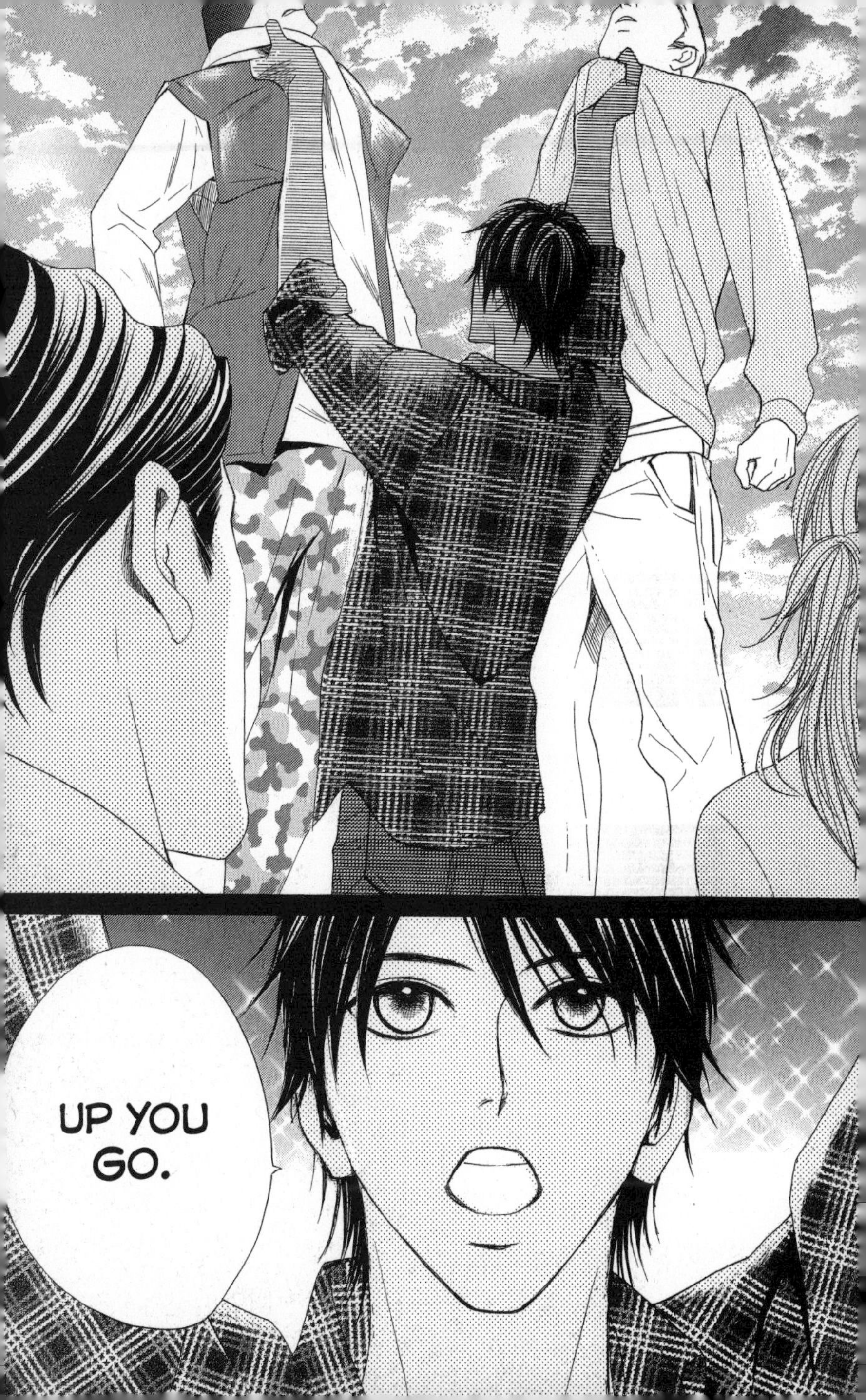
UP YOU GO.

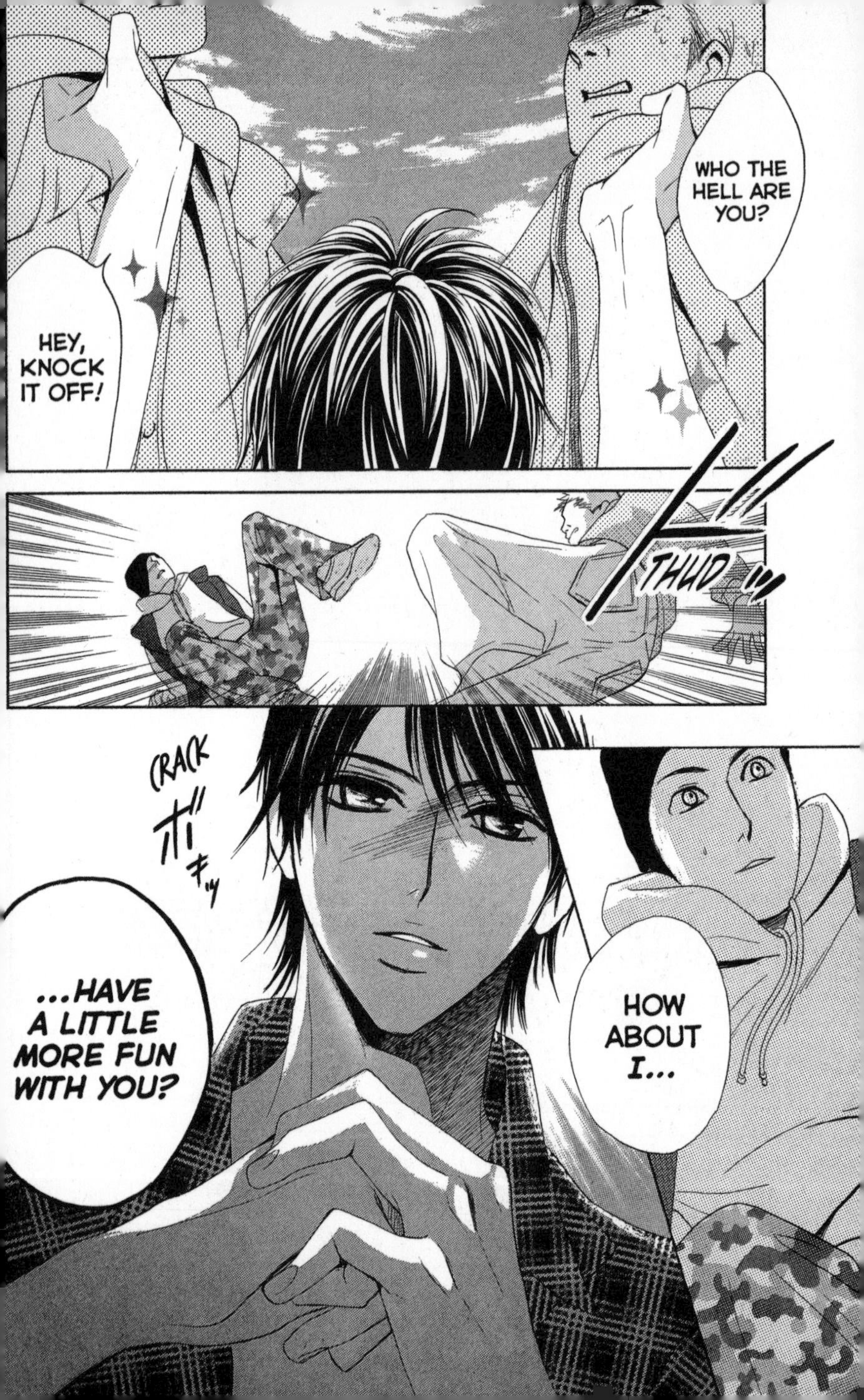
WHO THE HELL ARE YOU?
HEY, KNOCK IT OFF!
THUD
CRACK
ボキッ
HOW ABOUT I...
...HAVE A LITTLE MORE FUN WITH YOU?

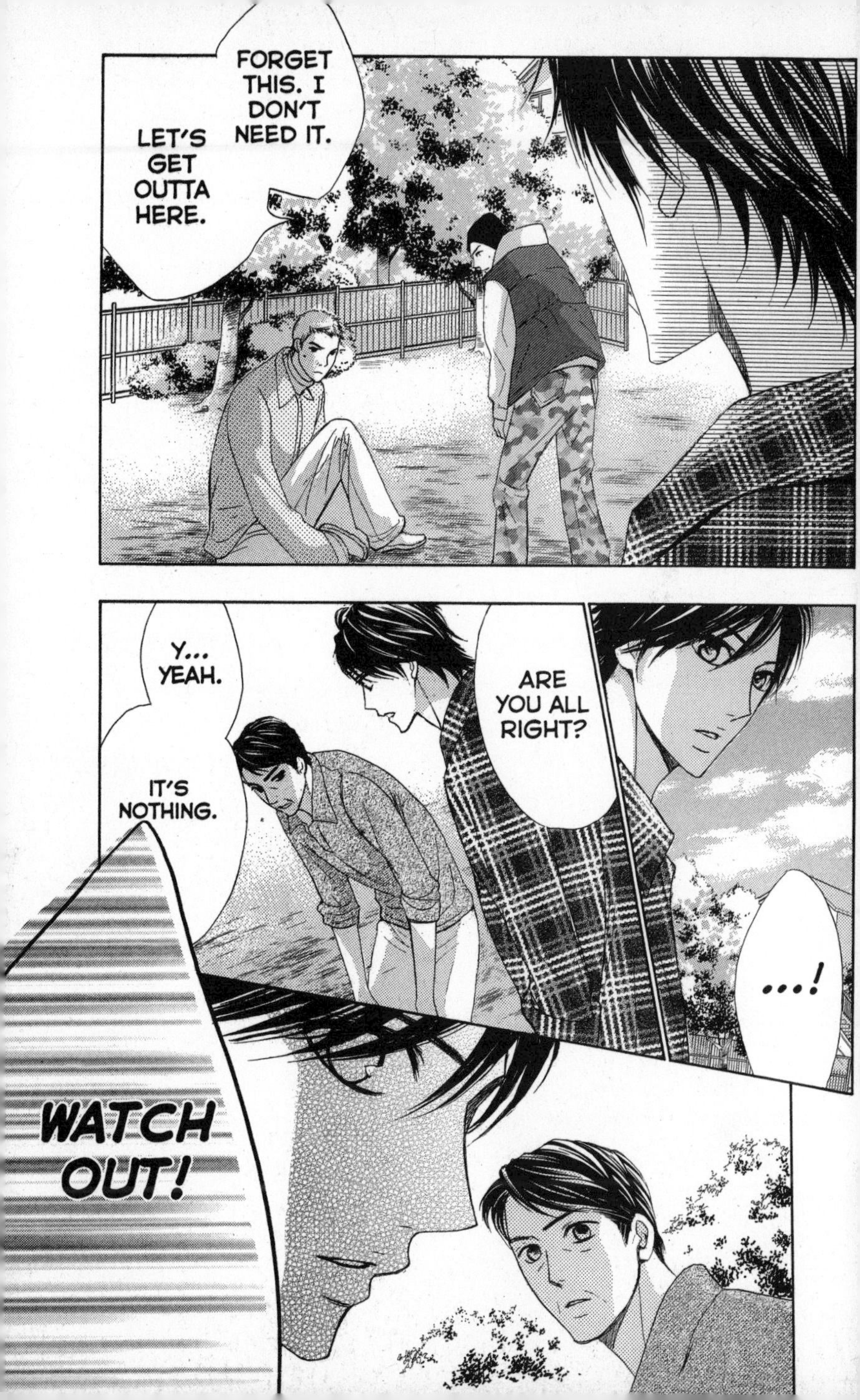
FORGET THIS. I DON'T NEED IT.
LET'S GET OUTTA HERE.
ARE YOU ALL RIGHT?
Y... YEAH.
IT'S NOTHING.
...!
WATCH OUT!

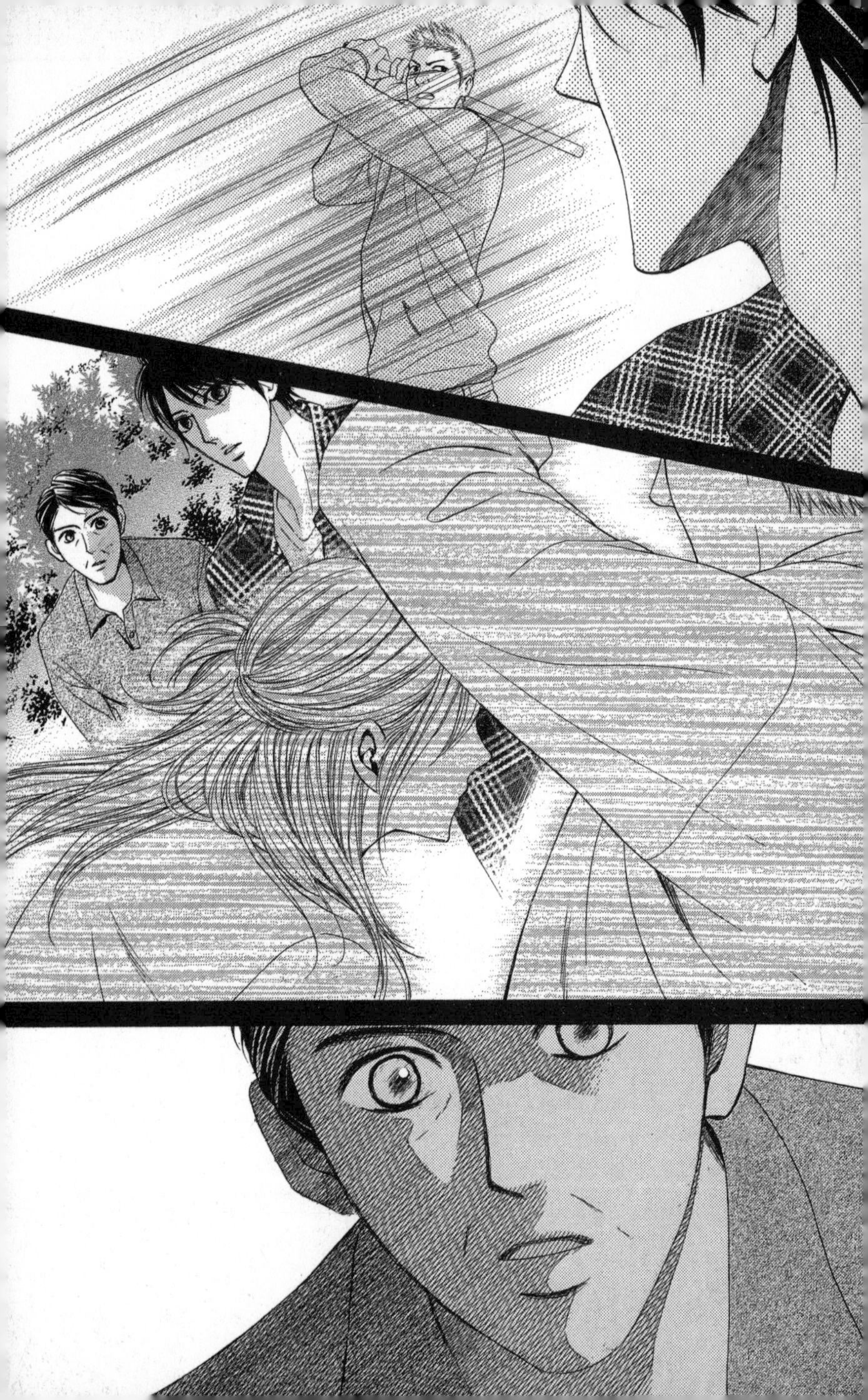

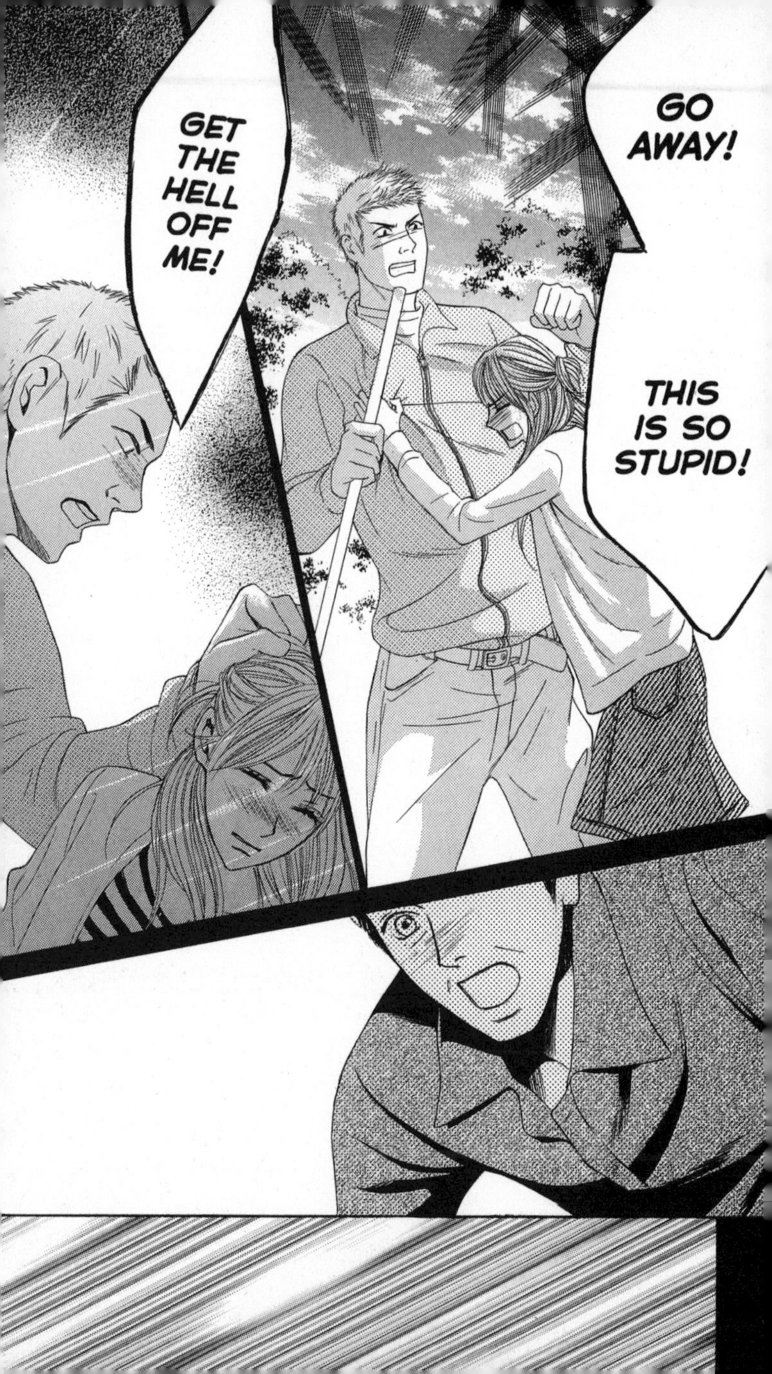
GO AWAY!
THIS IS SO STUPID!
GET THE HELL OFF ME!

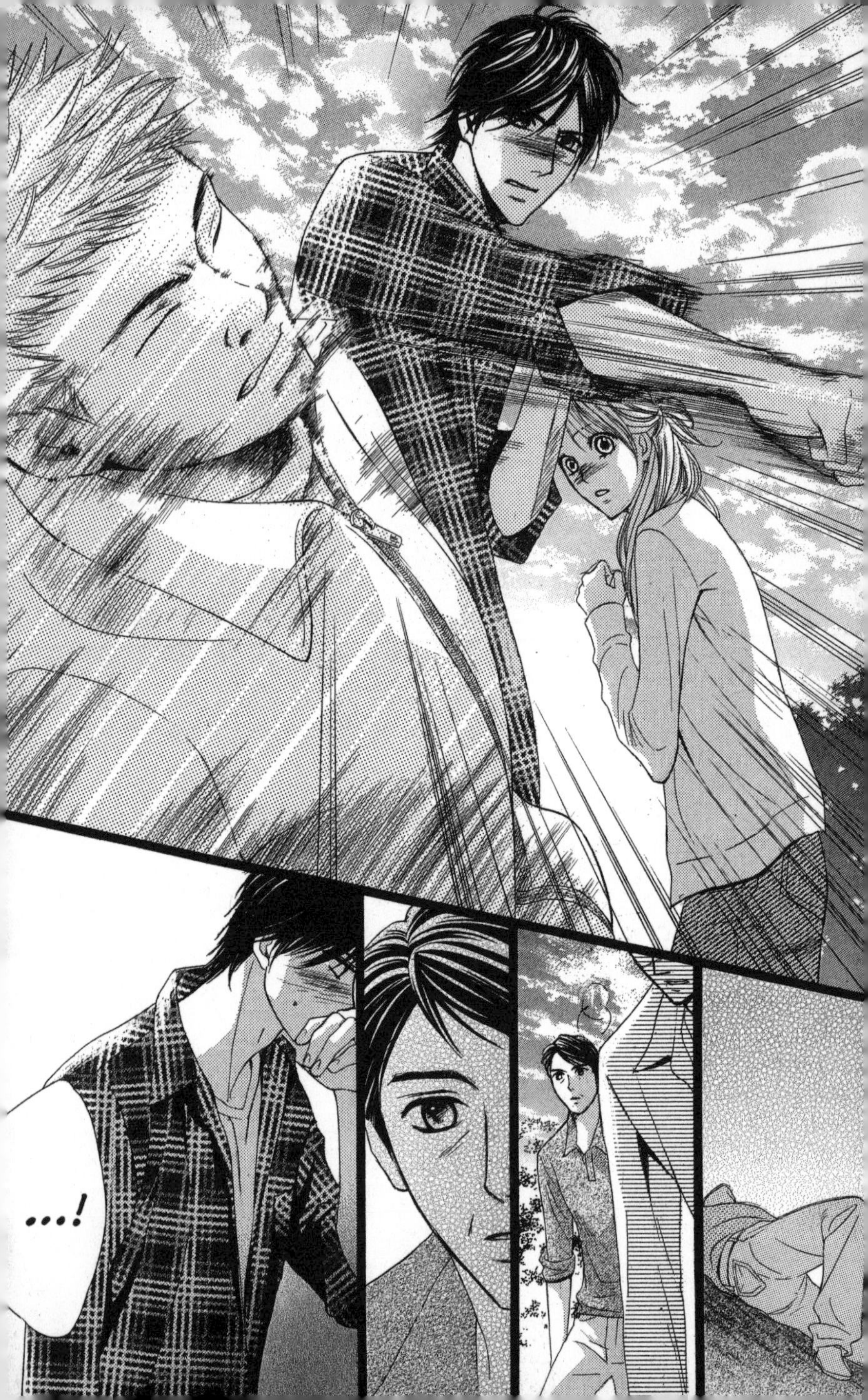
...!

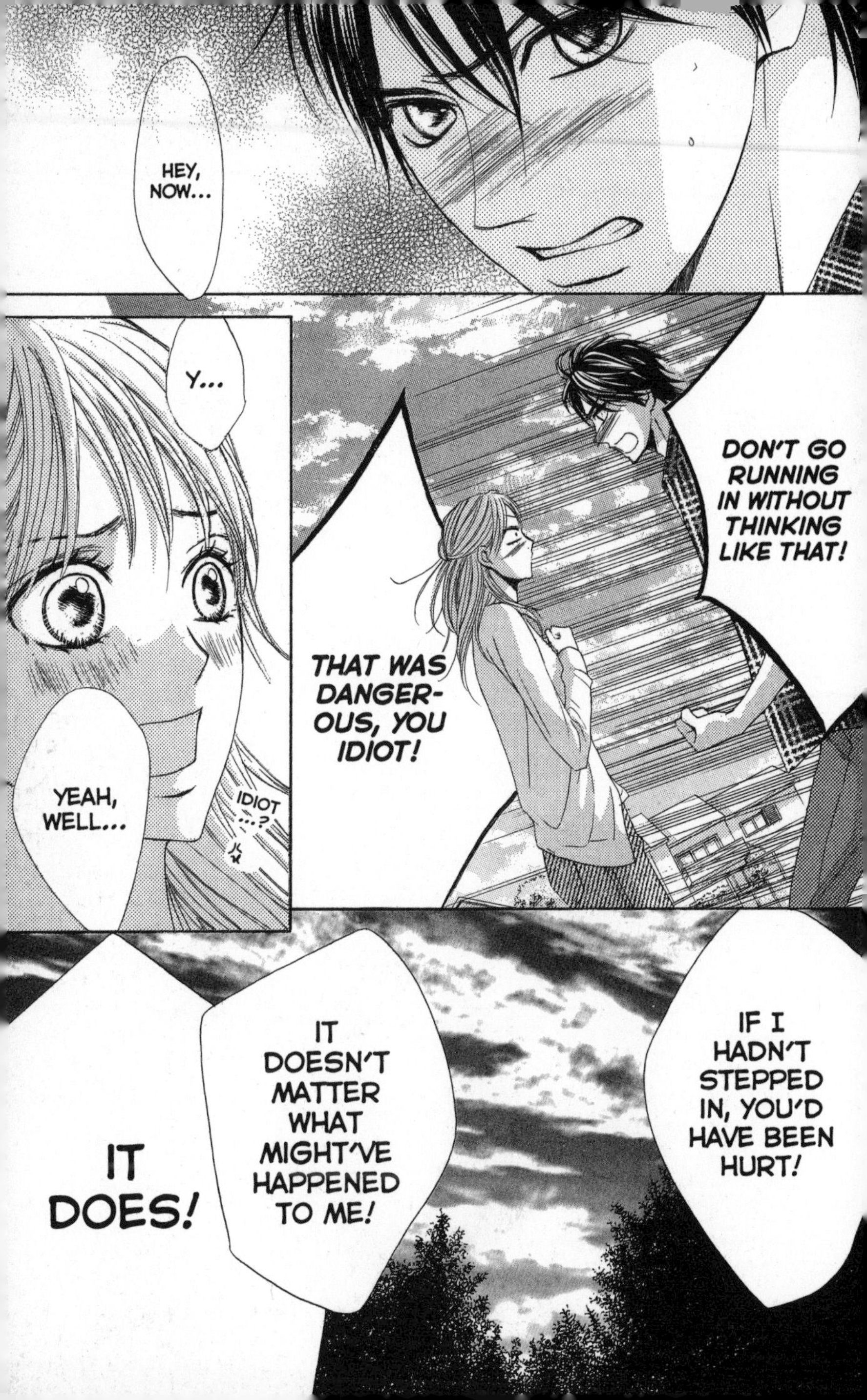
HEY, NOW...
DON'T GO RUNNING IN WITHOUT THINKING LIKE THAT!
THAT WAS DANGER-OUS, YOU IDIOT!
Y...
YEAH, WELL...
IDIOT ...?
IF I HADN'T STEPPED IN, YOU'D HAVE BEEN HURT!
IT DOESN'T MATTER WHAT MIGHT'VE HAPPENED TO ME!
IT DOES!

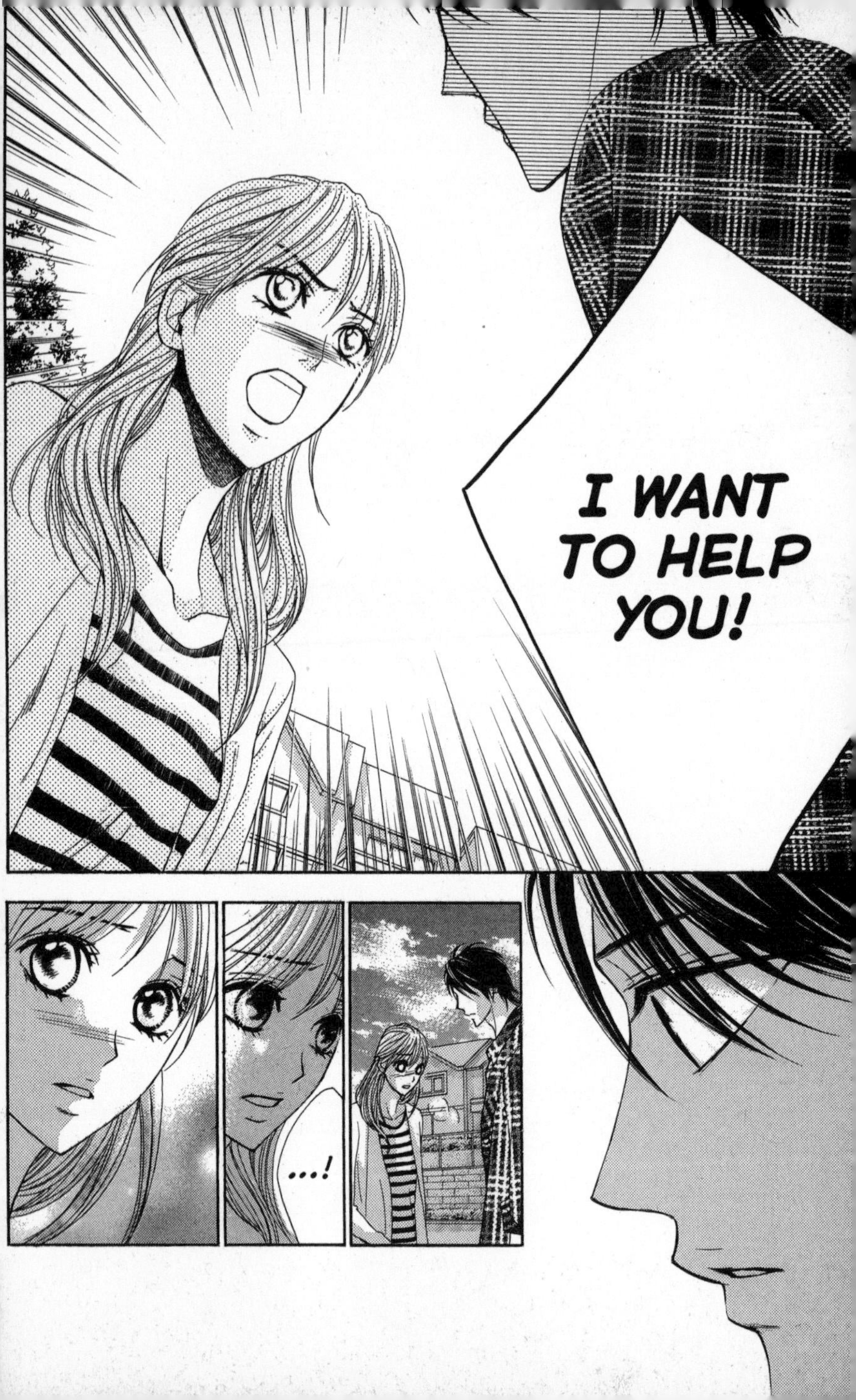
I WANT TO HELP YOU!
...!

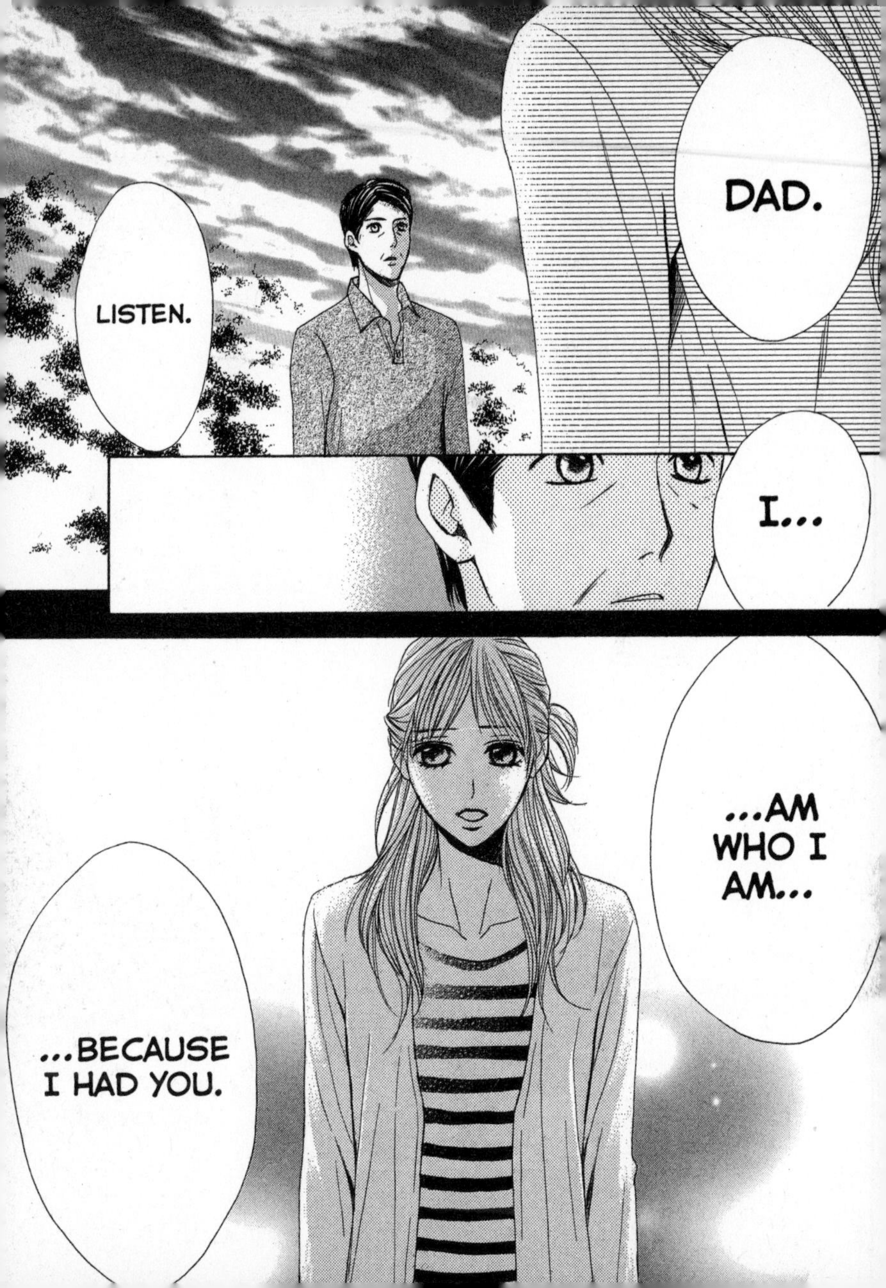
DAD.
LISTEN.
I...
...AM WHO I AM...
...BECAUSE I HAD YOU.

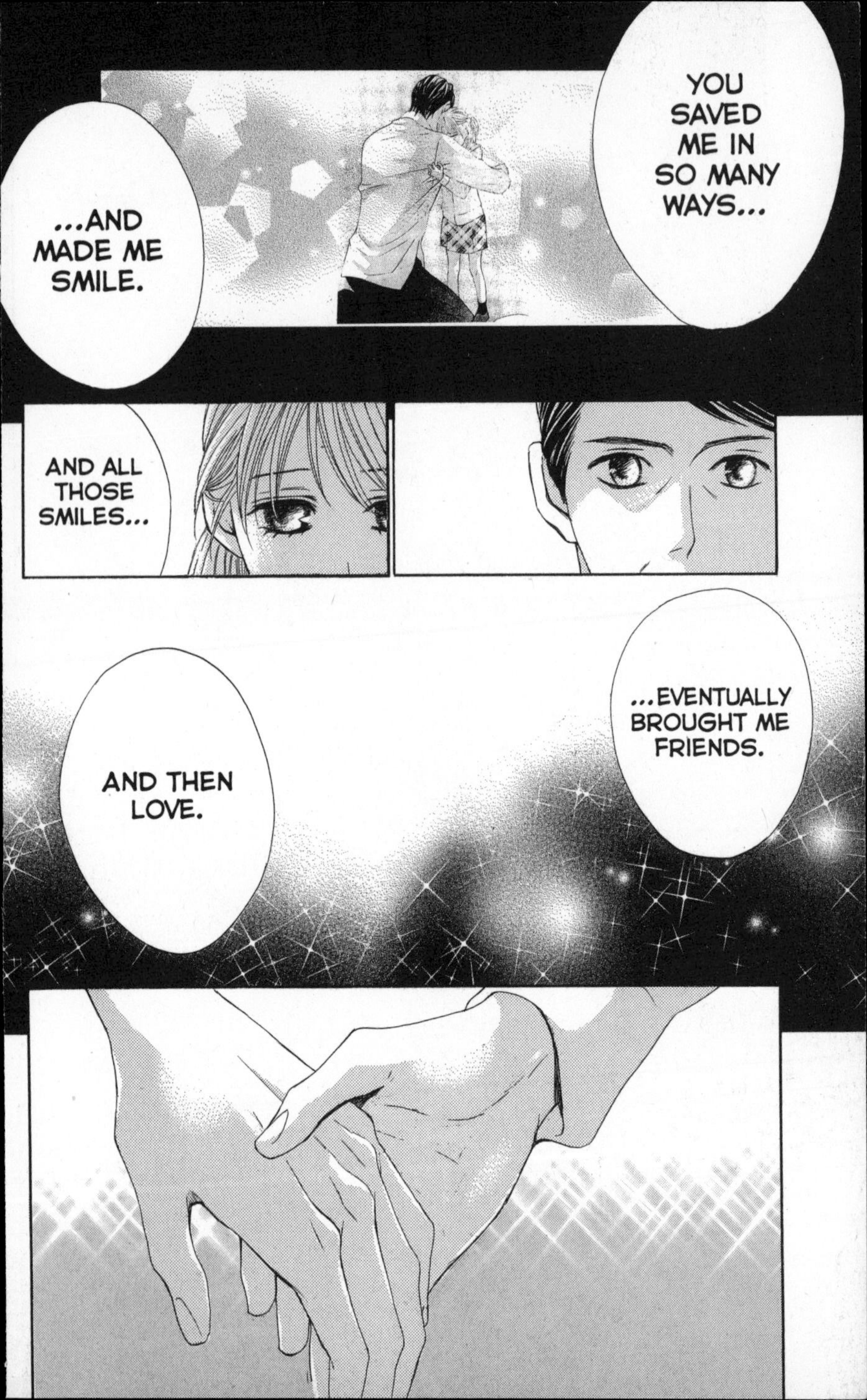
YOU SAVED ME IN SO MANY WAYS...
...AND MADE ME SMILE.
AND ALL THOSE SMILES...
...EVENTUALLY BROUGHT ME FRIENDS.
AND THEN LOVE.

I ALSO...

...HAVE SOMETHING I WANT TO PROTECT.

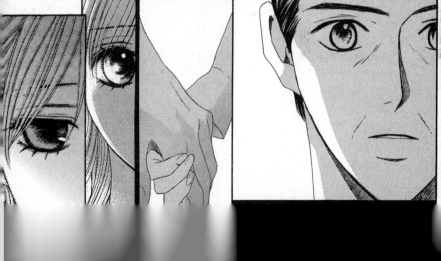

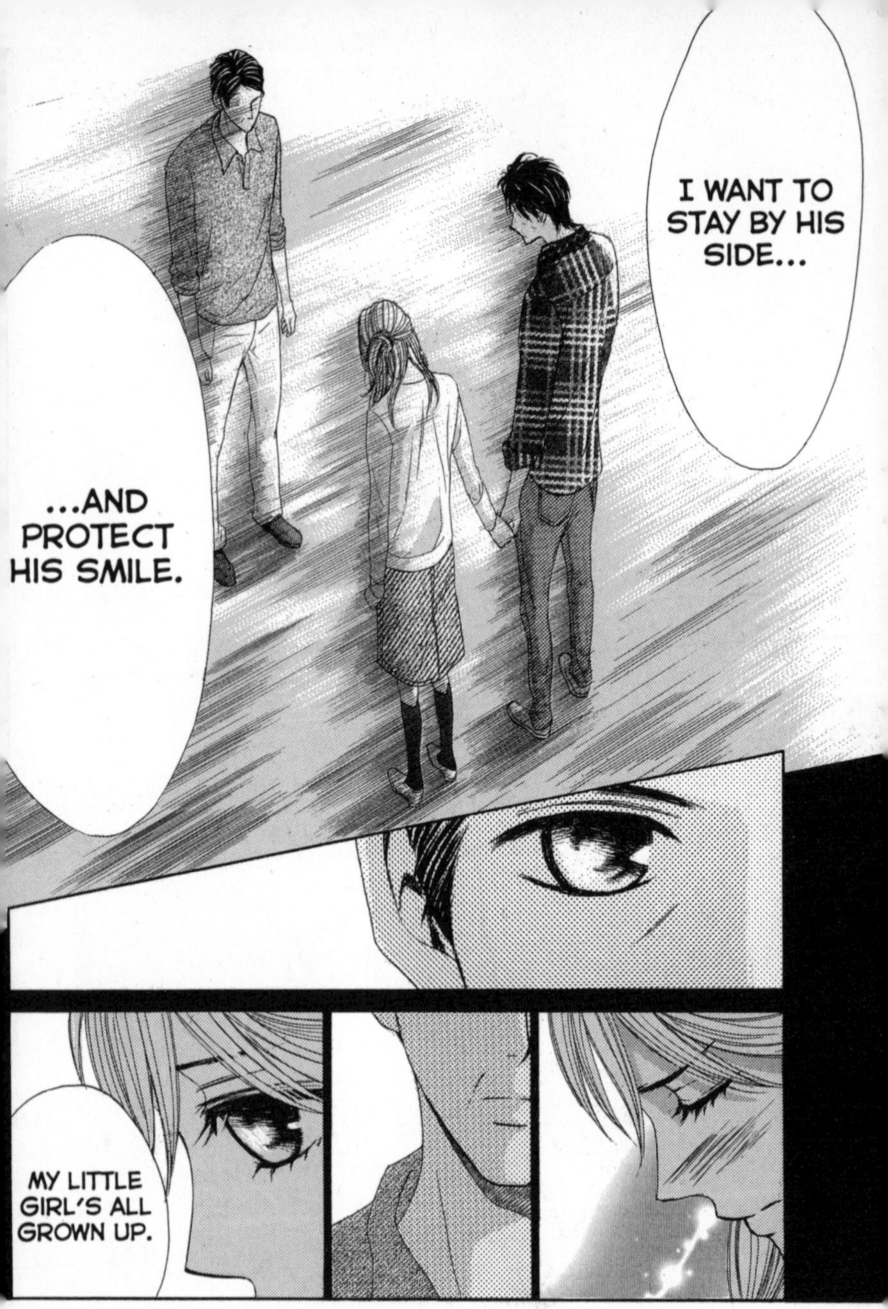
I WANT TO STAY BY HIS SIDE...
...AND PROTECT HIS SMILE.
MY LITTLE GIRL'S ALL GROWN UP.

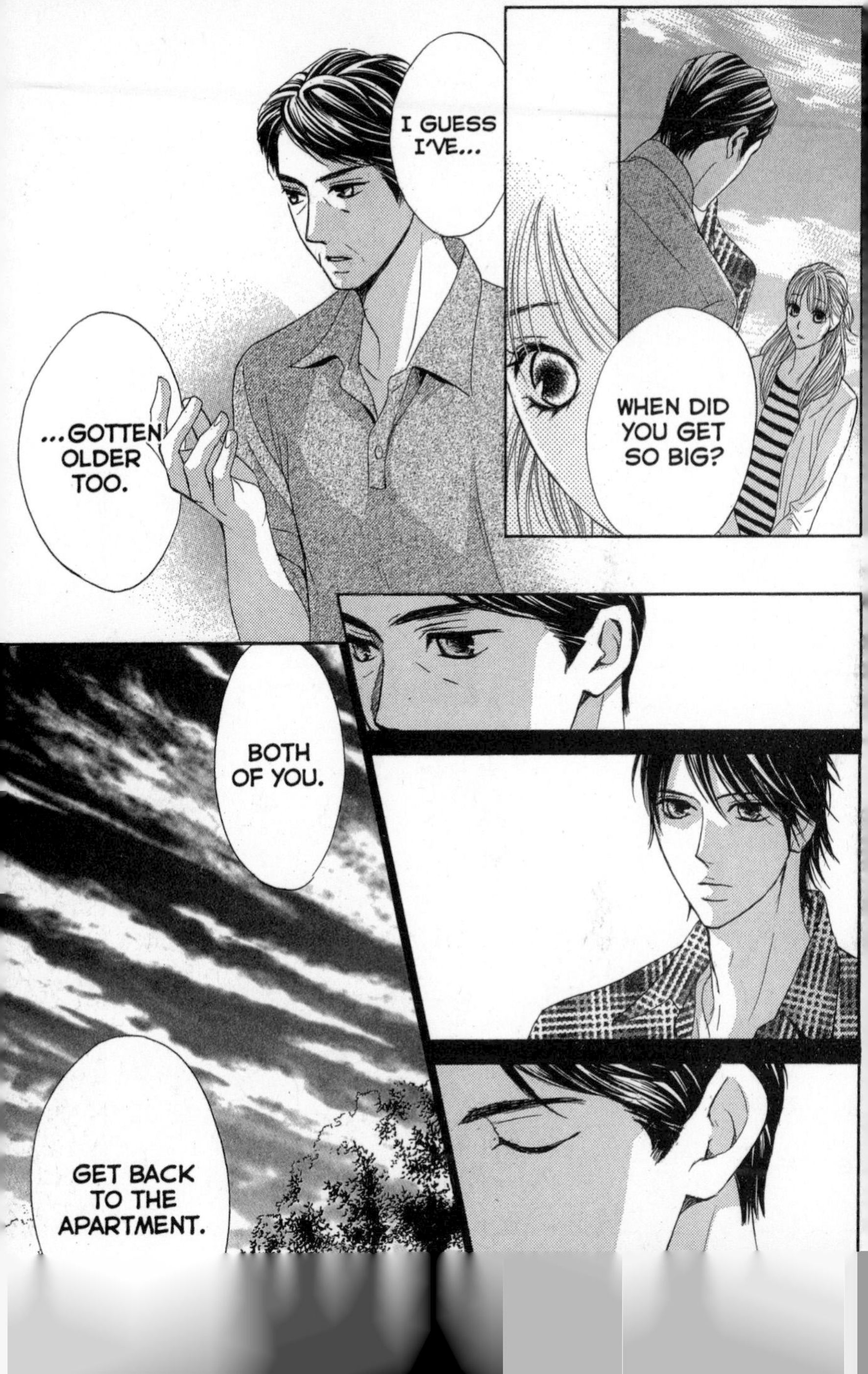
WHEN DID YOU GET SO BIG?
I GUESS I'VE...
...GOTTEN OLDER TOO.
BOTH OF YOU.
GET BACK TO THE APARTMENT.

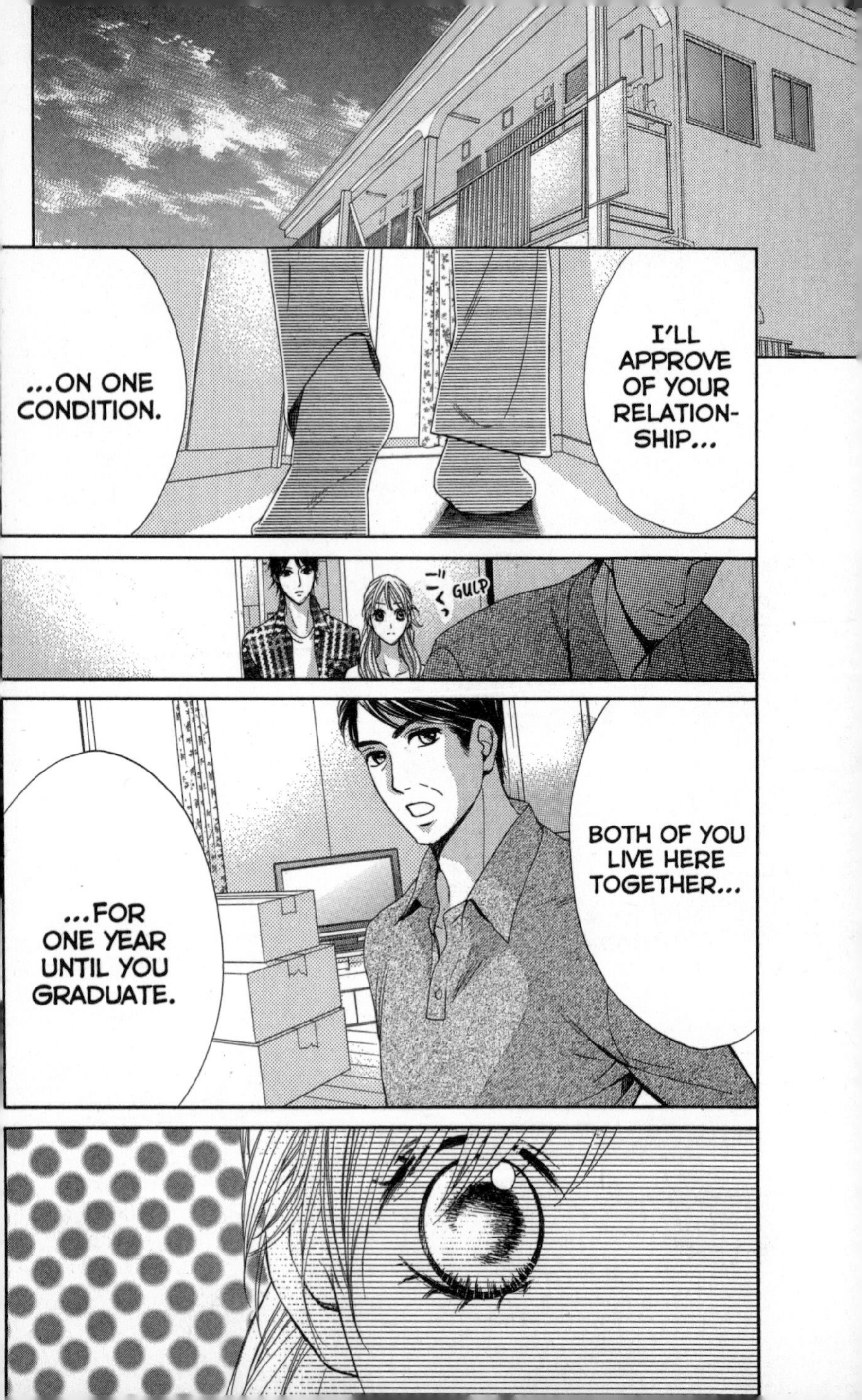
I'LL APPROVE OF YOUR RELATION-SHIP...
...ON ONE CONDITION.
ゴクッ GULP
BOTH OF YOU LIVE HERE TOGETHER...
...FOR ONE YEAR UNTIL YOU GRADUATE.

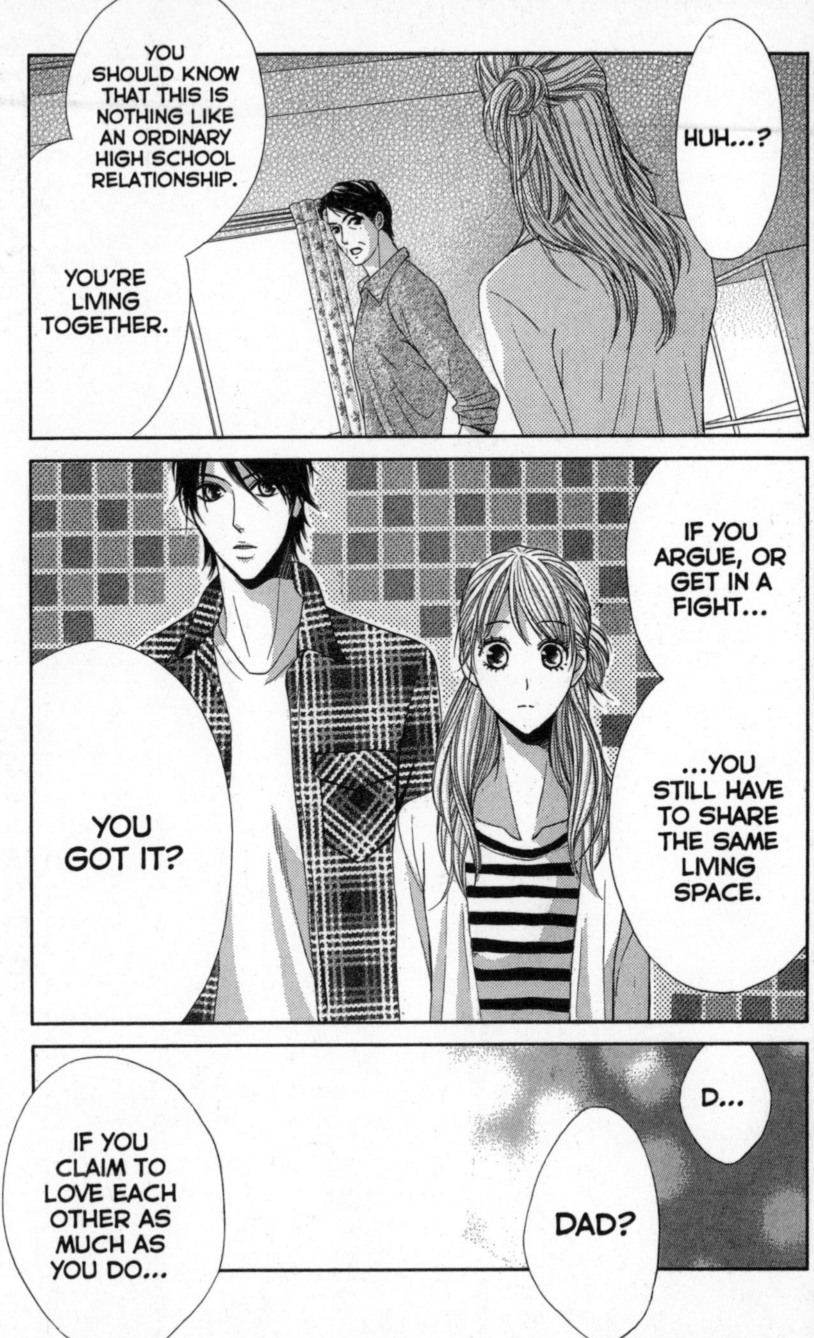
HUH...?
YOU SHOULD KNOW THAT THIS IS NOTHING LIKE AN ORDINARY HIGH SCHOOL RELATIONSHIP.
YOU'RE LIVING TOGETHER.
IF YOU ARGUE, OR GET IN A FIGHT...
...YOU STILL HAVE TO SHARE THE SAME LIVING SPACE.
YOU GOT IT?
D...
DAD?
IF YOU CLAIM TO LOVE EACH OTHER AS MUCH AS YOU DO...

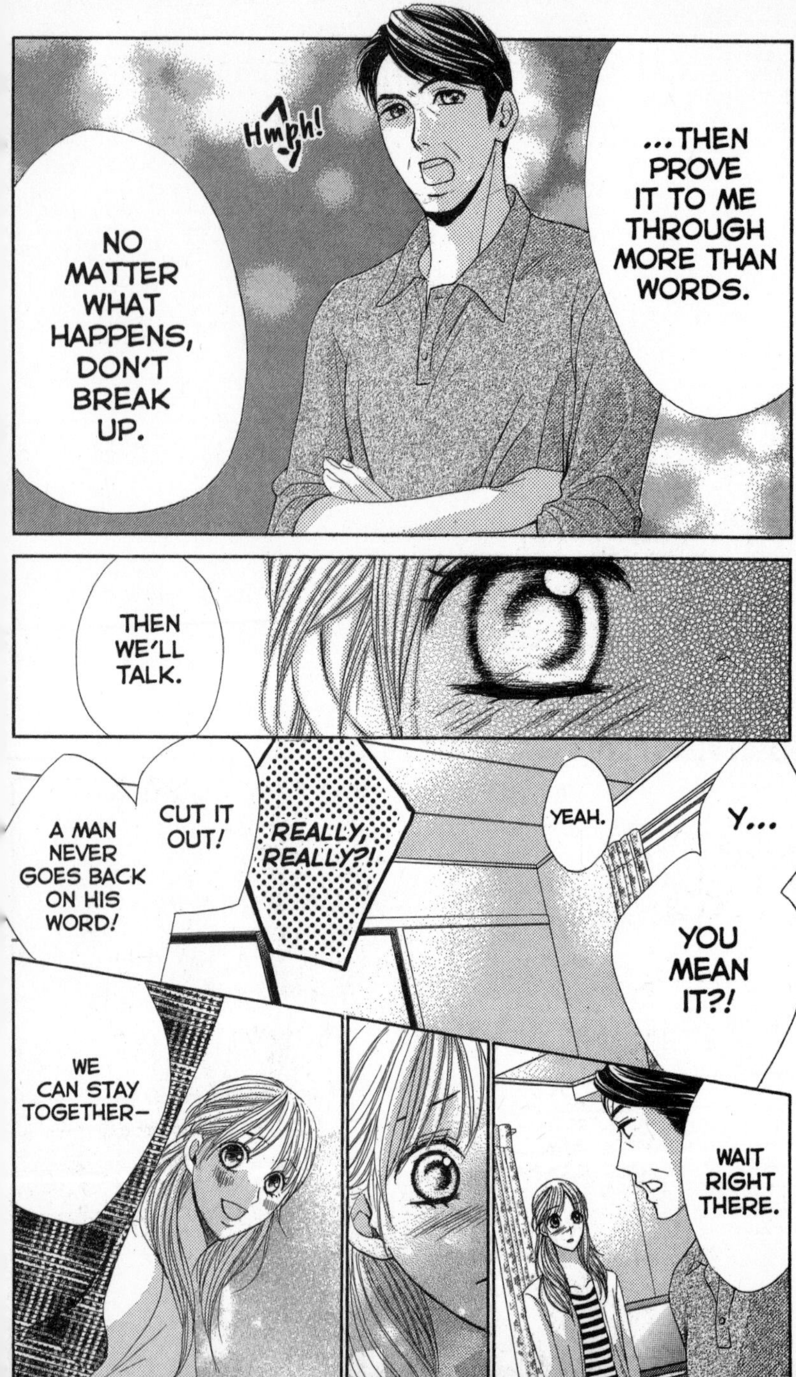
...THEN PROVE IT TO ME THROUGH MORE THAN WORDS.
Hmph!
NO MATTER WHAT HAPPENS, DON'T BREAK UP.
THEN WE'LL TALK.
Y...
YOU MEAN IT?!
YEAH.
REALLY, REALLY?!
CUT IT OUT!
A MAN NEVER GOES BACK ON HIS WORD!
WAIT RIGHT THERE.
WE CAN STAY TOGETHER—

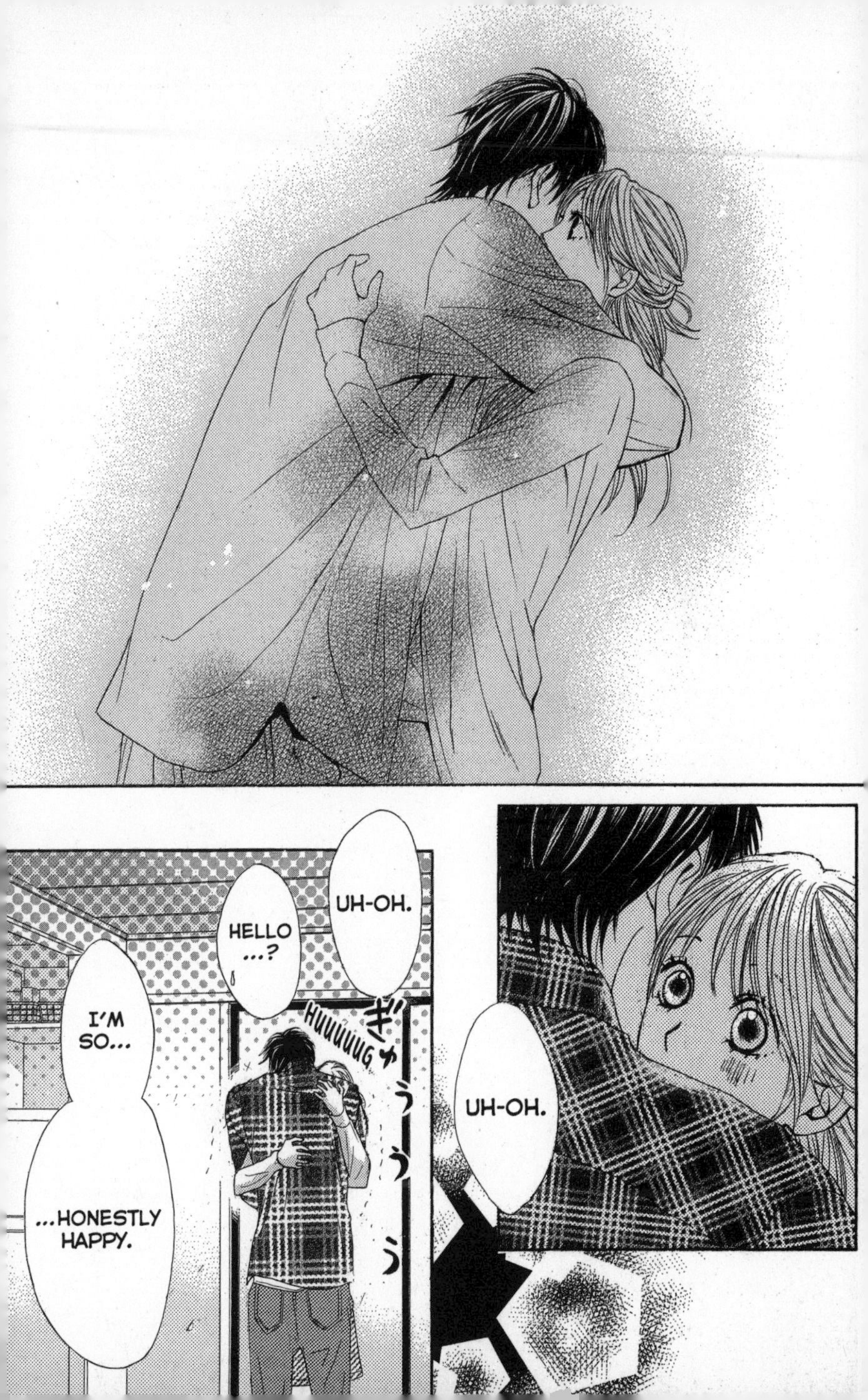
UH-OH.
UH-OH.
HELLO ...?
ぎゅううう
HUUUUUG
I'M SO...
...HONESTLY HAPPY.

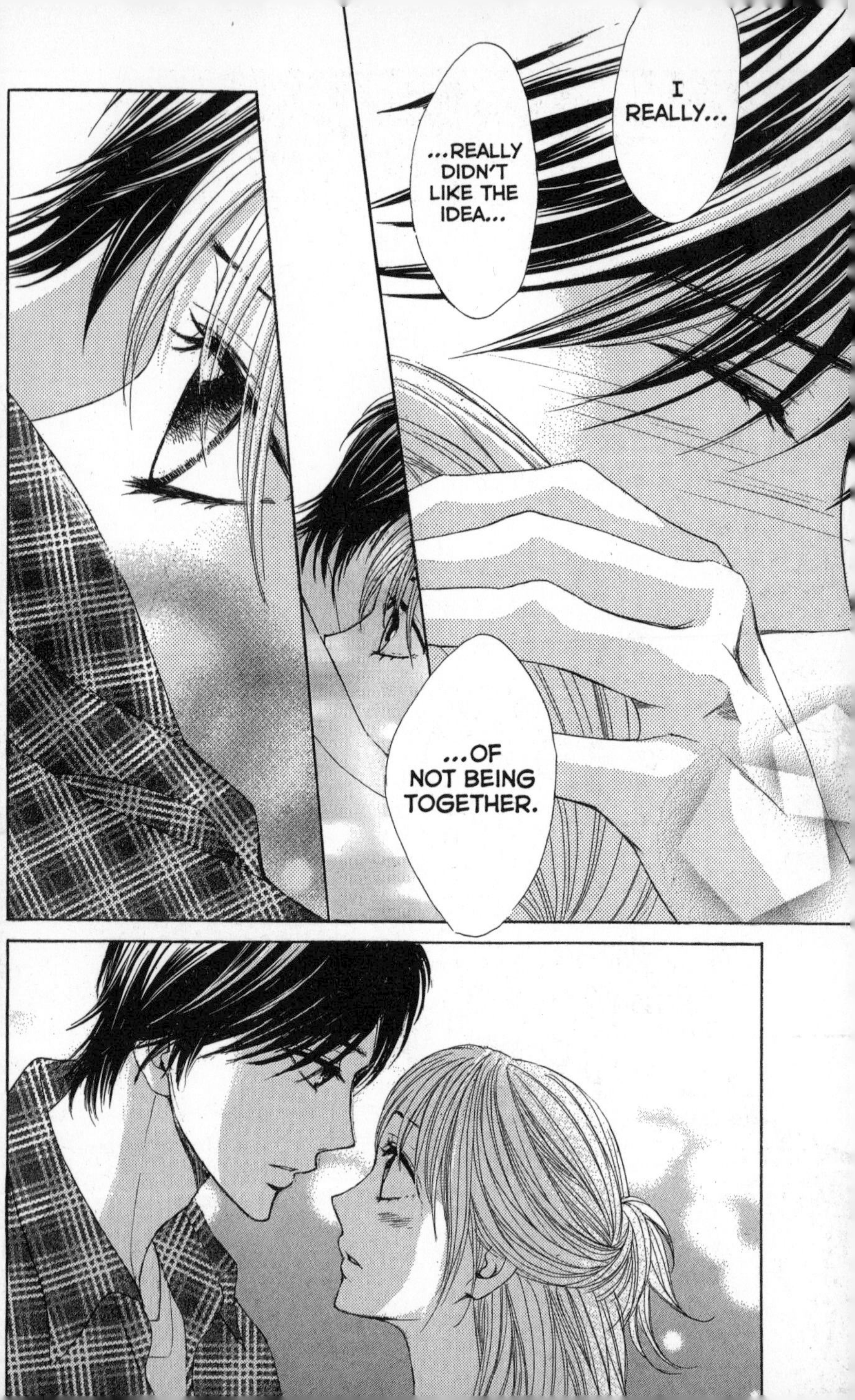
I REALLY...
...REALLY DIDN'T LIKE THE IDEA...
...OF NOT BEING TOGETHER.

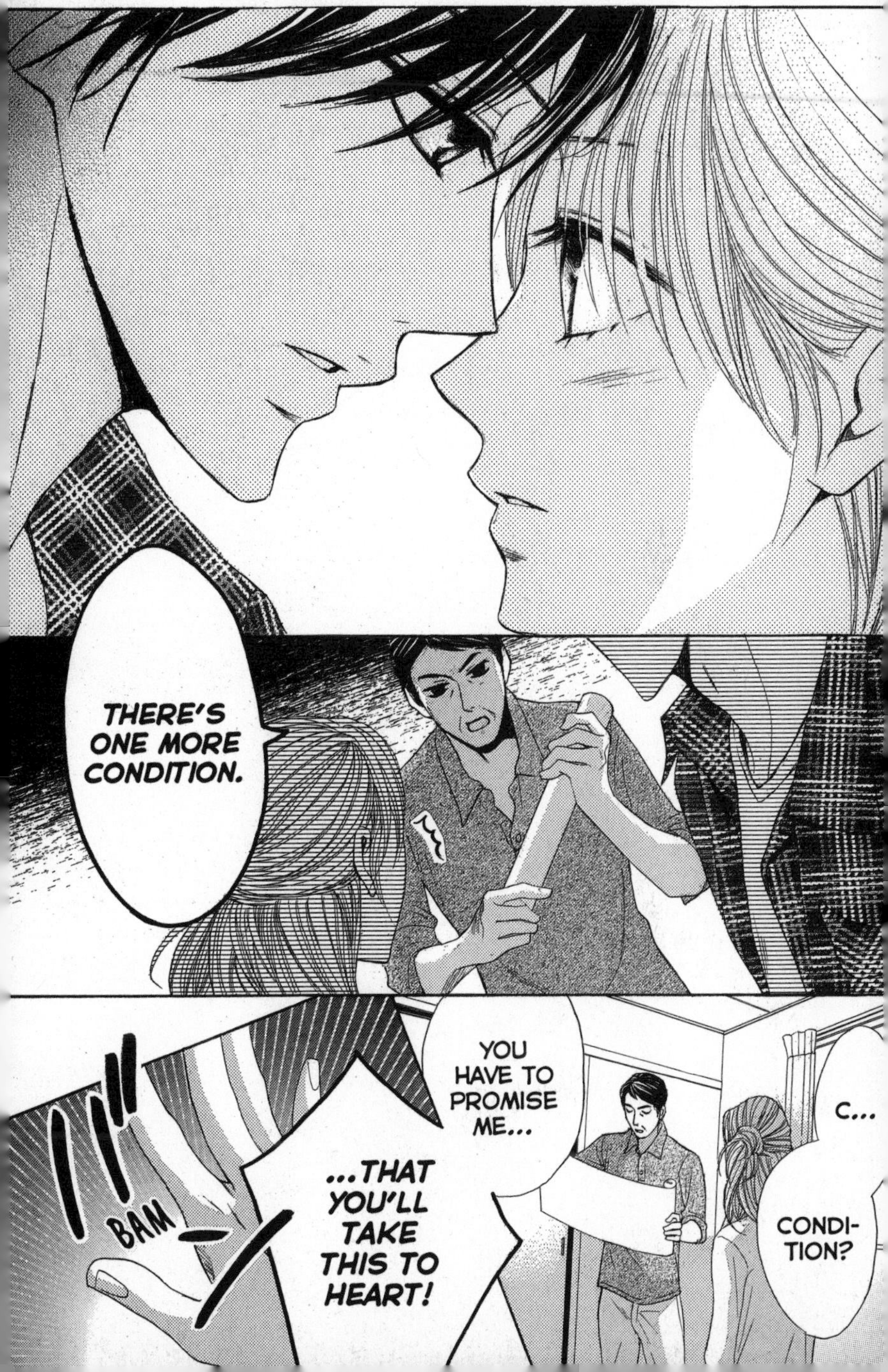
THERE'S ONE MORE CONDITION.
C...
CONDI-TION?
YOU HAVE TO PROMISE ME...
...THAT YOU'LL TAKE THIS TO HEART!
BAM

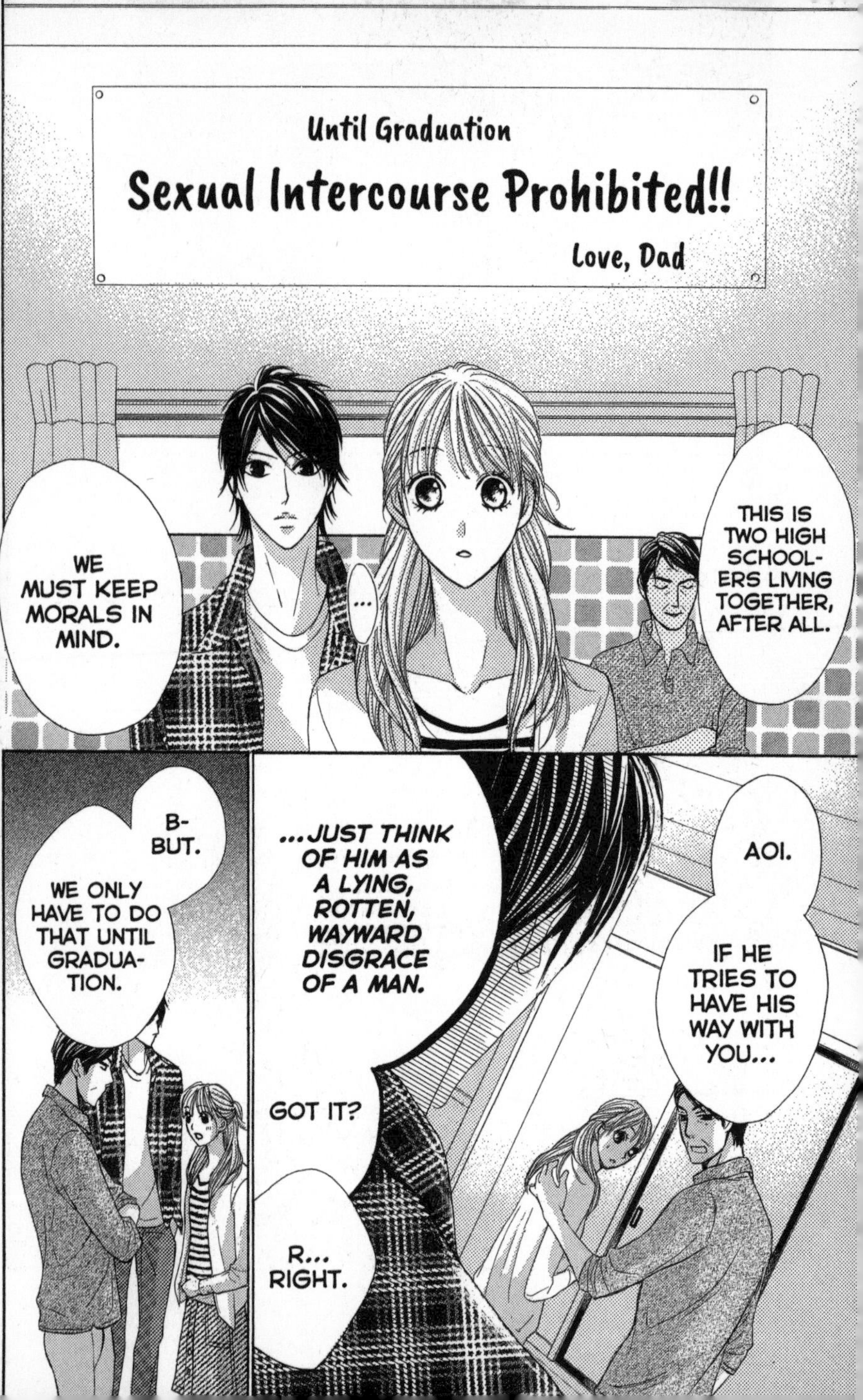
Until Graduation
Sexual Intercourse Prohibited!!
Love, Dad
THIS IS TWO HIGH SCHOOLERS LIVING TOGETHER, AFTER ALL.
...
WE MUST KEEP MORALS IN MIND.
AOI.
IF HE TRIES TO HAVE HIS WAY WITH YOU...
...JUST THINK OF HIM AS A LYING, ROTTEN, WAYWARD DISGRACE OF A MAN.
GOT IT?
R... RIGHT.
B-BUT.
WE ONLY HAVE TO DO THAT UNTIL GRADUATION.

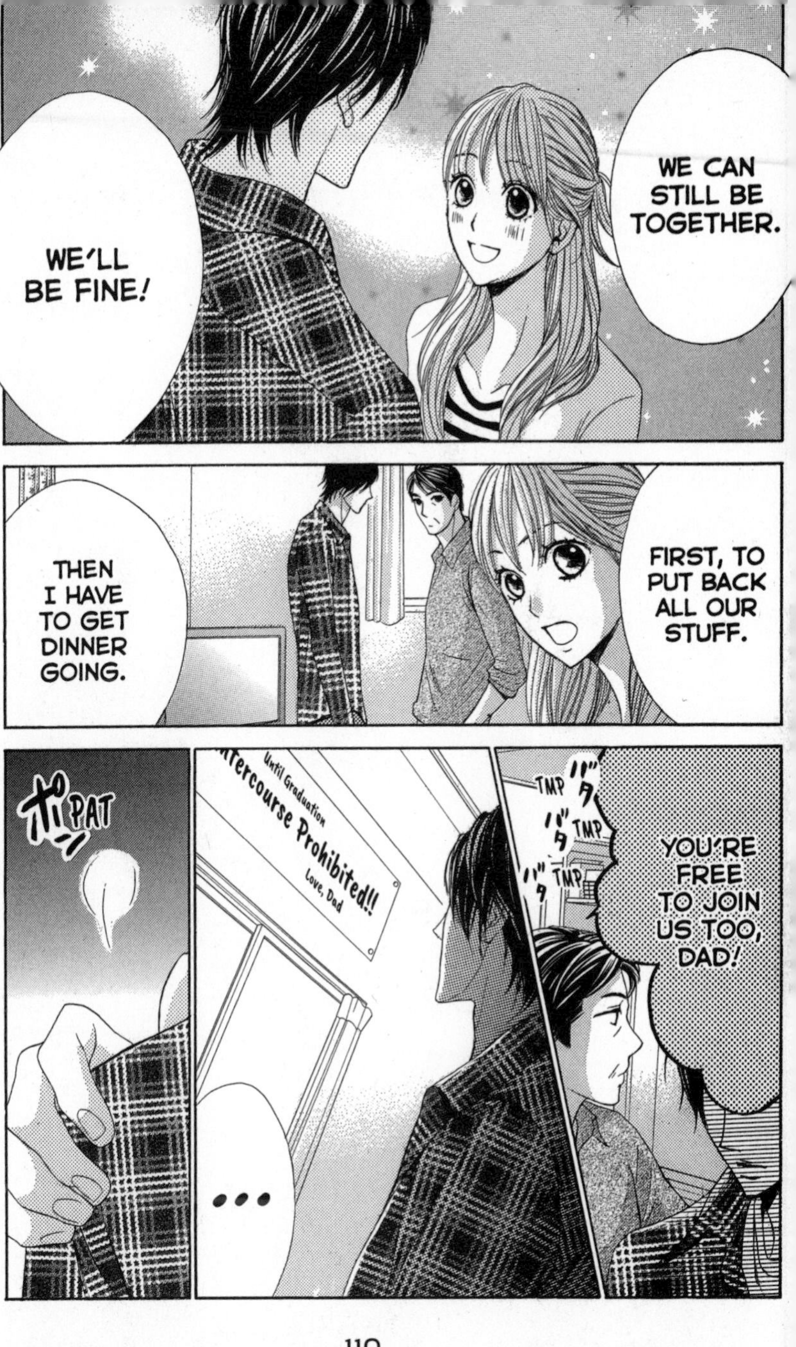
WE CAN STILL BE TOGETHER.
WE'LL BE FINE!
FIRST, TO PUT BACK ALL OUR STUFF.
THEN I HAVE TO GET DINNER GOING.
TMP TMP TMP
YOU'RE FREE TO JOIN US TOO, DAD!
Until Graduation
ntercourse Prohibited!!
Love, Dad
...
PAT

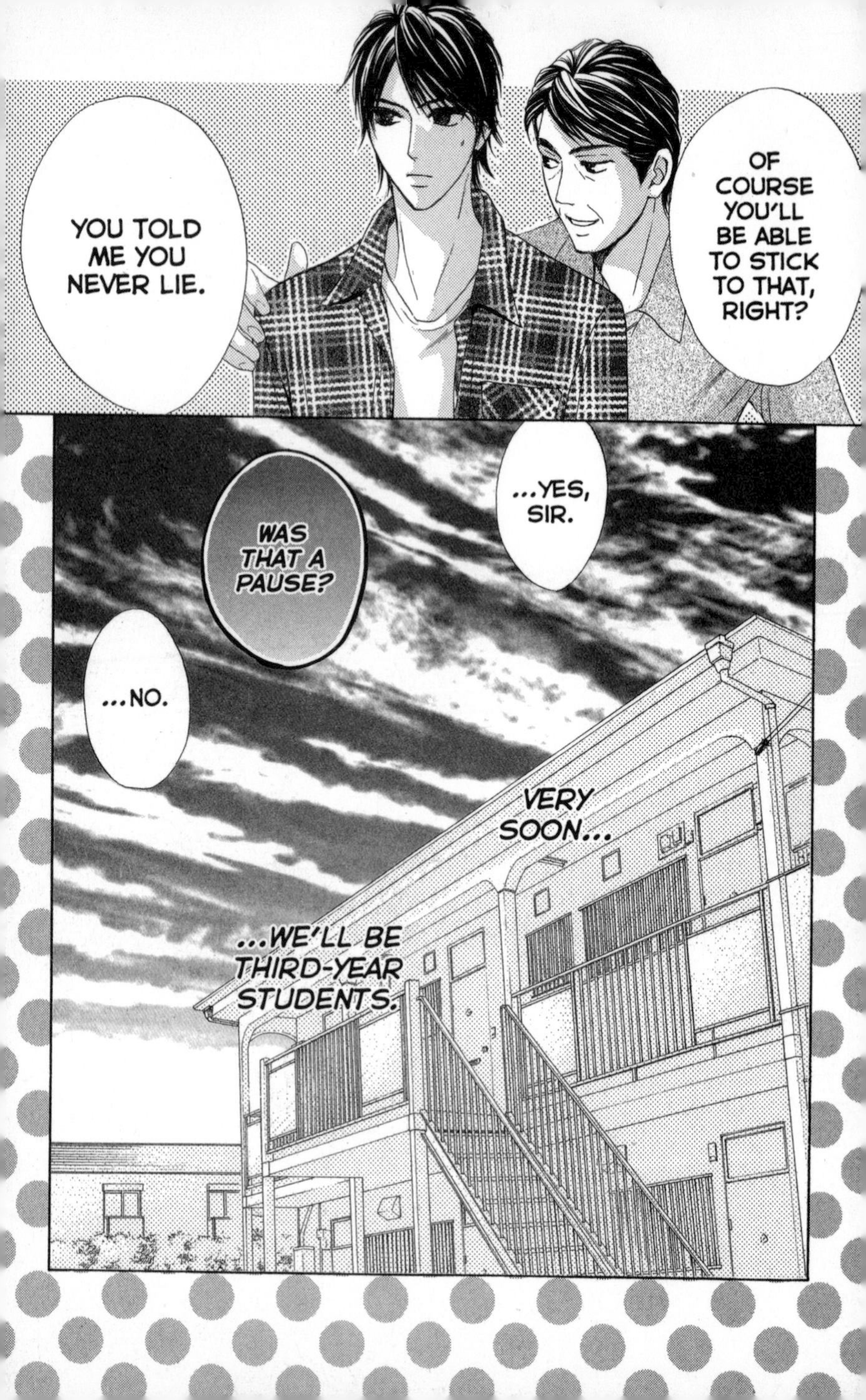

OF COURSE YOU'LL BE ABLE TO STICK TO THAT, RIGHT?
YOU TOLD ME YOU NEVER LIE.
...YES, SIR.
WAS THAT A PAUSE?
...NO.
VERY SOON...
...WE'LL BE THIRD-YEAR STUDENTS.

#36 Adult Time

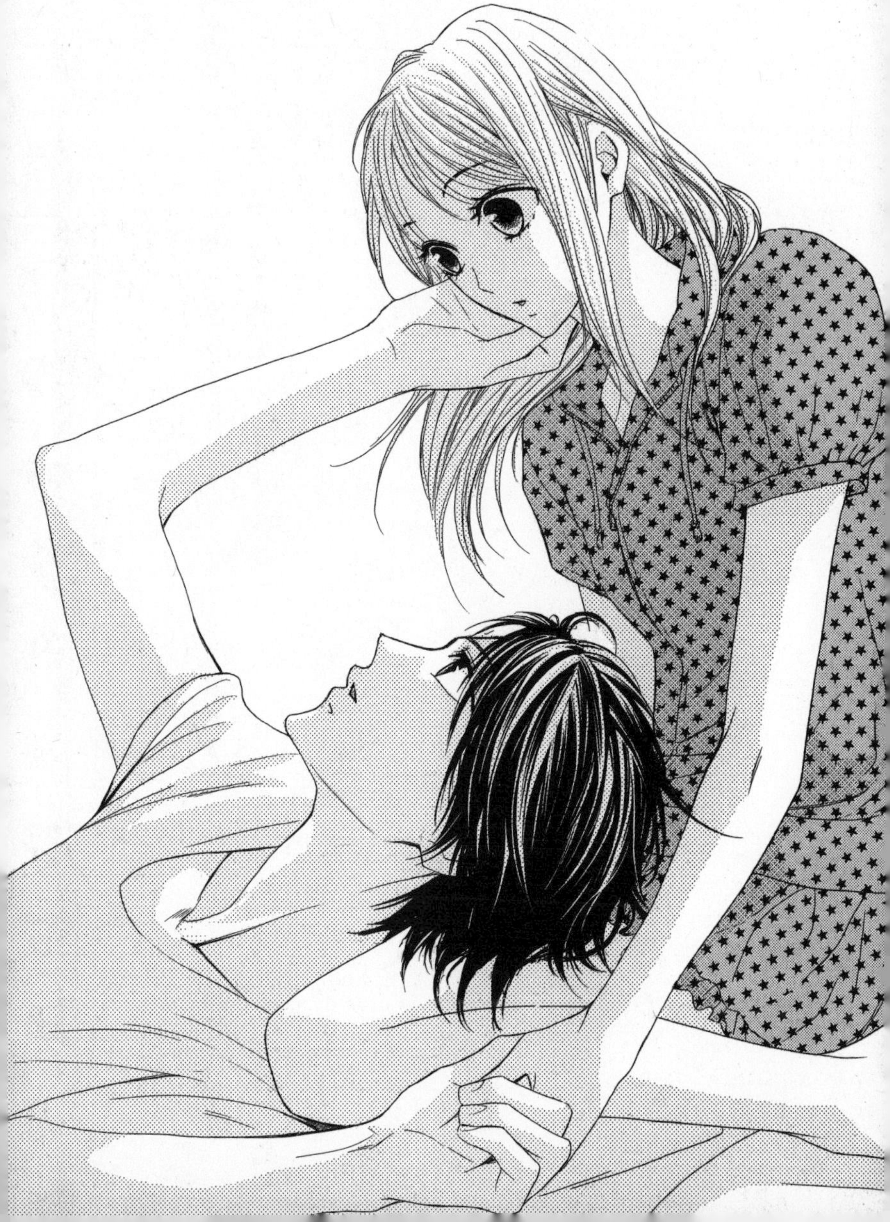

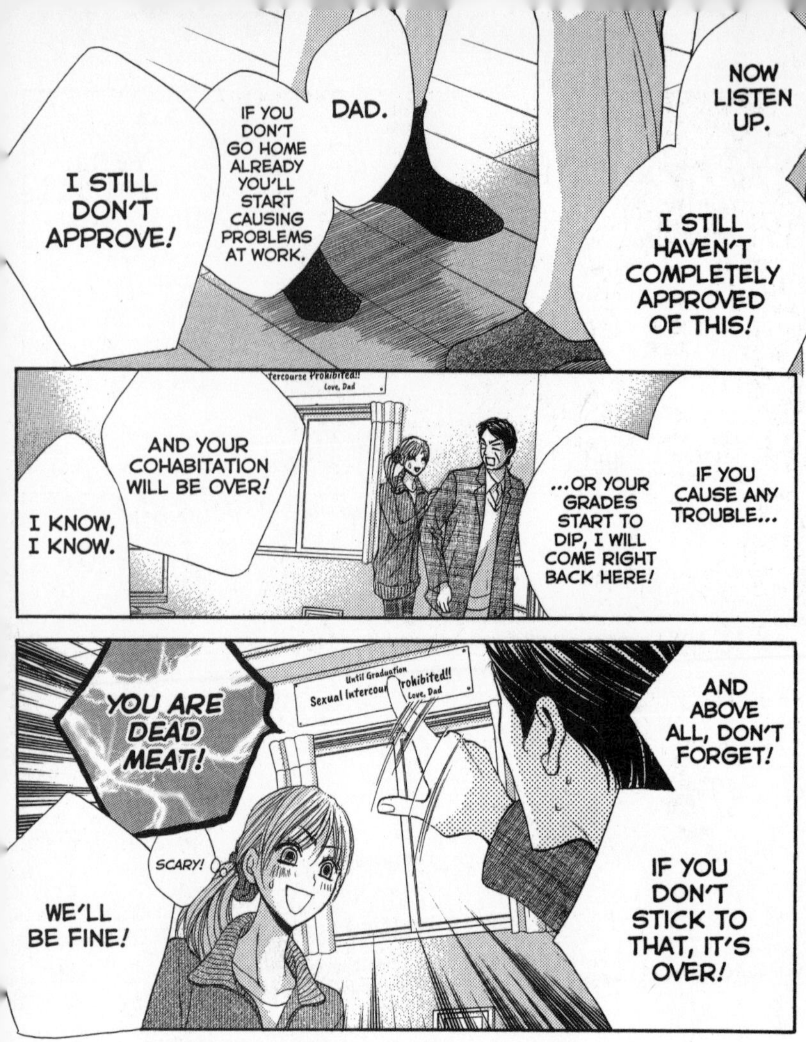
NOW LISTEN UP.
I STILL HAVEN'T COMPLETELY APPROVED OF THIS!
DAD.
IF YOU DON'T GO HOME ALREADY YOU'LL START CAUSING PROBLEMS AT WORK.
I STILL DON'T APPROVE!
Intercourse Prohibited!! Love, Dad
IF YOU CAUSE ANY TROUBLE...
...OR YOUR GRADES START TO DIP, I WILL COME RIGHT BACK HERE!
AND YOUR COHABITATION WILL BE OVER!
I KNOW, I KNOW.
AND ABOVE ALL, DON'T FORGET!
Until Graduation
Sexual Intercour
rohibited!!
Love, Dad
IF YOU DON'T STICK TO THAT, IT'S OVER!
YOU ARE DEAD MEAT!
SCARY!
WE'LL BE FINE!

L♥DK

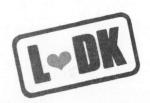

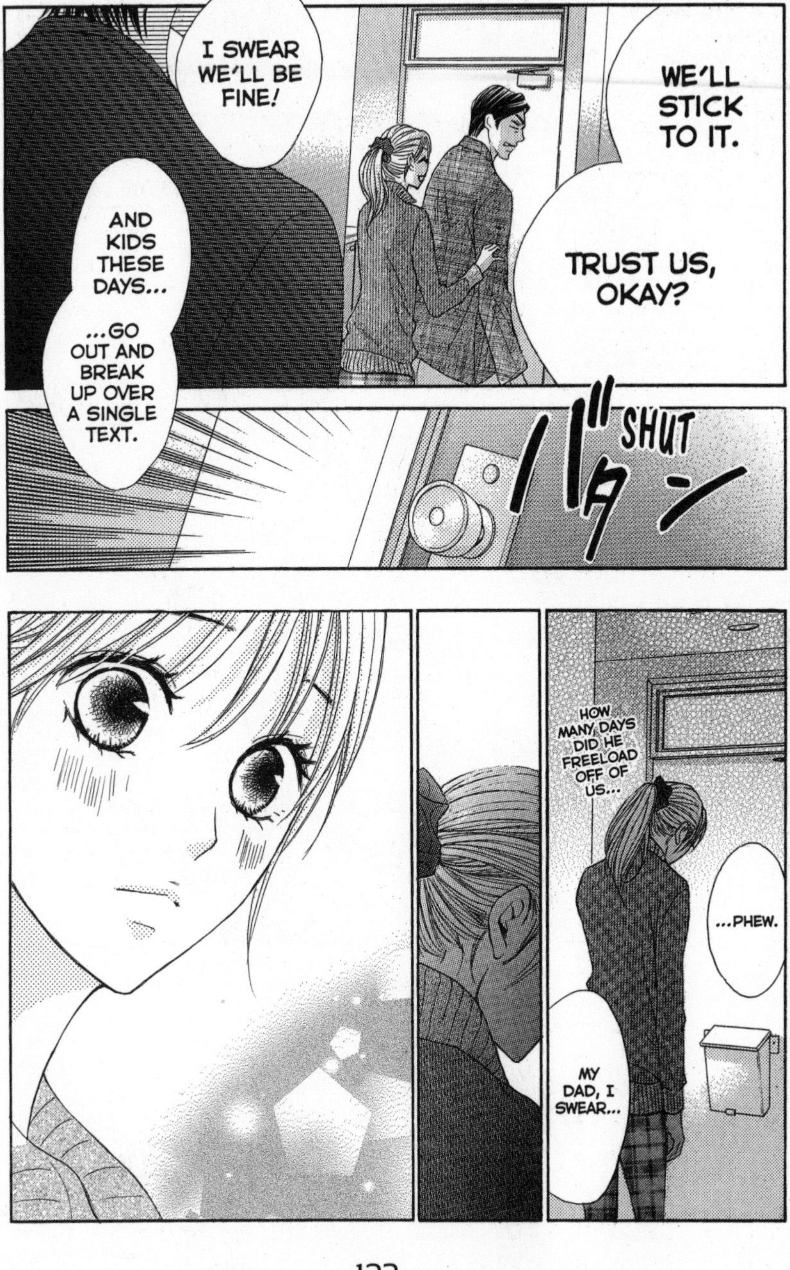
WE'LL STICK TO IT.
TRUST US, OKAY?
I SWEAR WE'LL BE FINE!
AND KIDS THESE DAYS...
...GO OUT AND BREAK UP OVER A SINGLE TEXT.
バタン
SHUT
HOW MANY DAYS DID HE FREELOAD OFF OF US...
...PHEW.
MY DAD, I SWEAR...

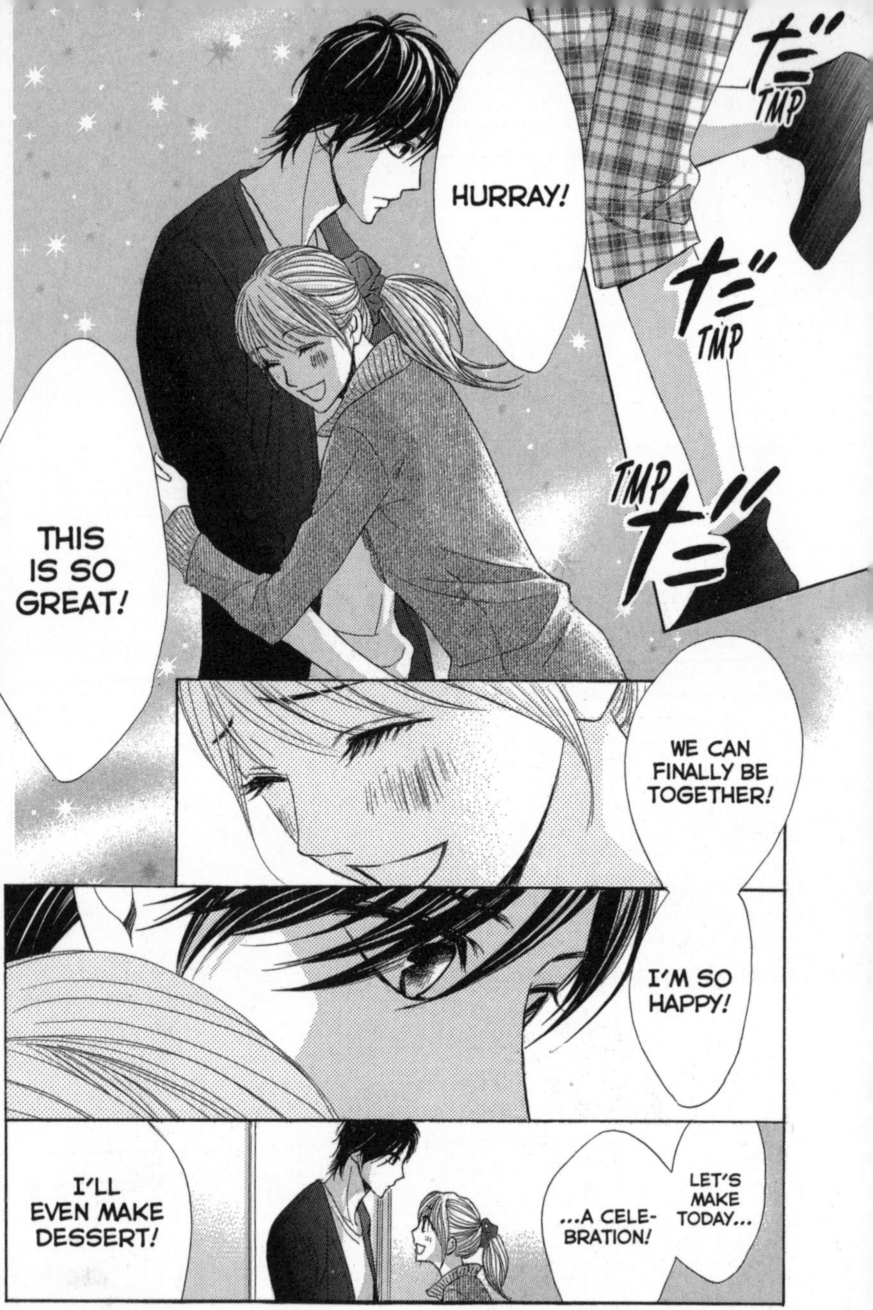
だ
TMP
だ
TMP
TMP
だ
HURRAY!
THIS IS SO GREAT!
WE CAN FINALLY BE TOGETHER!
I'M SO HAPPY!
LET'S MAKE TODAY...
...A CELE-BRATION!
I'LL EVEN MAKE DESSERT!

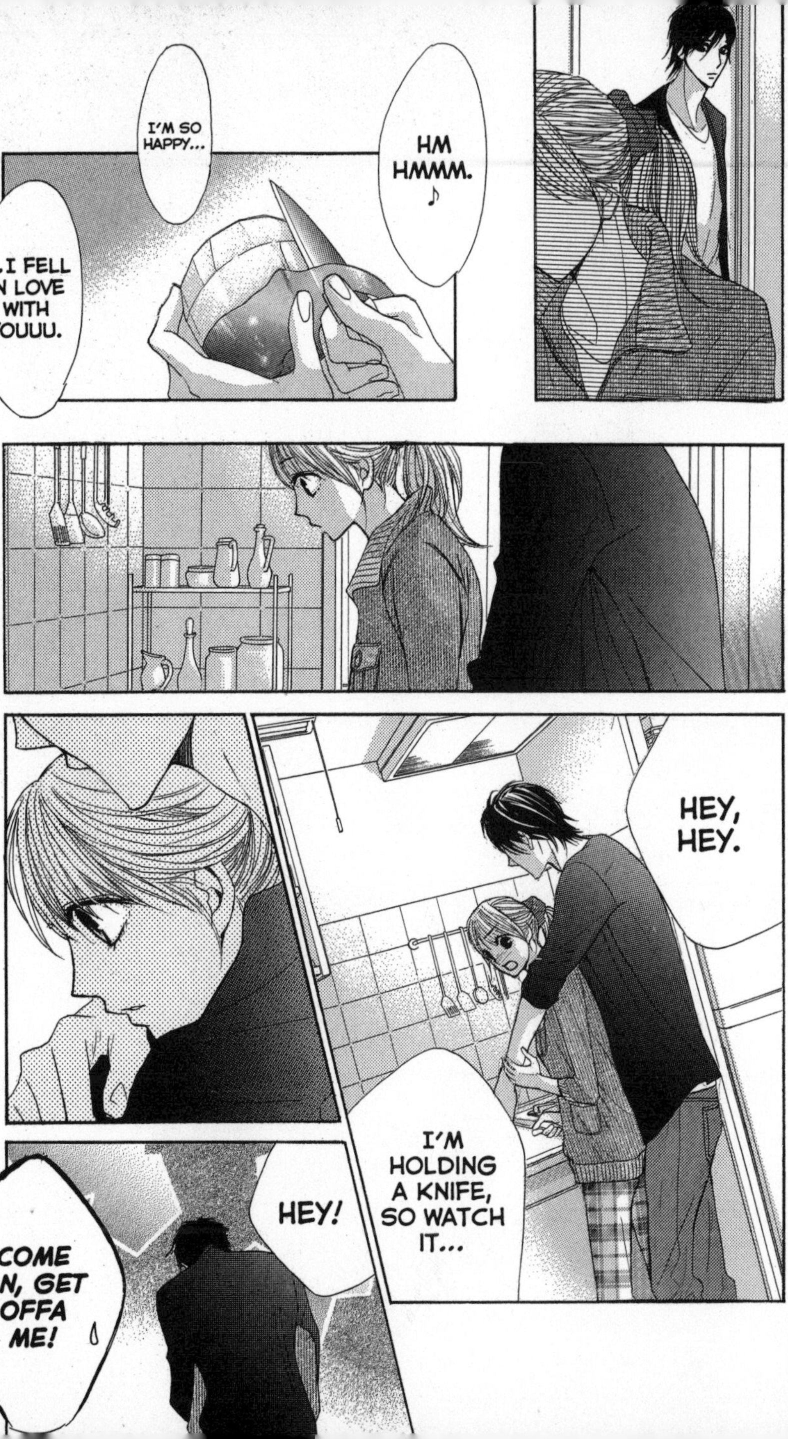
HM HMMM. ♪
I'M SO HAPPY...
...I FELL IN LOVE WITH YOUUU.
HEY, HEY.
I'M HOLDING A KNIFE, SO WATCH IT...
HEY!
COME ON, GET OFFA ME!

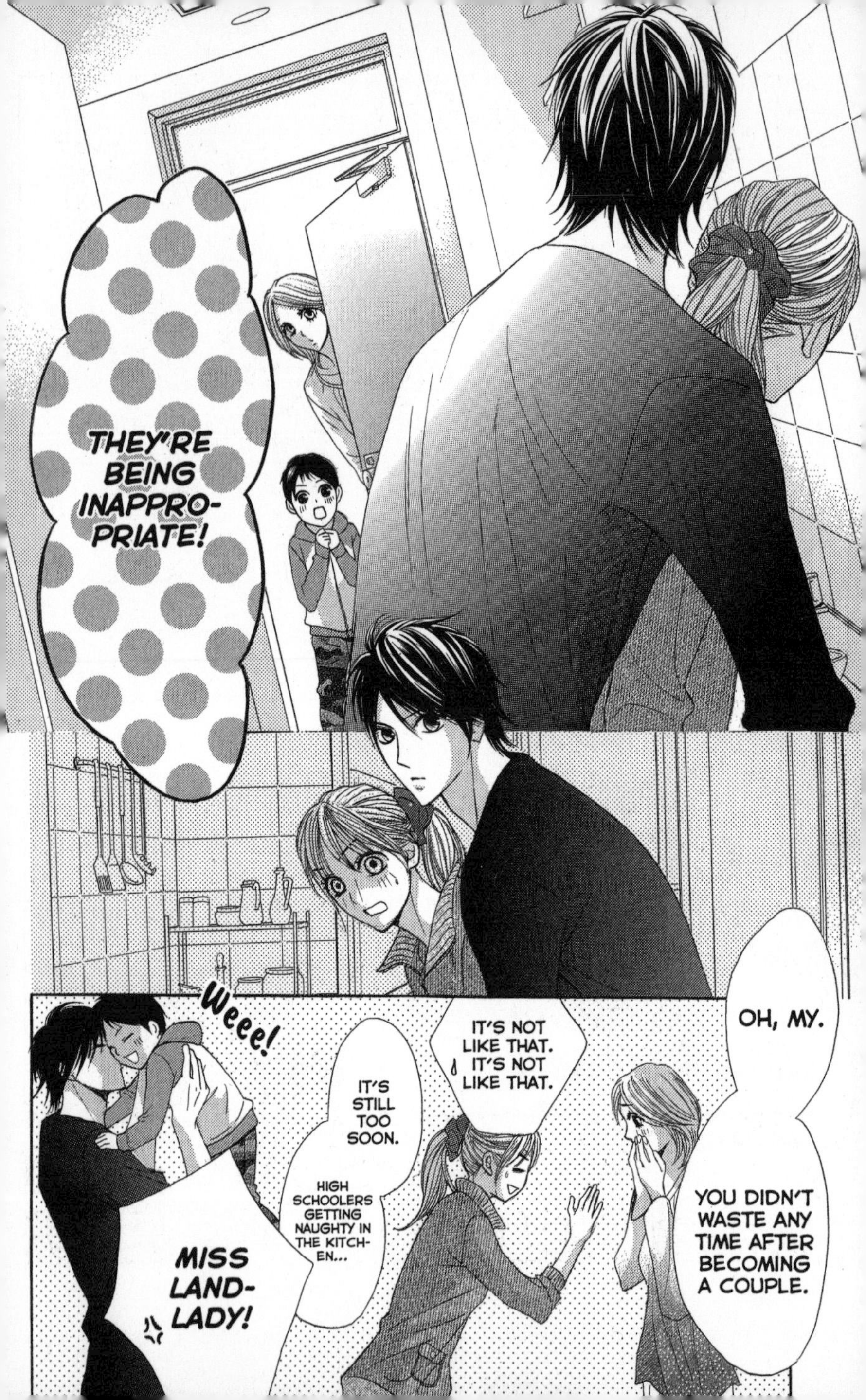
THEY'RE BEING INAPPRO- PRIATE!
OH, MY.
YOU DIDN'T WASTE ANY TIME AFTER BECOMING A COUPLE.
IT'S NOT LIKE THAT. IT'S NOT LIKE THAT.
IT'S STILL TOO SOON.
HIGH SCHOOLERS GETTING NAUGHTY IN THE KITCH- EN...
Weeee!
MISS LAND- LADY!

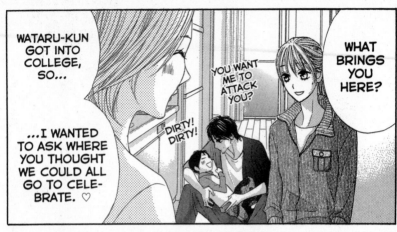

WHAT BRINGS YOU HERE?
YOU WANT ME TO ATTACK YOU?
DIRTY! DIRTY!
WATARU-KUN GOT INTO COLLEGE, SO...
...I WANTED TO ASK WHERE YOU THOUGHT WE COULD ALL GO TO CELEBRATE. ♡
WOW! IS THAT SO?
RIGHT NOW, KOUTA HAS HIS HEART...
...SET ON A HOT SPRING SPA.
THEY'VE GOT A WATER-SLIDE!
OH! WE'D LOVE TO GO!
PINCH PINCH
SOUNDS FUN!
Heh heh!
THEN LET'S GO PARTY! IT'S BEEN SO LONG! ♡

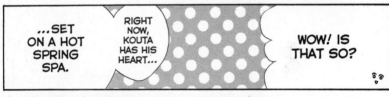

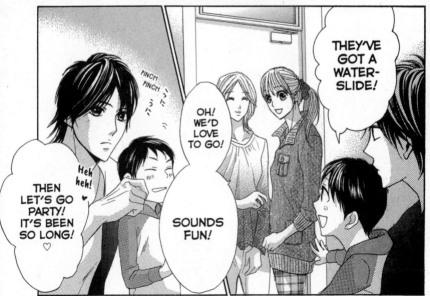

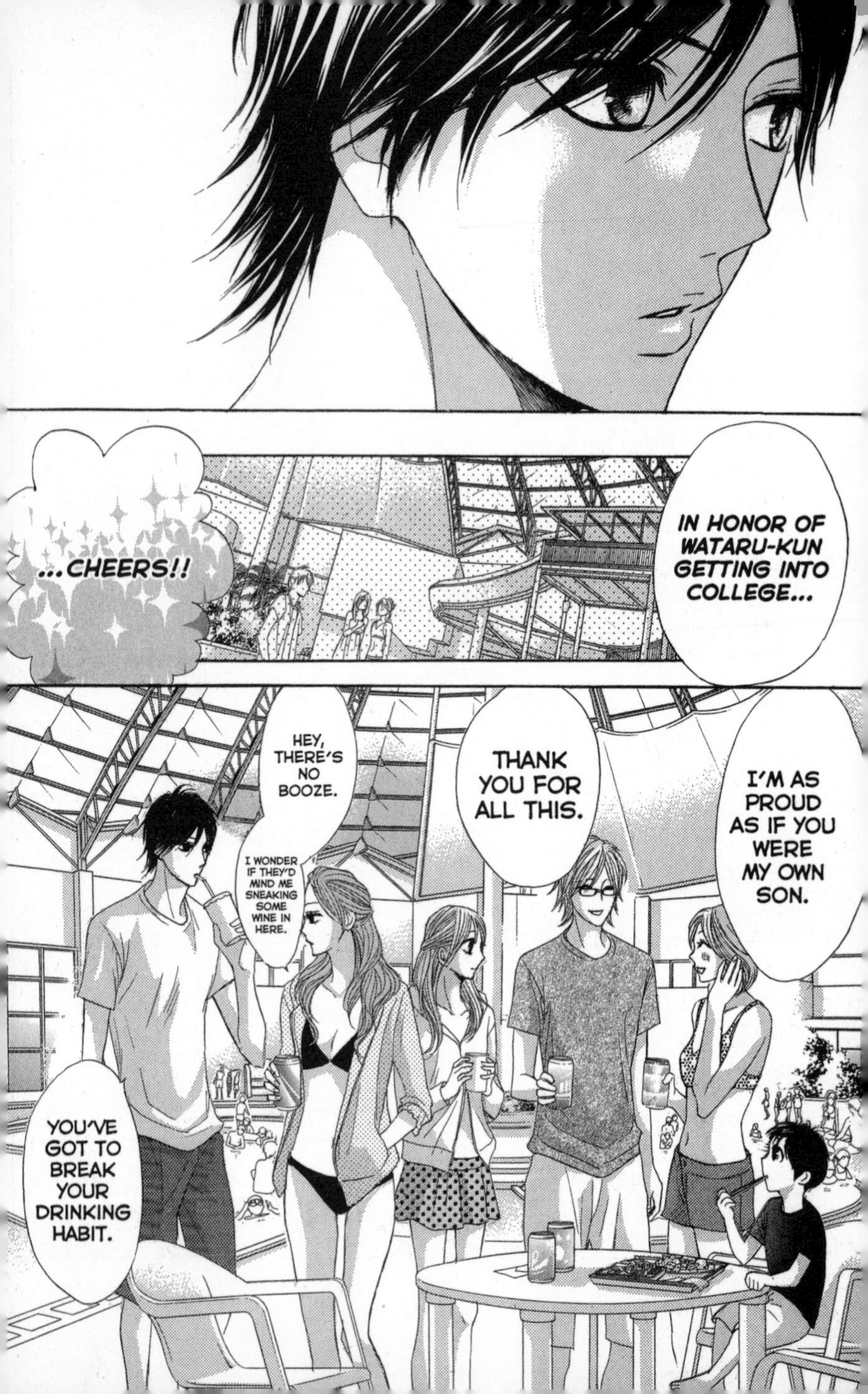
IN HONOR OF WATARU-KUN GETTING INTO COLLEGE...
...CHEERS!!
I'M AS PROUD AS IF YOU WERE MY OWN SON.
THANK YOU FOR ALL THIS.
HEY, THERE'S NO BOOZE.
I WONDER IF THEY'D MIND ME SNEAKING SOME WINE IN HERE.
YOU'VE GOT TO BREAK YOUR DRINKING HABIT.

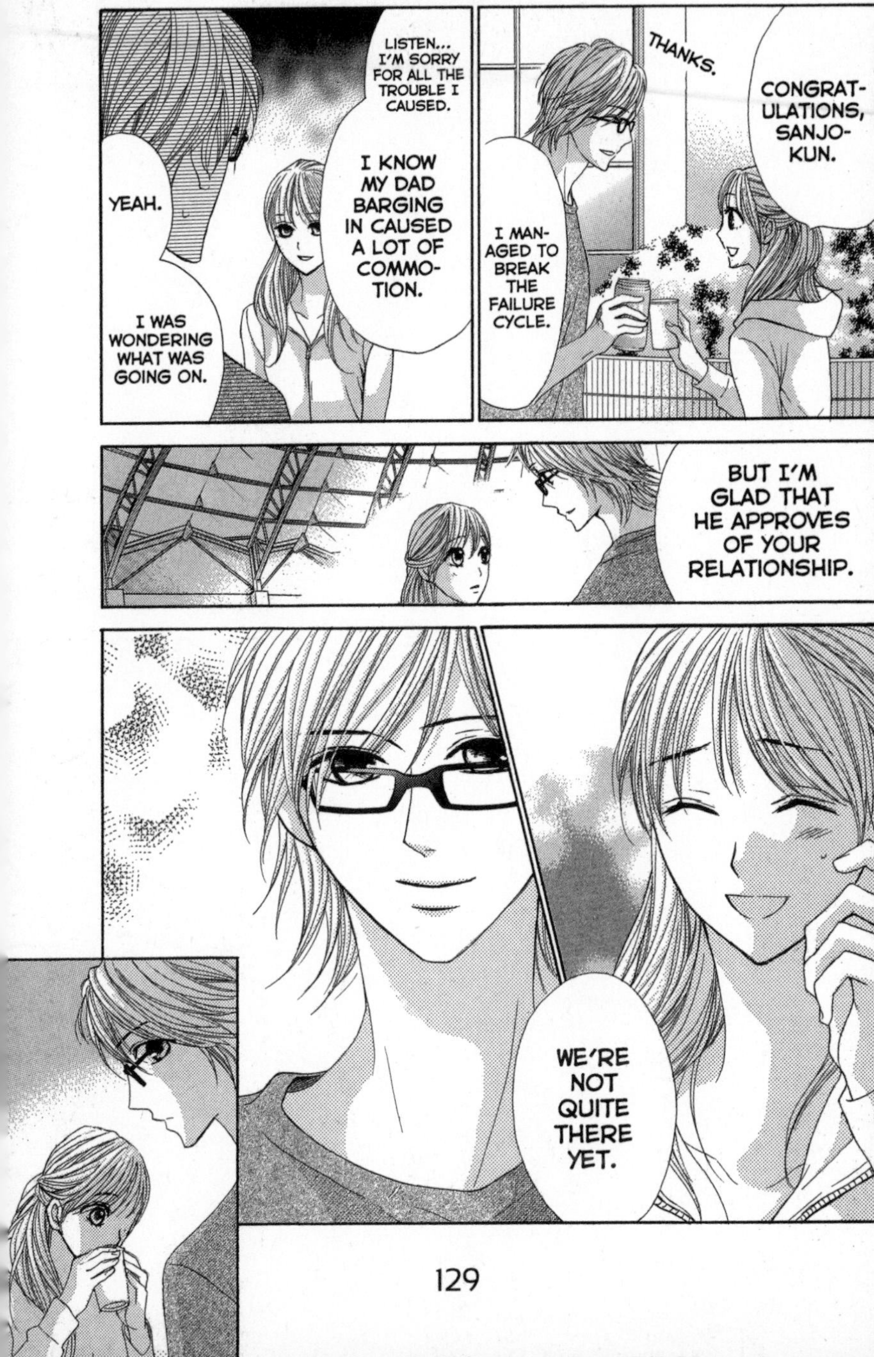
CONGRAT-ULATIONS, SANJO-KUN.
THANKS.
I MAN-AGED TO BREAK THE FAILURE CYCLE.
LISTEN... I'M SORRY FOR ALL THE TROUBLE I CAUSED.
I KNOW MY DAD BARGING IN CAUSED A LOT OF COMMO-TION.
YEAH.
I WAS WONDERING WHAT WAS GOING ON.
BUT I'M GLAD THAT HE APPROVES OF YOUR RELATIONSHIP.
WE'RE NOT QUITE THERE YET.

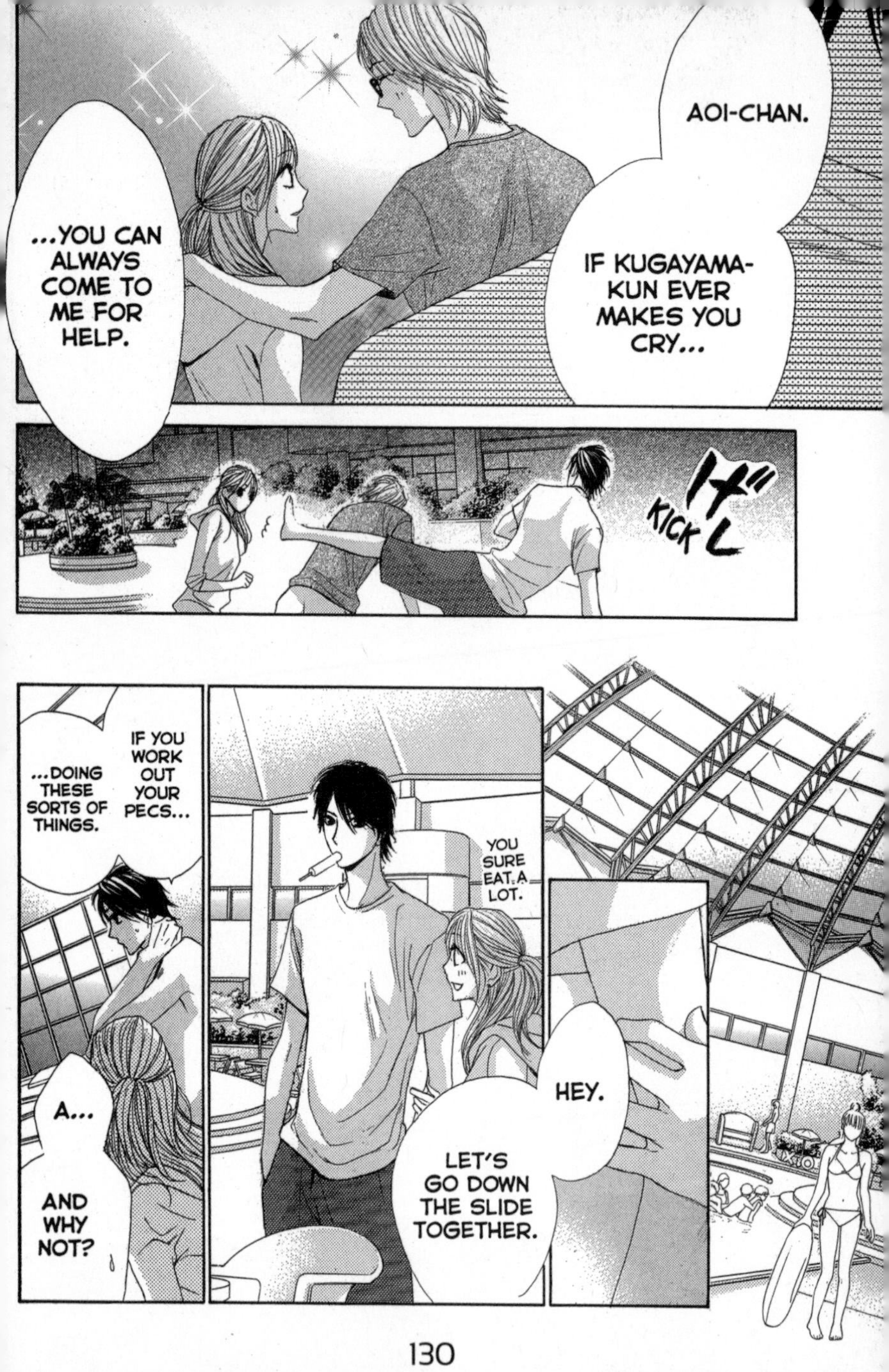
AOI-CHAN.
IF KUGAYAMA-KUN EVER MAKES YOU CRY...
...YOU CAN ALWAYS COME TO ME FOR HELP.
げし
KICK
HEY.
LET'S GO DOWN THE SLIDE TOGETHER.
YOU SURE EAT A LOT.
IF YOU WORK OUT YOUR PECS...
...DOING THESE SORTS OF THINGS.
A...
AND WHY NOT?

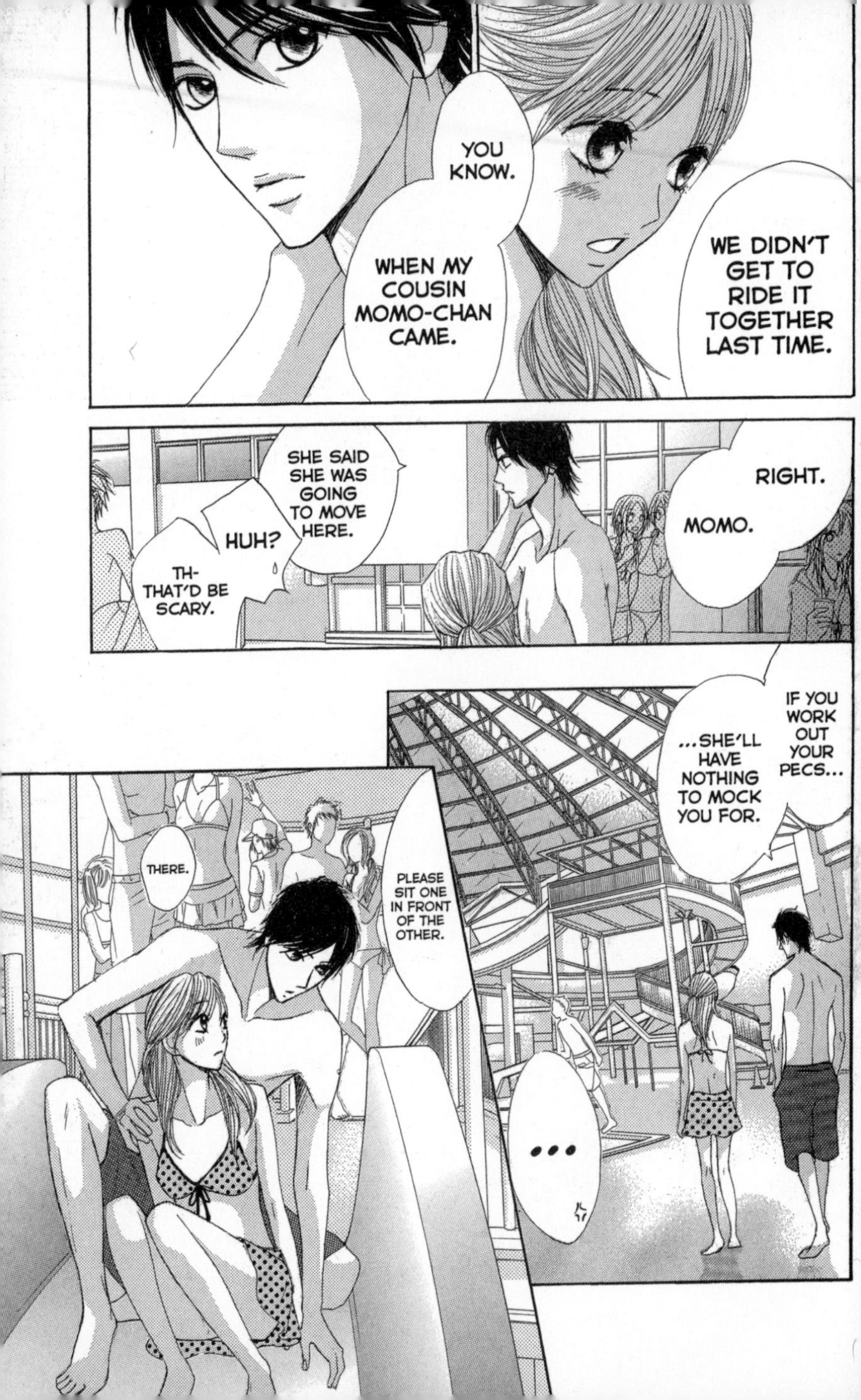
WE DIDN'T GET TO RIDE IT TOGETHER LAST TIME.
YOU KNOW.
WHEN MY COUSIN MOMO-CHAN CAME.
RIGHT.
MOMO.
SHE SAID SHE WAS GOING TO MOVE HERE.
HUH?
TH- THAT'D BE SCARY.
IF YOU WORK OUT YOUR PECS...
...SHE'LL HAVE NOTHING TO MOCK YOU FOR.
...
PLEASE SIT ONE IN FRONT OF THE OTHER.
THERE.

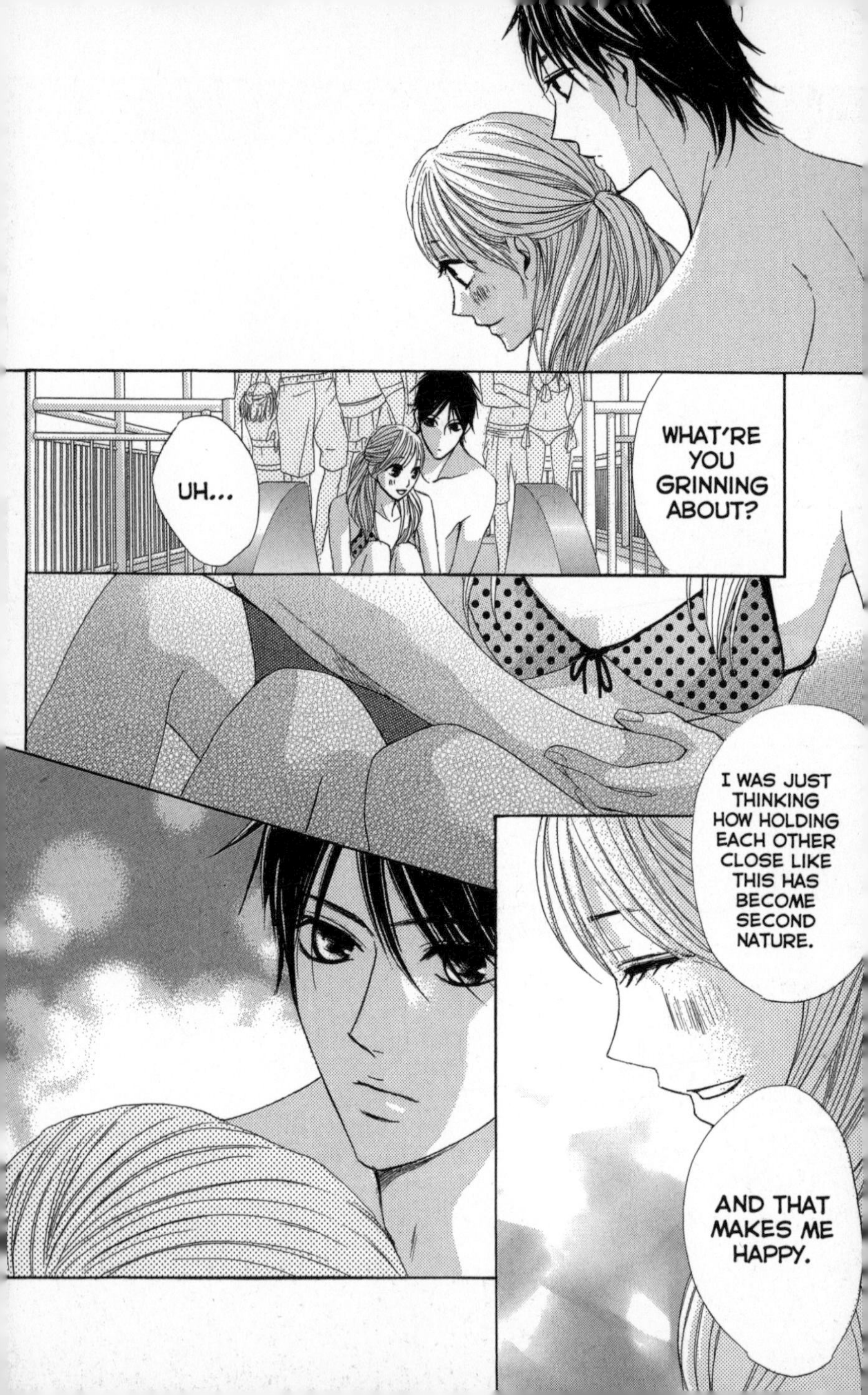
WHAT'RE YOU GRINNING ABOUT?
UH...
I WAS JUST THINKING HOW HOLDING EACH OTHER CLOSE LIKE THIS HAS BECOME SECOND NATURE.
AND THAT MAKES ME HAPPY.

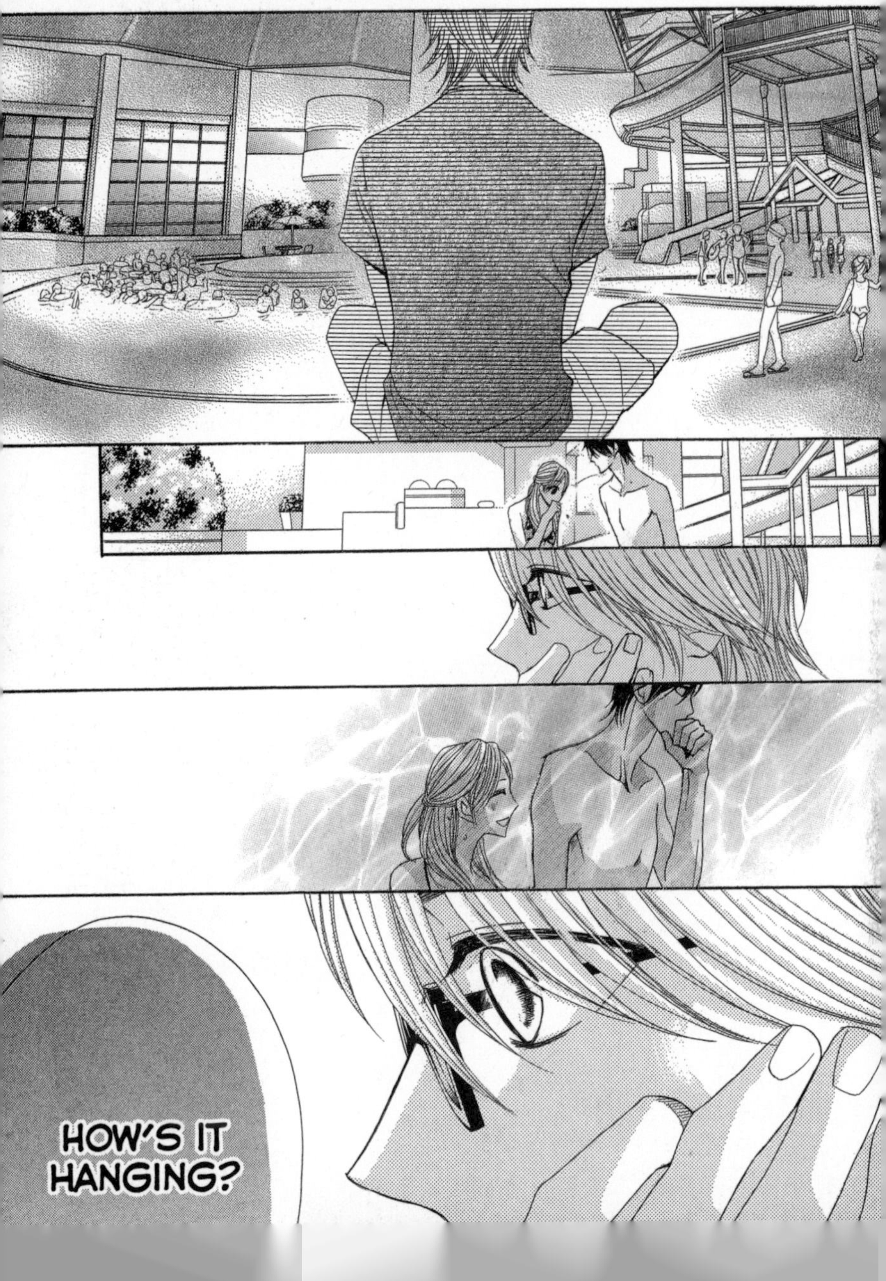
HOW'S IT
HANGING?

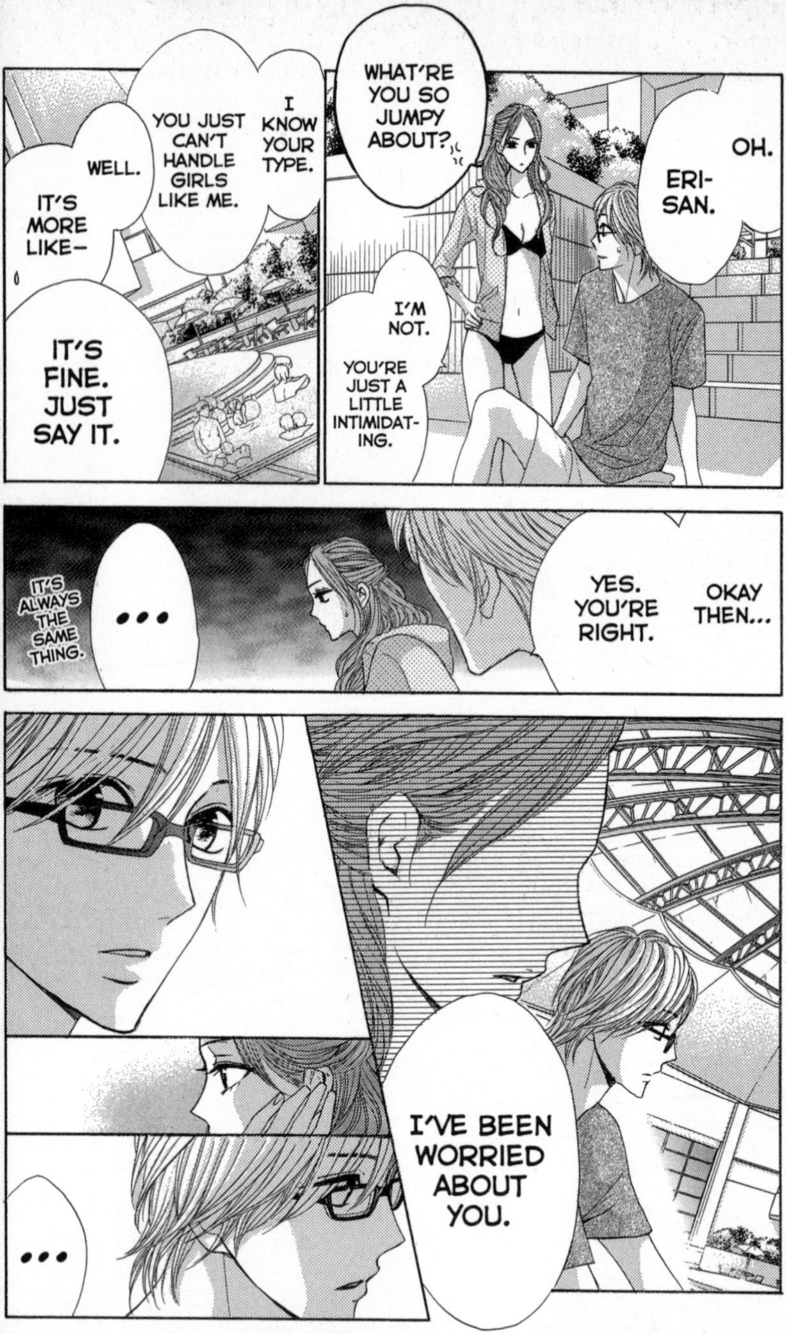
OH.
ERI-SAN.
WHAT'RE YOU SO JUMPY ABOUT?
I'M NOT.
YOU'RE JUST A LITTLE INTIMIDATING.
I KNOW YOUR TYPE.
YOU JUST CAN'T HANDLE GIRLS LIKE ME.
WELL.
IT'S MORE LIKE—
IT'S FINE. JUST SAY IT.
YES. YOU'RE RIGHT.
OKAY THEN...
...
IT'S ALWAYS THE SAME THING.
I'VE BEEN WORRIED ABOUT YOU.
...

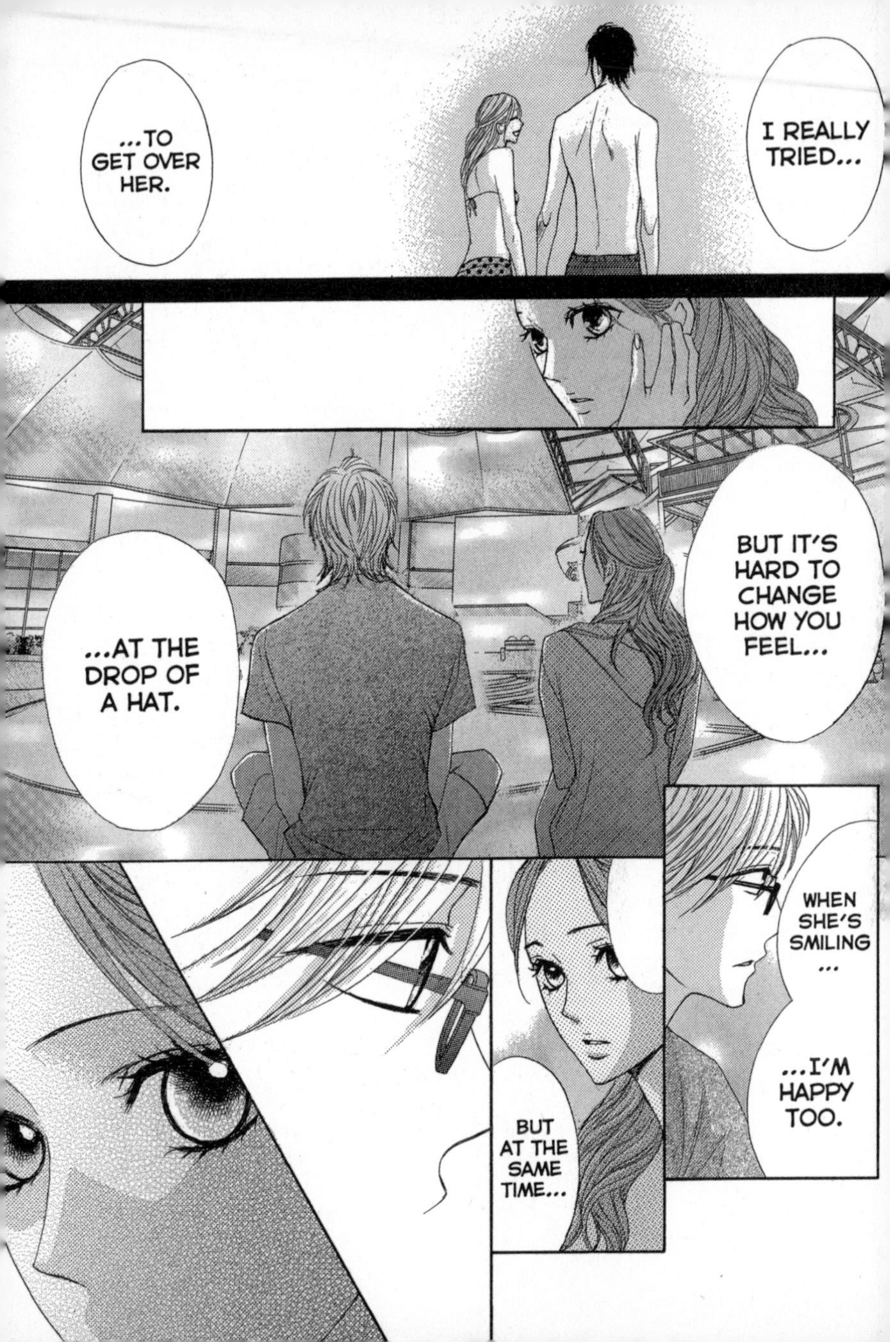
I REALLY TRIED...
...TO GET OVER HER.
BUT IT'S HARD TO CHANGE HOW YOU FEEL...
...AT THE DROP OF A HAT.
WHEN SHE'S SMILING ...
...I'M HAPPY TOO.
BUT AT THE SAME TIME...

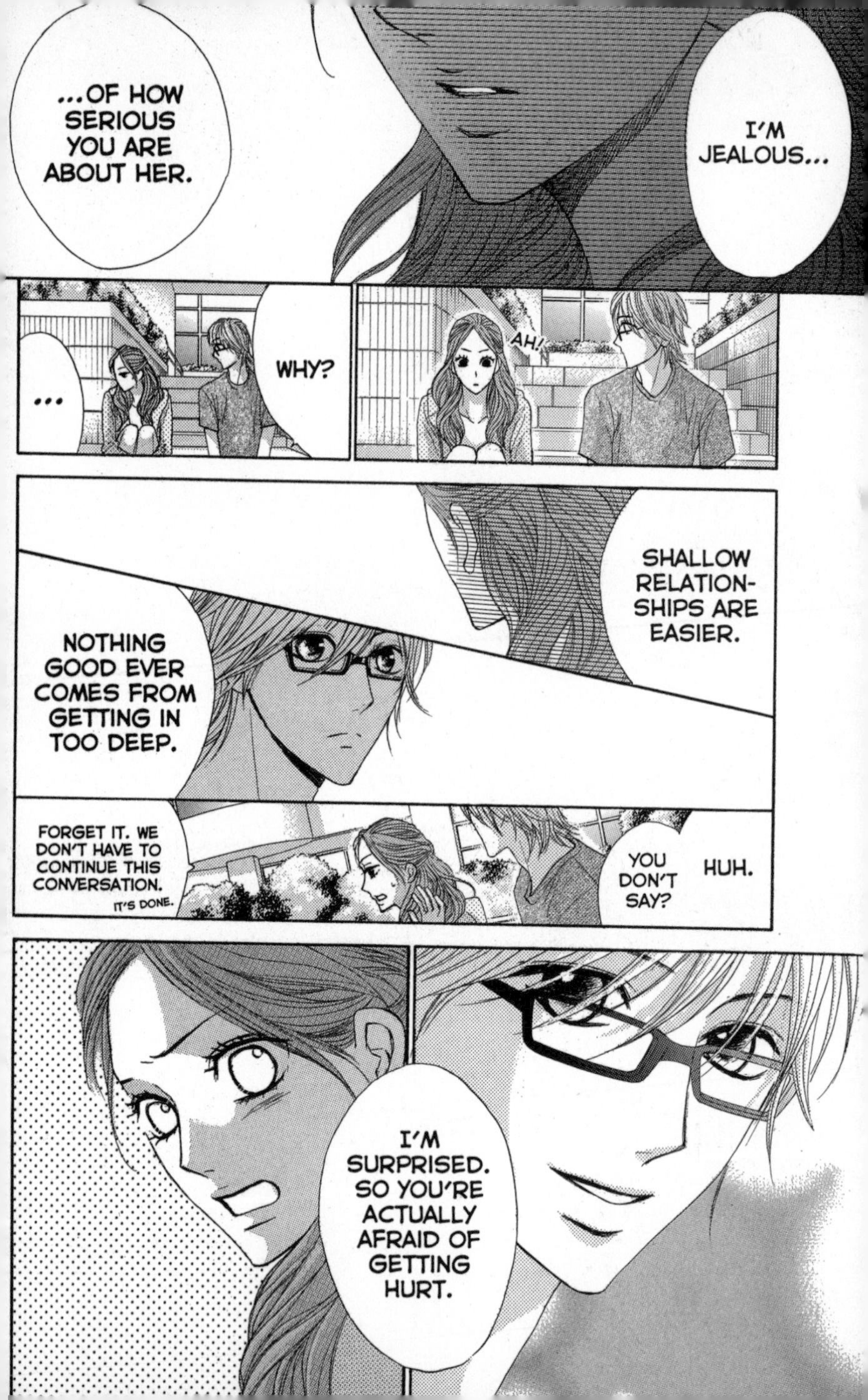
I'M JEALOUS...
...OF HOW SERIOUS YOU ARE ABOUT HER.
AH!
WHY?
...
SHALLOW RELATION-SHIPS ARE EASIER.
NOTHING GOOD EVER COMES FROM GETTING IN TOO DEEP.
HUH.
YOU DON'T SAY?
FORGET IT. WE DON'T HAVE TO CONTINUE THIS CONVERSATION.
IT'S DONE.
I'M SURPRISED. SO YOU'RE ACTUALLY AFRAID OF GETTING HURT.

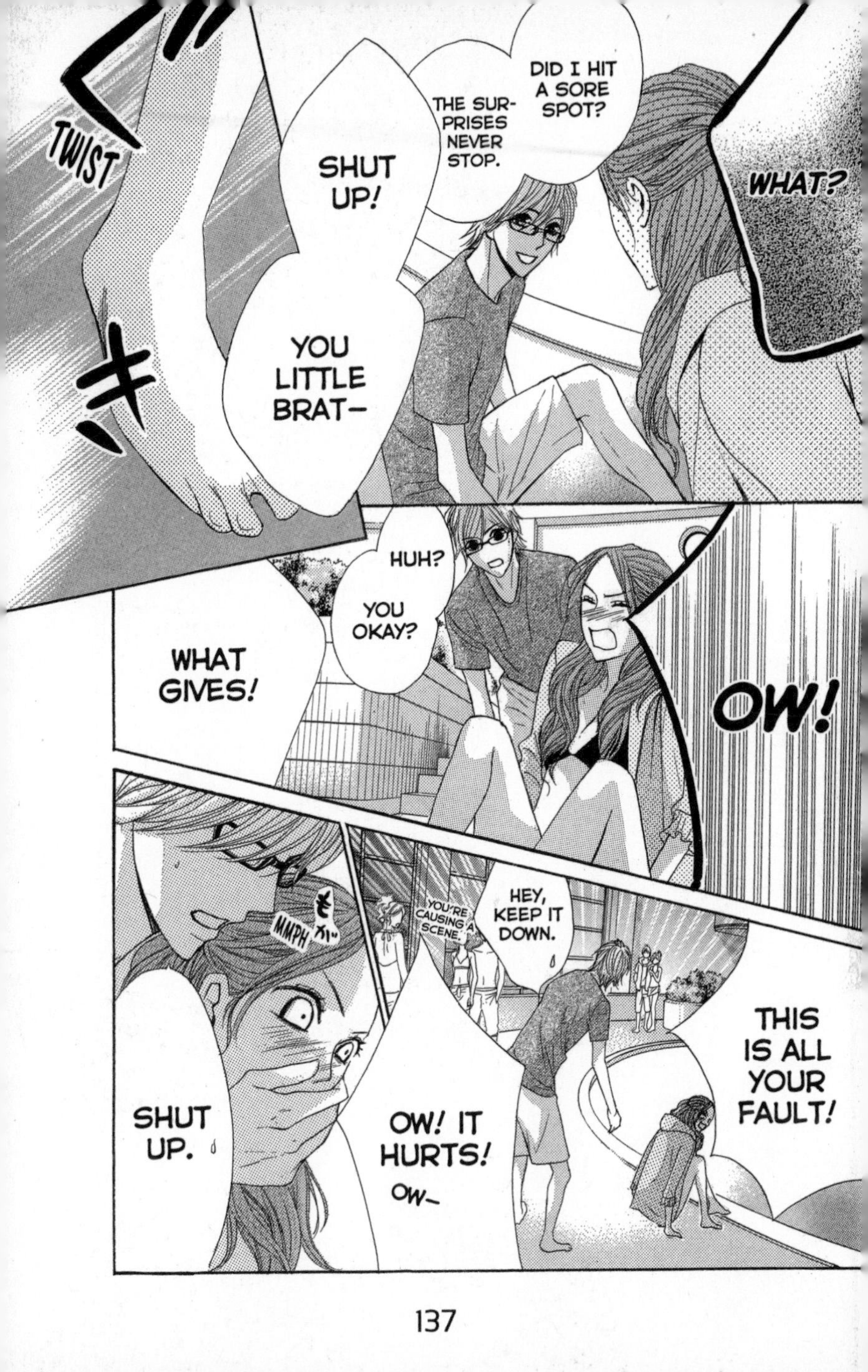
WHAT?
DID I HIT A SORE SPOT?
THE SUR-PRISES NEVER STOP.
SHUT UP!
YOU LITTLE BRAT—
TWIST
OW!
HUH?
YOU OKAY?
WHAT GIVES!
THIS IS ALL YOUR FAULT!
HEY, KEEP IT DOWN.
YOU'RE CAUSING A SCENE.
OW! IT HURTS!
OW—
MMPH
SHUT UP.

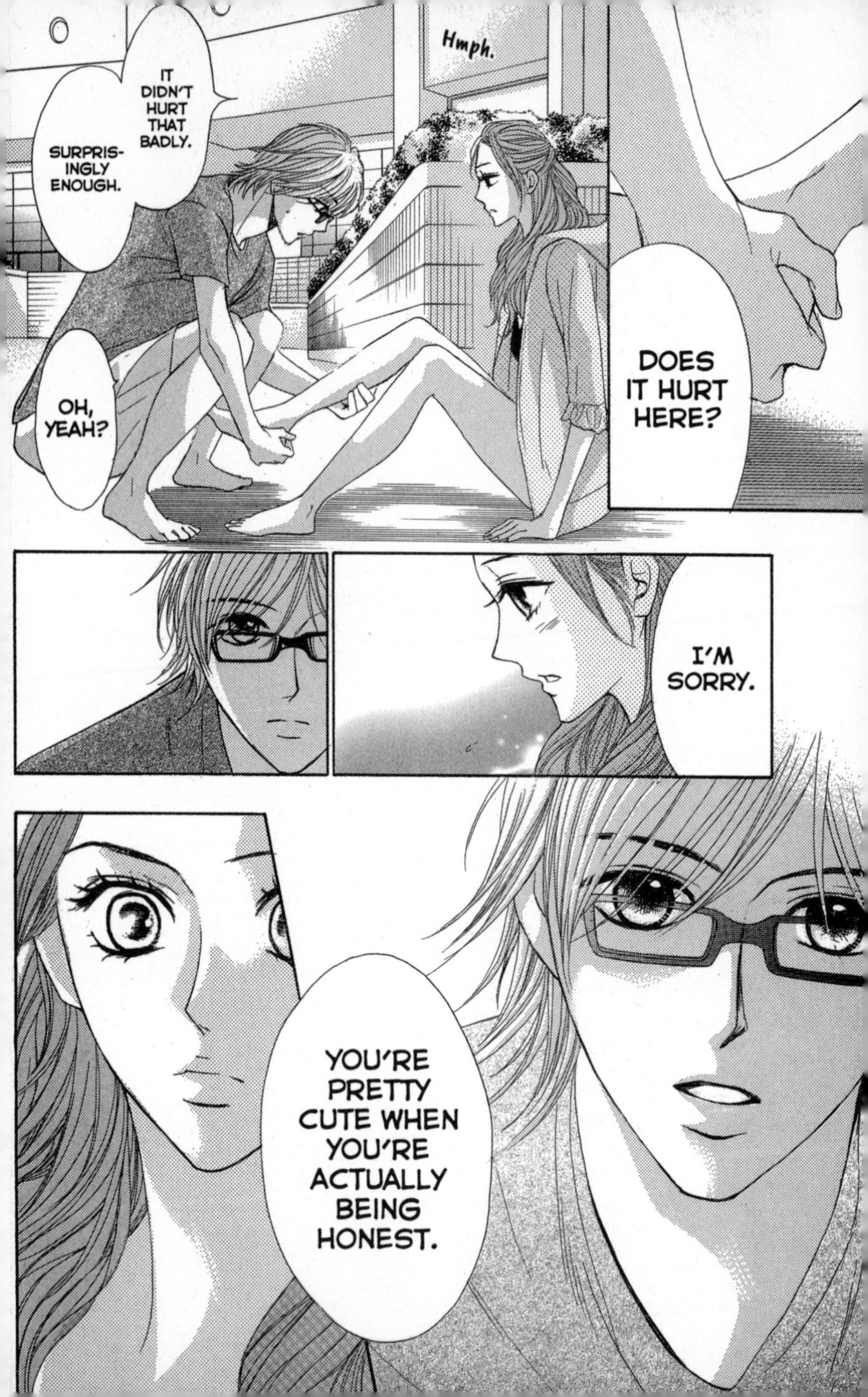
DOES IT HURT HERE?
Hmph.
IT DIDN'T HURT THAT BADLY.
SURPRIS-INGLY ENOUGH.
OH, YEAH?
I'M SORRY.
YOU'RE PRETTY CUTE WHEN YOU'RE ACTUALLY BEING HONEST.

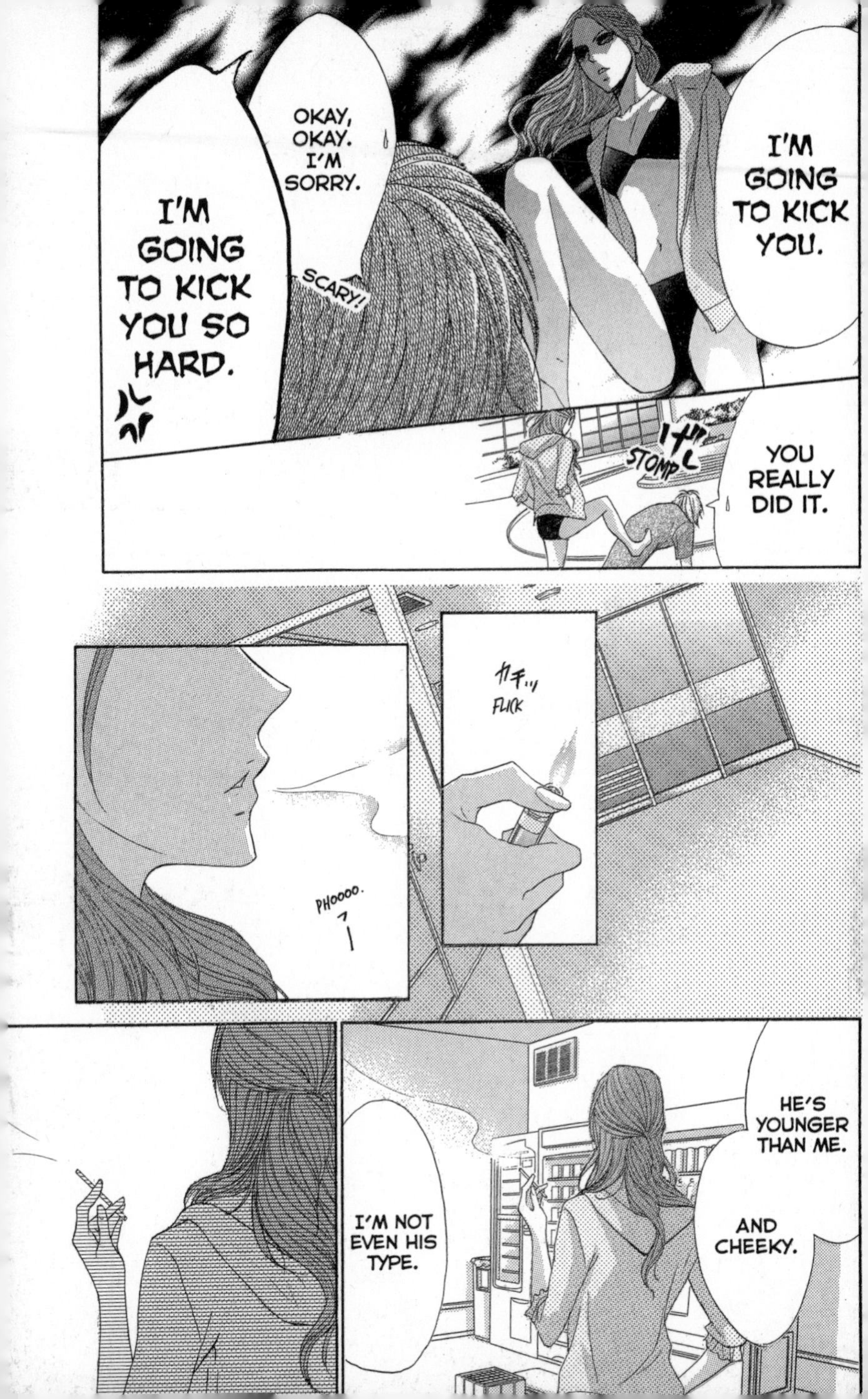
I'M GOING TO KICK YOU.
OKAY, OKAY. I'M SORRY.
SCARY!
I'M GOING TO KICK YOU SO HARD.
STOMP
YOU REALLY DID IT.
FLICK
PHOOOO.
HE'S YOUNGER THAN ME.
AND CHEEKY.
I'M NOT EVEN HIS TYPE.

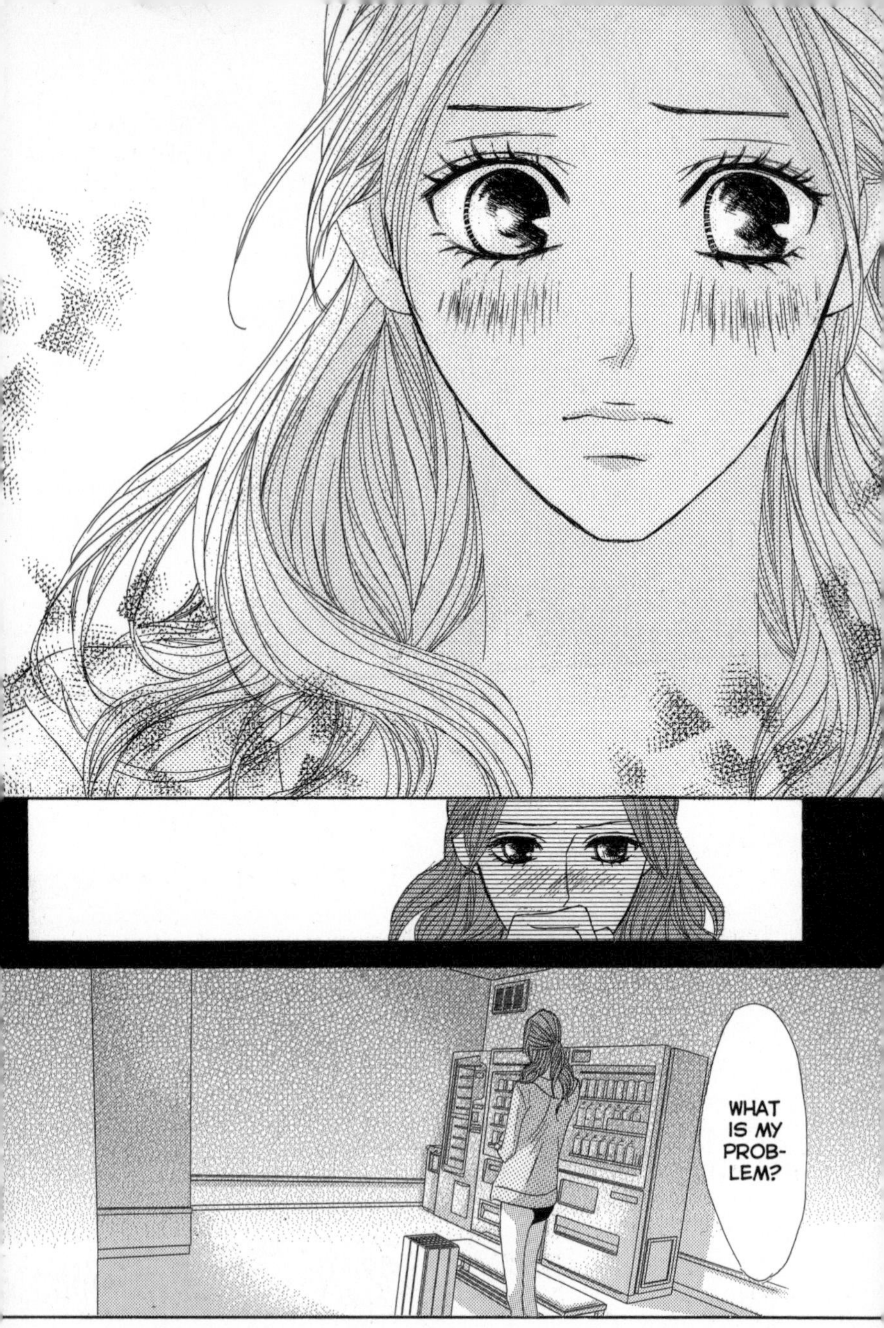
WHAT IS MY PROB-LEM?

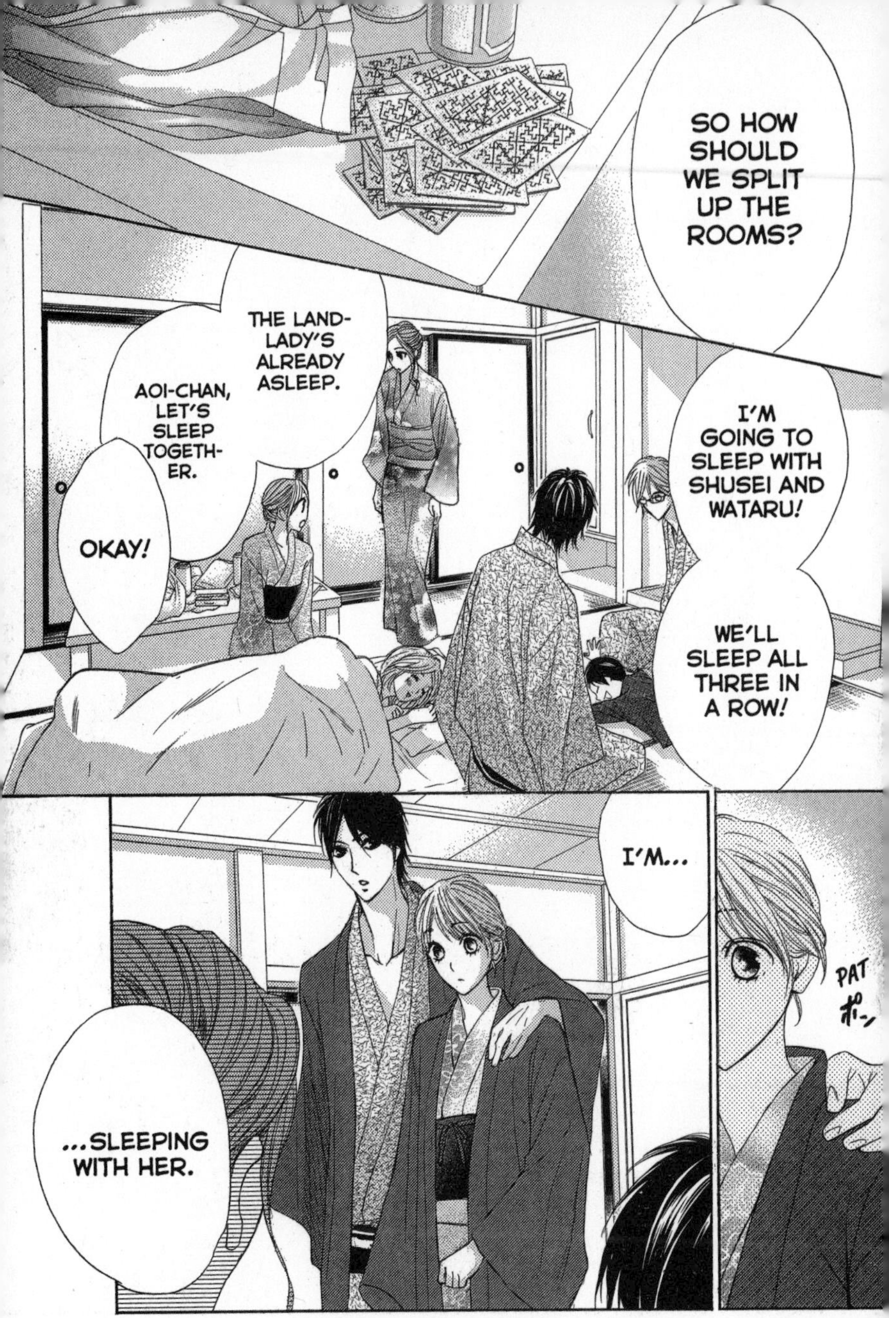
SO HOW SHOULD WE SPLIT UP THE ROOMS?
I'M GOING TO SLEEP WITH SHUSEI AND WATARU!
WE'LL SLEEP ALL THREE IN A ROW!
THE LAND-LADY'S ALREADY ASLEEP.
AOI-CHAN, LET'S SLEEP TOGETH-ER.
OKAY!
PAT
I'M...
...SLEEPING WITH HER.

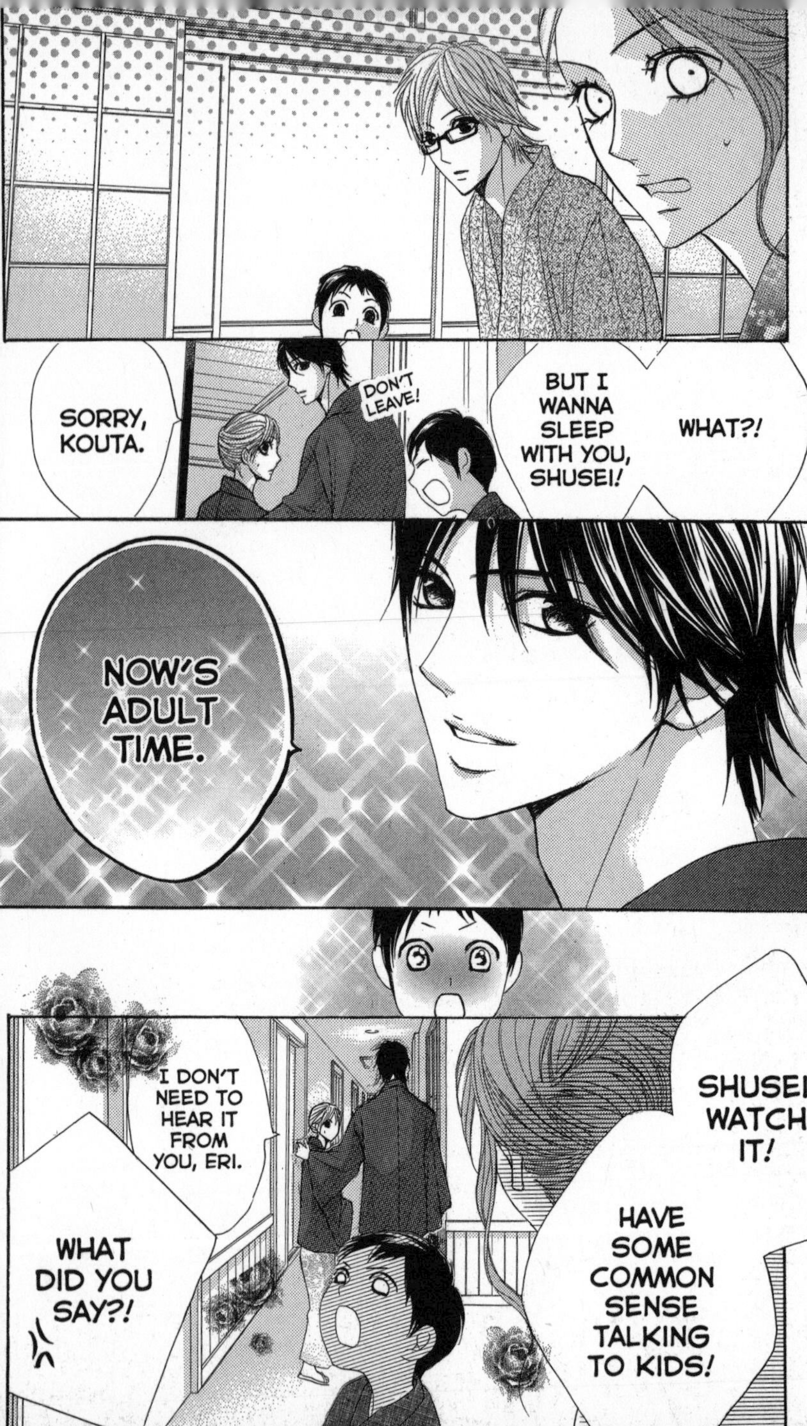
BUT I WANNA SLEEP WITH YOU, SHUSEI!
WHAT?!
DON'T LEAVE!
SORRY, KOUTA.
NOW'S ADULT TIME.
SHUSEI, WATCH IT!
HAVE SOME COMMON SENSE TALKING TO KIDS!
I DON'T NEED TO HEAR IT FROM YOU, ERI.
WHAT DID YOU SAY?!

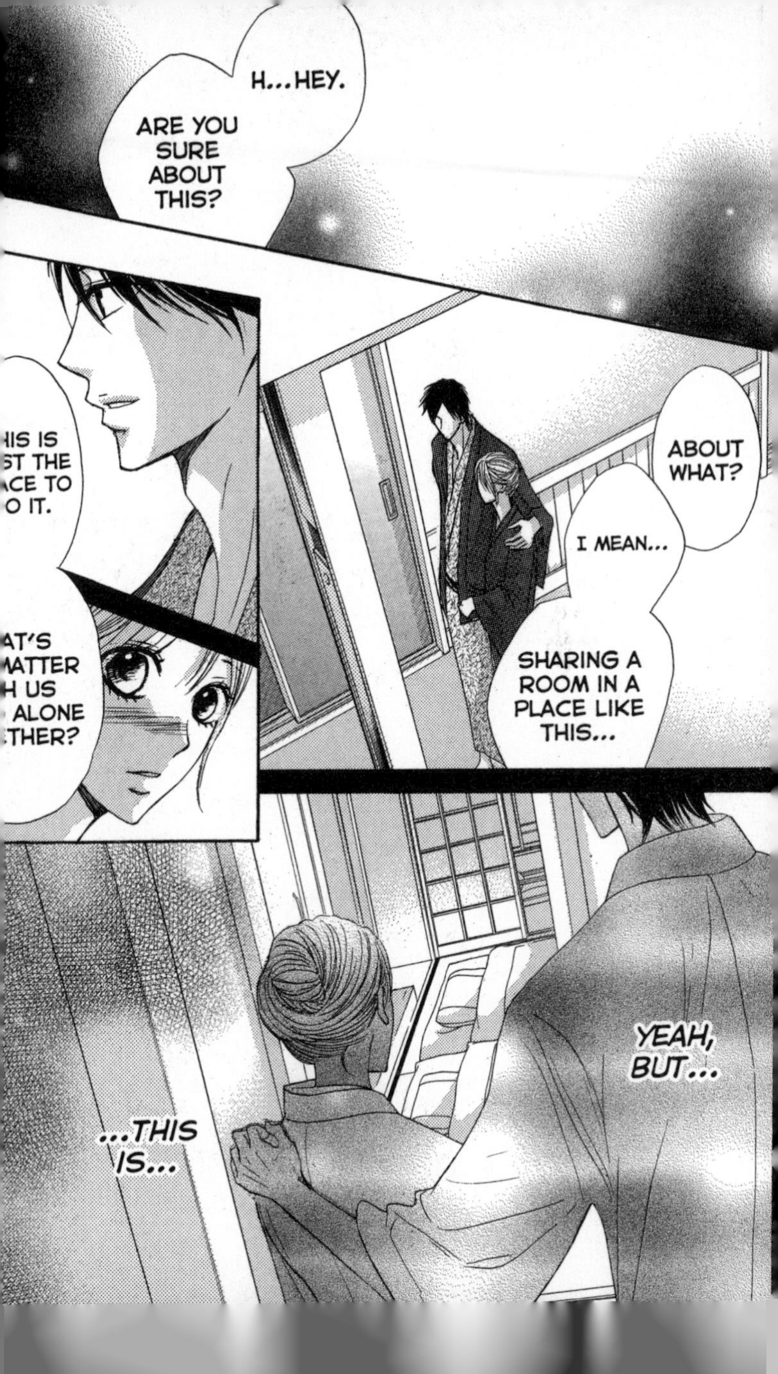
H...HEY.
ARE YOU SURE ABOUT THIS?
ABOUT WHAT?
I MEAN...
SHARING A ROOM IN A PLACE LIKE THIS...
HIS IS ST THE ACE TO O IT.
AT'S MATTER H US ALONE THER?
YEAH, BUT...
...THIS IS...

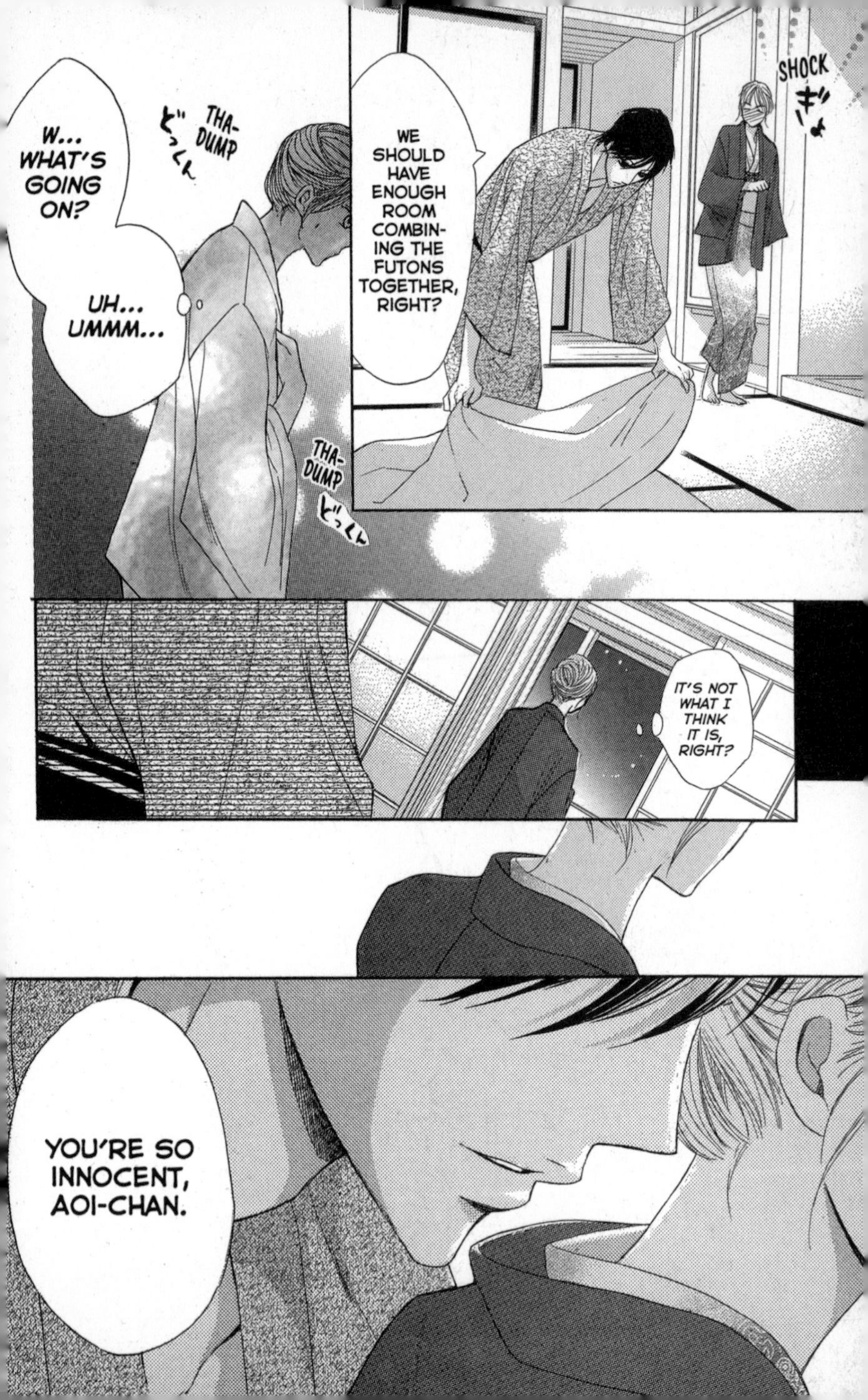
SHOCK
ギッ
WE SHOULD HAVE ENOUGH ROOM COMBINING THE FUTONS TOGETHER, RIGHT?
THA-DUMP
どっくん
W... WHAT'S GOING ON?
UH... UMMM...
THA-DUMP
どっくん
IT'S NOT WHAT I THINK IT IS, RIGHT?
YOU'RE SO INNOCENT, AOI-CHAN.

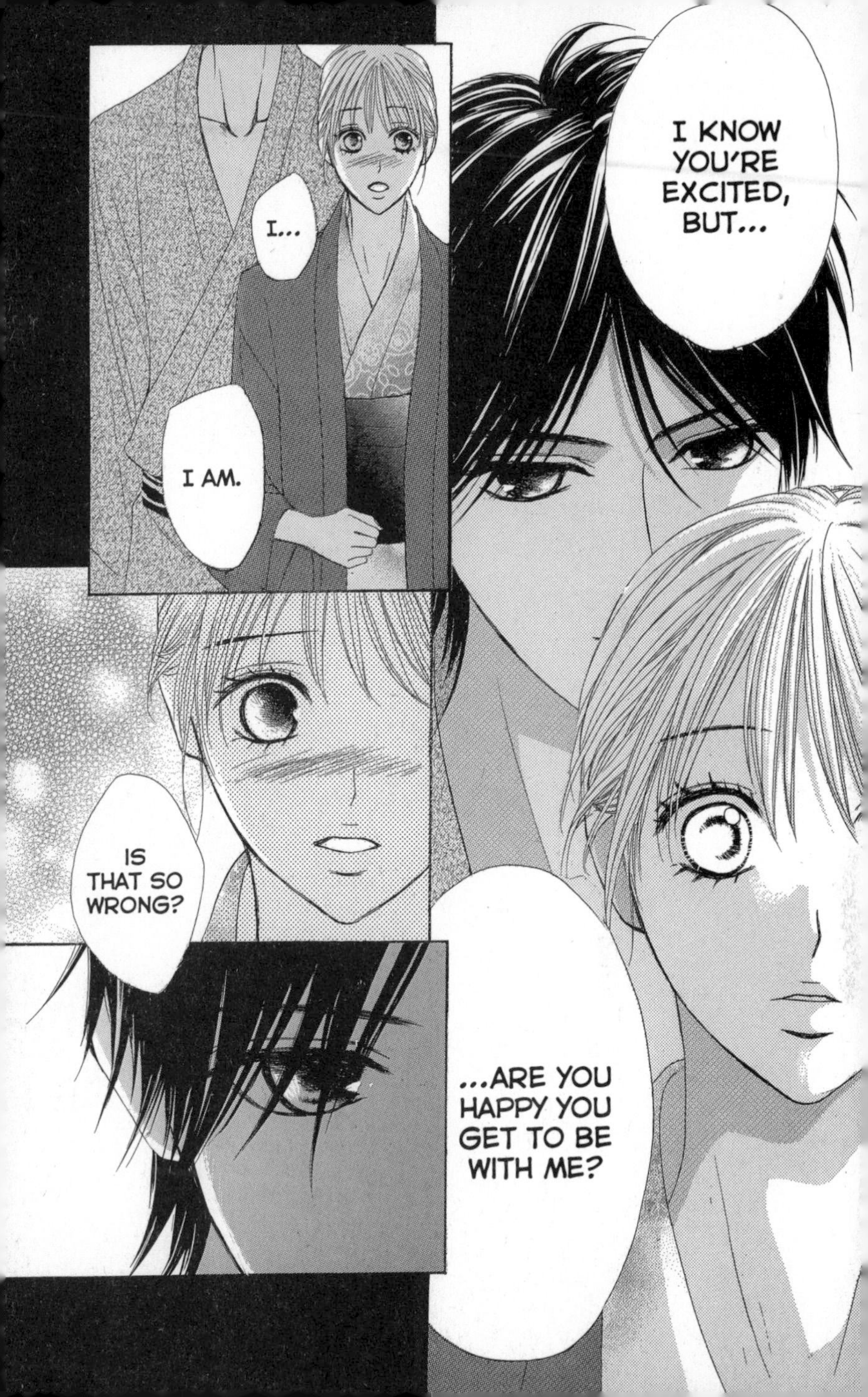
I KNOW YOU'RE EXCITED, BUT...
...ARE YOU HAPPY YOU GET TO BE WITH ME?
I...
I AM.
IS THAT SO WRONG?

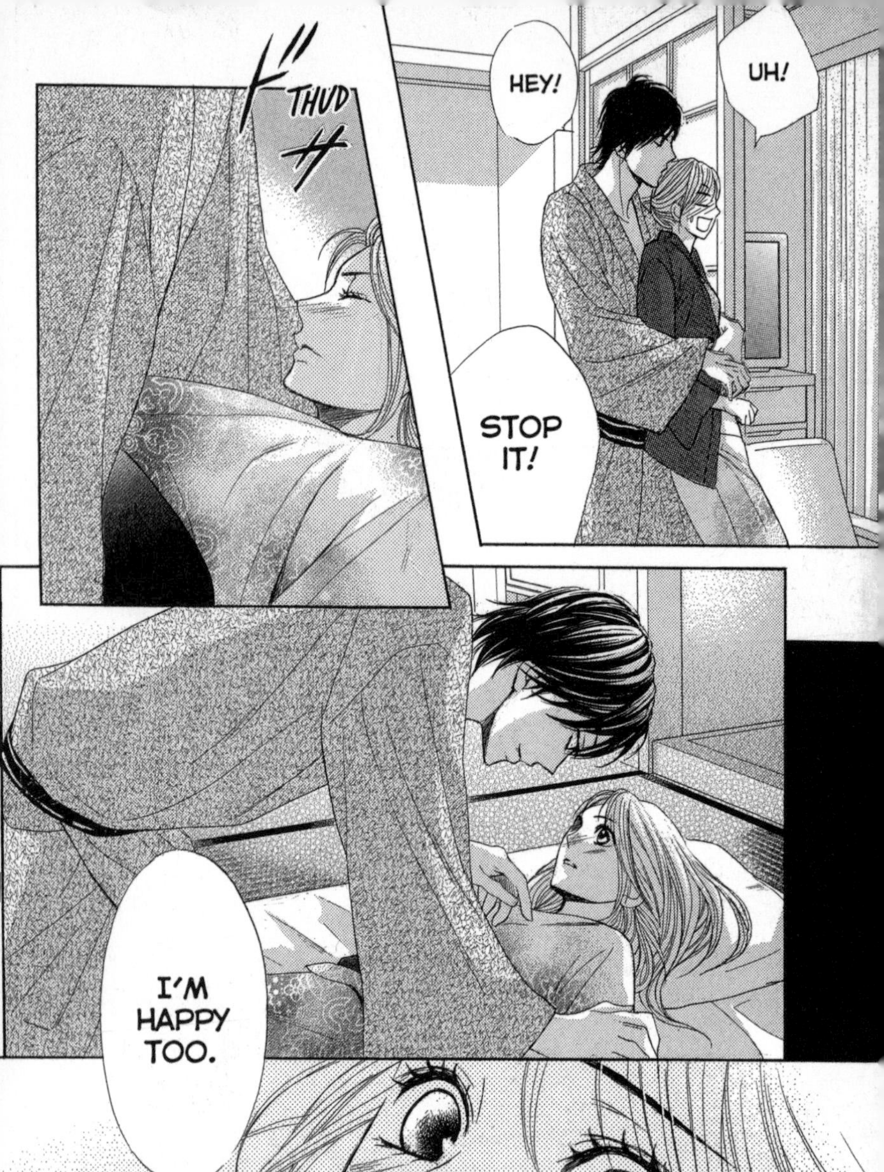
UH!
HEY!
STOP IT!
THUD
I'M HAPPY TOO.

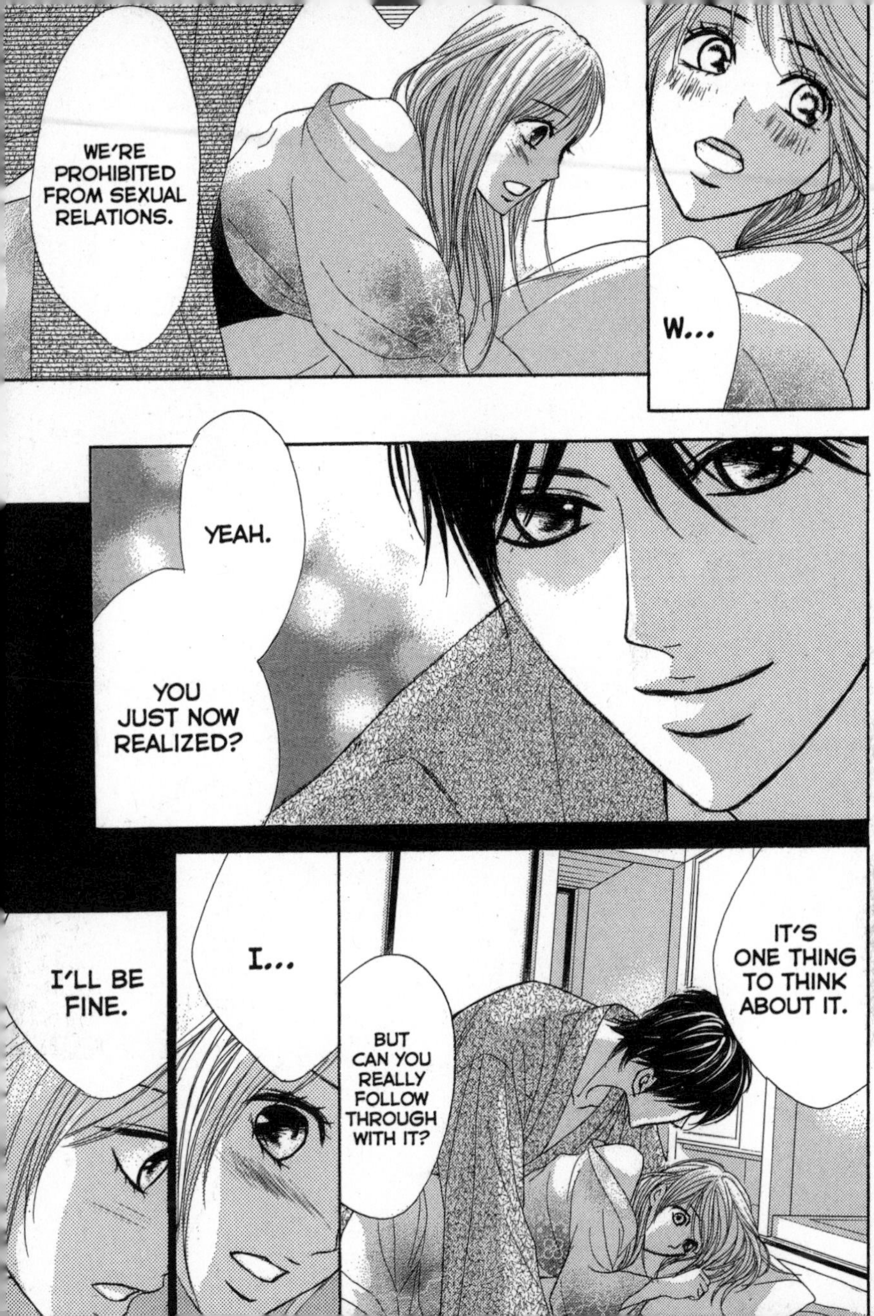
W...
WE'RE PROHIBITED FROM SEXUAL RELATIONS.
YEAH.
YOU JUST NOW REALIZED?
IT'S ONE THING TO THINK ABOUT IT.
BUT CAN YOU REALLY FOLLOW THROUGH WITH IT?
I...
I'LL BE FINE.

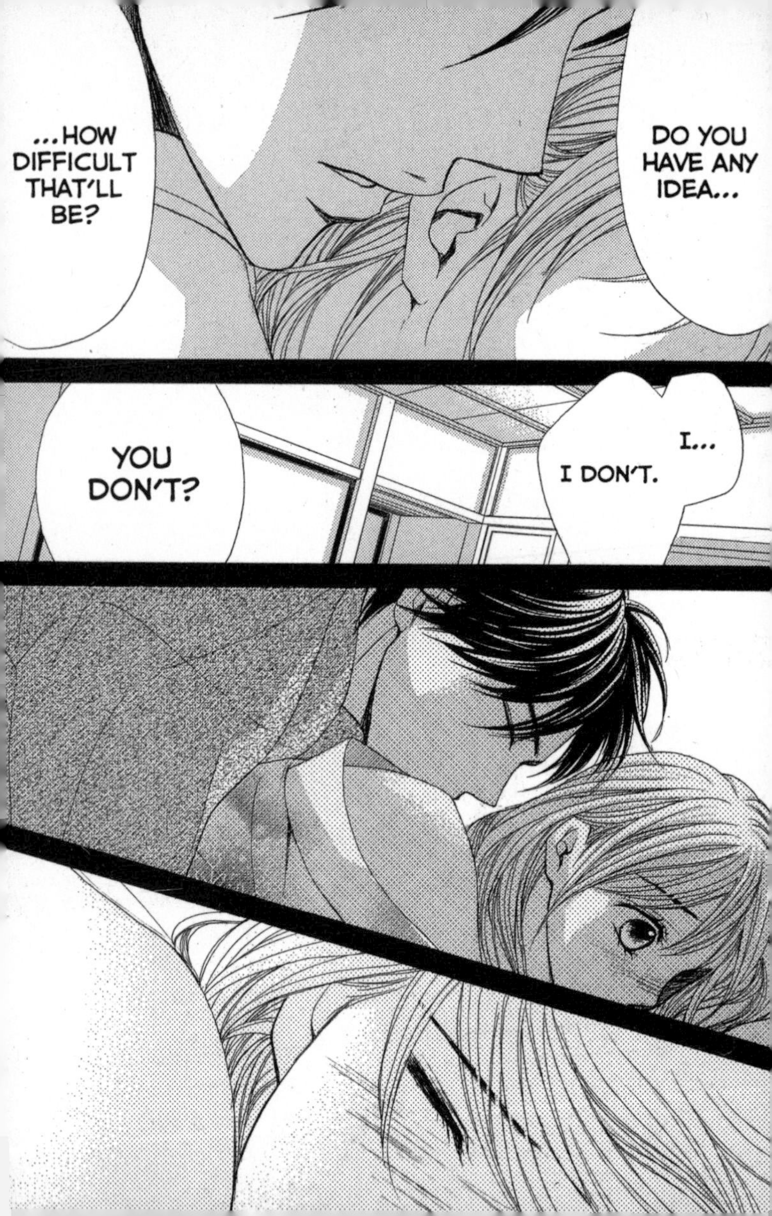
DO YOU HAVE ANY IDEA...
...HOW DIFFICULT THAT'LL BE?
I...
I DON'T.
YOU DON'T?

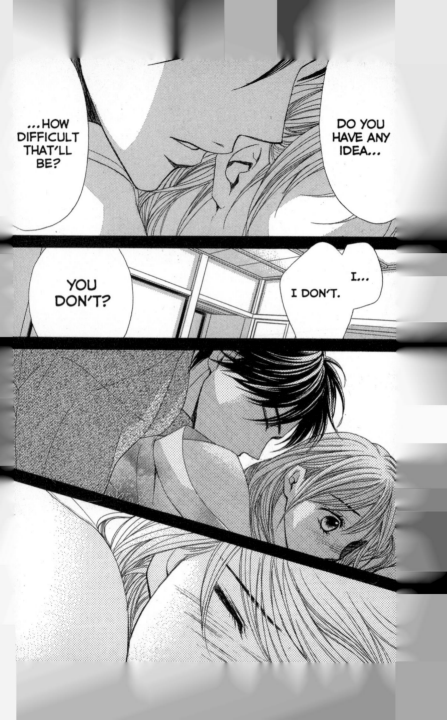

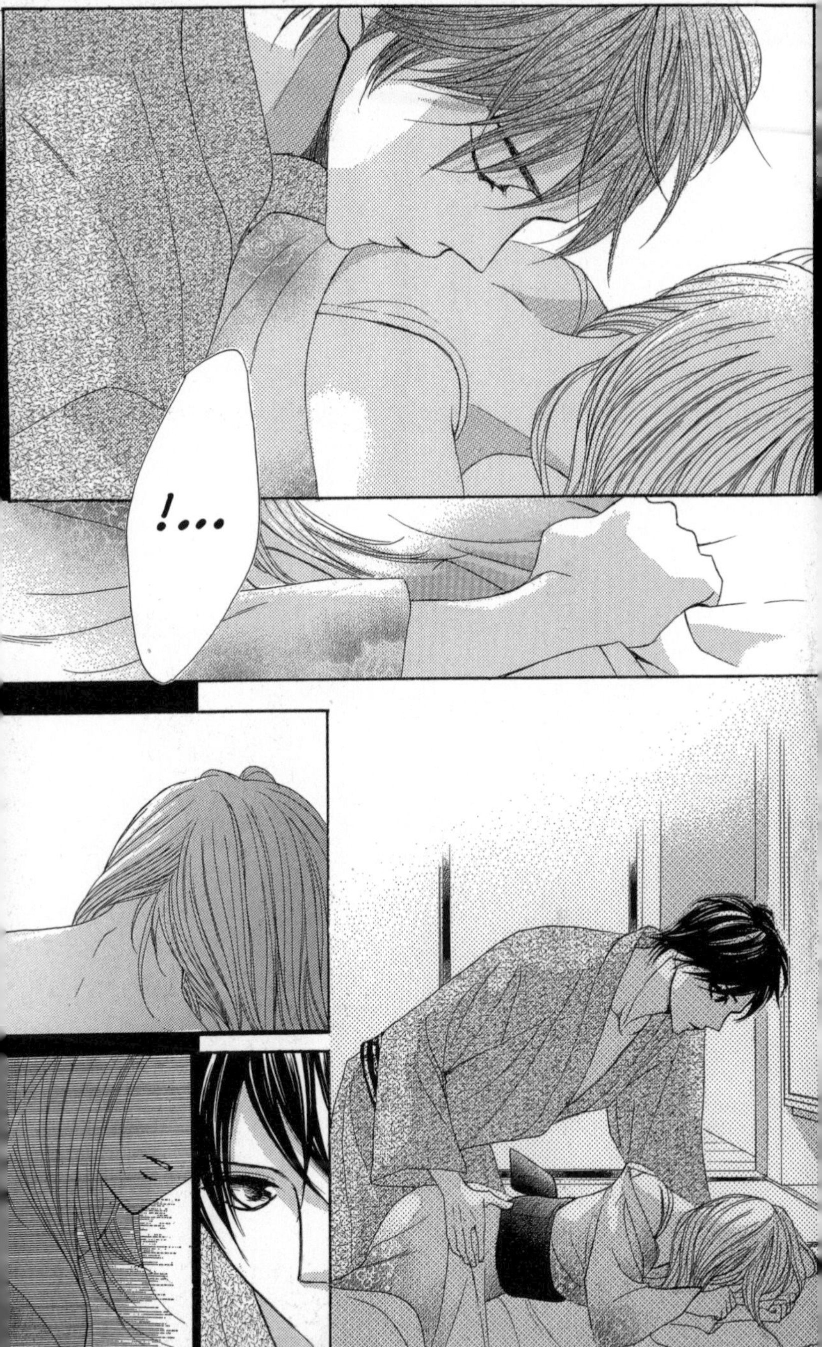
!...

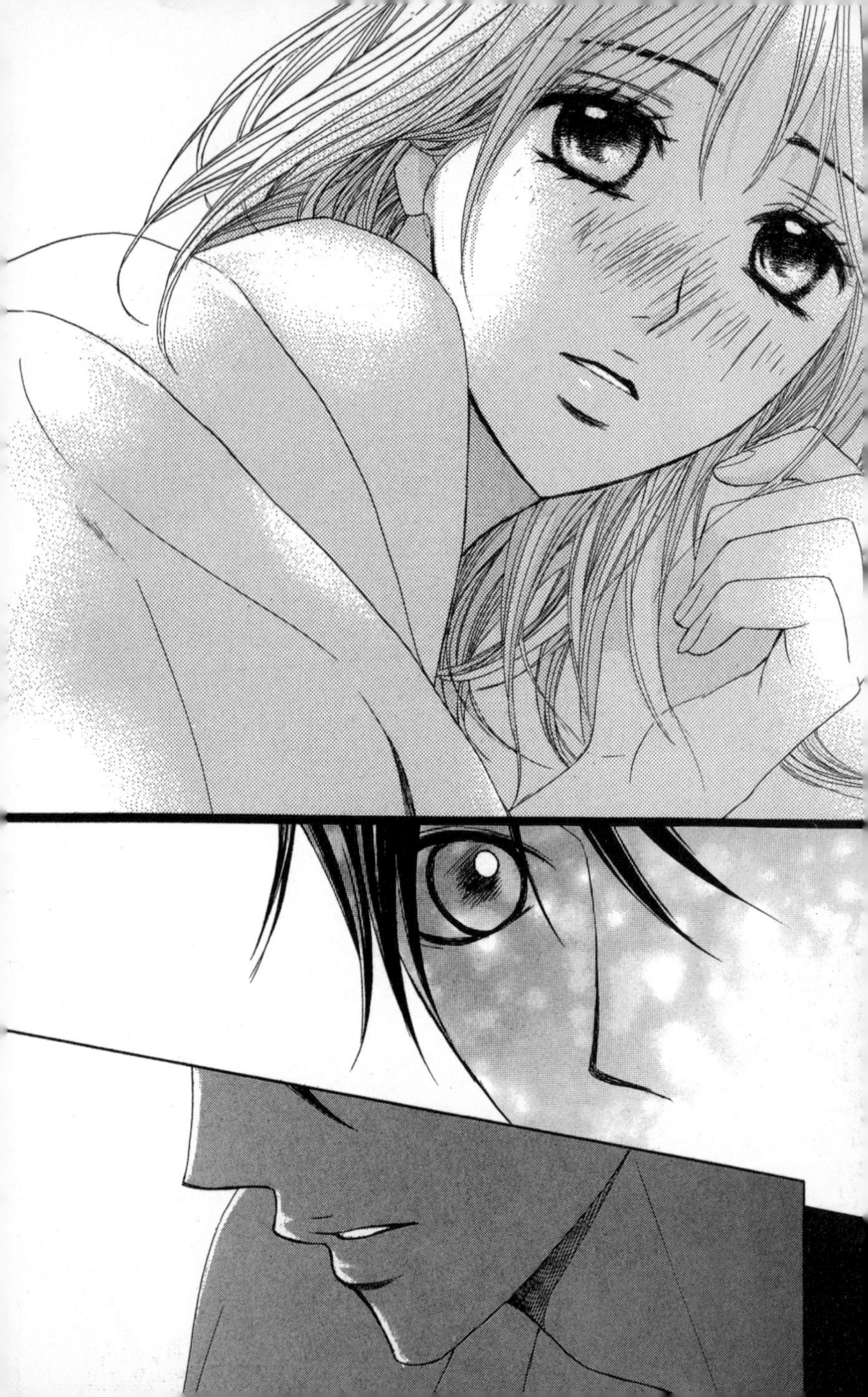

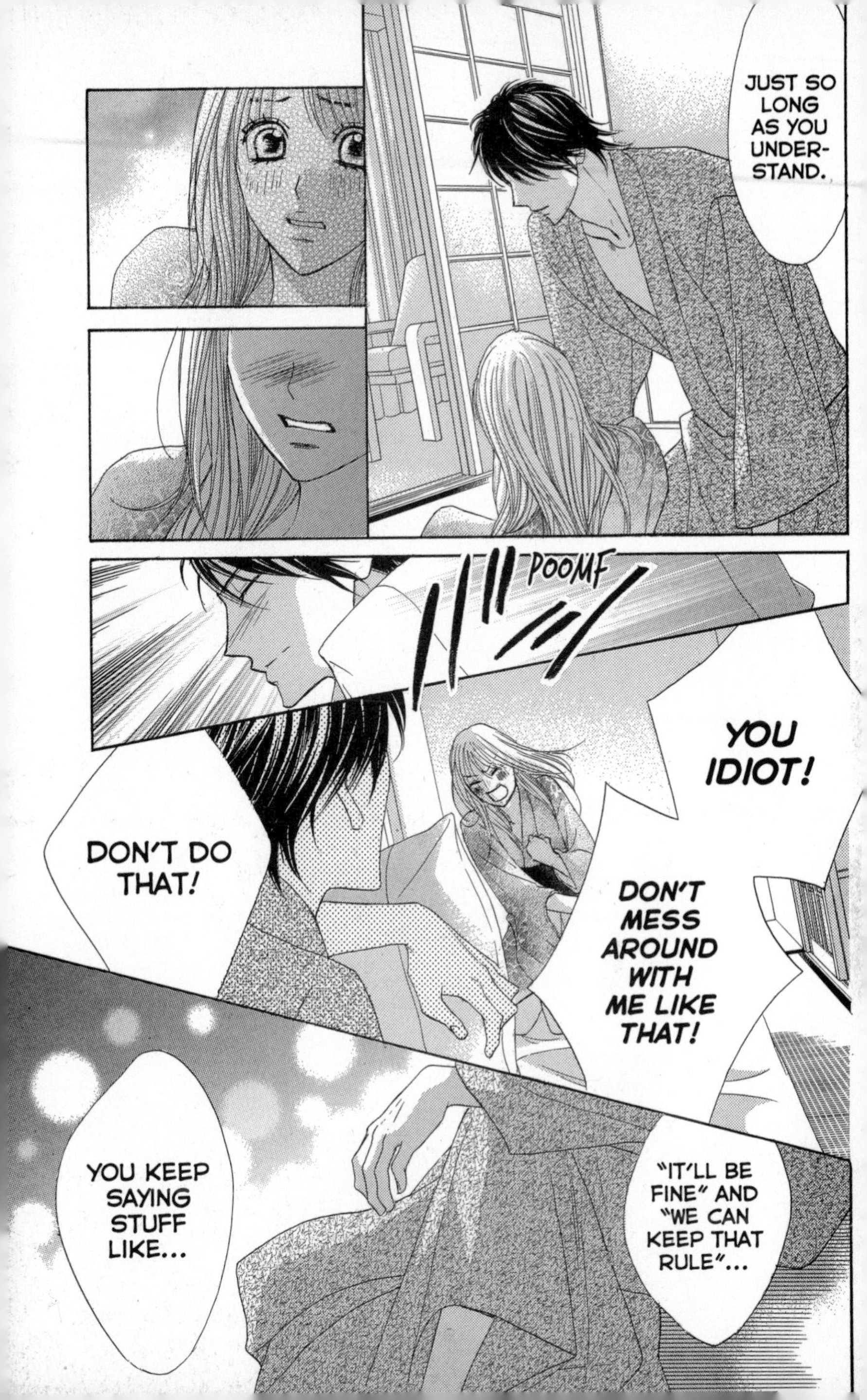
JUST SO LONG AS YOU UNDERSTAND.
POOMF
YOU IDIOT!
DON'T MESS AROUND WITH ME LIKE THAT!
DON'T DO THAT!
"IT'LL BE FINE" AND "WE CAN KEEP THAT RULE"...
YOU KEEP SAYING STUFF LIKE...

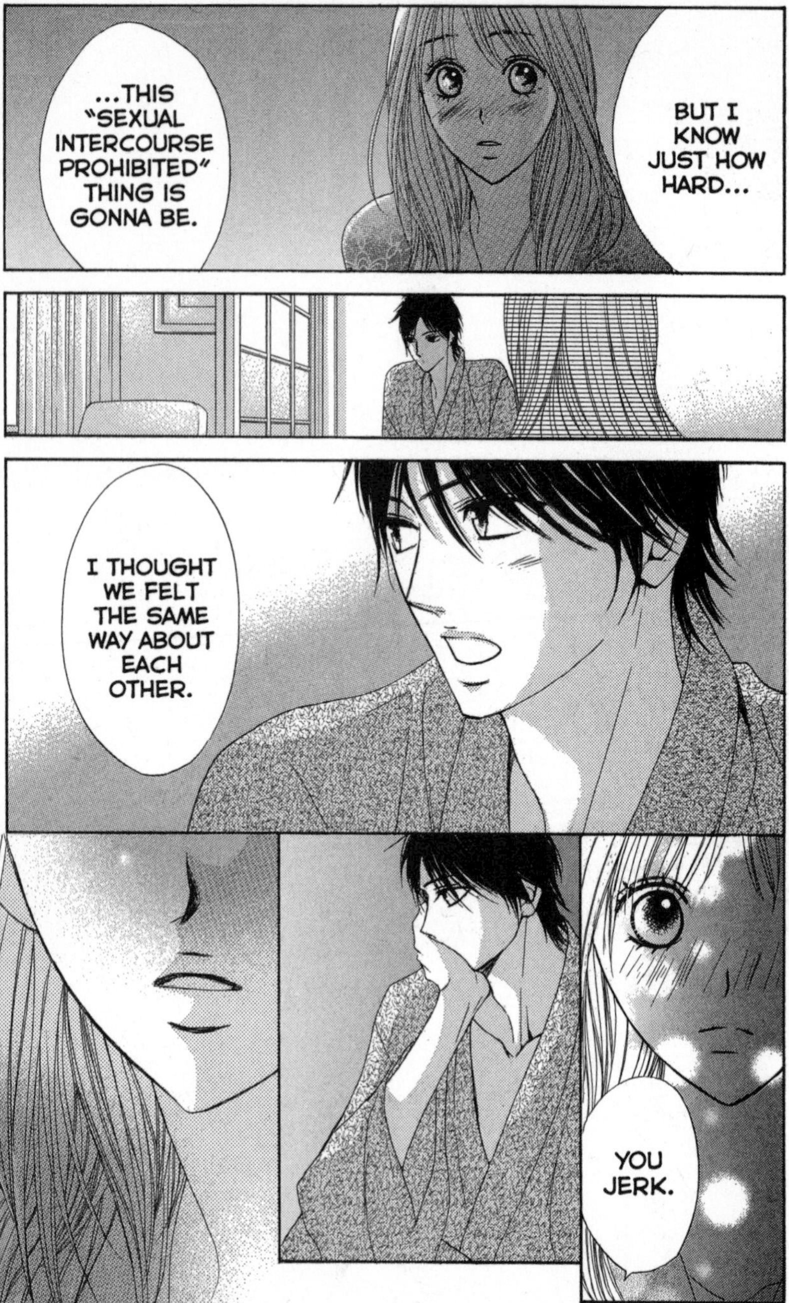
BUT I KNOW JUST HOW HARD...
...THIS "SEXUAL INTERCOURSE PROHIBITED" THING IS GONNA BE.
I THOUGHT WE FELT THE SAME WAY ABOUT EACH OTHER.
YOU JERK.

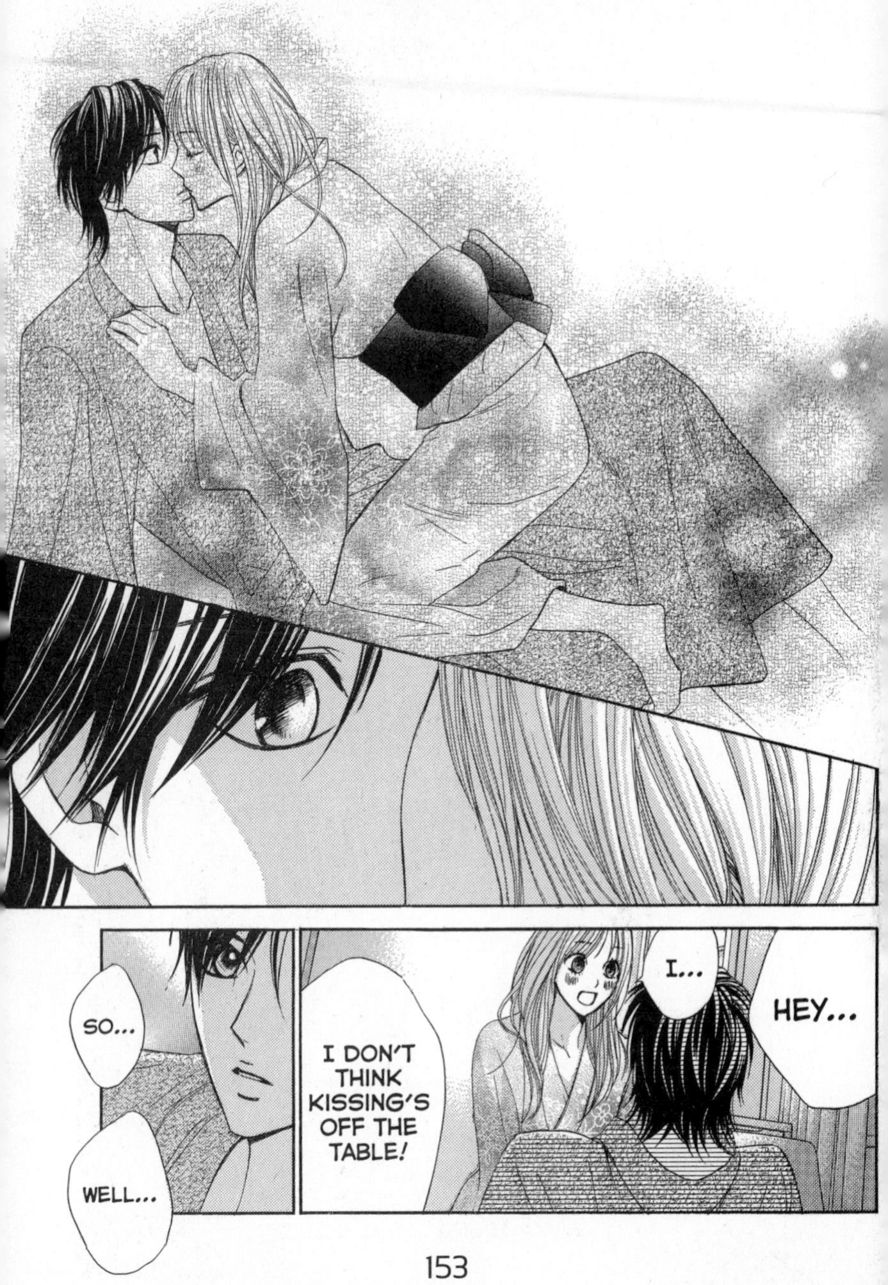
HEY...
I...
I DON'T THINK KISSING'S OFF THE TABLE!
SO...
WELL...

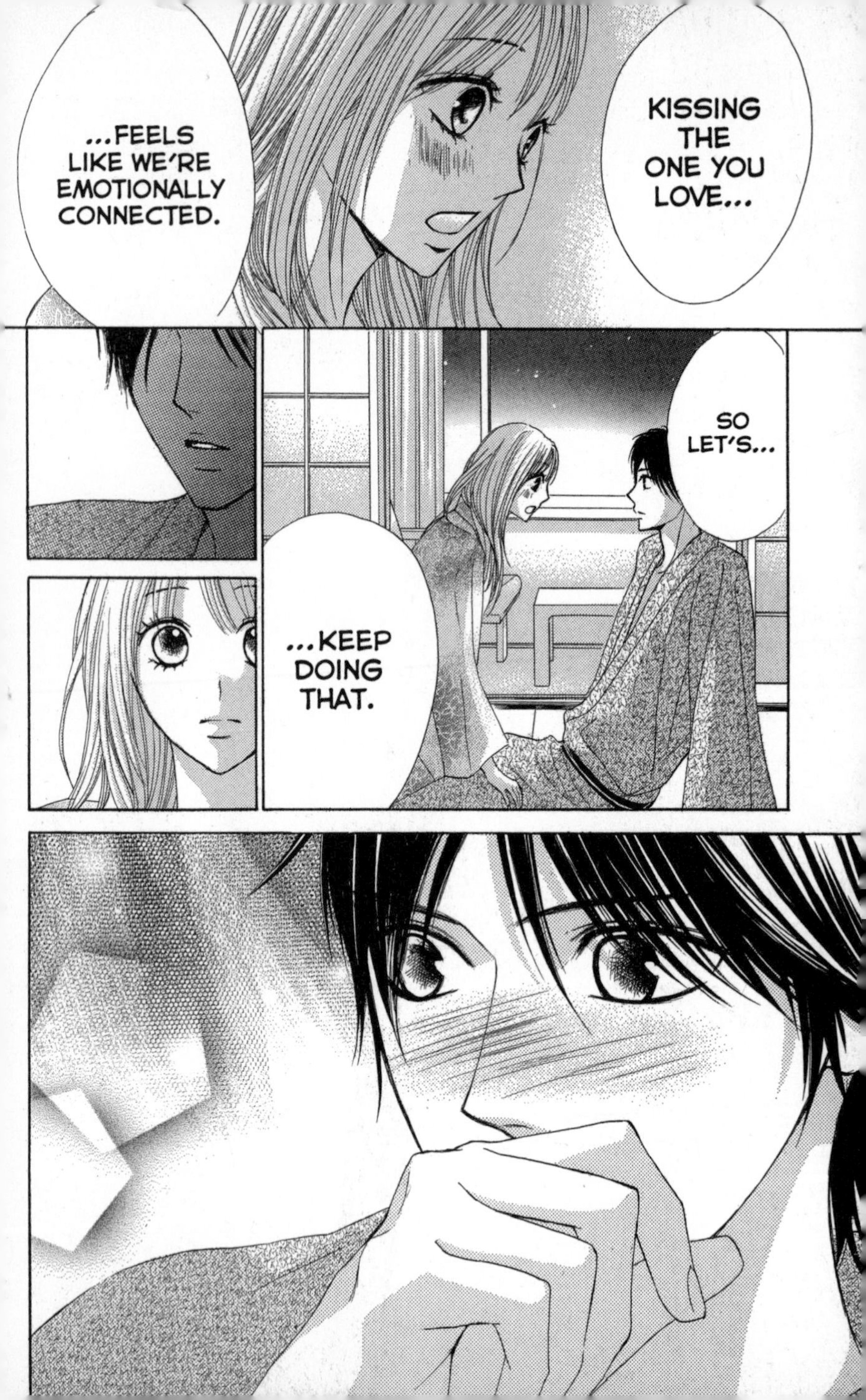
KISSING THE ONE YOU LOVE...
...FEELS LIKE WE'RE EMOTIONALLY CONNECTED.
SO LET'S...
...KEEP DOING THAT.

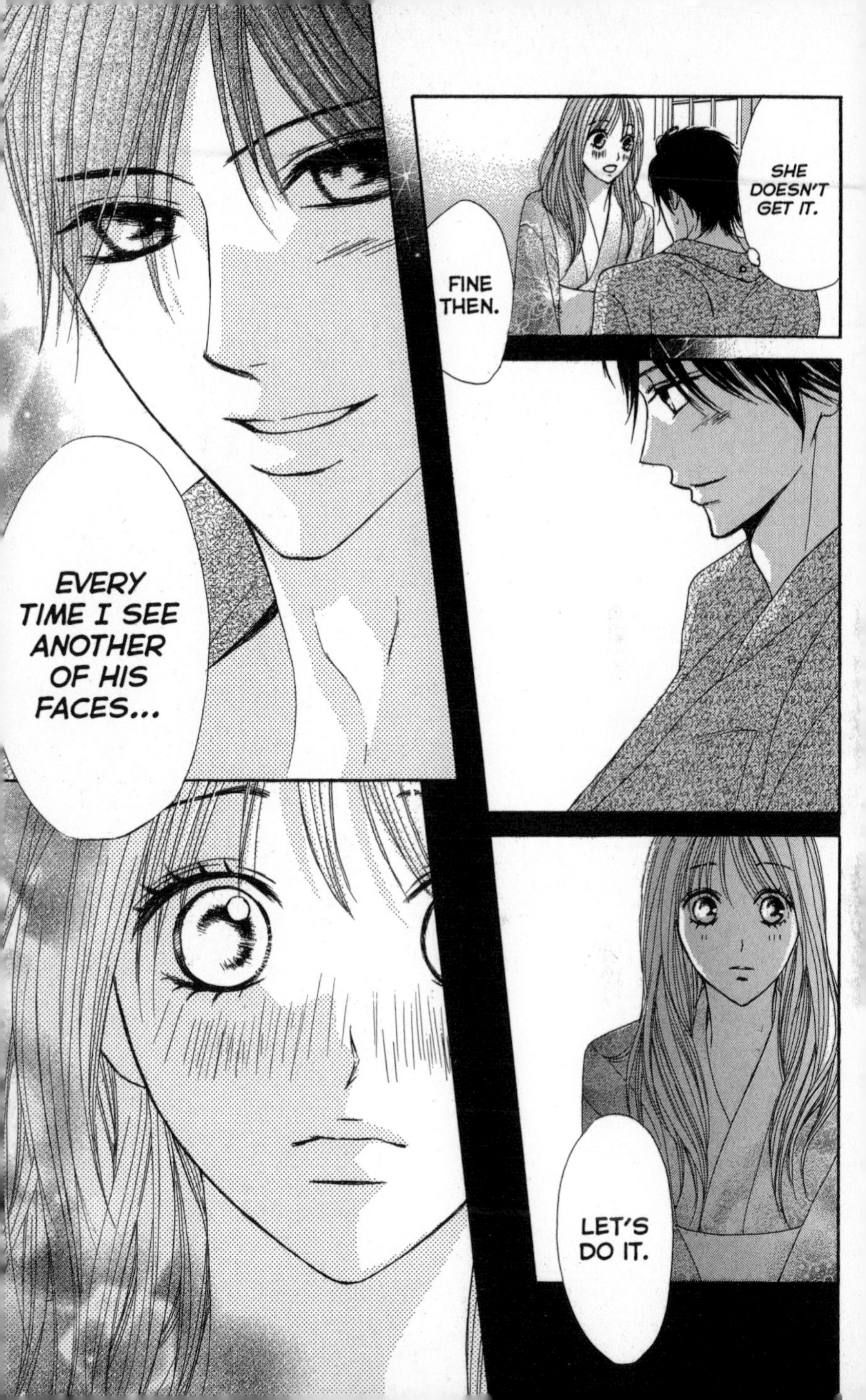
SHE DOESN'T GET IT.
FINE THEN.
LET'S DO IT.
EVERY TIME I SEE ANOTHER OF HIS FACES...

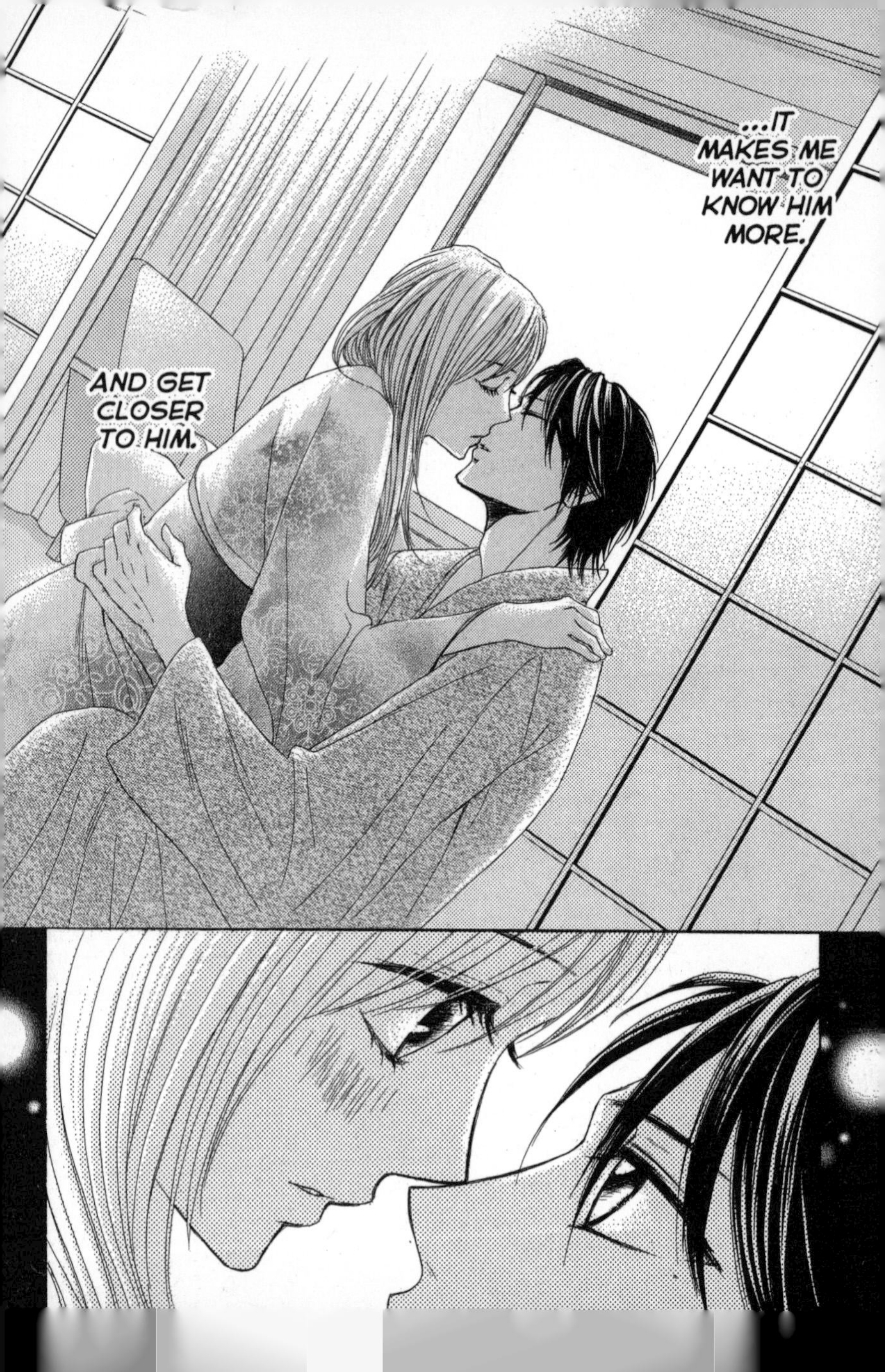
...IT MAKES ME WANT TO KNOW HIM MORE.
AND GET CLOSER TO HIM.

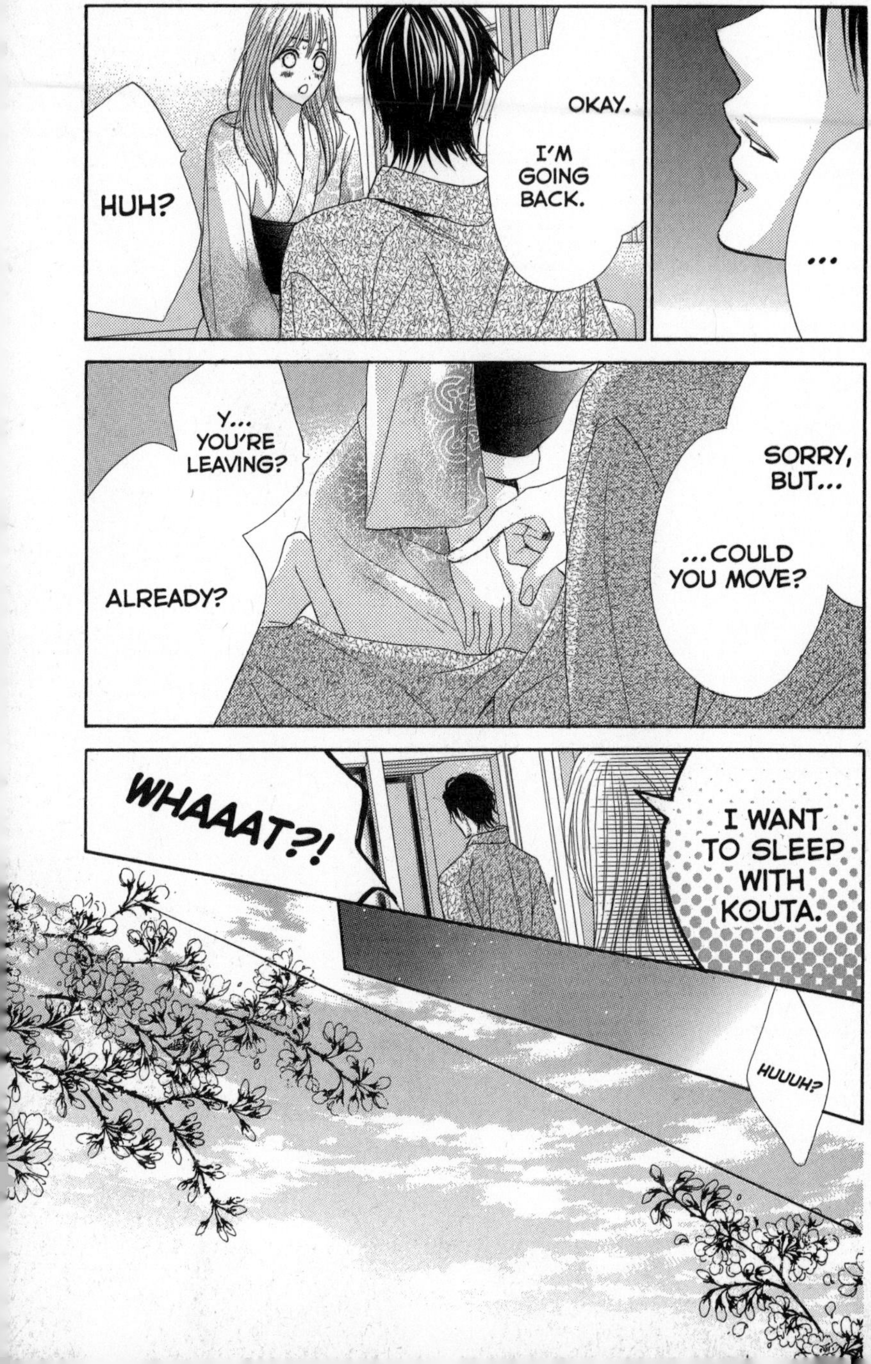
...
OKAY.
I'M GOING BACK.
HUH?
SORRY, BUT...
...COULD YOU MOVE?
Y... YOU'RE LEAVING?
ALREADY?
I WANT TO SLEEP WITH KOUTA.
WHAAAT?!
HUUUH?

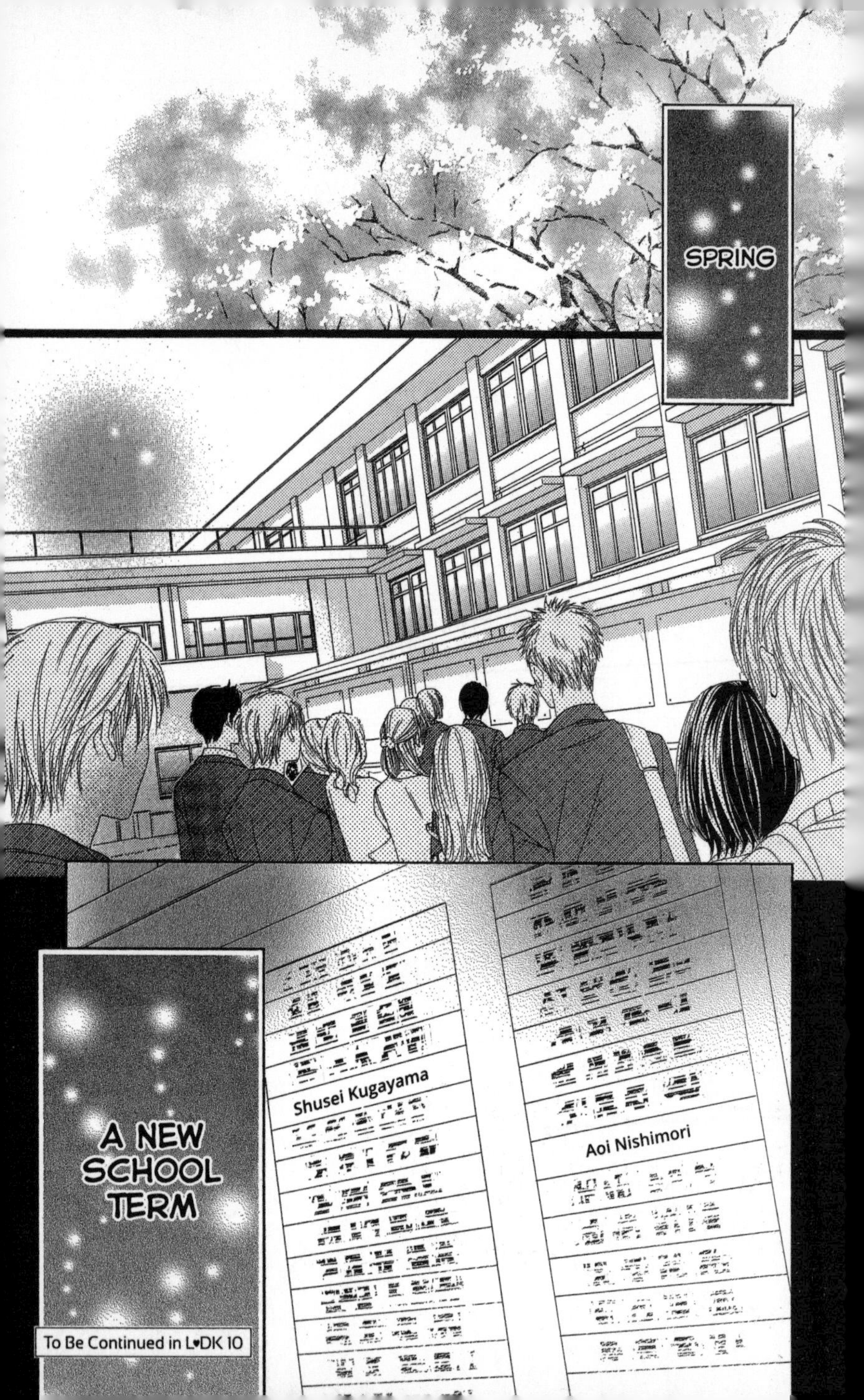
SPRING
Aoi Nishimori
Shusei Kugayama
A NEW SCHOOL TERM
To Be Continued in L♥DK 10

L♥DK

� Hello, everyone! Thank you very much for picking up Volume 9 of "L♡DK"! This is Ayu Watanabe. I say this every time, but it's really the encouraging voices of all of you that help me get through the month. I'm sorry I haven't been able to reply to all your fan letters. But I read them over with a happy grin on my face, and they're a source of energy for me when I'm feeing tired. Some people even include photo stickers of themselves, and their cuteness makes my heart squeeze swell. I can hardly take it. When I write, I tend to sound so old-fashioned, so please forgive that quirk of mine.

✶ Here we are in the middle of March, and I'm fighting a daily battle against allergies. How are all of you guys taking it?? I used to not have any symptoms, but somewhere along the way I developed a very severe reaction to pollen which I have to suffer with to this day. It sucks. My face itches and I can't stop sneezing!! It's especially difficult when working on storyboards. If I'm not careful with my medicine dosage, I also get suuuper sleepy, which only causes more stress for me. As my small attempt at fighting off all this irritation, I've developed a sneeze that would rival any old geezer's. And it really does make me feel better.

✿ Aaanyway. Ignoring Shusei's arm strength, it's actually the title of "L♡DK" that has been the topic of much discussion. I think I'd like to take this moment to discuss the origin story of the title. When coming up with a title for a book, the creator and editor put forth their own proposals for titles and have to discuss it with the editorial department before finally coming to a decision.

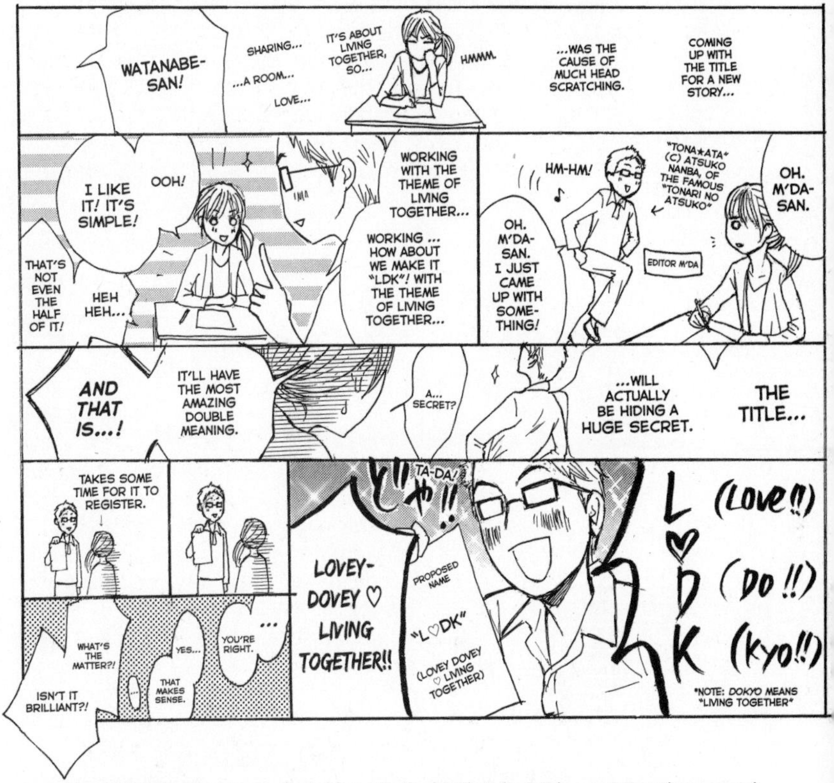
COMING UP WITH THE TITLE FOR A NEW STORY...
...WAS THE CAUSE OF MUCH HEAD SCRATCHING.
HMMM.
IT'S ABOUT LIVING TOGETHER, SO...
SHARING...
...A ROOM...
LOVE...
WATANABE-SAN!
OH. M'DA-SAN.
"TONA★ATA" (C) ATSUKO NANBA, OF THE FAMOUS "TONARI NO ATSUKO"
HM-HM!
EDITOR M'DA
OH. M'DA-SAN. I JUST CAME UP WITH SOMETHING!
WORKING WITH THE THEME OF LIVING TOGETHER...
WORKING ... HOW ABOUT WE MAKE IT "LDK"! WITH THE THEME OF LIVING TOGETHER...
OOH!
I LIKE IT! IT'S SIMPLE!
HEH HEH...
THAT'S NOT EVEN THE HALF OF IT!
THE TITLE...
...WILL ACTUALLY BE HIDING A HUGE SECRET.
A... SECRET?
IT'LL HAVE THE MOST AMAZING DOUBLE MEANING.
AND THAT IS...!
L (Love!!) ♡ D (Do!!) K (kyo!!)
*NOTE: DOKYO MEANS "LIVING TOGETHER"
TA-DA!
どや!!
PROPOSED NAME
"L♡DK"
(LOVEY DOVEY ♡ LIVING TOGETHER)
LOVEY-DOVEY ♡ LIVING TOGETHER!!
TAKES SOME TIME FOR IT TO REGISTER.
...
YOU'RE RIGHT.
YES...
THAT MAKES SENSE.
WHAT'S THE MATTER?!
ISN'T IT BRILLIANT?!

Now I totally approve of and love it. (heh) Thanks M'da-san! For the record, some other runners up we had were "Lovey Dovey Wivving Togever!", "The Last Boy in School", "Little Donkey Kong" (I still don't know why), and others. If there's anyone out there who fits this LDK description, please let me know!!

← On the next page is an On-Site Recording Report that was specially put together to come along with the drama CD that was released in January. I hope to see you again in the next volume! ♥♥

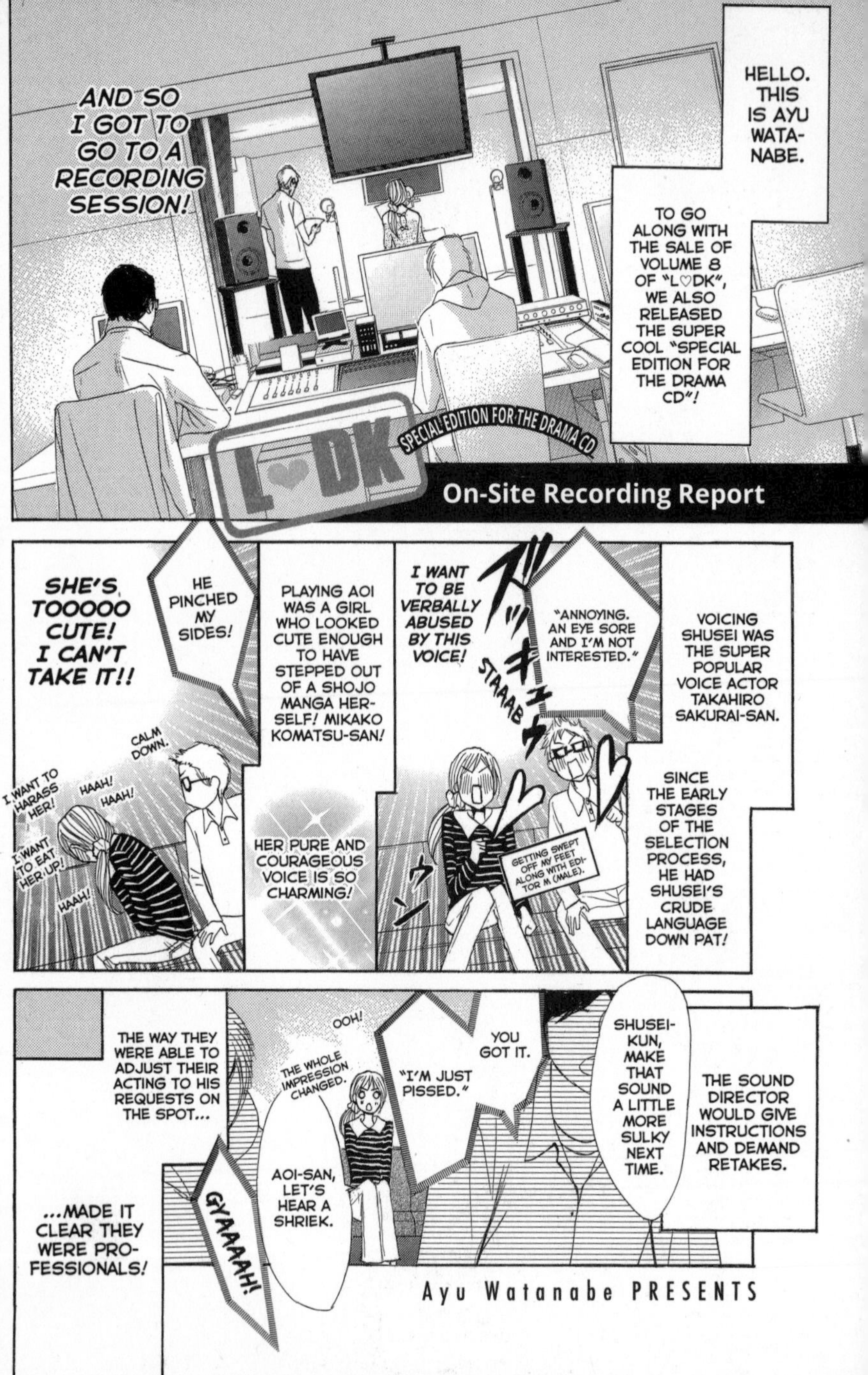
HELLO. THIS IS AYU WATANABE.
TO GO ALONG WITH THE SALE OF VOLUME 8 OF "L♡DK", WE ALSO RELEASED THE SUPER COOL "SPECIAL EDITION FOR THE DRAMA CD"!
AND SO I GOT TO GO TO A RECORDING SESSION!
L♡DK
SPECIAL EDITION FOR THE DRAMA CD
On-Site Recording Report
VOICING SHUSEI WAS THE SUPER POPULAR VOICE ACTOR TAKAHIRO SAKURAI-SAN.
SINCE THE EARLY STAGES OF THE SELECTION PROCESS, HE HAD SHUSEI'S CRUDE LANGUAGE DOWN PAT!
"ANNOYING. AN EYE SORE AND I'M NOT INTERESTED."
STAAAB
I WANT TO BE VERBALLY ABUSED BY THIS VOICE!
GETTING SWEPT OFF MY FEET ALONG WITH EDITOR M (MALE).
PLAYING AOI WAS A GIRL WHO LOOKED CUTE ENOUGH TO HAVE STEPPED OUT OF A SHOJO MANGA HERSELF! MIKAKO KOMATSU-SAN!
HER PURE AND COURAGEOUS VOICE IS SO CHARMING!
HE PINCHED MY SIDES!
SHE'S TOOOOO CUTE! I CAN'T TAKE IT!!
CALM DOWN.
HAAH! HAAH!
I WANT TO HARASS HER!
I WANT TO EAT HER UP!
HAAH!
THE SOUND DIRECTOR WOULD GIVE INSTRUCTIONS AND DEMAND RETAKES.
SHUSEI-KUN, MAKE THAT SOUND A LITTLE MORE SULKY NEXT TIME.
YOU GOT IT.
"I'M JUST PISSED."
OOH!
THE WHOLE IMPRESSION CHANGED.
AOI-SAN, LET'S HEAR A SHRIEK.
GYAAAAH!
THE WAY THEY WERE ABLE TO ADJUST THEIR ACTING TO HIS REQUESTS ON THE SPOT...
...MADE IT CLEAR THEY WERE PROFESSIONALS!
Ayu Watanabe PRESENTS

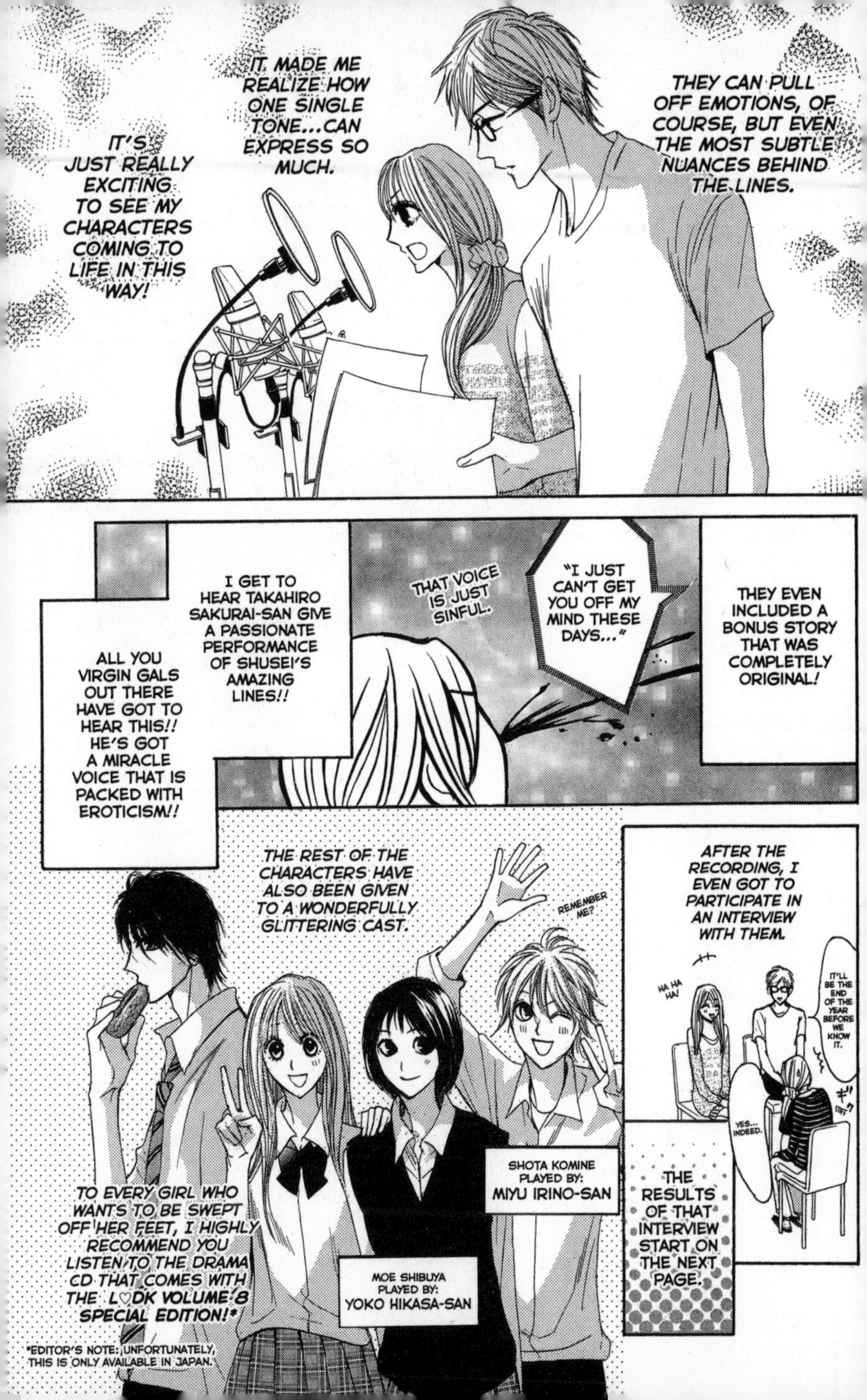

THEY CAN PULL OFF EMOTIONS, OF COURSE, BUT EVEN THE MOST SUBTLE NUANCES BEHIND THE LINES.
IT MADE ME REALIZE HOW ONE SINGLE TONE...CAN EXPRESS SO MUCH.
IT'S JUST REALLY EXCITING TO SEE MY CHARACTERS COMING TO LIFE IN THIS WAY!
THEY EVEN INCLUDED A BONUS STORY THAT WAS COMPLETELY ORIGINAL!
"I JUST CAN'T GET YOU OFF MY MIND THESE DAYS..."
THAT VOICE IS JUST SINFUL.
I GET TO HEAR TAKAHIRO SAKURAI-SAN GIVE A PASSIONATE PERFORMANCE OF SHUSEI'S AMAZING LINES!!
ALL YOU VIRGIN GALS OUT THERE HAVE GOT TO HEAR THIS!! HE'S GOT A MIRACLE VOICE THAT IS PACKED WITH EROTICISM!!
AFTER THE RECORDING, I EVEN GOT TO PARTICIPATE IN AN INTERVIEW WITH THEM.
IT'LL BE THE END OF THE YEAR BEFORE WE KNOW IT.
HA HA HA!
YES... INDEED.
THE RESULTS OF THAT INTERVIEW START ON THE NEXT PAGE.
THE REST OF THE CHARACTERS HAVE ALSO BEEN GIVEN TO A WONDERFULLY GLITTERING CAST.
REMEMBER ME?
SHOTA KOMINE PLAYED BY: MIYU IRINO-SAN
MOE SHIBUYA PLAYED BY: YOKO HIKASA-SAN
TO EVERY GIRL WHO WANTS TO BE SWEPT OFF HER FEET, I HIGHLY RECOMMEND YOU LISTEN TO THE DRAMA CD THAT COMES WITH THE L♡DK VOLUME 8 SPECIAL EDITION!*
*EDITOR'S NOTE: UNFORTUNATELY, THIS IS ONLY AVAILABLE IN JAPAN.

Commemorating the sale of the special edition for the Drama CD! ♥

Mikako Komatsu who plays Aoi x Takahiro Sakurai who plays Shusei x Ayu Watanabe

Special Interview

The special edition for the drama CD which is currently selling like hot cakes. ☆ We got to hear from the two voice actors who put their beautiful voices to work and ask questions Watanabe-sensei's always dreamed of. ♪ Take a peek at the content we've packed in to the special edition that includes never-before-seen illustrations too!

He was conscious of how tall Shusei-kun is. ☆

Sakurai-san, please let me hear your impressions of playing Shusei.

Sakurai-san (referred to as Sakurai from hereafter): Since Shusei-kun isn't very forthcoming with his feelings, the drama CD sort of ends with his love staying in the gray zone the whole while. It leaves you wondering "how does he really feel?" which I made sure to keep in mind. On a related note, Shusei-kun's really tall, right?

Watanabe-sensei (referred to as Watanabe from hereafter): That's right, he's about 180 cm tall.

Sakurai: I wanted to make sure that his looming height really came through.

Watanabe: Wow! I'm impressed you incorporated that into your acting!

Sakurai: That kind of quality that really fleshes out the image of the character is very important to the performance of his part. I made sure to envision him in my head when recording the dialogue.

I never expected to be so emotionally confused!

What scene from the drama CD would you recommend?

Komatsu-san (referred to as Komatsu from hereafter): When Aoi-chan and Shusei-kun get handcuffed together by Kouta-kun and the two have to go out in public like that. Shusei-kun does nothing but torment her throughout it, but in the end he does rescue her from the other female high school students. For some reason, I felt just as emotionally confused as Aoi-chan did from it (LOL). But since I think a lot of girls will relate to those rare bouts of kindness, I hope they'll imagine themselves in Aoi-chan's shoes when they listen to it. ♪

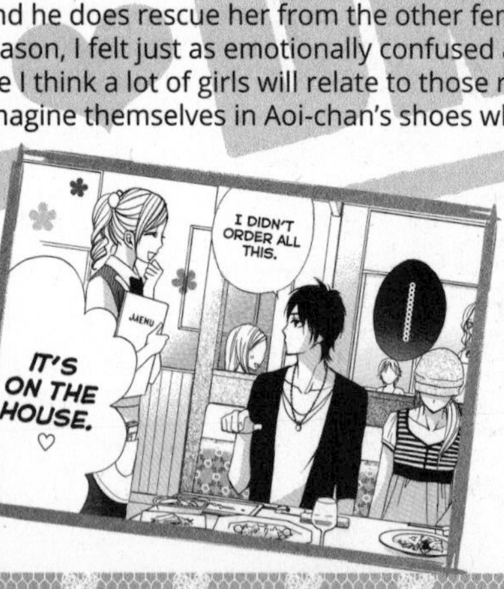
I DIDN'T ORDER ALL THIS.
IT'S ON THE HOUSE. ♡

It makes me want to be even meaner (LOL).

How did you enjoy the bonus side story that Watanabe-sensei wrote specifically for the special?

Sakurai: I'd have never expected the announcer from the psychic episode at the beginning would have that FM nuance to him, so it was a real shock!

OH, SHUSEI. YOU BIG BABY. ♡

Watanabe: It was really like a treat for voice actors, right? That was another of the finer points.
Komatsu: I want to see what happens after that episode. ☆
Sakurai: Aoi-chan's reaction when she's spooked is really adorable. It makes me want to tease her even more (LOL).

I see. So you mean that when that happens, it makes you want to be even meaner?
Sakurai: Yes. The two grow closer through that kind of teasing. And then he falls asleep (LOL).
Watanabe: It's just full of dreams!
Sakurai: Yes, full of dreams (LOL).
Watanabe: It's really packed full with that stuff, so I hope everyone can enjoy it. ♪

Falling hard for Shusei-kun's elegant voice. ♡

Lastly, we'd like to hear what Watanabe-sensei has to say as far as any particular points of interest regarding the CD.
Watanabe: They really did a marvelous job pacing the dialogue of these two characters. Aoi-chan's voice is really adorable and peppy and soulful, and I

Don't miss the exclusive features that come with the special edition!!

Two Big Items

fell hard for Shusei-kun's elegant voice when I heard it. So I hope everyone can also get a feel for the fun mood that the recording entails. And I hope everyone can enjoy the bonus story written just for it! Thank you very much!!

Ayu Watanabe's new drawing!! And a short story featuring Shusei's sweetly whispering voice!!

Two post cards with never-before-seen illustrations that you can only get here!!

BAM

PLEASE BE SURE TO RESTOCK THESE. ♡

渡辺あゆ

Retail Price: 1886 yen for the book itself (tax inc.)
* Please order it if it's not at your local bookstore.

special thanks

K.Hamano
N.Imai
S.Sato
Y.Negishi
I.Kozakura

my family
my friends

M.Morita
Y.Ikumi
A.Yamamoto

AND YOU

Ayu Watanabe
Mar.2012

Say I Love You.

KC KODANSHA COMICS

Mei Tachibana has no friends — and says she doesn't need them!

But everything changes when she accidentally roundhouse kicks the most popular boy in school! However, Yamato Kurosawa isn't angry in the slightest— in fact, he thinks his ordinary life could use an unusual girl like Mei. But winning Mei's trust will be a tough task. How long will she refuse to say, "I love you"?

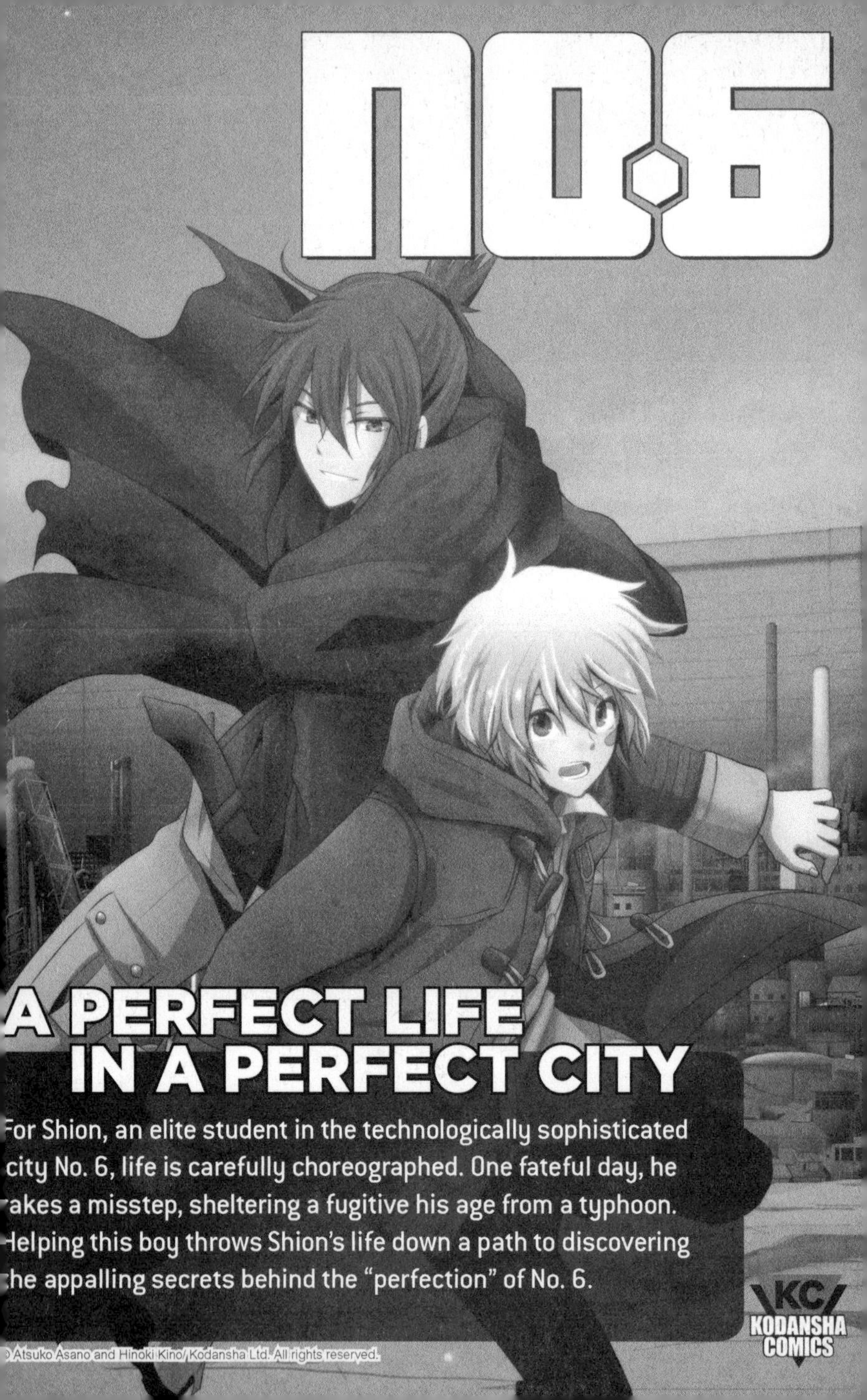
NO.6
A PERFECT LIFE IN A PERFECT CITY
For Shion, an elite student in the technologically sophisticated city No. 6, life is carefully choreographed. One fateful day, he takes a misstep, sheltering a fugitive his age from a typhoon. Helping this boy throws Shion's life down a path to discovering the appalling secrets behind the "perfection" of No. 6.
KC KODANSHA COMICS
© Atsuko Asano and Hinoki Kino/ Kodansha Ltd. All rights reserved.

My Little Monster

OPPOSITES ATTRACT...MAYBE?

Haru Yoshida is feared as an unstable and violent "monster." Mizutani Shizuku is a grade-obsessed student with no friends. Fate brings these two together to form the most unlikely pair. Haru firmly believes he's in love with Mizutani and she firmly believes

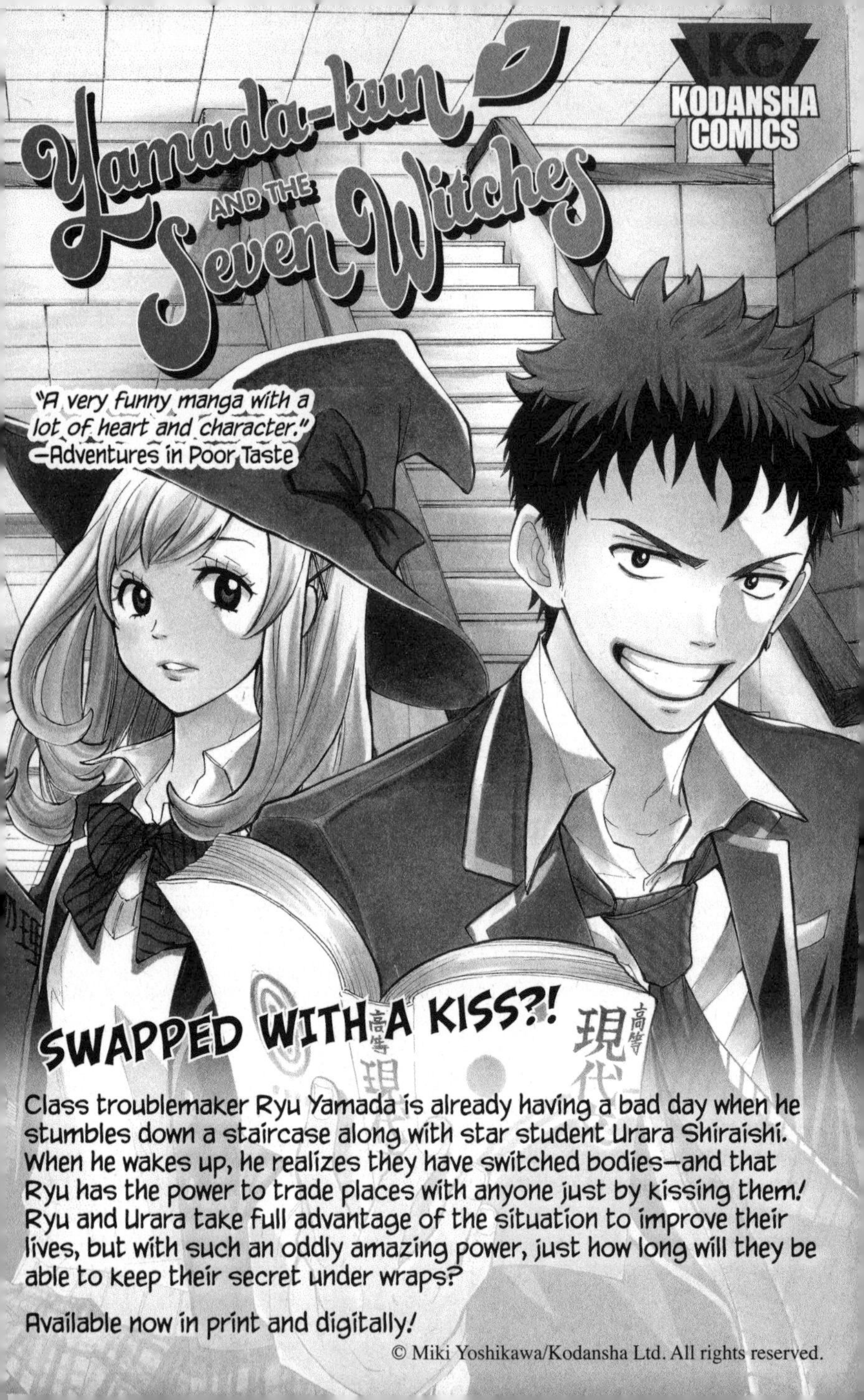
Yamada-kun AND THE Seven Witches
KODANSHA COMICS
"A very funny manga with a lot of heart and character." —Adventures in Poor Taste
SWAPPED WITH A KISS?!
Class troublemaker Ryu Yamada is already having a bad day when he stumbles down a staircase along with star student Urara Shiraishi. When he wakes up, he realizes they have switched bodies—and that Ryu has the power to trade places with anyone just by kissing them! Ryu and Urara take full advantage of the situation to improve their lives, but with such an oddly amazing power, just how long will they be able to keep their secret under wraps?
Available now in print and digitally!
© Miki Yoshikawa/Kodansha Ltd. All rights reserved.

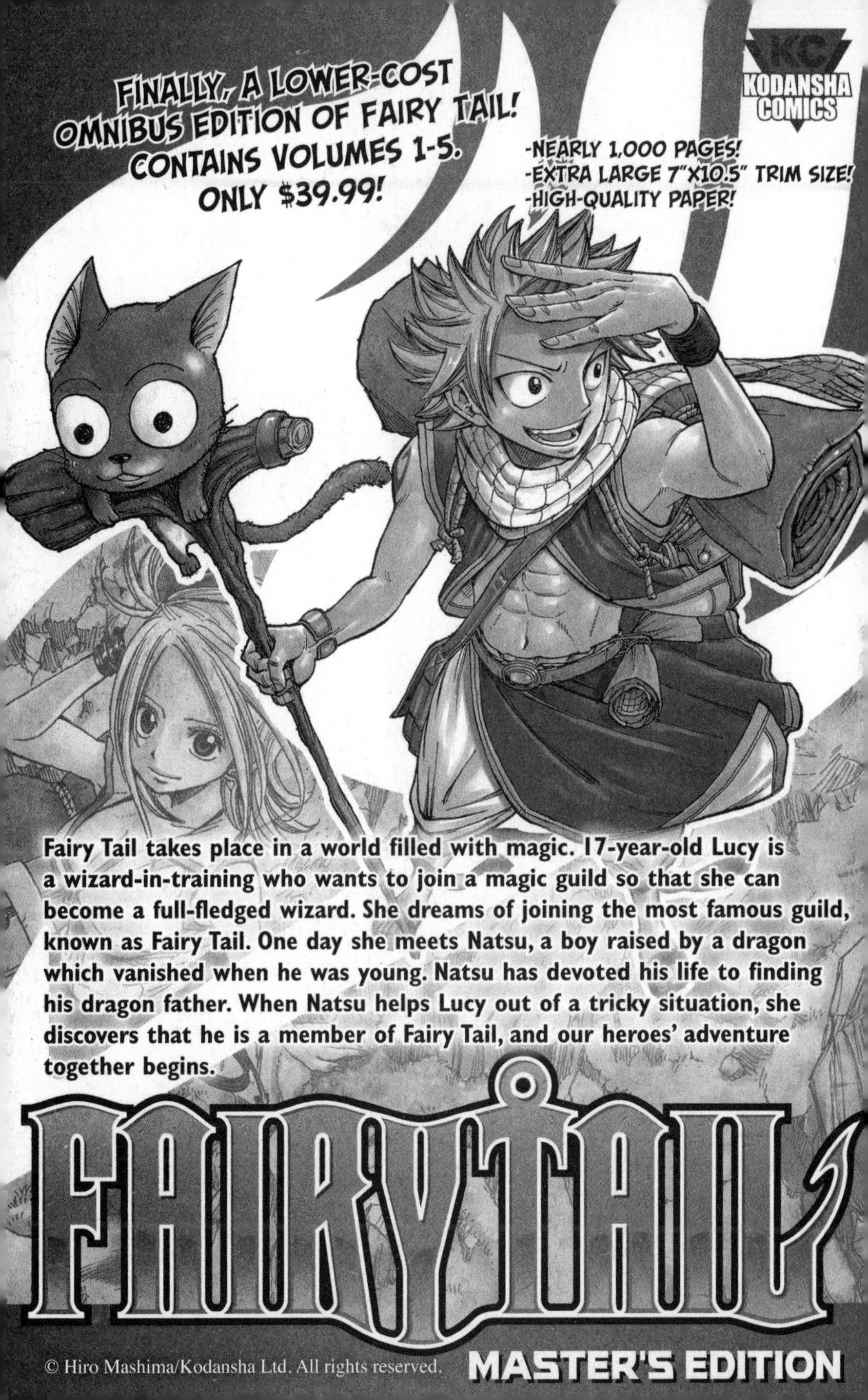
FINALLY, A LOWER-COST
OMNIBUS EDITION OF FAIRY TAIL!
CONTAINS VOLUMES 1-5.
ONLY $39.99!
KC
KODANSHA COMICS
-NEARLY 1,000 PAGES!
-EXTRA LARGE 7"X10.5" TRIM SIZE!
-HIGH-QUALITY PAPER!
Fairy Tail takes place in a world filled with magic. 17-year-old Lucy is a wizard-in-training who wants to join a magic guild so that she can become a full-fledged wizard. She dreams of joining the most famous guild, known as Fairy Tail. One day she meets Natsu, a boy raised by a dragon which vanished when he was young. Natsu has devoted his life to finding his dragon father. When Natsu helps Lucy out of a tricky situation, she discovers that he is a member of Fairy Tail, and our heroes' adventure together begins.
FAIRY TAIL
© Hiro Mashima/Kodansha Ltd. All rights reserved.
MASTER'S EDITION

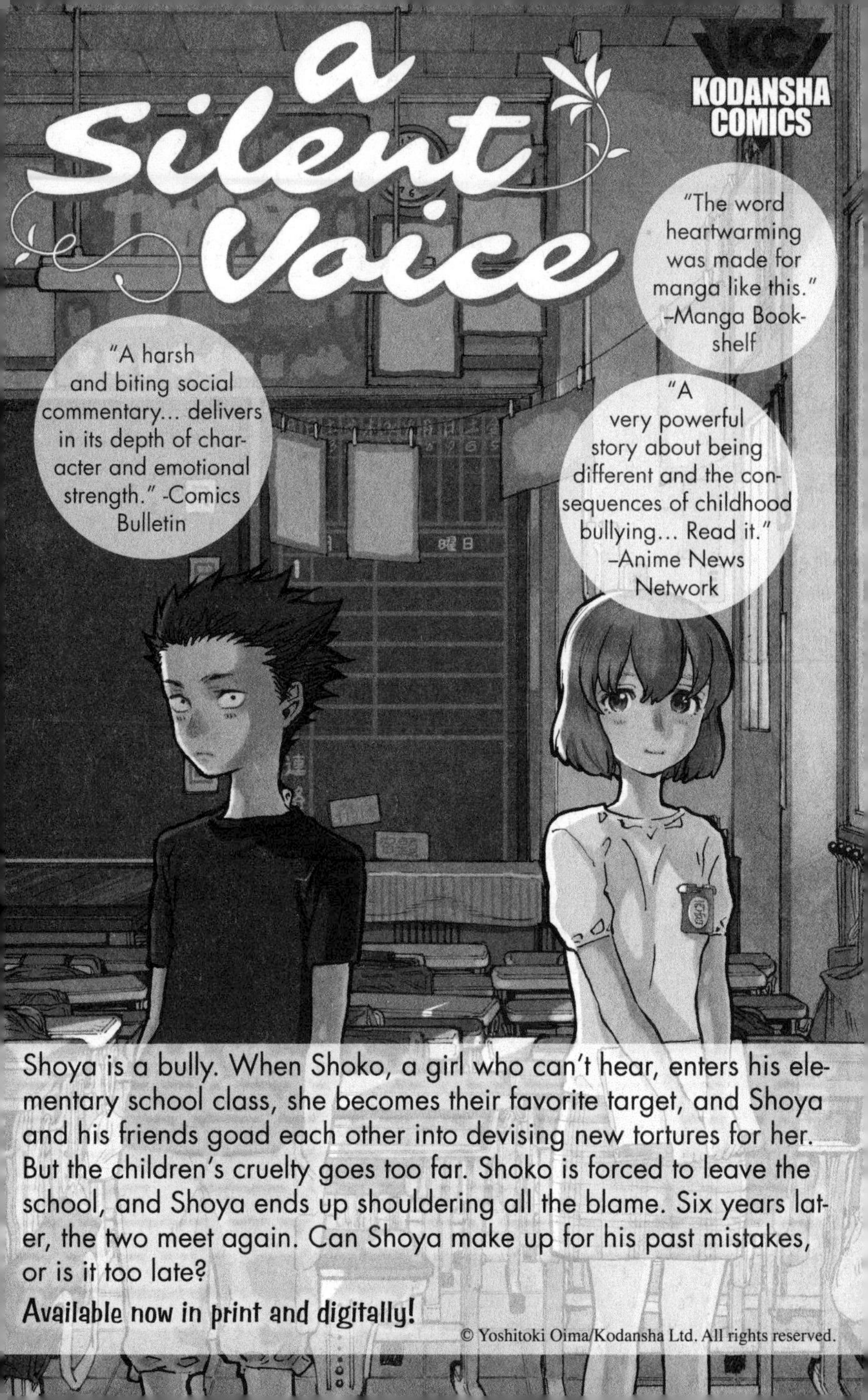
a Silent Voice
KODANSHA COMICS
"The word heartwarming was made for manga like this." –Manga Bookshelf
"A harsh and biting social commentary... delivers in its depth of character and emotional strength." -Comics Bulletin
"A very powerful story about being different and the consequences of childhood bullying... Read it." –Anime News Network
Shoya is a bully. When Shoko, a girl who can't hear, enters his elementary school class, she becomes their favorite target, and Shoya and his friends goad each other into devising new tortures for her. But the children's cruelty goes too far. Shoko is forced to leave the school, and Shoya ends up shouldering all the blame. Six years later, the two meet again. Can Shoya make up for his past mistakes, or is it too late?
Available now in print and digitally!
© Yoshitoki Oima/Kodansha Ltd. All rights reserved.

A Kodansha Comics Trade Paperback Original.

LDK volume 9 copyright © 2012 Ayu Watanabe
English translation copyright © 2017 Ayu Watanabe

Published in the United States by Kodansha Comics, an imprint of Kodansha USA Publishing, LLC, New York.

Publication rights for this English edition arranged through Kodansha Ltd., Tokyo.

First published in Japan in 2012 by Kodansha Ltd., Tokyo, as *L♡DK*, volume 9.

ISBN 978-1-63236-162-2

Printed in the United States of America.

www.kodanshacomics.com

9 8 7 6 5 4 3 2 1

Translation: Christine Dashiell
Lettering: Sara Linsley
Editing: Paul Starr
Kodansha Comics Edition Cover Design: Phil Balsman